Coverage of Interstate New Teacher Assessment and Support Consortium (INTASC) Standards for Beginning Teacher Licensing and Development

INTASC STANDARDS	CHAPTERS WHERE ADDRESSED
Standard 1: Central concepts, tools of inquiry, and structures of the subject being taught	6–8
Standard 2: Children's learning and intellectual, social, and personal development	4–8
Standard 3: Student differences in their approaches to learning and adaptations for diverse learners	4–8
Standard 4: Instructional strategies for students' development of critical thinking, problem solving, and performance skills	5–8
Standard 5: Individual and group motivation and behavior for positive social interaction, active engagement in learning, and self-motivation	5, 9–11
Standard 6: Effective verbal, nonverbal, and media communication techniques for inquiry, collaboration, and supportive interaction in the classroom	5, 9–11
Standard 7: Instructional planning based on knowledge of subject matter, students, the community, and curriculum goals	2–8
Standard 8: Formal and informal assessment strategies for intellectual, social, and physical development of the learner	5, 12, 13
Standard 9: Reflection to evaluate effects of choices and actions on others	1
Standard 10: Relationships with school colleagues, parents, and agencies to support students' learning and well-being	13, 14

THIRD EDITION

METHODS FOR EFFECTIVE TEACHING

PAUL R. BURDEN

Kansas State University

DAVID M. BYRD

University of Rhode Island

Boston   New York   San Francisco
Mexico City   Montreal   Toronto   London   Madrid   Munich   Paris
Hong Kong   Singapore   Tokyo   Cape Town   Sydney

Vice-president, Publisher: *Paul A. Smith*
Senior Editor: *Traci Mueller*
Editorial Assistant: *Erica Tromblay*
Marketing Manager: *Elizabeth Fogarty*
Editorial Production Service: *Whitney Acres Editorial*
Manufacturing Buyer: *JoAnne Sweeney*
Cover Administrator: *Linda Knowles*
Electronic Composition: *Omegatype Typography, Inc.*

For related titles and support materials, visit our online catalog at www.ablongman.com.

Between the time that Web site information is gathered and published, some sites may have closed. Also, the transcription of URLs can result in typographical errors. The publisher would appreciate notification when these occur so that they may be corrected in subsequent editions.

Cataloging and publication data not available at time of publication.

ISBN: 0-205-36774-7

Printed in the United States of America

10   9   8   7   6   5   4   3   2   1   RRD-VA   07   06   05   04   03   02

BRIEF CONTENTS

CONTENTS

CHAPTER THREE

Types of Teacher Planning   58

CHAPTER FOUR

The Inclusive and Multicultural Classroom   94

CHAPTER TEN

Classroom Management   234

CHAPTER ELEVEN

Classroom Discipline   277

PART V   ASSESSING STUDENT PERFORMANCE

CHAPTER TWELVE

Assessing Student Performance   303

CHAPTER THIRTEEN

Grading Systems, Marking, and Reporting   329

PART VI   WORKING WITH OTHERS

CHAPTER FOURTEEN

Working with Colleagues and Parents   355

PREFACE

This substantially revised third edition of *Methods for Effective Teaching* provides research-based coverage of general teaching methods while emphasizing contemporary issues, such as creating a learning community, differentiating your instruction, and making modifications in instruction due to student differences. The content is applicable for teachers at all levels: elementary, middle level, and high school. All content is aligned to PRAXIS/Principles of Learning and Teaching (see the inside front cover) and INTASC standards (page i).

Designed as a main textbook for courses in K–12 General Teaching Methods, Secondary/Middle Teaching Methods, or Elementary School Teaching Methods, this text's unique content includes motivating students for a learning community, working with colleagues and parents, differentiating your instruction, and managing lesson delivery. Thorough coverage of classroom management and discipline is provided, along with ways to create a positive learning environment. Each chapter clearly indicates the PRAXIS/PLT principles and the INTASC standards being addressed in the chapter. The numerous features, tables, and lists of recommendations ensure that the text is reader friendly and practically oriented.

CONTENT COVERAGE

The content of *Methods for Effective Teaching* is comprehensive, up to date, and authoritative. Each chapter reflects a synthesis of research and best practice. Part One, Foundations of Teaching Methods, provides an overview of the book and discusses the importance of teacher decision making and the creation of a successful learning community. Part Two, Planning Instruction, includes four chapters that consider the fundamentals of planning, types of teacher planning, and the standards movement as it relates to planning. Ways to plan for inclusive, multicultural classrooms are addressed, along with many practical ways to build motivational elements into lessons, with an emphasis on improving student interest and learning.

The three chapters of Part Three, Selecting Instructional Strategies, emphasize the need to differentiate instruction as a means to reach all learners. Ways to differentiate the curriculum and instructional strategies are highlighted when taking student characteristics into account. Two chapters examine various direct and indirect instructional strategies that can be used to differentiate instruction. The three chapters of Part Four, Managing Instruction and the Classroom, offer guidance for ways to manage various aspects of lesson delivery, along with specific principles of classroom management and discipline as part of a learning community.

Part Five, Assessing Student Performance, includes two chapters addressing the principles of effective assessment and the various ways to deal with grading systems, marking, and reporting. Finally, Part Six, Working with Others, examines how teachers can work with colleagues and parents in constructive ways.

New to This Edition

- Expanded coverage of instructional strategies, including a new chapter (Chapter 6) on differentiating your instruction
- New emphasis on creating a learning community in your classroom, as shown in a new feature and inclusion of related content in several chapters
- Three new features: Creating a Learning Community, Spotlight on Technology, and Modifications for Diverse Classrooms
- Major revision of Chapter 5, Motivating Students for a Learning Community
- Expanded discussion on assessing student performance, including portfolios, authentic assessment, and rubrics
- Expanded discussion on the role of colleagues and parents in the learning process
- Summary charts to show how the PRAXIS/Principles of Learning and Teaching principles and the INTASC standards are addressed in each chapter
- A new section of Web sites at the end of each chapter
- Twenty new Teacher in Action testimonials

Special Features

To maintain the reader's interest and to accommodate different learning styles and instructional settings, *Methods for Effective Teaching* contains a variety of pedagogical features.

- *Chapter Outline.* Each chapter begins with an outline of chapter headings and subheadings to provide an advance organizer for the reader.
- *Objectives.* Each chapter begins with a list of objectives that identify expected reader outcomes.
- *PRAXIS/PLT Principles and the INTASC Standards.* At the start of each chapter, there is a listing of the standards being addressed in the chapter. The codes (e.g., A5) and standards are identified in the tables on the inside front cover and page i.
- *Teachers in Action.* These features are included in each chapter to provide descriptions by actual elementary, middle school, and high school teachers of ways that they deal with particular topics addressed in the chapter. These teachers come from all parts of the country and different community sizes. There are about 70 Teachers in Action features, with an even balance for the elementary, middle, and high school levels.
- *Classroom Decisions.* Several features are placed in each chapter to consider the application of the content. Each Classroom Decisions includes several sentences describing a classroom situation concerning an issue in the chapter followed by a few questions asking the reader to make decisions about the application of the concepts.
- *Creating a Learning Community.* Several chapters include this feature, which provides a description of a classroom situation followed by three questions asking the reader to think, reflect, and decide on ways to create a learning community.

- *Spotlight on Technology.* This feature is included in several chapters; it presents specific content about ways that technology can be integrated into instruction. Contemporary uses of computers and technology are highlighted.
- *Modifications for Diverse Classrooms.* Several chapters include this feature, which presents a certain issue to illustrate the need to make modifications to help all students to learn. Three questions are posed to the reader asking for ways to modify some aspect of the classroom to meet learners' needs.
- *Key Terms.* A list of key terms at the end of each chapter draws the reader's attention to significant terms. Each term is highlighted in the text.
- *Major Concepts.* At the end of each chapter, a list of major concepts serves as a summary of the significant concepts.
- *Discussion/Reflective Questions.* Questions at the end of each chapter promote discussion and reflection in a classroom or seminar where a number of people are considering the chapter's content.
- *Suggested Activities.* These activities are listed at the end of each chapter for both clinical (on campus) settings and for field (school-based) settings to enable the reader to investigate and apply issues addressed.
- *Useful Resources.* An annotated list of recommended readings at the end of each chapter suggests readings for further enrichment.
- *References.* References cited in the chapters to document the research base of the content are all listed at the end of the book by chapter.

ACKNOWLEDGMENTS

Many people provided support and guidance as we prepared this book. A very special acknowledgment goes to our spouses and children: Jennie Burden and Mary Byrd, and to Andy, Kathryn, and Alex Burden and to David Byrd. Their support kept our spirits up when deadlines were pressing, and their understanding during our absences while preparing the content enabled us to complete the project.

Traci Mueller, our editor at Allyn and Bacon, facilitated the preparation of the manuscript, and we greatly appreciate her help.

A number of classroom teachers provided descriptions of their professional practice, which are included in the Teachers in Action features. Their experiences help illustrate the issues and bring life to the content.

Sandi Faulconer provided valuable assistance at Kansas State University in preparing several tables and the permissions log. Bridget Keane and Becky Donoghue at the University of Rhode Island were both careful readers and provided excellent suggestions for this effort. Finally, we would like to extend our gratitude to the following reviewers who provided constructive feedback for this revision: Jane Davis-Seaver, NCA&T University; Eric Groce, University of Texas at Tyler; and David Henderson, Sam Houston State University.

Paul Burden
David Byrd

ABOUT THE AUTHORS

Paul R. Burden is an assistant dean and professor in the College of Education at Kansas State University, Manhattan, where he has supervised student teachers and taught courses on teaching methods, classroom management and discipline, foundations of education, and instructional leadership. Previously, he was a middle-level science teacher in Buffalo, New York, and later earned his doctoral degree at the Ohio State University. He received the College of Education's Outstanding Undergraduate Teaching Award at Kansas State University in 1999.

Dr. Burden has presented over 70 papers at regional and national educational conferences and has written 15 articles and four book chapters on the topics of classroom management and discipline, staff development, teacher career development, working with beginning teachers, career ladders, writing for publication, school-based professional experiences, leadership skills, and diversity. In addition, he has been a presenter at over 40 staff development programs, and he currently serves as a reviewer for several journals.

From 1987 to 1998, he served as the editor of the *Journal of Staff Development,* a quarterly journal sponsored by the National Staff Development Council. He was a founding member of the Kansas Staff Development Council. Dr. Burden has served as president and a board member for the Association of Teacher Educators–Kansas, and has been active in several committees with the national Association of Teacher Educators.

Dr. Burden's other books include *Classroom Management* (Wiley & Sons, 2003); *Countdown to the First Day of School* (National Education Association, 2000); *Powerful Classroom Management Strategies: Motivating Students to Learn* (Corwin Press, 2000); and *Establishing Career Ladders in Teaching* (Charles C Thomas Publishers, 1987).

Married with three children, Dr. Burden enjoys traveling with his family and working on genealogy. He can be contacted at Kansas State University, 261 Bluemont Hall, Manhattan, Kansas 66506; (785) 532-5550; burden@ksu.edu.

David M. Byrd is a professor in the School of Education at the University of Rhode Island (URI). He is a graduate of the doctoral program in teacher education at Syracuse University. Prior to coming to Rhode Island, he was an associate professor at Southern Illinois University. He has a long-term professional and research interest in programs for beginning teachers and teacher professional development.

Dr. Byrd has authored and co-authored over 30 articles, books, and chapters, including chapters in both the *Handbook and Research on Teacher Education* (1996) and the *Handbook of Research on Supervision* (1998), both published by Macmillan. He has served as co-editor of the Association of Teacher Educators

Teacher Education Yearbook series, published by Corwin Press. Yearbook titles that he edited include *Preparing Tomorrow's Teachers: The Field Experience* (1996), *Research on the Education of Our Nation's Teachers* (1997), *Research on Career Long Teacher Education* (1998), *Research on Professional Development Schools* (1999), and *Research on Effective Models for Teacher Education* (2000). Presently he serves as chairperson of the Research Committee and the Commission on Field Experience Standards for the Association of Teacher Educators. Dr. Byrd can be contacted at the University of Rhode Island, 713 Chafee Hall, Kingston, Rhode Island 02881; (401) 874-5484; dbyrd@uri.edu.

CHAPTER ONE

INTRODUCTION TO TEACHER DECISION MAKING

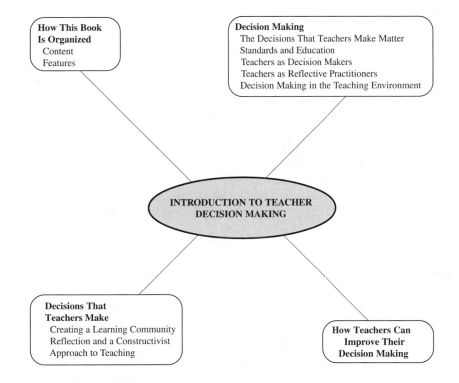

How This Book Is Organized
Content
Features

Decision Making
The Decisions That Teachers Make Matter
Standards and Education
Teachers as Decision Makers
Teachers as Reflective Practitioners
Decision Making in the Teaching Environment

INTRODUCTION TO TEACHER DECISION MAKING

Decisions That Teachers Make
Creating a Learning Community
Reflection and a Constructivist
Approach to Teaching

How Teachers Can Improve Their Decision Making

OBJECTIVES

This chapter provides information that will help you to:

1. Identify the ways this book is organized.

2. Define decision making.

3. Identify issues for which teachers need to make decisions.

4. Describe ways that teachers might improve their decision making.

1

PRAXIS/Principles of Learning and Teaching/Pathwise

The following principles are relevant to content in this chapter:

1. Reflecting on the extent to which the learning goals were met   (D1)
2. Demonstrating a sense of efficacy   (D2)

INTASC

The following INTASC standard is relevant to content in this chapter:

1. The teacher is a reflective practitioner who continually evaluates the effects of his or her choices and actions on others (students, parents, and other professionals in the learning community) and who actively seeks out opportunities to grow professionally.   (Standard 9)

Teachers engage in countless personal interactions with students each day. During instruction, teachers make decisions about the delivery of instruction, the use of instructional materials, evaluation of instruction, and many other issues. Teachers also make decisions about instruction while instruction is not taking place. These decisions may concern planning for issues such as the use of instructional strategies, classroom management, motivating students, student evaluation, and ways to create a successful learning community.

To examine teacher decision making and its relationship to teaching methods, the discussion in this chapter centers on four questions. How is this book organized? What is decision making? What decisions do teachers make? How might teachers improve their decision making?

HOW THIS BOOK IS ORGANIZED

Teachers make decisions about numerous aspects of instruction. Before considering the issue of teacher decision making, it is helpful to see how the content of this book is organized to address all aspects of teaching methods. Furthermore, it is useful to see how features in each chapter will be used to highlight and expand upon the content.

Content

Part One, which consists of Chapter 1, provides an introduction to the book and to teacher decision making. Part Two addresses decisions about *planning instruction;* it includes four chapters. Chapter 2 deals with the fundamentals of planning, including the reasons for planning, factors affecting planning, approaches to planning, and the standard movement. Chapter 3 examines types of teacher planning and the components of a daily lesson plan. Chapter 4 reviews decisions when addressing the diversity of students, including issues about student characteristics, student preferences for learning environments, and ways to create an inclusive, multicultural classroom. Motivating students for a learning community is examined in Chapter 5, with attention to motivational strategies and approaches to planning for motivation.

Part Three considers decisions when *selecting instructional strategies;* it includes three chapters. Chapter 6 examines the reasons and ways to differentiate your instruction to meet the needs of all learners. Teacher-centered, direct instructional strategies are discussed in Chapter 7, and student-centered, indirect strategies are presented in Chapter 8.

Part Four examines decisions related to *managing instruction and the classroom.* Chapter 9 addresses specific lesson delivery actions that teachers take when organizing and conducting the beginning, middle, and end of a lesson. Chapter 10 explores classroom management issues, such as preparing for the school year, organizing your classroom and materials, selecting and teaching rules and procedures, and establishing a cooperative classroom. Chapter 11 follows by discussing classroom discipline, misbehavior, interventions, and options for responding to misbehavior.

Part Five deals with *assessing student performance* within two chapters. Chapter 12 examines the characteristics of effective evaluation, various evaluation instruments, and details about preparing and administering teacher-made tests. Grading systems, marking, and reporting are explored in Chapter 13. Issues such as grading systems, assigning letter grades, gradebooks, and reporting grades and communicating with parents are included. Finally, Part Six on *working with others* (Chapter 14) identifies ways to work with colleagues and parents to better meet the needs of the students.

Features

Several features are included in each chapter to enhance understanding by showing how elementary and secondary teachers made decisions about chapter topics and by having you make decisions about chapter topics.

Each chapter begins with a *chapter outline* and a listing of *chapter objectives.* These features are intended to provide an advance organizer for chapter content. This is followed by a listing of *PRAXIS/PLT principles and INTASC standards* that are addressed in the chapter.

There are several additional features within the body of each chapter. Each chapter has three or four *Teachers in Action* case studies which were written by elementary and secondary teachers. The case studies illustrate how teachers decided to handle various topics in the respective chapters. There are four or five *Classroom Decisions* features in each chapter which include a statement about an issue covered in the chapter and then a question asking how you might deal with that particular issue in the classroom.

Several chapters include the *Creating a Learning Community* feature, which provides a description of a classroom situation followed by three questions asking the reader to think, reflect, and decide on ways to create a learning community. The *Spotlight on Technology* feature is included in several chapters to present specific content about ways that technology can be integrated into instruction. Contemporary uses of computers and technology are highlighted. Several chapters also include the *Modifications for Diverse Classrooms* feature, which presents a certain issue to illustrate the need to make modifications to help all students to learn.

At the end of each chapter, there is a list of *key terms,* along with a list of *major concepts* that were included in the chapter. These are followed by *discussion/reflective questions* about chapter content. *Suggested activities* to apply the chapter concepts are listed for clinical and field settings. A list of *useful resources* is provided for readers seeking additional information. Each chapter ends with a listing of *Web sites* that are related to chapter content. All the citations made in each chapter are listed in the references at the end of the book.

DECISION MAKING

Decision making involves (a) giving consideration to a matter and then selecting the identity, character, scope, or direction of something; (b) making choices; and (c) arriving at a solution that ends uncertainty. In relation to teaching, decision making is the basic teaching skill. Madeline Hunter (1984) defines teaching as "the constant stream of professional decisions that affects the probability of learning: decisions that are made and implemented before, during, and after interaction with the student" (pp. 169–170).

Shavelson (1976) reports that there are five features of decision making: (a) alternative acts; (b) states of nature (i.e., conditions not under direct teacher control); (c) outcomes; (d) utility for the teacher; and (e) goals. He contends that a teacher's understanding of the five features contributes to an awareness of alternatives and consequences, especially in planning.

Hurst, Kinney, and Weiss (1983) provide a research-based perspective for six stages of decision making: (a) problem awareness, (b) problem definition, (c) developing alternatives, (d) evaluating alternatives, (e) implementing a plan, and (f) evaluating results. For example, a teacher might notice that several students were having difficulty understanding and completing independent projects worked on in class. The teacher might observe and talk with the students in an attempt to more precisely define the problem, which in this case might be the need by several students to have more ongoing assistance. The teacher next would identify several approaches for solving the problem. After evaluating the appropriateness of these alternative solutions, the teacher might decide to have the students work in pairs or in small groups in an effort to provide each other with support. After trying this approach out, the teacher would evaluate whether the change in grouping actually solved the problem of students needing more assistance.

■ ■ ■ ■ ■

CLASSROOM DECISIONS

Hurst, Kinney, and Weiss (1983) indicate six stages of decision making that follow a step-by-step, linear approach. Do you make decisions in this way? How effective is your decision making? Are there other ways to make decisions?

Comprehensive reviews of research on teachers' pedagogical thought processes (e.g., Shavelson & Stern, 1981; and Clark & Peterson, 1986) and reports on decision making and teacher reflection (e.g., Clift, Houston, & Pugach, 1990) suggest that teachers make decisions in a variety of ways. This literature focuses on two approaches to decision making by teachers—teachers as decision makers and teachers as reflective practitioners.

The Decisions That Teachers Make Matter

As attempts are made to improve schools and school systems and increase student achievement, one constant has remained. Teachers are the most important factor in improving schools. Attempts to reform or improve education rise or fall based on the knowledge, skills, and commitment of teachers. This point is made quite clearly by Linda Darling-Hammond (1997) in *Doing What Matters Most: Investing in Quality Teaching.* Teachers need to know how to implement new practices, but they must also take ownership or the innovation does not succeed. As a teacher, you should expect to face huge challenges; our society is diverse and rapidly changing, our economy needs an educated work force, and our nation expects students to be educated to the highest academic standards in our history.

What you know and can do as a teacher affects all the core tasks of teaching. This book's goal is to ensure the following:

- You have a deep understanding of the content that you will teach.
- You know how students learn and develop.
- You are able to select activities and learning materials that have interest and the potential to motivate student learning.
- You select teacher strategies and activities that engage and involve students in the learning process.
- You can assess students' progress and have the ability to interpret students' oral and written work.

Your decisions can make all the difference for a child. No other factor or attempt at educational improvement has the influence on children's learning that an effective teacher has. Consequently, no other innovation can compensate for a teacher's lack of skill, knowledge, or commitment. Research has shown that teacher expertise is one of the most important of the factors that influence student growth and achievement. As a teacher, you need the support and resources necessary to succeed, including the expenditures necessary to create small schools and small class sizes. Therefore, teachers who know the subject(s) that they teach, who understand how children learn, and who know their students well and can meet their individual needs tend to be successful.

Ronald Ferguson (1991) is one of many researchers who have provided data on the importance of teacher expertise (Darling-Hammond, 1997). In a study of Texas teachers, Ferguson used scores on a licensing examination, master's degrees, and experience as his outcome measures. He found that these variables accounted for about 40 percent of the measured variance in students' reading and mathematics achievement at grades 1 through 11. In other words, teacher expertise varies widely, and expert teachers can make a huge difference in how well students achieve. This finding is especially important in light of the fact that teacher expertise is something that can be effected over time both by you as an individual preparing to teach and by schools and districts through their hiring practices and efforts at supporting teacher continuing education and professional development.

Standards and Education

The move to increase teacher expertise is not the only educational reform effort taking place in America. Education abounds with vigorous attempts to determine how to improve teaching and learning. These efforts often fall into two broad categories:

1. What should children learn?
2. What is the most effective way to teach children?

The most recent rush to declare a state of emergency and mobilize resources to improve education can be traced back to the 1983 publication of the National Commission on Excellence in Education's *A Nation at Risk.* The report, which called for reform in education, included recommendations for stronger graduation requirements, academic standards, and standards-based testing and more time spent on the basics of education. It also included recommendations for improved standards for teachers.

As supporters of the standards movement in education point out, standards are designed to improve education through increased rigor, consistency, and accountability. Indeed, in theory, it is difficult to imagine who would not be in favor of their adoption (Shepard & Bliem, 1995; Brady, 2000). However, as with all reform efforts, there are supporters and detractors, pluses and minuses, regarding standards-based reform. As a teacher, you will be asked to provide an environment in which children can succeed. Therefore, take some time to understand what is possibly the most important educational reform of the last 20 years.

Specific information on the standards movement and examples of standards for particular subject areas are discussed in Chapters 2 and 3. These chapters introduce the topic of teacher planning and the types of plans that teachers prepare. In tandem with this movement to content standards and assessment of students is a similar movement to develop criteria for the knowledge, skills, and dispositions that teachers need to promote student achievement (Ambach, 1996). These standards (see Figure 1.1) have been developed for beginning teachers through the *Interstate New Teacher Assessment and Support Consortium* (INTASC, 1998) and for experienced master teachers through the *National Board for Professional Teaching Standards* (NBPT, 1987). These standards are also being used as models for the development of state standards for beginning teachers, as well as state program approval standards for teacher education programs. They also serve as a foundation for the *National Council for Accreditation of Teacher Education*'s (NCATE, 2001) accreditation process for teacher education programs at colleges and universities. Clearly, current views on education reform stress the need for systematic change (Pajak, 2001).

At the beginning of each chapter of this book, you will see that we have referenced the INTASC standards being addressed in the chapter. In this way, you will know which INTASC standards are matched to the particular knowledge or skill that you are reading about or practicing. These standards serve as the basis for state standards for teacher preparation around the country and are likely to be a central feature in both your assessment as you go through your teacher education program and during your first few years as a teacher. Although your state may have adapted these standards, it is likely that it did so after extensive state review and reflection. Therefore, you will likely recognize the similarities be-

FIGURE 1.1   Model Standards for Beginning Teacher Licensing and Development

These standards were developed by the Interstate New Teacher Assessment and Support Consortium (INTASC).

- *Standard 1.* The teacher understands the central concepts, tools of inquiry, and structures of the discipline(s) that he or she teaches and can create learning experiences that make these aspects of subject matter meaningful for students.
- *Standard 2.* The teacher understands how children learn and develop and can provide learning opportunities that support their intellectual, social, and personal development.
- *Standard 3.* The teacher understands how students differ in their approaches to learning and creates instructional opportunities that are adapted to diverse learners.
- *Standard 4.* The teacher understands and uses a variety of instructional strategies to encourage students' development of critical thinking, problem solving, and performance skills.
- *Standard 5.* The teacher uses an understanding of individual and group motivation and behavior to create a learning environment and encourages positive social interaction, active engagement in learning, and self-motivation.
- *Standard 6.* The teacher uses knowledge of effective verbal, nonverbal, and media communication techniques to foster active inquiry, collaboration, and supportive interaction in the classroom.
- *Standard 7.* The teacher plans instruction based on knowledge of subject matter, students, the community, and curriculum goals.
- *Standard 8.* The teacher understands and uses formal and informal assessment strategies to evaluate and ensure the continuous intellectual, social, and physical development of the learner.
- *Standard 9.* The teacher is a reflective practitioner who continually evaluates the effects of his or her choices and actions on others (students, parents, and other professionals in the learning community) and who actively seeks out opportunities to grow professionally.
- *Standard 10.* The teacher fosters relationships with school colleagues, parents, and agencies in the larger community to support students' learning and well-being.

A full text of these standards, along with the listing of knowledge, dispositions, and performances, can be found at this Web site: http://www.ccsso.org/intascst.html.

CLASSROOM DECISIONS

As you review the INTASC standards, think about ways that you can provide evidence of your competence as a teacher as related to each standard. For example, what evidence can you produce to show the following:

- You know the discipline(s) that you will teach.
- You can use a variety of instructional strategies to encourage students' critical thinking, problem solving, and performance.
- You can create a positive motivational environment for learning.
- You can assess students to ensure their intellectual, social, and physical development.
- You reflect on and evaluate the effects that you as a teacher have on your students.

tween INTASC standards and those used by your state or teacher education program. Ownership at the state and local level is a central tenet of the INTASC improvement model.

The standards movement, as it relates to teacher performance, received a major push with the publication of *What Matters Most: Teaching for America's Future* by the National Commission on Teaching and America's Future (1996). In addition to calling on policy makers to "get serious" about standards for students and teachers, it promoted the notion that if all students are to reach high standards then teachers must be supported as they develop the capacity to meet the learning needs of diverse learners (Pajak, 2001). Without excellence in teaching—high standards and the related tests required by some states for graduation—we could, as some critics fear, have schools that do not support the continuous education of *all* children.

The standards movement calls for high standards for all, but will repeated failure lead some children and adolescents to leave school earlier than they might have and without the skills to succeed? Many critics raise this issue as their greatest fear that the standards movement could lead to even greater marginalization of those most in need (see Cuban, 1995; Kohn, 2000). As a teacher, you will be the most important factor in whether children are empowered by their education or demoralized.

Teachers as Decision Makers

The teacher decision-making research includes studies of teacher planning, interactive decision making, and judgments. This work has been summarized by a number of researchers, most notably Shavelson and Stern (1981), Clark and Peterson (1986), Borko and Niles (1987), and Borko and Shavelson (1991). Diagnosis and prescription, problem solving, and decision making have been named as basic teaching skills. In addition, research convincingly points out that successful teachers are thoughtful teachers (Glickman, Gordon, & Ross-Gordon, 2001).

With the teachers as decision makers approach, decision making is seen as a step or a series of steps in reaching conclusions. It is a concrete, linear process. For example, the decision-making model developed by Shavelson and Stern (1981) suggests that teachers operate automatically within well-established routines and make decisions when something unacceptable occurs during the routines.

Many teacher education programs teach instructional planning using the Tyler model (1950), which is a linear process of planning and implementing instruction. (This approach is more fully discussed in Chapter 2 on the fundamentals of planning.) Briefly, though, teachers planning with this decision-making approach would sequentially formulate aims and goals, specify instructional objectives, assess student needs, determine instructional strategies, and decide how to evaluate student performance. Decisions made at each point lay the foundation for decisions made on the subsequent issues. In a similar way, teachers might follow a linear process in decision making when dealing with issues such as instructional media, classroom management, motivating students, guiding student study, and evaluating student performance.

In the early 1980s, research on teaching began to focus on the beliefs teachers hold about students, classrooms, and learning, and on the decisions teachers make while planning, teaching, or reflecting on past teaching. This research addresses how teachers think, make decisions, and reflect about their classrooms. It has often attempted to make distinctions between "novice" and "expert" teachers (Berliner, 1987; Sabers, Cushing, & Berliner, 1991; Carter, Doyle, & Riney, 1995; Kagan, 1995). From this research come the following findings.

1. *The ability to think is the basis of effective teaching.* Expert teachers differ from novices not only in what they are able to do during the act of teaching but, perhaps more importantly, in what they know and how they use this knowledge to improve their teaching. Expert teachers remember how events turned out when they were in similar teaching situations in the past. These remembrances help teachers construct classroom management routines and confidently employ varied instructional strategies. Expert teachers also use their experience and knowledge of classrooms to refocus quickly to ensure that lessons progress in a positive manner.

2. *Classrooms are complex places, and expert teachers understand how variables such as time, motivation, student learning, curriculum, and learning strategies all play out as a series of events in classrooms.* Expert teachers know that students also have agendas and that they must adjust to ever-changing classroom events and changes in atmosphere. For example, in any given lesson, students may vary in their attention span, prior knowledge, or level of motivation. Therefore, teachers must be able to anticipate when to change strategies or routines to maximize student learning.

3. *Expert teachers know about the types of classroom events they deal with on a regular basis.* On the other hand, expert teachers are not necessarily able to anticipate how new events or strategies will unfold in their classrooms. Therefore, rapid changes in classroom structures are not easily adapted to, even by expert teachers.

4. *Novice and expert teachers differ vastly in their knowledge of how to shape and extend learning opportunities for students.* No one should expect beginning teachers to have instant expertise. Teachers need experience, time for reflection, and a supportive environment if they are to become expert.

5. *Novice teachers have strong opinions about teaching and how they will act as teachers.* To improve, novice teachers need to reflect upon these opinions and judge them against primary measures of educational success. While this sounds like common sense, novice teachers can become overwhelmed by issues of content coverage, choice of strategy, time constraints, and their own level of stage presence. When this happens, novice teachers can lose sight of the primary measure of success—student motivation and learning.

Beginning teachers who reflected most often on these issues tended to work in schools where they had responsibility for major curricular decisions (Kilgore, Ross, & Zbikowski, 1990). The perception that teachers have control over the design of their classroom seems to enhance their ability to reflect deeply about teaching.

While teachers can be viewed as decision makers, the term does not seem to fully indicate how teachers make decisions. As teachers become more experienced, they tend to rely less on sequential planning and more on the simultaneous processing of information to make planning decisions. In fact, decision making by experienced teachers during planning has been described as being cyclical and reflective (Yinger & Clark, 1982). Much has been written about this reflective process to teacher decision making, which is discussed in the next section.

Teachers as Reflective Practitioners

The second approach to teacher decision making views teachers as reflective practitioners who reflect upon and evaluate the success of past decisions in an effort to make better decisions in the future. As compared to viewing teachers as decision makers, Schön (1987) stated that there is "knowledge in action" which does not rely on a series of conscious steps in a decision-making process. Instead, the knowledge is inherent in the action; it is based, in part, on the past experiences of the teacher interacting with the particular situation. Thus, it may not be possible for a teacher to describe the decision-making process that led to the action since it is not linear or conscious. The knowledge-in-action concept legitimizes a way of thinking that seems to go on constantly in teaching (Richardson, 1990).

Teachers reflecting on their practice may be one means to better understand this type of decision making. *Reflection* can be defined as a way of thinking about educational matters that involves the ability to make rational choices and to assume responsibility for those choices (Ross, 1990). Reflection, as defined by Ross, requires that the teacher be introspective, open-minded, and willing to accept responsibility for decisions and actions.

John Dewey's writings are often cited as an early influence and source of ideas on teacher reflection (e.g., Beyer, 1984; Cruickshank, 1985; Glickman, 1986; Schön, 1987). Dewey (1933) contends that teachers should be trained in analyzing and defining principles behind reflective techniques. Reflection, for Dewey, involves active, persistent, and careful consideration of behavior or practice. He says reflection is the means for meeting and responding to the problems. The more teacher reflectivity that occurs, the better the quality of teaching. For example, teachers should constantly consider what made an activity successful, or not. New ways of enhancing the process should be constantly pursued.

Schön (1987) stresses that reflective practice is grounded in the practitioner's appreciation systems (i.e., repertoire of values, knowledge, theories, and practices). Thus, the appreciation system of the teacher influences the situations that will be recognized, the way the teacher frames and reframes the situation, and the judgments made about the desirability of various solutions.

As reflective practitioners, teachers need to be willing to analyze their own traits and behaviors in relation to the events that take place in the classroom (Zeichner & Tabachnick, 1981). Teachers, therefore, need to observe and attempt to make sense of situations by checking their insights against prior experience. Information they receive from their students can also be helpful. When viewing a videotape of their instruction, for example, teachers might express a variety of reflective concerns about issues such as their appearance or mannerisms; techniques, materials, or classroom environment; and ethical and moral issues (Byrd, Foxx, & Stepp, 1990).

Being reflective involves constant self-analysis. Zeichner (1981–1982) proposes that teachers constantly ask "Why?" For example, "Why is this objective important to all of my students?" or "Why is this test relevant to my objectives as applied by the students in my class?" or "How do I know if students learned the content, and how do I check that?"

TEACHERS IN ACTION

REFLECTIONS ON WEEKLY PLANS

Sue Garver, third grade teacher, Riley, Kansas

I find myself constantly evaluating and reevaluating what I do in my classroom on a daily and yearly basis. Being a reflective person has allowed me to grow and improve in my teaching. There are several things that I do on a regular basis that help me be more reflective in my teaching.

First, I meet with other teachers during our breaks or after school in order to compare notes—two heads are always better than one. During this time, we talk, compare ways we teach a subject, share new ideas, and just give each other moral support. This is a time when I reflect on the methods I currently use to present a subject and on ways that I could improve my teaching methods.

Second, I take a few minutes at the end of each day to evaluate the lessons I taught that day. I think this has helped me improve my teaching skills. In addition, I have included a column for these evaluative and reflective comments right in my plan book next to the plans for each lesson.

Throughout the day, I often make notes on a sticky pad concerning the lessons I teach. Then at the end of the day, I transfer those notes to my plan book in the column for my reflections. I make notes concerning the success of the lesson, what I could do differently next time, what could be done to meet the needs of individuals, what I did right in the lesson, and anything else that might be helpful next time I teach that lesson. I keep those lesson plans close by when planning for the following year.

Third, reflecting upon my teaching enables me to set goals for myself more easily. My school asks that each teacher set yearly goals. I have found that I can set goals easily when I make these reflective notes during the school year and when I take time at the end of the school year to reflect on my teaching. I leave for the summer knowing what goals I have set for the following school year. By doing this, I can attend conferences, take classes, and read up on the areas where I feel I need improvement.

Decision Making in the Teaching Environment

Researchers of classroom behavior have concluded that the practice of teaching is complex and uncertain (e.g., Clark, 1988) and that teachers need to make decisions within this environment. Dealing with complex problem situations, in fact, is a dominant element in the life of a teacher (Shulman, 1987). The complex life of teachers can be better understood by considering the relationship of teachers' thoughts and decisions to their behaviors and to the behaviors and achievement of their students (Clark & Peterson, 1986). Five aspects of decision making in the teaching environment are worth considering.

First, teachers make decisions to achieve varied academic, social, and behavioral goals. For instance, a teacher might make decisions about monitoring student behavior while working with a single small group of students. At the same time, the teacher might have expectations for students' social and academic performance. Thus, the teacher must consider these varied goals and decide on ways to plan and implement the goals.

Second, teachers make decisions in a complex environment interacting with students in a variety of ways. For example, teachers do a number of things to monitor and respond to student off-task behavior. Effective teachers have a high degree of *withitness,* which is the ability to be aware of what is happening in the classroom and to communicate that awareness to the students through their actions (Kounin, 1970). Decisions related to with-itness are continually made by teachers.

Third, teachers need to consider multiple perspectives when making decisions. In fact, teachers may interpret a situation far differently than their students. For example, a teacher might try to reinforce a student when, in fact, the student might be embarrassed by the attention or comments. Reflective teachers should use their experience, knowledge about effective teaching, intuition, and insight to help understand how events in the classroom influence learning. Beginning teachers, of course, have limited experience and may not have a broad knowledge base when being reflective.

Fourth, teachers need to make moment-by-moment adjustments of their plans to fit the continually changing and uncertain conditions found in classrooms (Lampert & Clark, 1990). Teachers learn to make these adjustments through the knowledge they have gained from the context of their classrooms, the interactive nature of their thinking, and their speculations about how these adjustments will affect the classroom environment.

Fifth, teachers need to make decisions to plan for instruction. Once instruction begins, teachers might find that they need to modify the lesson delivery because the lesson may not proceed in the way intended. The teacher must choose to strengthen the lesson and not simply continue with a nonproductive event when the lesson did not meet the teacher's expectations.

DECISIONS THAT TEACHERS MAKE

Teachers make decisions about a number of issues. First, when planning and preparing for instruction, teachers make planning decisions about goals and objectives, needs assessment, instructional strategies and activities, and evaluation of student performance. Second, when presenting instruction, teachers need to select instructional strategies that help achieve the lesson objectives. Also, teachers need to decide how to structure the lesson and to conduct themselves during the delivery of the lesson. Furthermore, instructional materials and resources need to be selected.

Third, teachers also make decisions about organizing and managing instruction, with special emphasis on classroom management and classroom discipline. This includes decisions about issues such as organizing the classroom and materials, choosing rules and procedures, reinforcing desired behaviors, holding students academically accountable, creating a positive classroom climate, and determining options for responding to misbehavior.

Fourth, teachers consider learners' instructional needs when making instructional decisions. This includes making provisions for individual differences, motivating students, and guiding student study. Fifth, teachers make decisions about evaluating student performance. This includes ways to evaluate student performance, establish a grading system, and report to parents. Finally, teachers make decisions about steps they could take to improve their teaching.

Creating a Learning Community

Over the years, the way that teachers have gone about instruction has changed as more is known about the nature of teaching and learning. In recent years, more emphasis has been

TEACHERS IN ACTION

DECISIONS ARE AFFECTED BY MY TEACHING PHILOSOPHY

Donna Erpelding, third grade teacher, Manhattan, Kansas

Decisions that I make in the classroom are affected by my views of teaching. An effective teacher understands the "art of teaching." Teaching is not just opening a book, making assignments, and grading papers. It's about understanding and supporting the development of a child. I believe that the classroom of an effective teacher is child-centered, where student needs are understood and met. Students themselves need to be valued, respected, and appreciated. I believe that I am in the *learning success business* rather than the materials coverage business. There are no losers in my classroom—only winners!

Effective teachers draw talents and uniqueness from their students, and then capture and build on that talent in a variety of ways using teaching methods and strategies. An effective teacher can "go with the flow" and change a lesson to capture a "teachable moment." Kids are so much more capable than we give them credit for.

My students may not score any higher on a standardized test than students from a more traditional classroom. But, I know my students leave my room with many talents and strategies for learning that are not measured on a standardized test. They have had a year of many and varied learning experiences—not just doing paper and pencil activities, reading the chapter, and answering the questions at the end. My hope is they love learning and they believe in themselves and their unique talents when they go out to face the unknowns of a future world.

placed on building learning communities in the classroom because students appear to be most successful in that environment. Problems with student misbehavior are also minimized in an environment where students are actively involved in their classroom and instruction. As a result, considerable decision making centers on ways to create a successful learning community.

A *learning community* is a classroom designed to help all students to feel safe, respected, and valued in order to learn new skills. Anxiety, discomfort, and fear are incompatible with the learning process and make teaching and learning difficult. Successful classrooms are those in which students feel supported in their learning, are willing to take risks, are challenged to become fully human with one another, and are open to new possibilities.

With increasing diversity in classrooms, the need to create supportive classroom communities becomes even more important. Teachers must identify community building as a high priority if we are to have classrooms that include diverse students and make them welcome, appreciated, and valued members of the classroom environment. Actions can be taken to build an inclusive classroom learning community (Baloche, 1998).

In *Because We Can Change the World,* Sapon-Shevin (1999) identified five characteristics of learning communities:

1. *Security.* A safe, secure community allows for growth and exploration. A nurturing community is a place where it is safe to be yourself, take risks, ask for help and support, and delight in accomplishments. A safe environment helps to protect students from distractions and disruptions that interfere with the learning process.

2. *Open communication.* In a cohesive environment, there is open communication. All forms of communication—oral, written, artistic, and nonverbal—are encouraged. In safe, accepting environments, students' individual differences and needs are openly acknowledged. Students share freely what is happening, what they need, and what they are worried about. Because all students have the right to feel safe, for example, this communication should be encouraged to address their concerns.

3. *Mutual liking.* In supportive classroom communities, students are encouraged to know and like their classmates. Opportunities are provided for students to interact with one another, and students are given many chances and strategies for learning to see and say nice things about classmates.

4. *Shared goals or objectives.* Cooperative communities are those in which students work together to reach a shared goal or objective. This can be achieved with whole-class projects in which students work toward a goal while interacting with and supporting one another.

5. *Connectedness and trust.* In learning communities, students feel a part of the whole. They know that they are needed, valued members of the group. They know that others are depending on them to put forth their best effort. Trust and connectedness mean sharing the good things, as well as any concerns or problems.

To create a learning community, teachers often plan lessons designed to involve students in cooperative learning activities. These activities seem to have three elements that are critical to their success: face-to-face interactions, a feeling of positive interdependence, and a feeling of individual accountability (Johnson, Johnson, & Holubec, 1994). In addition, it is necessary to teach students social skills and to process group functioning for these learning activities to be successful.

Teachers also need to arrange the physical environment for instruction, guide and correct behavior, and create a supportive classroom. All these responsibilities for creating a learning community relate to classroom management.

Reflection and a Constructivist Approach to Teaching

A related concept to teacher decision making and reflection is constructivist theory. *Constructivist theory* holds that individuals construct meaning and understanding through their prior knowledge and apply this knowledge in new current situations (Resnick, 1987). Therefore, a constructivist approach to teacher education involves teachers and their students constructing meaning out of information they have been exposed to through active participation and interaction (Doyle, 1990). This process values the student's point of view, teacher/student interaction, questioning to promote student thought, and the importance of nurturing student reflection and thought rather than a primary focus on a single "correct" answer or product.

The constructivist approach to reflection and teacher decision making not only provides insight into how teachers make decisions and why but also provides a framework for

CREATING A LEARNING COMMUNITY

FACILITATING OPEN COMMUNICATION

One way to create a learning community is to facilitate open communication in an environment where all students feel safe, respected, and valued. Communication between the teacher and the students is important, but communication among students is also valued.

As you develop your manner of teaching, you need to make decisions to facilitate this open communication. This task may seem daunting, and it may be easier to address when it is broken down into smaller parts, as follows:

1. How might you arrange for students to *orally* share their ideas and comments about what is happening, what they need, and what they are worried about? How might you gather input from them about ways to improve the learning community?
2. How might you facilitate this communication in *written* form?
3. What steps could you take to ensure that all students feel safe when communicating, that they are not threatened, and that they do not receive put-downs from others?

how teachers structure their classrooms. A teacher using the constructivist framework provides students with the opportunity to investigate concepts and creates an environment in which students can actively discuss and investigate the new content.

Students should be challenged by the activities and stimulated by their own and the teacher's questions. A key feature of this model is that students are encouraged to actively seek understanding and knowledge; this is done by using prior understandings to help to understand new material. The development of new insights requires relating new investigations to previous understandings. Teachers who reflect on their own practice employ a constructivist perspective. They constantly review significant events which take place in the classroom and try to clarify and improve their understanding of teaching and learning.

As you read this text, you will encounter many concepts related to teaching and have the opportunity to reflect on how these concepts can help you become a better teacher and help your students become better learners. A constructivist teacher is always thinking about both of these questions.

HOW TEACHERS CAN IMPROVE THEIR DECISION MAKING

Teachers may improve their decision making through a variety of means, but reflection about their decision making and instructional practice has proven to be a very helpful approach for many teachers (Wildman, Niles, Magliaro, & McLaughlin, 1990).

Three perspectives support this notion of teacher growth through reflections (Grimmett et al., 1990). First, reflection helps teachers replicate effective classroom practices and continue to use effective teacher behaviors. Second, reflection helps teachers deliberate among competing views of teaching. It enables teachers to be informed about events within a context. Third, reflection can help teachers reorganize or reconstruct experiences. This, in effect, can help transform practice.

Many strategies supporting the development of reflection exist in the literature (e.g., Zeichner, 1987; Clift et al., 1990; Freiberg & Waxman, 1990; Ross, 1990; Wildman et al., 1990; Griffin, 1997). Several strategies described here might be used in conjunction with a college class. Some activities such as journal writing and questioning can be accomplished independently as you reflect on teaching experiences, observations, microteachings, and readings.

1. *Reflective teaching.* This is a procedure that provides a person with repeated opportunities to teach and analyze brief lessons developed by program designers specifically for this purpose (Cruickshank, 1985; Phi Delta Kappa, n.d.). Lessons are commonly videotaped, thus enabling replay and critique. Reflective teaching might be included in preservice teacher education programs.

2. *Microteaching.* Microteaching involves a person, commonly a preservice teacher, teaching a brief lesson to peers in an effort to exhibit specific teaching behaviors, such as nonverbal cues, wait time for questions, and probing questions (Allen & Fortune, 1966). The brief lesson is videotaped, and the student receives feedback from the instructor. Assessment procedures can be modified to have the process serve as a reflective tool. For example, there might be formative feedback, peer feedback, and self-assessment of the microteaching lesson (Freiberg & Waxman, 1990).

3. *Inquiry activities.* Preservice and beginning teachers may enter the profession with images and common sense knowledge about learning, teaching, and students (Calderhead, 1988). Inquiry activities such as action research about teaching techniques, case studies of teaching episodes, ethnographic descriptions of classroom events, and curriculum analysis and development can be used to encourage continuous inquiry by teachers about the relationship between entering knowledge and knowledge derived from theories and research (Ross, 1990). Inquiry activities might be used in preservice education programs to encourage reflection.

Written descriptions of classroom events or case studies are one of the most popular methods used to help preservice students gain understanding of the culturally diverse, complex world teaching has become. Often dilemma-based, these cases provide students with the opportunity to recognize specific educationally significant events during teaching; gain understanding of the event; reflect on how problems or dilemmas were handled by the teacher and the adequacy of the outcome; and most importantly reflect on sensible, moral, educationally sound practices they might themselves use in the future (Harrington, Quinn-Leering, with Hodson, 1996).

4. *Reflective writing.* Reflective writing is a way for preservice teachers to practice critical analysis and reasoning (Copeland, 1986). It also provides teacher education faculty with a way to challenge and support each student's reflective thinking. Journal writing is the most common way to stimulate reflection (Copeland, 1986; Zeichner, 1987). With journal writing, preservice teachers keep a daily or regular journal in which they record their experiences and raise questions about teaching (Freiberg & Waxman, 1990). Journals are sometimes used during introductory phases of a preservice teacher education program

or during student teaching. Journals enable prospective teachers to systematically reflect on their development as a teacher and on their actions in the classroom (Zeichner & Liston, 1987). Experienced teachers may also write journals for their development.

To illustrate the use of journal writing, students in a preservice teacher education program might be required to write a journal for microteaching lessons they teach. Sample guidelines for preparing a journal for this situation are displayed in Table 1.1, illustrating both the format and the content of a typical journal. Additionally, these guidelines are included to provide a model as you begin to reflect on your own teaching through journal writing.

5. *Portfolio development.* This involves development of portfolios in which preservice and beginning teachers collect and organize materials and artifacts such as lesson plans and examples of students' work, photographs from classrooms, and videotapes of lessons with self critique. Purposefully collecting sets of artifacts demonstrates the ability to reflect on important indicators of success. Reflective teaching portfolios provide a concrete representation between teacher expectations, student performance, and teacher reflection about teaching and learning (Wenzlaff & Cummings, 1996).

6. *Supervisory approaches.* The development of reflection requires a different orientation to supervision than is provided in traditional clinical supervision which focuses on the rational analysis of instructional behavior. Inquiry-oriented supervision differs from clinical supervision by (a) including analysis of the intentions and beliefs of students, (b) viewing institutional form and social context of teaching as topics of analysis, (c) analyzing the content as well as the behaviors of instruction, and (d) analyzing unintended as well as intended outcomes of instruction (Zeichner & Liston, 1987).

7. *Faculty modeling.* Modeling of reflection by teacher education faculty can also play an important role in helping teachers learn complex knowledge (Ross, 1990). This type of modeling provides a generalized role model of the reflective practitioner.

8. *Questioning and dialogue.* Teacher educators and others can use questions to stimulate teachers to use newly acquired concepts, to discuss relationships among concepts and

---

TEACHERS IN ACTION

REFLECTIVE WRITING

Sandy Peer, high school math teacher, Wichita, Kansas

The most valuable graduate course I took was one that required me to express my philosophy in writing. Then I had to videotape myself and look for evidences of my philosophy. I also had to interview my students to find out, if possible, what they thought about my philosophy of teaching. Students' perceptions of teachers are reality for them. Thus, I make it a personal goal to have their perceptions agree with what I am doing—or at least what I think I am doing. This whole process caused me to be more reflective about decisions I made in my teaching—decisions about planning, instructional strategies, media, the ways I interact with students, evaluation, and other areas.

TABLE 1.1   Sample Guidelines for Preparing a Journal Format

These guidelines are for students who have just completed teaching a microteaching lesson in a college classroom. This format can also be used by teachers who have just finished teaching a lesson in an actual classroom.

What Are the Parts of a Log?

A. *Heading*

Name: (Your name)

Date of the lesson: (A log entry should cover only one day and should be written immediately after reviewing your videotape—short notes of your impressions on the day you teach may also prove helpful. Otherwise, memories tend to fade.)

Time spent: (e.g., 1:30–1:45 PM)

B. *Sequence of Events*

Make a brief list describing what happened. By making a list, you keep a record of what happened. This record may be useful for future reference. It allows you to mention all events, even those that seemed insignificant to you at the time. One way for you to do this sequence is to follow the headings from your lesson plan.

C. *Elaboration of One or Two Significant Episodes*

An episode is an "event or sequence of events complete in itself but forming a part of a larger one." Select one or two episodes that are significant to you. An episode may be significant because what happened bothers you, excites you, causes you to rethink your initial ideas (i.e., your perspective, goals, or plans), or convinces you that your initial ideas were valid. Therefore, whether the episodes reflect your successes or your failures, they are significant if you learned something important from them.

Once you have selected one or two significant episodes, you should describe them in detail. When you describe the episodes, try to relive them. Reliving the experiences will enable you to think about what you felt during the episode, how you perceived the responses of learners and other people (e.g., the supervisor) to your actions and words, and who or what contributed significantly to shaping the events. This type of reflection will provide you with material for further reflection in the next section of the log.

D. *Analysis of Episode(s)*

An analysis of episodes includes a description of why they were significant to you and how you interpret them. Try to figure out what you accomplished, identify problems that emerge, and determine how you plan to follow up. Also distill from the episodes what you learned. This last point is the most important.

You may have learned what works in this situation and what does not. If so, describe what you conclude. But you may also have learned something about your philosophy of teaching (your perspective). Does the episode confirm your ideas or force you to reconsider them? Maybe some initial ideas you held depend to a large extent on the situation in which you apply them. If so, what was it about the situation that affected the applicability of the ideas?

Many experiences raise more questions than they answer. You might use your logs as an opportunity to note questions that arise during your microteaching experiences which you want to discuss with your supervisor during a microteaching lab or a class lecture.

CREDIT: Adapted from *Field Experience: Methods of Reflective Teaching* (5th ed.) by George J. Posner. Copyright © 1985, 1989, 2000 by Longman Publishing Group. Pages 26–28. Reprinted with permission.

teaching experiences, and to pose their own questions (Simmons & Schuette, 1988). The purpose of the questions is to encourage dialogue and to stimulate teachers to view situations from multiple perspectives.

CLASSROOM DECISIONS

Sometimes two student teachers meet to discuss their teaching. What might they discuss? How might this process help the teachers be more reflective and better decision makers?

Pugach and Johnson (1990) describe peer collaboration as a structured interaction in which pairs of teachers rehearse new ways of thinking. Peer collaboration allows the meaning of problematic classroom situations to be constructed jointly by teachers through the process of dialogue. The collaborative construction of new meaning is intended to be the reflective act that can lead to alternative classroom interventions. Specifically, the peer collaboration process has four steps: (a) clarify problems of practice by self-questioning in a guided learning situation, (b) summarize the redefined problem, (c) generate possible solutions and predict what might happen if they are used, and (d) consider various ways of evaluating the effectiveness of the solution chosen.

Opportunities for teachers to reflect with other teachers can also be an important aid to introspection. Teachers meeting with others to investigate and discuss reform efforts, research on teaching, and their own ideas and classroom practices, has been found to enhance teachers' ability to think about their own teaching. In addition, teachers who reflect and analyze their teaching with teachers of different races, experience levels, and academic subjects find themselves thinking about new viewpoints, and this helps them to more clearly define their own perspectives on teaching and learning (Newell, 1996).

Teachers are becoming more involved in shared decision making with principals regarding the management and governance of schools. This movement, called "site-based or school-based management," raises the level of importance of teachers as a community of educators, developing the skills and attitudes necessary to evaluate and implement reform agendas to improve the education of children (Leino, 1995; Conle, 1997).

SUMMARY

This chapter is intended to serve as an organizer for the content in the rest of the book. Each subsequent chapter addresses issues that will require teacher decisions. While information about teachers as decision makers and reflective practitioners is useful, it is important to recognize that decisions are made within the complex teaching environment. There are no roadmaps for how decisions are made, and teachers will need to give attention to how they make decisions in an effort to improve their decision making for issues discussed in the following chapters. Through journal writing, questioning, or other techniques, reflection might provide the means for you to improve your decision making as you consider content in the following chapters.

KEY TERMS

A Nation at Risk
Constructivist theory
Decision making
Inquiry activities
Interstate New Teacher Assessment and Support Consortium (INTASC)

Learning community
Microteaching
National Board for Professional Teaching Standards (NBPT)
National Council for Accreditation of Teacher Education (NCATE)

Reflection
Reflective teaching
Reflective writing
Withitness

MAJOR CONCEPTS

1. Teaching is centrally the act of decision making—teachers plan and act through the process of thought and reflection.

2. Decision making involves making choices and arriving at a solution that ends uncertainty.

3. Decision making might be seen as a step or a series of steps in reaching conclusions.

4. Reflection can be defined as a way of thinking about educational matters that involves the ability to make rational choices and to assume responsibility for those choices.

5. Teachers make decisions about a number of issues when preparing for, presenting, organizing, managing, and evaluating instruction.

6. A learning community is designed to help all students to feel safe, respected, and valued in order to learn new skills. Characteristics of a learning community include security, open communication, mutual liking, shared goals or objectives, and connectedness and trust.

7. A number of approaches can be used to help teachers improve their reflective process and their decision making.

DISCUSSION/REFLECTIVE QUESTIONS

1. Why is decision making a basic teaching skill?

2. What factors influence the decisions that teachers make?

3. What aspects of the classroom could teachers give their attention to when making decisions to create a successful learning community?

4. What might you do now and at other points in your teacher education program to improve your reflection and decision making?

SUGGESTED ACTIVITIES

For Clinical Settings

1. Using the journal format in Table 1.1 as a guide, select a significant event from a class you have attended on campus during the last three weeks to analyze.

2. Teach a brief lesson to a small group of peers. Write and reflect about a significant event which took place in your lesson.

3. Think of ways that you might examine and reflect about content in the subsequent chapters in this book.

For Field Settings

1. Talk with several teachers to explore how they make decisions related to teaching.

2. Ask several teachers to describe lessons that they changed after the lesson began. Explore their thinking and decision making.

3. Ask several teachers about the ways that they try to create a successful learning community.

USEFUL RESOURCES

Brooks, J. G., & Brooks, M. G. (1993). *The case for constructivist classrooms.* Alexandria, VA: Association for Supervision and Curriculum Development.

Reviews the rationale for constructivist teaching approaches, and then provides thorough descriptions and examples about the guiding principles of constructivism and ways to create constructivist settings. Well referenced.

Reagan, T. G., Case, C. W., & Brubacher, J. W. (2000). *Becoming a reflective educator: How to build a culture of inquiry in the schools* (2nd ed.). Thousand Oaks, CA: Corwin Press.

Examines ways that teachers can become creative and innovative agents of inquiry in their schools and classrooms.

York-Barr, J., Sommers, W. A., Ghere, G. S., & Montie, J. (2001). *Reflective practice to improve schools: An action guide for educators.* Thousand Oaks, CA: Corwin Press.

A very useful guide providing a framework for reflective thinking and acting. Offers examples of strategies to guide individual, small group, or schoolwide reflection.

WEB SITES

- Survival Guide for New Teachers: How New Teachers Can Work Effectively with Veteran Teachers, Parents, Principals, and Teacher Educators

  http://www.ed.gov/pubs/survivalguide/

- Weekly newspaper on education filled with helpful articles and special reports.

  http://www.edweek.org/

- Teacher certification requirement in various states

  http://www.uky.edu/education/tep/usadcert.html

- An educational index of top education-related sites

  http://www.educationindex.com

- The Educational Resources Information Center (ERIC), a federally funded, nationwide information network designed to provide access to education literature. It is a program of the National Library of Education, U.S. Department of Education.

  http://www.ericsp.org

- The National Center on Education and the Economy, a not-for-profit organization based in Washington, D.C. Standards-based education is the hallmark of the center's work. Information and materials on a number of national programs are available on this site.

  http://www.ncee.org/default.html

- The Interstate New Teacher Assessment and Support Consortium (INTASC) is a consortium of state education agencies, higher education institutions, and national educational organizations dedicated to the reform of the education, licensing, and ongoing professional development of teachers. Created in 1987, INTASC's primary constituency is state education agencies responsible for teacher licensing and professional development. Most states now have incorporated or adapted the INTASC *Model Standards for Beginning Teachers,* for preparation and professional development.

  http://www.ccsso.org/intasc.html

- National Board Certification measures experienced teacher's practice against high and rigorous standards. The process is an extensive series of performance-based assessments that includes teaching portfolios, student work samples, videotapes, and thorough analyses of the candidates' classroom teaching and student learning. Teachers also complete a series of written exercises that probe the depth of their subject-matter knowledge, as well as their understanding of how to teach these subjects to their students.

  http://www.nbpts.org/

CHAPTER TWO

THE FUNDAMENTALS OF PLANNING

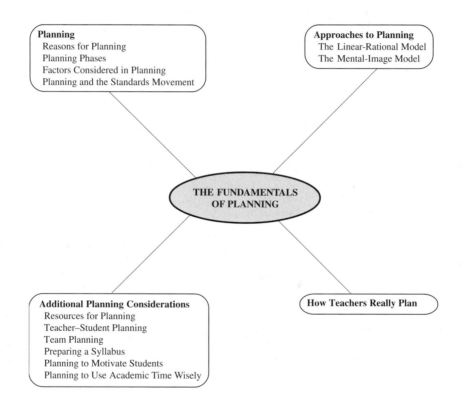

Planning
  Reasons for Planning
  Planning Phases
  Factors Considered in Planning
  Planning and the Standards Movement

Approaches to Planning
  The Linear-Rational Model
  The Mental-Image Model

THE FUNDAMENTALS
OF PLANNING

Additional Planning Considerations
  Resources for Planning
  Teacher–Student Planning
  Team Planning
  Preparing a Syllabus
  Planning to Motivate Students
  Planning to Use Academic Time Wisely

How Teachers Really Plan

OBJECTIVES

This chapter provides information that will help you to:

1. Describe the reasons for instructional planning.

2. Identify factors that you might consider when planning for instruction.

3. Describe the two predominate approaches to instructional planning.

4. Identify resources that can be used when planning.

5. Prepare a syllabus and plan to motivate students.

6. Describe changes that teachers often experience in their approach to planning.

PRAXIS/Principles of Learning and Teaching/Pathwise

The following principles are relevant to content in this chapter:

1. Creating or selecting teaching methods, learning activities, and instructional materials or other resources that are appropriate for the students and that are aligned with the goals of the lesson   (A4)

2. Creating or selecting evaluation strategies that are appropriate for the students and that are aligned with the goals of the lesson   (A5)

INTASC

The following INTASC standard is relevant to content in this chapter:

1. The teacher plans instruction based upon knowledge of subject matter, students, the community, and curriculum goals.   (Standard 7)

Planning for instruction is a critical element in the instructional process. Carefully designed, comprehensive plans will have a positive effect on student learning. To help you to understand and be prepared to plan for instruction, this chapter will examine the planning process, approaches to planning, and related planning issues. The chapter ends with a discussion about how teachers really plan.

PLANNING

Planning for instruction refers to decisions that are made about organizing, implementing, and evaluating instruction. Planning is one of the most important tasks that teachers undertake. When making planning decisions, you also need to consider who is to do what, when and in what order instructional events will occur, where the events will take place, the amount of instructional time to be used, and resources and materials to be used. Planning decisions also deal with issues such as content to be covered, instructional strategies, lesson delivery behaviors, instructional media, classroom management, classroom climate, and student evaluation.

The goal of planning is to ensure student learning. Planning, therefore, helps create, arrange, and organize instructional events to enable that learning to occur. Planning helps arrange the appropriate flow and sequence of instructional events and also manage time and events.

The amount of time spent on planning varies greatly by individual teachers. It is influenced by factors such as pupil needs, the complexity of the teaching assignment, facilities and equipment, and the experience of the teacher. Some teachers estimate that they spend 10 to 20 percent of their time in planning (Clark & Yinger, 1979).

To more fully understand instructional planning, it is useful to consider the reasons for planning, the phases in which planning occurs, and factors that are considered while planning.

Reasons for Planning

When looking at the entire school year, planning is needed for the year, each term, each unit, each week, and each lesson. Written weekly plans are typically required by school districts, and these plans for beginning teachers are often reviewed by the school principal. Plans for the year, term, and units are not commonly reviewed by the principal. There are a number of reasons to prepare thorough plans for all the time frames, with some plans written in detail and some not so thoroughly written (Clark & Yinger, 1979; Freiberg & Driscoll, 2000).

Planning can help you to do the following:

- Give you a sense of direction, and through this, a feeling of confidence and security. Planning can help you stay on course and reduce your anxiety about instruction.
- Organize, sequence, and become familiar with course content.
- Collect and prepare related instructional materials, and plan to use various types of instructional media. This planning will help when ordering instructional supplies.
- Use a variety of instructional strategies and activities over time.
- Prepare to interact with students during instruction. This may include preparing a list of important questions or guidelines for a cooperative group activity.
- Incorporate techniques to motivate students to learn in each lesson.
- Take into account individual differences and the diversity of students when selecting objectives, content, strategies, materials, and requirements.
- Arrange for appropriate requirements and evaluation of student performance.
- Become a reflective decision maker about curriculum and instruction.
- Provide substitute teachers and members of a teaching team with a specific plan to follow if you are absent.
- Show other members of a teaching team what you are doing and how you are doing it.
- Satisfy administrative requirements. Teachers are often required to turn in their weekly plans for review by their principal.
- Use written plans as resources for future planning.

Planning Phases

There are four phases in the planning process (Freiberg & Driscoll, 2000). Each phase has a function in the planning process, and key decisions are made at each level, which in turn affects subsequent decisions in the next planning phase.

First, *preplanning* is a time when a mental plan is made before instruction actually begins. These tentative mental plans are made concerning the design and implementation of a lesson or a larger instructional unit. This is a time when you might gather information about the students' needs and interests, review and gather content, and consider the conditions in which instruction is to take place. During the preplanning phase, you may visualize what might occur in a unit or a lesson, mentally sequence the content, consider alternative instructional activities, and make tentative decisions about all aspects of the upcoming instruction.

Next, *active planning* is a time when decisions are made about instruction and a commitment to a specific plan is made. This occurs before instruction and is the time when written plans are prepared. During active planning, you will make final decisions and preparations before instruction concerning issues such as the content, teaching strategies, instructional activities, instructional materials, motivational strategies, instructional media, and evaluation procedures. In addition, in this phase all resources and materials are prepared and gathered in preparation of instruction.

Third, *ongoing planning* occurs during instruction itself and involves fine-tuning the plan based on events that take place during instruction. Even with thorough, well-thought-out plans, you may find that you need to make some adjustments in the plan based on events that take place during instruction. For example, when asking students questions to check their understanding, you might find that you need to reteach a part of the lesson, or that students are taking less time than expected for a certain activity. Adjustments may include adding or dropping certain planned activities, extending the time for an activity, or changing your instructional strategy.

Finally, *postplanning* occurs after instruction takes place and involves evaluation of the instruction that just took place. It is often helpful to make notes of your experiences with the lesson. This is useful information in planning future lessons concerning that subject matter. Notes can be made in the margins of a plan book, in looseleaf notebooks, or journals.

CLASSROOM DECISIONS

While you are teaching a lesson, you may realize that it isn't turning out exactly as you had planned. As a result, you may need to make some changes as you proceed. When teaching a class, what signals might you see to indicate that you need to shift away from your lesson plan? How might these signals be different in classes with a different subject matter or at a different grade level?

This reflective time after instruction can help you to evaluate strengths and weaknesses of the planned lesson and consider how to improve instruction. You may ask yourself questions about whether the lesson objectives were met, how many students mastered the objective, the appropriateness and effectiveness of the activities and materials, the sequencing and pacing of the instruction, the degree of student involvement, or changes you might make next time to improve the lesson.

Factors Considered in Planning

When making plans for instruction, you will need to take into account factors related to your beliefs about teaching and the role of teachers, the instructional activities, routines of teaching, your own personal and professional characteristics, and your reflections on your practice (Borko & Niles, 1987; Kagan, 1995). Taken together, these factors will affect the decisions that you make about your instructional plans.

Factors Related to Instructional Activities.   Instructional activities are the basic means through which teachers interact to present concepts and skills to students. There are a number of factors which you may consider when you plan any given instructional activity (Clark & Yinger, 1987).

1. *Content.* Content refers to the knowledge, skill, rule, concept, or creative process that you wish students to learn. Students are expected to achieve school district goals stated in curriculum guides, and you select content related to the goals. While you have some autonomy, you are expected to teach and deal with content that is consistent with the district-approved goals.

Planning for content varies with the level of instruction, whether it be an advanced course, general content, or remedial material. Also, the nature of the content may affect teachers' planning decisions. For example, you might plan and teach in different ways for mathematics, reading, laboratory-related content, and social studies. Thus, what is taught determines to a great extent how you might plan and teach your lessons.

2. *Materials.* Materials are the tangible written, physical, or visual stimuli that are used in instruction. Textbooks, workbooks, computers, videotapes, software, and Web sites are some materials that you might use.

The availability of these materials influences your planning decisions. For example, when planning a lesson in which the students are painting with watercolors, an art teacher would need to be sure that certain materials are available. If the materials are not available, the teacher would need to make alternative plans. Teachers also need to consider how closely matched the materials are to the instructional objectives. For example, when considering using a film in a lesson, you would need to check on the nature and level of the content and also be sure the equipment is available when needed.

3. *Instructional strategies.* Selecting a variety of instructional strategies used to teach content is a central planning decision for teachers. These instructional strategies will be reviewed more thoroughly in Chapters 6, 7, and 8. Briefly, though, you might use lectures, demonstrations, questions, recitations, practice, and drills. Or you could use discussions, panels and debates, or small groups. Or, you might select inquiry and discovery approaches through the use of gaming, role playing and simulation, laboratory work, or computer-assisted instruction.

4. *Teacher behaviors.* Teachers do a number of things during a lesson to conduct the lesson and to help engage students in learning activities; these will be discussed in Chapter 9 on managing lesson delivery. Briefly, though, you need to make plans to state expectations, provide a set induction, maintain a group focus, provide smooth transitions, clearly present lesson content, provide closure and a summary, and handle other aspects of conducting a lesson.

5. *Structure of the lesson.* Structure of the lesson refers to actions that take place at certain points in the class period or the lesson presentation, and you need to plan for the structure of a lesson. For example, the start of the class period you may provide directions, pass out materials, or direct students to new locations. As the lesson proceeds, students might be reading, discussing, writing, or be participating in a particular instructional strategy. At the end of the class, students may return to their seats, clean up, or collect materials. These phases of a lesson are more thoroughly discussed in Chapter 9 on managing lesson delivery. When delivering lesson content, you might use a certain sequence of actions reflecting a certain approach to instruction.

6. *Learning environment.* When planning for instructional activities, consider the type of learning environment you would like to create. While many factors need to be taken into account, several issues warrant special attention. First, an effective classroom management system needs to be planned for and established, dealing with issues such as establishing classroom rules and procedures, reinforcing desired behaviors, holding students academically accountable, and creating a positive classroom climate (all discussed in Chapter 10). Second, a plan of dealing with misbehavior needs to be established (see Chapter 11). Third, you need to plan for ways to provide for individual differences (see Chapter 6). Fourth, you need to plan for ways to motivate students to learn (see Chapter 5). All of these issues contribute to the learning environment, and you need to plan for ways to address them.

7. *Students.* When planning for instructional activities, consider characteristics of the particular students you have in your classroom. Take into account students' motivation needs, academic needs, and physical and psychological needs. Furthermore, consider how students will be grouped for instruction (i.e., whole group, small group, independent work) and consider which particular students will be in groups. As you plan, take into account the ability level of the students and the ways in which students might be grouped to achieve instructional objectives. In addition, take into account the number of students who are involved in the instructional activities.

8. *Duration of the lesson.* Make plans for the time that is available or allocated. Instructional activities tend to last from 10 to 60 minutes. In a kindergarten class, 10 minutes of an activity may be the limit of student concentration and attention. Class lengths in primary and intermediate elementary grades are commonly up to the discretion of the teacher, but they often last no longer than 20 to 30 minutes. Classes in middle schools, junior high schools, and high schools commonly have predetermined lengths, ranging from 45 to 60 minutes or as much as 90 minutes in a block schedule. Within the time available, teachers need to use a variety of activities and resources to achieve lesson objectives and maintain student motivation. You need to be a good time manager to ensure that students have the opportunity to achieve the goals of the lesson during this time period.

9. *Location of the lesson.* When planning for instructional activities, plan for where the lesson will take place. The location of an activity may change based on the need for (a) space to work on a set of materials (i.e., a computer station or a learning center), (b) additional new references, materials, or experiences (i.e., the library, a field trip), or (c) a different social structure (i.e., a debate, a play, or any activity in which students work together).

Routines of Teaching.   In addition to decisions about instructional activities, another important planning factor is the development of teaching routines or established procedures. A *routine* is a standard operating procedure to achieve a certain task. These procedures enable you to create a learning environment in which the students are knowledgeable about classroom procedures and teacher expectations. In fact, routines are like scripted segments of behavior that help you and your students move to a shared goal (Leinhardt et al., 1989).

TEACHERS IN ACTION

PLANNING TO INTEGRATE ALL SUBJECTS

Donna Erpelding, third grade teacher, Manhattan, Kansas

Over the years working with children, I have observed and have come to the conclusion that children learn more if they can see how everything fits together. Several years ago one of my students made a comment when I wanted a written paper corrected for spelling errors. He said, "Why should I rewrite this paper to correct the spelling? This isn't spelling class." Now I strive for integration of my lessons. I think integration of knowledge aids in understanding, critical thinking, and problem solving.

Content in my classroom, therefore, revolves around a theme. A week long study of Mexico can be used to illustrate theme integration. Everything we studied during the week focused on Mexico. The stories we read in reading had a Spanish or Mexican emphasis. The lessons in social studies were centered around the history of Mexico and map studies. Major geographical features—mountains, lakes, sea coasts, plains—were part of the week's experiences and assignments. In science we looked at how simple machines helped in the building of the

Mayan temples. We made an inclined plane and pulled a basket of "rocks" (books). Spelling words that week were Spanish words that are familiar to us in our daily lives. We learned a few Spanish phrases, listened to Spanish music, and completed some artwork dealing with a Mexico influence. In math, we wrote word problems dealing with products in Mexico's agriculture. The librarian shared slides and articles of pottery, clothing, baskets, and other materials she obtained on a recent trip to Mexico.

We did some critical thinking about a variety of influences on Mexico's food production. We had a problem-solving discussion on the transportation of fruits, fresh flowers, and other products to destinations in the United States. Among other questions, we asked how fruits and flowers are kept fresh. By the end of the week, the students had a better understanding and appreciation of Mexico. I deliberately planned the integration of all the subjects around the theme of Mexico.

Thus, general procedures become an organizational structure around which you organize activities, and, therefore, content and materials.

Routines serve two important purposes. First, they ease the task of planning by providing a framework that allows you to spend time selecting content and monitoring student performance. Second, once familiar with the procedures and expectations, students may be less anxious about their work. When students know the guidelines for acceptable behavior, the length of the activity, and the means of feedback, then they can focus on the learning tasks. There are four types of routines.

1. *Activity routines.* Teachers often use established procedures to help organize the activities they implement with students. These routines help you avoid having to consider separately each of the factors related to the instructional activities (discussed previously). By standardizing some aspects of an activity, you have more time to spend thinking about other aspects. For example, if the duration and location are standardized during an activity, you can focus on the structure and sequence or the instructional techniques and methods. For instance, you might establish a routine location and length of time for reading groups, discussion activities, or lab activities. Activity routines become even greater timesavers as students have greater awareness of teacher expectations for student behavior during various activities.

CLASSROOM DECISIONS

Activity routines can help organize and standardize instructional activities. If you planned to have students at work tables, what activity routines might you establish to have the students go to the work area, obtain supplies, clean up, and return materials? How might you change any of these routines for different grade levels?

---

2. *Instructional routines.* Instructional routines are the established procedures that teachers attach to the techniques and methods they use during instruction. For example, you may develop certain practices for questioning, monitoring, and giving instructions. Instructional routines are often used in the presentation of concepts, skills, rules, or creative acts. In this way, you form patterns of behavior that are used on a number of different occasions.

For example, you might use instructional routines in classroom discussions. Through the use of instructional routines, you do not have to tell students how to have a class discussion each time they begin a discussion. Students are aware of the procedures from having had class discussions in the past. After you reinforce the procedures during the first few classes, the procedures become part of the structure of the class.

3. *Management routines.* Management routines involve the use of established procedures to maintain order and to coordinate student behavior at the start and close of the school day and between instructional activities. Management routines help regulate behaviors such as passing out or collecting materials, leaving the room, cleaning the room, starting the school day, or having transitions between activities.

For some of these tasks, students may understand the teacher's purposes and goals. For example, when you ask students to hand in a set of papers in alphabetical order, students understand that this saves time for you as you score the papers and record the grades.

Students might not be aware of the purposes for certain teacher behaviors. For example, when you stand by the door as students exit the classroom, you are achieving a number of management goals. First, by blocking half of the doorway and speaking to students as they leave, you can monitor the flow of students and ensure small quiet clusters of students exit rather than a large unruly mass. Second, you have the opportunity to comment to students about their day and, thereby, end the day on a positive personal note. Though students may not be aware of your purposes for this management routine, they nevertheless are affected by them.

4. *Executive planning routines.* Executive planning routines are procedures that teachers follow when they are preparing instructional plans. For example, you may follow a pattern of actions when preparing lesson plans. You may gather materials related to the topic, look through the materials, list activities that might serve as part of the unit, decide on a sequence of the activities, and so on. These actions are executive planning routines.

Teacher Characteristics.   Planning decisions about instructional activities and instructional routines are affected by the characteristics of the teachers themselves (Evertson, Neely, & Hansford, 1990).

First, the amount of teaching experience you have influences planning decisions. Previous experiences provide you with a more complete mental image of lessons and, thus, your initial lessons need less adjustment. Second, your philosophy of teaching and learning will have an effect on planning decisions. Third, your knowledge of content also affects planning decisions. Teachers who know their content usually can plan more varied and flexible lessons because they can readily use and arrange information. Fourth, your organizational style affects planning decisions. This style is reflected by your need for structure, planning routine, and style of solving problems. Fifth, expectations that you set for your classes, for student learning, and for your own teaching also influence your planning and lesson images. Finally, general feelings of security and control about teaching play an influential role in the planning process. When you feel secure in all dimensions of teaching, teaching plans tend to be less rigid. When not so secure, teachers tend to be more structured and plan in greater detail. In summary, your characteristics serve as a filter through which instructional activities and routines are considered.

Planning and the Standards Movement

The standards movement has lead to the development of standards or criteria for student performance. These standards are especially helpful when you are considering the content, materials, and instructional strategies outline in the preceding section.

The standards movement began with the development of content standards in areas such as mathematics (National Council of Teachers of Mathematics, 1989), science (American Association for the Advancement of Science, 1993) and English (National Council of Teachers of English & International Reading Association, 1996). A central feature of this process has been to involve education stakeholders (e.g., policy makers, educators, parents, students and community members) in the identification of what students should know and be able to do to be productive citizens. Samples of these standards are listed in Table 2.1.

The National Center on Education and the Economy and the Learning Research and Development Center (LRDC) at the University of Pittsburgh have taken the standards in the areas of language arts, science, and mathematics and developed an assessment system to measure student performance against the standards at the elementary, middle, and high school levels (New Standard Student Performance Standards, 1997). This assessment system can be used by teachers, and it is available directly from the National Center. The standards are matched to a series of examinations and are sold by Harcourt Brace Educational Measurement. Professional development is available through the National Center to support the implementation of standards and assessment systems.

The standards address what should be taught, and the performance assessment indicates the level of performance that students should demonstrate. The goal of these new standards is to benchmark or match these assessments to those of other countries whose students achieve highly on international assessments. The tests include a mix of traditional test items and performance tasks that ask students to use their knowledge to solve complex problems.

TABLE 2.1   Sample Content Area Standards

CONTENT AREA	ORGANIZATION AND WEB SITE	STANDARDS
English language arts	National Council of Teachers of English (NCTE) http://www.ncte.org/	1. Reading 2. Writing 3. Speaking, Listening, and Viewing 4. Conventions, Grammar, and Usage of the English Language 5. Literature
Foreign language	American Council on the Teaching of Foreign Language (ACTFL) http://www.actfl.org/	1. Communication: Communicate in Languages Other Than English 2. Cultures: Gain Knowledge and Understanding of Other Cultures 3. Connections: Connect with Other Disciplines and Acquire Information 4. Comparisons: Develop Insight into the Nature of Language 5. Communities: Participate in Multilingual Communities at Home and around the World
Mathematics	National Council of Teachers of Mathematics (NCTM) http://www.nctm.org/	1. Number and Operations 2. Algebra 3. Geometry 4. Measurement 5. Data Analysis and Probability 6. Problem Solving 7. Reasoning and Proof 8. Communication 9. Connections 10. Representations
Science	National Science Teachers Association (NSTA) http://www.nsta.org/	1. Physical Science and Concepts 2. Life Science and Concepts 3. Earth and Space Sciences and Concepts 4. Scientific Connections and Applications 5. Scientific Thinking 6. Scientific Tools and Technologies 7. Scientific Communication 8. Scientific Investigation
Social studies	National Council for the Social Studies (NCSS) http://www.socialstudies.org/	1. Culture 2. Time, Continuity, and Change 3. People, Places, and Environment 4. Individual Development and Identity 5. Individuals, Groups, and Institutions 6. Power, Authority, and Governance 7. Production, Distribution, and Consumption 8. Science, Technology, and Society 9. Global Connections 10. Civic Ideals and Practices

The National Assessment of Educational Progress (NAEP) is the only nationally representative, continuing assessment of what America's students know and can do in various subject areas. As such, the NAEP is often called the Nation's Report Card. Assessment has taken place since 1969. As the only measure given over time to assess educational achievement, the NAEP plays a primary role in evaluating the progress of the nation's educational system. Currently, the commissioner of education statistics, the head of the National Center for Education Statistics (NCES) in the U.S. Department of Education, is responsible for administering and reporting on the NAEP assessments. The National Assessment Governing Board, appointed by the secretary of education but independent of the department, governs the program.

Proponents of the standards movement would say that you only need to review the student performance data to recognize the importance of the standards movement. Table 2.2 shows the percentage of students who are scoring at or above proficient in reading, writing, or science or in standards-based language at or above the standard. For example, 29% of fourth grade students in New York State scored proficient or above on the NAEP reading

SPOTLIGHT ON TECHNOLOGY

USING TECHNOLOGY TO ACCESS TEST DATA

How well have the students performed on the NAEP assessments? As a teacher, what do you think should be done if performance is low? The NAEP data can be found on Education Week's Special Reports Web page: http://www.edweek.org/sreports/ or directly from the NAEP Web site: http://nces.ed.gov/nationsreportcard/.

Your individual state also has its own testing program. The data on how well students are performing on standards-based state assessments and other important measures of school success (e.g., dropout rates for high school students; SAT scores) are, in most cases, listed on your state Department of Education's Web site (e.g., state averages and data for Rhode Island schools and school districts can be found at http://infoworks.ride.uri.edu/2001/default.asp).

One of your goals as a teacher should be to improve your ability to critically analyze information and data on student success in your classroom and school. Using information from the World Wide Web (see the following Web sites of interest), you can gather valuable data on children. In many cases, you can even find information on individual schools or districts. You might find it interesting to review data on a school that you attended or one in which you have had or will have a field experience. Interviews and classroom visits can also be invaluable to your review.

Web Sites of Interest

- K–12 State Education Departments, with directories of schools and districts. From the Council of Chief State School Officers. www.ccsso.org.   http://www.ccsso.org/seamenu.html
- The Annie E. Casey Foundation funds a nationwide network of state-level KIDS COUNT projects that provides a more detailed, community-by-community picture of the condition of children.   http://www.aecf.org/links.htm KIDS COUNT Projects Online
- Kids count national data on the status of children; information from positive lead testing rates to teenage pregnancy rates.   http://www.kidscount.org/
- Census data. http://www.census.gov/-U.S.

TABLE 2.2   Summary of National Assessment of Educational Progress Grades by State

STATE	STUDENT ACHIEVEMENT (% SCORING AT OR ABOVE PROFICIENT)					
	Fourth Grade NAEP Reading (1998)	Eighth Grade NAEP Reading (1998)	Eighth Grade NAEP Writing (1998)	Fourth Grade NAEP Math (1996)	Eighth Grade NAEP Math (1996)	Eighth Grade NAEP Science (1996)
Alabama	24	21	17	11	12	18
Alaska	?	?	?	21	30	31
Arizona	22	28	21	15	18	23
Arkansas	23	23	13	13	13	22
California[a]	20	22	20	11	17	20
Colorado	34	30	27	22	25	32
Connecticut	46	42	44	31	30	36
Delaware	25	25	22	16	19	21
Florida	23	23	19	15	17	21
Georgia	24	25	23	13	16	21
Hawaii[b]	17	19	15	16	16	15
Idaho	?	?	?	?	?	?
Illinois	?	?	?	?	?	?
Indiana	?	?	?	24	24	30
Iowa	35	?	?	22	31	36
Kansas	34	35	?	?	?	?
Kentucky	29	29	21	16	16	23
Louisiana	19	18	12	8	7	13
Maine	36	42	32	27	31	41
Maryland	29	31	23	22	24	25
Massachusetts	37	36	31	24	28	37
Michigan	28	?	?	23	28	32
Minnesota	36	37	25	29	34	37
Mississippi	18	19	11	8	7	12
Missouri	29	29	17	20	22	28
Montana	37	38	25	22	32	41
Nebraska	?	?	?	24	31	35
Nevada	21	24	17	14	?	?
New Hampshire	38	?	?	?	?	?
New Jersey	?	?	?	25	?	?
New Mexico	22	24	18	13	14	19
New York	29	34	21	20	22	27
North Carolina	28	31	27	21	20	24
North Dakota	?	?	?	24	33	41
Ohio	?	?	?	?	?	?
Oklahoma	30	29	25	?	?	?
Oregon	28	33	27	21	26	32

(continued)

TABLE 2.2   CONTINUED

	STUDENT ACHIEVEMENT (% SCORING AT OR ABOVE PROFICIENT)					
STATE	Fourth Grade NAEP Reading (1998)	Eighth Grade NAEP Reading (1998)	Eighth Grade NAEP Writing (1998)	Fourth Grade NAEP Math (1996)	Eighth Grade NAEP Math (1996)	Eighth Grade NAEP Science (1996)
Pennsylvania	?	?	?	20	?	?
Rhode Island	32	30	25	17	20	26
South Carolina	22	22	15	12	14	17
South Dakota	?	?	?	?	?	?
Tennessee	25	26	24	17	15	22
Texas	29	28	31	25	21	23
Utah	28	31	21	23	24	32
Vermont	?	?	?	23	27	34
Virginia	30	33	27	19	21	27
Washington	29	32	25	21	26	27
West Virginia	29	27	18	19	14	21
Wisconsin	34	33	28	27	32	39
Wyoming	30	29	23	19	22	34
United States	29	31	24	20	23	27

Percentages may not add up to 100% because of rounding.

? Indicates that state did not participate in national assessment, survey, or data collection.

[a]California did not receive a grade for school climate because the state has dramatically reduced class size, but the data do not reflect it.

[b]Hawaii has a single statewide district.

assessment. Students in Connecticut scored at the top of the performance range for fourth grade reading, with 46% at or above the proficient level. The average for fourth grade reading across the United States was also 29%. With only 29% scoring proficient in reading, 71% are, by definition, not proficient in reading.

APPROACHES TO PLANNING

There are two prominent approaches to instructional planning. The linear-rational model involves sequential decisions about goals, objectives, needs assessment, strategies, and evaluation. The mental-image approach involves forming mental images of lessons you plan to teach after considering factors related to instructional activities and instructional routines (Juarez, 1992).

The Linear-Rational Model

The type of planning taught most often in teacher education programs is a sequential process based on clear goals and objectives. The *linear-rational model* of instructional planning involves sequential decisions about the (a) formulation of goals, (b) specification of objectives, (c) assessment of student needs relative to the stated goals and objectives, (d) selection of strategies and learning activities linked to the objectives, and (e) evaluation of student performance (see Figure 2.1).

It is a logical and organized way to plan for instruction. With this model, you build on the knowledge gained from each step. Insights gained in one step lead to changes in other steps. In this way, objectives, methods, and evaluation are logically linked and are given consideration in the initial planning. For example, you must think about evaluation even when making decisions about objectives, activities, content, and sequence.

This model is the traditional approach used in both teaching and studying the planning process. The rational model was originally proposed by Tyler (1950) and later refined by Taba (1967), Popham and Baker (1970), Gagné, Briggs, and Wager (1992), and Gagné and Driscoll (1988). The rational model is sometimes referred to as "instructional design" or "the systems approach to planning." It requires the analysis of the components of planning in a logical order with an orderly but flexible sequence. Each of the five steps in the linear-rational model for instructional planning is discussed in the following sections.

Formulation of Aims and Goals.   The first step of the linear-rational model of instructional planning involves the formulation of goals. Educational goals are the broad statements of purpose that educators use to provide a direction for the courses they plan. The purposes of education are stated at a number of levels: nation, state, school district, subject, grade level, unit plan, or lesson plan. The terms *aims, goals,* and *objectives* are commonly used to identify the educational purposes at each of these levels.

Aims.   The term *aim* refers to broad statements about the intent of education. Aims are often written by national or state panels, commissions, or policy-making groups. Aims express a philosophy of education and concepts about the social role of schools and the needs of children. They guide our schools and give educators direction.

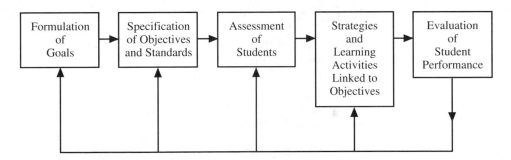

FIGURE 2.1   The Linear-Rational Model for Planning

The terms *philosophy, aims,* or *goals* are often used interchangeably in reference to any statement associated with the broad purposes of education. As a rule, statements of philosophy and aims are the most abstract and general statements for the purposes of education. Furthermore, statements of philosophy are often written in paragraph form, with short statements of aims following them in an attempt to further clarify and delineate the educational mission.

Historically, aims of education have changed very little. For example, the "Seven Cardinal Principles of Secondary Education," written by the Commission on the Reorganization of Secondary Education in 1918 include many beliefs found in current statements of educational philosophy, aims, or goals. The seven principles include (a) health, (b) command of the fundamental processes, (c) worthy home membership, (d) vocation, (e) citizenship, (f) worthy use of leisure time, and (g) ethical character. Courses in elementary and secondary schools address these aims of education. Furthermore, many recent reports produced by national and state panels, commissions, and policy-making groups include aims that are similar to the Seven Cardinal Principles.

In 1991, six national education goals were identified by members of the National Education Goals Panel (1991), comprised of six governors, four members of the administration, and four members of Congress. The goals were intended to set a direction for school districts around the country.

The president challenged every community to become an America 2000 Community (Department of Education, 1991) by doing four things: (a) adopt the six National Education Goals, (b) develop a community-wide strategy to achieve them, (c) design a report card to measure results, and (d) plan for and support a New American School. Since that time, many districts have adopted the goals as the focus of their district's curricular efforts. Several objectives were identified for each goal. As mentioned previously, the terms *aims* and *goals* are often used interchangeably, but the six national goals fit our definition of aims since they are broad statements of intent. The six National Education Goals state that by the year 2000:

1. All children in America will start school ready to learn.
2. The high school graduation rate will increase to at least 90 percent.
3. American students will leave grades four, eight, and twelve having demonstrated competency in challenging subject matter, including English, mathematics, science, history, and geography; and every school in America will ensure that all students learn to use their minds well, so they may be prepared for responsible citizenship, further learning, and productive employment in our modern economy.
4. United States students will be first in the world in science and mathematics achievement.
5. Every adult American will be literate and will possess the knowledge and skills necessary to compete in a global economy and to exercise the rights and responsibilities of citizenship.
6. Every school in America will be free of drugs and violence and will offer a disciplined environment conducive to learning.

Goals.   Educators need to translate general aims into statements that will describe what schools are expected to accomplish. These translations of aims into more specific, subject-related terms are called *goals.*

Goals are more definite than aims. Goals are nonbehavioral and provide direction for educators, but they do not specify achievement levels. Goals are often written by professional associations and state and local educational agencies to serve as guidelines for school and curriculum guides for what all students should accomplish over their entire school career. General school goals are then written by school district personnel in more specific terms for each subject area in curriculum guides.

A number of school districts now use outcomes-based education, which affects goal statements and the subsequent translation into objectives and the evaluation of student performance. *Outcomes-based education* (OBE) involves focusing and organizing all the school's programs and efforts with an emphasis on clearly defined outcomes which all students must demonstrate upon exit from the course, program, or grade level. With OBE, there is more emphasis on the product of learning instead of the process, and more emphasis on individualized learning. Various labels are used to describe OBE. Master learning and total quality performance are terms that are sometimes used to describe these same ideas. A curriculum guide reflecting OBE would state the content and also what the student should be able to demonstrate.

Subject-specific educational goals are written as a bridge to even more explicit learning objectives. Luckily, the task of translating general school goals to subject area goals is not left solely on the shoulders of the individual teacher. Most school districts have curriculum guides that the district prepares, adopts, and makes available for teachers to use. These curriculum guides are based on goals selected by the district.

Curriculum guides commonly include subject-specific course goals, a fairly detailed outline of curricular content, and recommended instructional activities and materials. Curriculum guides are prepared by teachers in the district and are formally adopted by the school board. The guides ensure that the goals have proper coverage at appropriate grade levels. Teachers are expected to use these curriculum guides in their planning.

In summary, aims are translated into general school goals which, in turn, are translated into subject-specific course goals. These course goals are in the curriculum guides that are made available to teachers. You would use the course goals in the curriculum guide to identify learning objectives for unit and weekly plans. When you prepare daily lesson plans, you translate the learning objectives into performance objectives. As displayed in Figure 2.2, general aims undergo a series of translations and ultimately result in a number of specific performance objectives used in daily lesson plans.

There are some interesting influences at work as the aims undergo this series of translations. For example, the process of the selection and division of goals into subject areas by grade is largely controlled at the local school district level, but not without input at the state and national levels. State departments of education often provide a listing of general subject area goals or standards by grade level. These goals influence individual school districts in their selection of subject-specific course goals, in part due to the growing phenomenon of statewide competency exams. In fact, some state departments of education develop curriculum guides that are to be used throughout the state. The curriculum guides may contain goals, activities, the means of assessment, resources, and other information. Standardized tests at the national level, such as the National Assessment of Educational Progress (NAEP), the Stanford Achievement Test, the Metropolitan Achievement Test, and the California Achievement Test, also influence the development of goals at the state and local level.

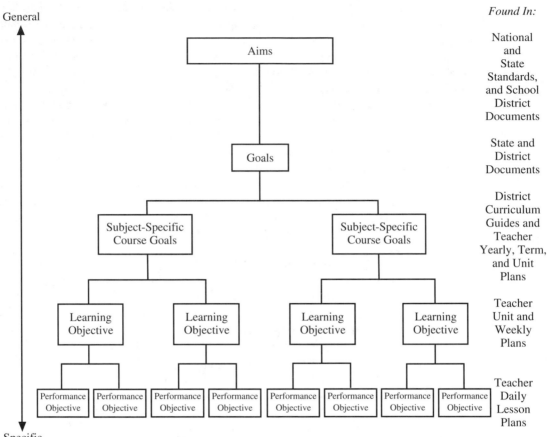

FIGURE 2.2   Aims, Goals, and Objectives

Textbooks, student workbooks, and other published instructional materials have great influence on the interpretation of aims and goals, and on the curriculum in schools. When preparing the content of printed materials and textbooks, publishing companies seek input from teachers through surveys and interviews. The companies also take into account goals for courses that have been developed by the state departments of education. Teachers, especially new teachers, tend to rely heavily on curriculum guides and textbooks for a large portion of their planning.

To illustrate one step in the translation of the aims, we can look at the process of developing subject-specific goals in the state of Illinois. A committee of representatives from education, business, and the general public were brought together to develop subject-specific goals for language arts, mathematics, biological and physical sciences, fine arts, physical development, and health. The goals were developed as "relatively timeless expressions of what the state of Illinois wants and expects its students to know and be able to do as a consequence of their elementary and secondary schooling" (Illinois State Board of

Education, 1986, p. iv). The broad listings of goals with sample learning objectives to aid schools in the process of developing their own lists of district level objectives were disseminated to schools. This process was established to have all school districts prepare lists of objectives representing the "skills and understandings" that would be required of all students (p. v). These goals and the resulting objectives would then serve as the basis for a testing program to assess student performance.

Specification of Objectives.   When preparing unit plans, teachers commonly look at the subject-specific course goals and curriculum content in the curriculum guide for their subject. You would then translate that material into learning objectives for unit or weekly plans. When preparing daily lesson plans, unit learning objectives are translated into performance objectives (see Figure 2.2).

Subject-specific course goals are more specific translations of district goals and are stated in curriculum guides. Subject-specific course goals can be translated and broken down into more specific learning objectives used in unit or weekly plans (Gronlund, 2000). *Learning objectives* are statements of what is hoped that students will achieve through instruction, and they are narrower in scope than subject-specific goals. For example, a subject-specific course goal concerning increasing student literacy might lead to a more narrow and specific learning objective about students writing a well organized business letter.

To write learning objectives, look at the subject-specific course goals that are printed in the curriculum guide for the subject they are teaching. Then translate these subject-specific course goals into more specific learning objectives which are included in your unit and weekly plans. From these learning objectives, you can then write more specific performance objectives for daily lesson plans.

Performance objectives are written for daily lesson plans and are stated in behavioral terms to indicate what is to be observed and measured. When writing performance objectives, you need to consider the parts of the stated objective and the learning domains represented. These issues are considered next.

Assessment of Student Needs.   The next step in the linear-rational model of planning is *needs assessment* or *diagnosis.* Diagnosis means looking at a situation to fully understand it and to find clues for deciding what to do. Successful diagnosis reveals (a) the students' aptitudes, aspirations, backgrounds, problems, and needs; (b) the level of learning your students have reached; and (c) where your students are weak and strong.

This information will help you make a number of planning decisions about both curriculum and instruction. With this information, you will be able to capitalize on students' strengths and intrinsic motivation, and to help correct their deficiencies. It also can serve as the basis for placing students in appropriate groups and for adjusting assignments; this is especially useful when assigning students to groups, such as for cooperative learning. Information obtained through diagnosis also helps you make decisions about curricular material to be covered. Areas of need can vary widely within the same classroom and therefore you need to be aware of both the general needs of their students and the specific needs of individual students.

The process of diagnosis involves seeing what the situation is and what should be done next. The steps of diagnosis are (Clark & Starr, 1996) (a) assess the situation; (b) determine if there is any difficulty; (c) if there is any difficulty, identify what it is, determine its cause, and search for factors in the situation that would help you to make your teaching more effective and eliminate the difficulty and its cause; (d) make a final estimate of the situation in view of the information obtained in the earlier steps; and (e) make decisions on the basis of the final estimate of the situation.

Information for needs assessment or diagnosis comes from a variety of sources (Clark & Starr, 1996). A number of printed records are available, such as the cumulative record folder kept for each student, test results, anecdotal records, and even reports of physical exams. Indirect contacts also provide information. These include contacts with parents, other teachers who have had involvement with the student, the guidance counselor, and others. Direct contacts with the students also provide very useful information. This can be done through personal observations, through student autobiographies or questionnaires, or through diagnostic, formative, or summative tests.

CLASSROOM DECISIONS

Before selecting specific content and instructional activities for a unit, it would be useful to find out what students already know about the content in the unit. If you were teaching about the electoral process in the state and federal government, how would you assess your students' current knowledge? What are some alternative assessment approaches that would bring some novelty and variety to the class?

Futhermore, an important skill in diagnosis is the ability to decide *if* as well as *why* instructional problems exist. Is the student having problems because of a lack of understanding? An alleged instructional problem can be due to poor directions given for a task or a lack of rewards for completion of the task, rather than a lack of understanding of a required skill or knowledge of the topic. In a similar vein, students who do not hand in their homework are more likely to be doing so based on a lack of motivation, reward, consequence, or perceived value as compared to a lack of knowledge. Sometimes the solution to a problem of poor student performance is not reteaching, but rather specific feedback and/ or additional practice and reinforcement.

Taken together, information that teachers gather through diagnosis or needs assessment can be very useful when making decisions on curriculum and instruction. Diagnosis is an important step in the linear-rational model that takes place after the specification of objectives and before deciding about strategies and learning activities.

Strategies and Learning Activities.   In the linear-rational model to instructional planning, teachers formulate goals, specify objectives, and assess students' needs before getting to the point where they select strategies and learning activities. After carefully selecting the precise performance objectives in different levels of the learning domains, you need to select strategies and learning activities that will help students achieve those objectives.

There are many instructional strategies that the teacher could select to achieve the instructional objectives for a particular lesson. These include lectures, demonstrations, practice and drills, reviews, group and discussion methods, inquiry approaches, discovery learning and problem solving, role playing, community involvement, and other approaches. Instructional strategies will be considered in detail in Chapters 6, 7, and 8.

Here, it is useful to consider an important aspect in the delivery of the content and the choice of instructional strategies—planning for the sequence of instructional tasks. Sequencing has two basic purposes (Orlich, Harder, Callahan, & Gibson, 2001). First, it can be used to isolate knowledge (a fact, concept, generalization, or principle) so that students can understand the unique characteristics of the selected information or to isolate a thinking process so that students can master the process under varying conditions. This makes learning more manageable. Second, sequencing can be used to relate the knowledge or process being taught to the larger organized body of knowledge. This makes learning more meaningful. A sequence is process-related in that it establishes a schedule for learning the various parts of the related content.

There are several principles that apply to all kinds of sequencing (Orlich et al., 2001). First, start with a simple step. Structure the presentation so the students can easily identify content. It is helpful to provide numerous examples. Second, proceed to the concrete. This means that you should illustrate the objective or content with materials, models, simulations, or artifacts. Third, plan to structure a lesson or learning sequence so that it becomes more complex. This means that you might introduce additional variables, generate new sets of criteria, or establish relationships between the content of the lessons and other content. Fourth, you may introduce abstractions in which students are asked to generalize, predict, or explain information generated.

Lessons and units can be organized in a variety of ways. In relation to sequencing, there are four models of lesson or unit organization that can be considered (Orlich et al., 2001). Each model has advantages, and no single model is superior. The teacher needs to choose the model that provides the greatest assistance in lesson planning, organizing, and implementing.

1. *Task analysis model.* This model involves careful sequencing entry-level objectives, ultimately leading to the terminal objectives. Intermediate or entry-level objectives are those which need to be addressed as a foundation for later objectives. Terminal objectives are those which generally are the ending point of instruction and involve complex cognitive skills.

Therefore, break down the tasks of instruction into small pieces and sequence them from the most concrete to the most abstract. In doing so, you lead from facts to concepts to generalizations and ultimately to principles. Thus, content in a single lesson might need to be sequenced from intermediate to terminal knowledge and skills. For example, before students can achieve the terminal objective of dribbling in to shoot a layup in basketball, the students must first be accomplished in several entry-level objectives such as dribbling, dribbling while running, and then shooting from a dribble. These entry-level objectives are sequenced for increasing complexity.

2. *Concept analysis model.* This model involves sequencing concept facts and examples, and then relating the concept to a concept hierarchy. You may sequence content by (a) describing the concept first, followed by an analysis of facts and a series of examples, or (b) providing examples of the concept first and then allowing the student to discover the underlying concept.

One of the most effective methods in teaching concepts is the use of examples. For instance, you might teach the concept of mineral hardness by testing the hardness of several minerals at the start of a lesson. Then you could guide students, through questions and discussion, to conclusions about the principles of hardness.

3. *Advance organizer model.* There are three sequential parts to lesson presentation with this model. First, an advance organizer is used to introduce the lesson. It could be a generalization, a definition, a story, or some information that enables the learner to relate the lesson material to previous knowledge. An advance organizer provides an overview and focus. Second, new content that is presented is subdivided into more complex ideas to make it easily understood; this is called progressive differentiation. Third, attempts are made to help students understand the relationships among the elements of the content being taught; this is called integrative reconciliation. For example, a lesson in health on first aid might begin with a news article about a house fire and personal injuries, which would serve as an advance organizer. Then the content could be covered dealing with aspects of first aid.

4. *A diagnostic-prescriptive model.* This is a four-step teacher–student interaction model based on student entry-level knowledge and skills. The steps include (a) observation, (b) diagnosis, (c) prescription, and (d) evaluation. If some students do not experience success the first time they are exposed to a topic, it is useful to prepare some type of educational diagnosis. This is followed with a prescription of an explicit set of instructional objectives for the students who have not achieved at a standard the teacher believes to be adequate. After students have completed their prescribed activities, they need to be evaluated. If learning has not improved, the cycle may be repeated. For example, activities that require a progression of physical skills lend themselves to this model.

Each of these four models provide teachers ways to organize and sequence lesson content, and each approach has advantages and disadvantages. Consider your objectives, curriculum, students, and teaching style when determining which model to use for your particular teaching situation.

Evaluation of Student Performance.   The last step in the linear-rational model of instructional planning involves evaluating student performance. The issue of student evaluation will be thoroughly covered in Chapter 12, including selecting instruments of evaluation and preparing and administering teacher-made tests. But, you need to make decisions about evaluating student performance even *before instruction occurs,* and thus it should be considered when making planning decisions.

While details about establishing a framework for evaluation will be covered in Chapter 12, it is useful to examine aspects of evaluation that need to be addressed when planning for instruction. The reasons for evaluation must first be determined. A classroom test, for instance, can serve a variety of purposes such as judging student mastery, measuring growth over time, ranking students, and diagnosing difficulties. Different purposes lend themselves to various evaluation measures. Evaluation measures include tests, observations, discussions, interviews, work samples, experience summaries, rating instruments, questionnaires, and other approaches.

Course content which is to be evaluated must be specified, and general objectives (learning objectives at the unit level of planning) must be identified. Then performance objectives need to be prepared in the cognitive, affective, and psychomotor domains. A table of specifications (discussed in Chapter 12) then must be created with the content and objectives placed within a grid. All these steps for evaluation need to be done before instruction occurs. Therefore, you need to plan for the evaluation of student performance when you are preparing your instructional plans.

The Mental-Image Approach

Despite the logic of using the linear-rational model for instructional planning, many teachers do not use that approach. Instead, they tend to develop mental images about how they think a particular lesson or activity ought to unfold (Clark & Yinger, 1987). This approach is called the *mental-image approach* to instructional planning, which involves teachers forming mental images of the lessons they plan to teach after considering instructional routines and other factors (Morine-Dershimer, 1977, 1979; Juarez, 1992).

Teachers think about and visualize lessons in greater detail than is generally written in a plan book. Teachers realize they must take into consideration their past experiences, goals for the children, the topics or content that needs to be covered, materials available, the length of time available, and many other factors when they plan. When considering these factors, many teachers go through a cycle of comprehension, planning and preparation, teaching, evaluation, and reflection. This cycle is influenced by many factors including their level of experience; beliefs about teaching, learning, and classroom management; philosophy of education; materials available; and the particulars of the setting or context in which they teach (Lee & Huang, 1997).

When planning, effective teachers take a variety of factors into account and are more apt to focus on activities necessary to manage students more effectively during the instructional process (Tursman, 1981). As a result, mental images often focus on activities that can serve as vehicles to teach various subjects or objectives. For example, you might have a videotape available on a selected topic and then think of several parts of a lesson using the videotape—a warmup activity, the viewing of the videotape, the creation of a content outline together with the class after the viewing, and the preparation of a story, report, or drawing by each student.

A number of studies on teacher planning show that planning is mainly a mental process, not entirely committed to paper (e.g., Clark & Yinger, 1979). First, Taylor (1970) studied the way secondary teachers plan course syllabi. Teachers began planning by considering the context of teaching and only later considered the purposes that their teaching would serve. Of course, this is not the sequence proposed in the linear-rational model.

Second, Zahorik (1975) continued this line of inquiry by examining teachers' use of behavioral objectives and planning models. He found the decision most frequently made first in planning related to content, followed by objectives, needs assessment, and others. Zahorik concluded from this study that teacher planning decisions do not always follow linearly from a specification of objectives.

Third, Peterson, Marx, and Clark (1978) studied the planning process of junior high teachers by observing and audiotaping the teachers as the teachers thought aloud during the process of planning. They found that teachers spend the largest amount of their planning time considering the content they will teach, followed by the teaching strategies and activities they will use, and the least amount of time on objectives.

Fourth, Clark and Yinger (1979) found that many elementary teachers in their study on teacher planning did not begin with goals and objectives. Instead, the teachers first considered activities they would use, the content they would teach, specific student needs, and materials or resources available. The teachers also used information gained from evaluating previous lessons.

Fifth, Morine and Vallance (1975) described the outcomes of teachers' comprehensive planning activities as "lesson images." The images contain details of the plans, but the teachers seldom recorded written plans with the same degree of detail. In fact, teachers' written plans are often lists of topics linked to the *lesson images* or general mental plans that teachers use to guide instruction (Morine-Dershimer, 1977, 1979).

Features of the Mental-Image Approach.   The mental-image approach to instructional planning is portrayed in Figure 2.3. Each component of the mental image approach is described in the following sections, drawing upon the research review by Clark and Peterson (1986).

1. *Factors related to instructional activities and routines.* When making mental images of a lesson, teachers often give primary consideration to the instructional activities and instructional routines described earlier in this chapter. Based on their mental review of these factors, teachers make tentative decisions about the instructional plans.

2. *Teacher characteristics.* The tentative planning decisions are affected by the characteristics of the teacher, as described earlier in this chapter. These characteristics serve as a filter through which the instructional activities and routines are considered. Thus, your tentative instructional plans may be modified as you reflect upon your teaching experience, philosophy, knowledge of the content, and collective life experiences.

3. *Mental images of lessons.* Teachers begin to form mental images of lessons after they have considered the factors related to instructional activities and instructional rou-

---

TEACHERS IN ACTION

MENTAL PLANNING

Mary Joyce Grinsell, grades 9–12 home economics, Pawtucket, Rhode Island

Overall, I think a lot of mental activity is necessary in planning before anything is put on paper. I find planning is a constant activity. I even review in my mind each day what needs to be completed before the next day's teaching can take place. Evaluation is also a constant activity. My plan book is completed in pencil; this allows me to make needed changes as the school week progresses.

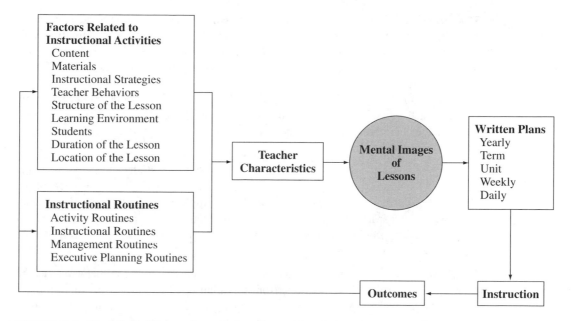

FIGURE 2.3   The Mental-Image Approach to Instructional Planning

tines, and these decisions are filtered by the characteristics of the teachers. Effective teachers usually plan by thinking of long-term and short-term plans at the same time. To plan effectively, teachers must consider specific, daily, and short-term plans simultaneously as they consider how semester goals and long-range planning will be accomplished.

A teacher's mental image of a lesson will commonly take into account objectives, materials, content, instructional strategies, instructional behaviors, and the like. The mental image will also include plans for weekly and longer-term planning. Once a teacher develops the mental image, then the plans can be written, but usually not in the degree of detail that was in the teacher's mental image.

While the arrows in Figure 2.3 indicate a regular sequence of events, teachers develop a personal approach to considering the factors related to instructional activities and instructional routines. This personal approach to addressing all these factors is affected by the teacher's thought processes (Clark & Peterson, 1986).

4. *Written plans.* As teachers become more experienced, they have more to draw upon as they create mental images of plans. As a result, experienced teachers tend to write fewer detailed plans than beginning teachers. Written plans include yearly, term, unit, weekly, and daily plans. An experienced teacher may have just a few notes or statements in the written plan, whereas the teacher's mental image of the plan may be rich in detail.

Principals commonly review teachers' weekly plans, especially for beginning teachers. It is also important to have written weekly plans in the event that a substitute teacher is needed. While you may write yearly, term, unit, and daily plans, they are commonly not reviewed by the principal.

5. *Instruction.* After mental images of lessons have been developed and plans have been written, instruction takes place one lesson at a time. Thus, teachers actually implement the plans they developed after taking into account the factors related to instructional activities and instructional routines. Teachers use instructional strategies in an effort to have students meet instructional objectives.

Once again, the teacher's plan is not intended to be a rigid script but rather a flexible framework for the lesson. You may need to make a number of changes from the intended plan due to student interest and performance, the relative success of the instructional delivery, and other factors.

6. *Outcomes.* After instruction, the teacher needs to assess student learning, which is one gauge of the success of the planning. In addition, teachers assess many aspects of the lesson to determine whether it was successful. For example, you might reconsider the factors related to the instructional activities and the instructional routines. The experience of teaching the lesson provides additional information to draw upon when creating mental images of lessons in the future.

7. *Adjusting plans.* Planning establishes a proposed course of action that serves as the teacher's guide. Appropriate deviations from this plan can be made as instruction takes place. Teachers anticipate what is likely to happen during a lesson, but they may realize that the lesson needs to be changed somewhat as the events unfold during instruction. For instance, student enthusiasm, attention, and interest may cause you to make changes from the original plan. In addition, you may change the structure and sequence for ending class activities such as cleaning up, returning materials, returning to seats, and summarizing.

Good teachers expect to adjust their plans as they go along, and they plan alternatives so they are prepared to do so. Even during instruction, teachers might need to call upon their mental images of lessons and alternative lessons to deal with the changing conditions of the classroom. The ability to adjust plans and instruction is a combination of forethought, insight, experience, and common sense. Middle-level and secondary teachers often have several sections of the same course. This enables them to modify a lesson and teach it differently in the same day. In doing so, they can make adjustments to the lesson, teach it to the next class that comes in, and see the effects immediately.

It is very helpful to write your reactions to lessons and suggestions for modification directly in the plan book. In that way, you can take these reactions into account when planning to teach the lesson the next time. By saving your lesson plans and weekly plans from one year to the next, you can refer back to the plans and the extra notations when planning the lesson in the new year.

ADDITIONAL PLANNING CONSIDERATIONS

In addition to the fundamentals of planning already discussed, there are a few other issues that you should consider as you plan for your instruction.

Resources for Planning

There are a number of resources available when you begin planning for the school year and for each unit and lesson. Many of these resources relate to the *curriculum,* which is the content to be taught. Resources are also available concerning how you go about instruction and how you might take into account related issues such as meeting the diversity of student needs, guiding student study, using instructional media, and evaluating student learning. Many resources commonly used by K–12 teachers are outlined here.

1. *Curriculum guides.* A *curriculum guide* is a document that identifies the objectives and content that are to be included in a given grade level for a given subject. Not all districts have curriculum guides available. But for those that do, the curriculum guides are approved by the local school board, and teachers are expected to help students master that material during the school year.

Curriculum guides commonly include subject-specific course goals, a fairly detailed outline of curricular content, recommended instructional activities, an annotated bibliography, and an annotated list of films, filmstrips, videotapes, computer software, and other instructional resources. Curriculum guides are often revised every few years, and teachers in the district who teach in the subject area of the curriculum guide usually have an opportunity to serve on this committee.

2. *Curriculum bulletins or materials published by the state department of education or by professional organizations.* The state department of education in each state may have additional curricular materials available such as curriculum bulletins, suggested curriculum guides for the various subject areas, and related materials concerning the content. You could contact the state department of education in your state to inquire about materials that might be available in the subject area that you teach.

Many professional organizations prepare materials that relate to the middle-level and secondary curriculum. These materials may include resource books on the particular subject matter, but also may include thorough descriptions of objectives, outcomes, and content for the various grade levels. The National Council of Teachers of Mathematics (NCTM), for example, has prepared comprehensive documents that outline and describe standards for K–12 mathematics instruction. These are significant resources for teachers of mathematics. In varying degrees, professional organizations in the other subject areas have similar resources available about curriculum and instruction.

3. *The teacher's edition of the textbook being used, or instructor's manuals.* Most textbook companies provide a teacher's edition for each textbook that is used by students. The teacher's edition often includes chapter objectives, suggested activities and resources, suggested time frames for each chapter, lists of vocabulary words, suggested questions, and other guides. It may also include transparencies, lists of suggested test questions, and other resources.

4. *Other textbooks for the course.* In addition to the textbook that you use for your course, there probably are several textbooks for that course available from other companies. Even though the material might be slightly different, these books and their accompanying teacher's editions can be a good source of additional information. You might be able to use suggested activities, resources, or test questions listed in the teacher's edition, or you might be able to use photocopies of certain tables or figures.

5. *Professional journals and publications.* Most subject fields have a professional organization that produces journals, books, monographs, videotapes, and other resource materials

TEACHERS IN ACTION

RESOURCES WHEN PLANNING FOR SIX WEEKS

Valerie Garnier, high school U.S. history teacher, Irving, Texas

I plan for six weeks at a time, since that is how our academic year is broken up. When planning, I gather the following materials:

- The teacher's edition of the textbook (This includes good introductory materials, critical thinking questions, and odd bits of fun information.)
- The curriculum guides for the courses that I teach (These include suggested timelines for units, among other things.)
- A resource kit (This contains masters for all maps, and reinforcement and enrichment sheets.)
- My film list (This is organized by chapters; it lists films for each chapter with a brief description of the film and the length of the film.)
- Last year's plans (This includes notes that I wrote to myself about how long I spent on each activity, what worked and what didn't, and how I had to adjust various activities.)

- A school calendar (I need to see when there are holidays, staff development days, or other days that we don't have class.)

I spread these materials in neat stacks on the floor of my study. Then I sit in the middle with a blank calendar and plenty of scratch paper. I make a list of chapters I want to cover and how much time I'd like to spend on each.

I then list the activities that I want for each chapter, trying to aim for variety. There's no need to do three maps in one week and not do another one for several weeks. I also try to space tests two or more weeks apart, and never on Mondays! I usually have an interesting project due for every other unit, but I allow students to work on them at least a week.

I have no real secrets here. But I always try to plan too much, since it's hard to think of fillers on the spot. You can always cut out an activity if time runs short, or carry it over to the next day.

that relate to the curriculum and instruction of that discipline. These organizations include the National Council of Teachers of English, the National Council for the Social Studies, the National Association of Biology Teachers, the Home Economics Education Association, and the National Art Education Association.

6. *Other sources.* Additional resources may be obtained from a variety of sources. Many public and private agencies have prepared materials that are suitable for middle-level and secondary instruction. For example, the National Dairy Council can be contacted about nutrition-related content and instructional materials. Similarly, many state and national governmental agencies have materials available. The extension departments of many public universities provide materials upon request. Museums may have some curricular materials, and resources may be available from many community agencies. Parents and other teachers should not be overlooked as resources for additional information about curriculum and instruction.

Teacher–Student Planning

Teacher–student planning means that the teacher does not make all the decisions about the curriculum and instruction, and that students are involved in some degree in the planning

■ ■ ■ ■ ■ ▬▬▬▬▬▬▬▬▬▬▬▬▬▬▬▬▬▬▬▬▬▬▬▬▬

MODIFICATIONS FOR DIVERSE CLASSROOMS

USING TEACHER'S EDITIONS OF TEXTBOOKS FOR PLANNING

Many K–12 textbooks come with a teacher's edition that includes recommended objectives, instructional activities, additional resources, timelines for covering the chapters, and other guidelines for teachers. However, this material will need to be modified to fit your particular setting.

1. What are the advantages and disadvantages of relying on the teacher's edition of the textbook for a large part of your instructional planning?

2. There may be some inconsistencies between what is recommended in the teacher's edition and what is included in the curriculum guide for the course. What should a teacher do in this case?

3. What should a teacher do if the textbook does not include some content that is included in the curriculum guide?

and decision making. The amount of freedom that you give students in cooperative planning will depend on many things, such as student maturity, student ability levels, the subject area, your educational philosophy, and the students' previous experience with cooperative planning. Teacher–student planning may not be suited to every teacher or every subject area.

There are several ways that students might be involved in this cooperative planning (Clark & Starr, 1996). One way is to present alternative plans to the students and allow them to select the plans they prefer. For example, you might give students the choice of several activities related to the unit objectives and let students select which activities will be used. Second, you might let students, individually or as a whole class, select their goals from a list of behavioral objectives. Third, you could propose a plan of action and then ask students for their suggestions and approval. It is best to start by giving students limited choices and to have successful experiences with those choices before moving to approaches involving more student freedom.

Team Planning

Teachers in some schools plan together, but that does not necessarily mean that they also are involved in team teaching. *Team planning* occurs when two or more teachers collaboratively prepare instructional plans. Planning procedures that a group of teachers use are often similar to the steps you might take when planning alone. The success of teams can be enhanced through the use of team-building activities and clarification of team roles and procedures (Merenbloom, 1991). Time to plan and the authority to make changes are issues related to team collaboration (DiPardo, 1997). There are two ways that team planning may occur.

First, all teachers who teach the same course may get together to plan cooperatively. For example, all teachers of algebra may meet on a regular basis to plan a common curriculum for the students going through that course. These teachers may agree to a common set of course objectives, activities, and outcomes. They may even meet on a weekly basis

TEACHERS IN ACTION

STUDENT INPUT TO TEACHER PLANNING

Sue Watson, high school history teacher, Columbus, Georgia

I begin each course and each unit by asking the students to identify WHY we need to study this particular subject and WHAT we expect to learn. While I have already selected my goals and objectives, I will often find a way to tie in their ideas into the course or unit. I can add some of their ideas into the course and also can better understand what their interests are. This is particularly helpful when it is a required course that they are not excited about taking.

I encourage the students to write down the Whys and the Whats that we identified at the start. I want them to refer back to these ideas to see if we have met the goals that we set for ourselves. This What and Why procedure helps me to stay in tune with the students' interests and to tailor the course to the students.

to share ideas about weekly and daily lesson plans. This type of team planning for the same course occurs most often at the junior and high school levels where there may be several teachers teaching a given course.

Second, teachers from several different subject areas may meet to arrange for *interdisciplinary planning,* which involves planning and coordinating instructional activities and assignments for each subject area represented by the teachers. Thus, an interdisciplinary team may consist of the teachers of social studies, mathematics, English or language arts, science, and perhaps teachers in other subject areas. The team may meet several times a week. This type of planning is more common at the middle level where there may be blocked courses involving investigation of an issue from the perspective of several subject areas.

There are several advantages of team planning (Muth & Alvermann, 1999). First, groups can help complement the talents of each team member. Each person has strengths and weaknesses, and ideas coming from others in the group may help cover a weakness of an individual member. For example, one teacher on the team may not be very familiar with the computer software available for the unit under discussion. Collectively, other team members may be able to provide this information that the teacher would not have had. Second, team planning can help teachers address the interdisciplinary nature of the content they teach. Further, team planning can enhance classroom management. Teams may plan common rules and procedures that are consistently implemented and enforced by all team members. Finally, teams can help establish collegiality among teachers, which provides support and encouragement for all team members.

For interdisciplinary planning to be most effective, teachers must fully commit to the concept and the additional time necessary to ensure success. Important features include: administrative support and vision; identification of the unit theme, including objectives, activities, and evaluation methods; time to plan, implement, and evaluate as a team; time for staff development; adequate resources; incentives for participants; talented and committed teachers; and patience and flexibility on the part of the team to enable the program to develop and work effectively (Furner, 1995; Panaritis, 1995).

Preparing a Syllabus

A *syllabus* is a written statement about the content, procedures, and requirements of a particular course. A course syllabus can serve the following purposes (Kellough & Kellough, 1999):

- States requirements, rules, expectations, and other policies, and thus helps eliminate misconceptions about the course.
- Serves as a plan to be followed by the teacher and the students.
- Helps students feel at ease by providing an understanding of what is expected of them.
- Helps students organize, conceptualize, and synthesize their learning experiences.
- Serves as documentation about the course for those outside the classroom (e.g., the principal, parents, other teachers).
- Serves as a resource for members of a planning team. In fact, each team member should have a copy of each other member's syllabus.

Many teachers prepare a course syllabus before the school year begins and give it to the students on the opening day of school and thoroughly discuss it at that time. Some teachers, however, prefer to provide students with an opportunity for input into the course syllabus. To do so, you could provide time for students to meet in small groups sometime in the opening days of the school year. Have them brainstorm the development of their course syllabus; you might mention some issues that are commonly included in a course syllabus to guide their discussion. Each group could report its ideas, and consensus could be developed for the content of the syllabus. You could then prepare a copy of the syllabus that was agreed upon and provide each student with a copy.

Whether developed only by yourself or in cooperation with your students, a course syllabus typically has the following information (e.g., Kellough & Kellough, 1999):

- *General information about the course.* The teacher's name, course title, class period, beginning and ending times, and room number. This may include times when you are available for a conference, and perhaps your phone number.
- *Course description.* Describe the course, and mention how students will profit from it. This may also include a list of course goals and expected outcomes.
- *Materials required.* Mention the textbook, notebook, or other supplies needed by the student. Indicate what is provided by the school and what the student should provide. Mention what should be brought to class each day.
- *Instructional approaches and activities.* Indicate the type of instructional approaches you plan to use during the course, and also mention any special events or activities that are planned (field trips, experiments, guest speakers, special projects).
- *Course requirements and evaluation procedures.* Indicate the means of evaluating student learning: tests, quizzes, homework, projects, group work, work samples, etc. Indicate the point value or relative weight for each of these items when the report-card grade is determined.
- *Policies on various issues.* Include your policy on late homework or papers, tardiness, absenteeism, extra credit, makeup work, plagiarism, rules for classroom behavior,

procedures for completing classroom tasks, procedures for various classroom tasks, and others.

- *A course outline of content.* Provide an outline of the content to be covered in the course. This should include some headings to reveal some details about the course.

CLASSROOM DECISIONS

A course syllabus includes much useful information for the students concerning course content, procedures, and requirements. Would you want your students to participate in the preparation of your course syllabus? Why or why not? Would the grade level or the subject of the course that you teach make a difference in your decision about student involvement? How might you accommodate student learning style differences as you develop your syllabus?

Planning to Motivate Students

Motivating students to learn is a vital teaching role. *Motivation* is the process of arousing, directing, and maintaining behavior. But the way to motivate students is complex, and you must deliberately plan for it. When planning for instruction, there are aspects of student motivation that need to be taken into account when planning for the week, the unit, and each lesson.

The issue of motivating students is more thoroughly covered in Chapter 5. As a preview for that chapter, there are a number of strategies to motivate students to learn, including capturing student interest in the subject matter, highlighting the relevance of the subject matter, designing the lesson to maintain interest and promote student success, and providing feedback and rewards for performance. There are also certain actions that you can plan for at the start, the middle, and the end of the lesson to facilitate student motivation to learn. To enact all of these actions, you need to deliberately plan to motivate students to learn.

Planning to Use Academic Time Wisely

When considering how to use academic time wisely, it is first useful to examine the time that actually is available for instruction. Students are in school for several hours a day, yet much of that time is used for lunch, time between classes, and homeroom or announcement times. Of the allocated time, some time is used for announcements, collecting or distributing papers and supplies, transitions between activities, and other noninstructional events. Thus, the actual academic time is less than the allocated time.

Some students may be daydreaming or be off-task, so the time spent in learning is less than the allocated time. The time students are actually paying attention and are engaged in action is called *time-on-task. Academic learning time* refers to the amount of time a student engages in learning tasks that yield fairly high rates of success (Strother, 1984). What really counts is for students to be successful during that allocated time. As you can see, the amount of engaged time is much less than the time students are in school.

To illustrate this, consider a 45-minute class. Within this allocated time, 5 minutes may be spent on taking attendance and making announcements, 5 minutes on describing an activity and giving directions, and 5 minutes for cleanup and preparation to finish the class. That leaves 30 minutes of actual academic time, but students may not even be fully engaged during all that time. Furthermore, their engagement during this time may not be entirely fruitful.

The amount of time students are engaged in learning academic content is positively related to their achievement in that content area. A student who is continually off-task will not achieve as well as one who remains on-task. Students often are off-task in rather obvious ways, such as getting out of their seats, reading notes or materials, or talking to other students. Off-task behavior can often manifest itself in daydreaming or other forms of mental or emotional disengagement that may be difficult to detect.

To engage students in the learning process, you could (a) elicit the desired behavior; (b) provide opportunities for feedback in a nonevaluative atmosphere; (c) use group and individual activities as motivational aids when necessary; (d) use meaningful verbal praise; and (e) monitor seatwork and check it (Borich, 2000). You can begin and end lessons precisely on time, reduce transition time between tasks and activities in a lesson, and minimize waste time in an effort to maximize time-on-task and student engagement (Wyne & Stuck, 1982). The time available for instruction increases when you (a) follow schedules; (b) begin and end activities on time; (c) facilitate transitions from activity to activity; and (d) assign scheduled activities first priority rather than engaging in spontaneous alternative activities (Rosenshine, 1980).

Effective classroom management and scheduling can lead to increased learning and a reduction of discipline problems (Berliner, 1979). Good and Brophy (2000) indicate that time-on-task is important, but the task itself must be relevant, appropriate, lead to a reasonably successful outcome (such as designing the difficulty of the assignment to enable the student to have at least 80 percent of the problems correct), and be followed by timely feedback. Instructional time should be allocated in relation to the importance of the academic task.

HOW TEACHERS REALLY PLAN

In teacher education programs, preservice teachers are taught the linear-rational model for planning because novice teachers need a sequence and structure to their planning. As a result, beginning teachers tend to rely more on this model for planning, which is a straightforward process moving from specification of objectives, through diagnosis of student needs and selection of instructional strategies, to instruction and evaluation (Neely, 1985, 1986).

While beginning teachers seem to have an understanding of the importance of planning, they often do not have a deep enough understanding of the subject they are teaching to explain it to their students (Reynolds, 1992). In addition, during the planning process they are often unable to tailor materials and instruction to meet the needs of individual students.

As beginning teachers gain experience, they often plan through the use of lesson images and through varied and personal ways to planning. This shift might occur because experienced teachers have more knowledge to draw upon and feel more secure in planning without detailed written plans, or because they may not be required to write detailed lesson plans once they are tenured.

TEACHERS IN ACTION

FLEXIBILITY IN THE COURSE SYLLABUS

Sue Watson, high school history teacher, Columbus, Georgia

When developing a course syllabus for high school students, I find that it is helpful to keep some flexibility in the plans. As a young teacher, I found I was much too specific regarding what would be covered each day in class, and this set up myself and my students for frustration if we did not stay on track with the plans due to assemblies or other circumstances.

Now I prepare a syllabus for the students that states the expectations for the grading period and the objectives to be covered. However, exact due dates are not listed in the syllabus. Instead, dates for major tests and projects are posted on a calendar at my classroom door. These are usually posted 7 to 10 days in advance for tests and 3 to 4 weeks in advance for major projects. Students can then record these due dates on their syllabus, which is kept in the front of their notebook.

The syllabus gives the students and myself an important tool to use in planning time. The flexibility in the syllabus lowers our frustration level and also helps the students to see the need to plan for the unexpected.

Because of their prior knowledge and experiences with students, experienced teachers think about and approach teaching differently than do novice teachers. These differences are reflected in the teachers' ability to recall classroom events and in their analysis of classroom situations (Peterson & Comeaux, 1987). Experienced teachers are more likely to plan for contingencies, for rules and procedures, and for ways to assess student progress and give feedback (Gagné, 1985).

Experienced teachers often have plans in memory from previous teaching experience, while novice teachers may have plans that are more superficial and not as carefully thought out (Calderhead, 1987). Experienced teachers know what to expect in terms of student interest and behaviors and, as a result, are able to develop plans that are more likely to motivate students to learn. Novice teachers, however, are more likely to have a trial-and-error approach to planning until they have developed the knowledge and experience that will help them predict student responses to planned activities.

During actual instruction, experienced teachers are significantly more responsive to cues from students than are novice teachers (Berliner, 1988). These cues can help teachers make adjustments in their plans to help improve the effectiveness of their lessons. Adjustments may include changing things such as instructional activities, grouping arrangements, learning expectations, lessons pace, or time allocated for selected activities. In fact, overly rigid planning that is not adapted to student progress may have a negative effect on learning (Calderhead, 1984). When teachers monitor the implementation of their plans, there is a positive effect on student learning (Neely, 1986).

Experienced teachers who have been identified as experts are likely to have developed sophisticated planning processes (Leinhardt, 1986). Their plans build on prior student learning, include lesson agendas, allow for fluid movement within the lesson structure, and meet goals with well-rehearsed actions. In contrast, novice teachers often have ambiguous goals, give unclear signals, have fragmented lessons, and have limited integration of topics.

Planning is central to good teaching, and a plan must be first and foremost of value to the person who writes it. It must be in a useful form and should contain information needed by the teacher to arrange for instruction. As a beginning teacher, you may prefer to use the linear-rational model of instructional planning since it provides a more structured framework to make planning decisions. As you become more experienced, you might adapt that model into a planning process that fits you and your teaching situation.

KEY TERMS

Academic learning time	Interdisciplinary planning	Performance objectives
Active planning	Learning objectives	Planning for instruction
Activity routines	Lesson images	Postplanning
Aims	Linear-rational model of planning	Preplanning
Content	Management routines	Routine
Curriculum	Materials	Standards
Curriculum guide	Mental-image approach to planning	Subject-specific course goals
Diagnosis	Motivation	Syllabus
Executive planning routines	Needs assessment	Teacher–student planning
Goals	Ongoing planning	Team planning
Instructional routines	Outcomes-based education	Time-on-task

MAJOR CONCEPTS

1. Planning for instruction refers to decisions teachers make about organizing, implementing, and evaluating instruction. The goal of planning is to ensure student learning.

2. Planning is needed for the school year, each term, each unit, each week, and each lesson.

3. There are four phases of the planning process: preplanning, active planning, ongoing planning, and postplanning.

4. When making plans for instruction, you need to take into account factors related to instructional activities, routines of teaching, and your own personal and professional characteristics.

5. The linear-rational model of instructional planning emphasizes planning in a linear sequence when formulating goals, specifying objectives, assessing student needs, developing strategies and learning activities, and evaluating student performance.

6. Aims are broad statements about the intent of education. Goals are the translation of the aims into more specific subject-related terms.

7. Aims are translated into general school goals, which are translated into subject-specific course goals. These course goals are in curriculum guides and are used by teachers when they translate the course goals into more specific learning objectives. These, in turn, are translated by teachers into performance objectives for daily lesson plans.

8. Diagnosis of student needs provides information about student abilities, needs, interest, and background. There are a number of sources for this information.

9. Instructional strategies and learning activities can be sequenced in a variety of ways to promote effective learning.

10. Plans for evaluation of student performance need to be made prior to instruction to be sure that objectives and content covered in instruction match those measured in the final assessment.

11. The mental-image approach to instructional planning involves teachers forming mental images of lessons they plan to teach after considering the factors related to instructional activities and instructional routines. With this approach, teachers think about and visualize lessons in greater detail than is written in a plan book.

12. Additional considerations for planning include resources for planning, teacher–student planning, team planning, preparing a syllabus, planning to motivate students to learn, and planning to use academic time wisely.

13. Beginning teachers tend to rely on the linear-rational model for instructional planning since it provides a more structured framework to make planning decisions. As you become more experienced, you might adapt that model into a planning process that fits you and your teaching situation.

DISCUSSION/REFLECTIVE QUESTIONS

1. Select one class session you recently experienced. Identify and discuss factors related to instructional activities that the instructor might have taken into account when planning the lesson.

2. What are the merits for beginning teachers of using the linear-rational model for instructional planning?

3. Who should serve on a district-wide curriculum development committee to translate general goals into course specific goals and to prepare curriculum guides?

4. Why should you consider aspects of student evaluation even before instruction takes place?

5. What does the term *lesson image* mean to you? What are the merits of using the mental-image approach to instructional planning?

6. What might be the merits and disadvantages of involving your students in instructional planning? What factors might affect your decision about involving students in planning?

7. What are some ways that teachers can maximize the amount of time-on-task?

SUGGESTED ACTIVITIES

For Clinical Settings

1. Select a course you are now taking and consider how content was sequenced in several class sessions. Consider why content was sequenced in that way. Describe alternative ways to successfully sequence the content.

2. List possible merits and disadvantages for both the linear-rational model and the mental-image approach to instructional planning.

3. With one or more other people in this class as a team, prepare instructional plans for three class sessions to cover one of the later chapters in this book. Include decisions about content to be covered, sequence of content, instructional activities, use of materials, and evaluation of student learning.

4. Examine the course syllabus for several courses that you have taken. Identify features and content that contribute to an effective course syllabus. What information was missing on any of these syllabi that would have been useful to you?

For Field Settings

1. Examine several curriculum guides that are produced by the district. Look at the goals, objectives, content outline, recommended activities, instructional materials, and other features of the curriculum guides.

2. Ask several teachers how they planned for instruction during their first year of teaching. Ask them to describe how their approach to planning might have changed as they became more experienced. How do they plan now?

3. Ask several teachers to explain instructional routines which they use in their classrooms. Identify the merits of these approaches.

4. If there are teachers in the school who are team planning, ask one or more of them to discuss the planning procedures they use and to identify the strengths of this process as well as any problems with it.

USEFUL RESOURCES

Berliner, D. C., & Biddle, B. J. (1995). *The manufactured crisis: Myths, fraud, and the attack on America's public schools.* New York: Longman.

Discusses facts about the success of schools that dispute many of the publicized complaints about schools.

Morrison, G. R., Ross, S. M., & Kemp, J. E. (2001). *Designing effective instruction* (3rd ed.). New York: John Wiley & Sons.

Designed for prospective educators, this book presents a 10-element model of instructional design. Includes real-life examples to reinforce concepts.

Tucker, M., & Codding, J. (1998). *Standards for our schools.* San Francisco: Jossey-Bass.

Provides a review of the issues related to standards and the implications for teachers and school districts.

WEB SITES

- This site is designed to serve as a resource using the WebQuest model to teach with the Web. Examples and materials available online.

  http://edweb.sdsu.edu/webquest/webquest.html

- Classroom Connect: A very good education-based search engine.

  http://www.classroom.net

- Search portal: A well-organized portal for searching resources on the Internet.

  http://www.sau.edu/Internet/

- Education World Search Engine

  http://www.education-world.com

- Web site for the *National Geographic.*

  http://www.nationalgeographic.com/explore/classic/

- Web site tied to the History Channel. Site has lesson plans and source materials.

  http://www.historychannel.com/classroom/

- A PBS-sponsored site that showcases issues of culture and culture shock throughout history.

  http://www.pbs.org/wgbh/cultureshock/index_1.html

- The WordMasters Challenges are competitions for students in grades 3 to 12 that address high-level reading and reasoning skills.

  http://wordmasterschallenges.com/elem.htm

- Prize-winning dictionary program with a number of interesting features: buzzword of the day, verse composer, build your own dictionary, and at companion site http://www.m-w.com/ get word pronunciations online.

  http://www.wordcentral.com/

- This site has biographies of women who contributed to our culture in many different ways. There are writers, educators, scientists, heads of state, politicians, civil rights crusaders, artists, entertainers, and others

  http://www.DistinguishedWomen.com/

CHAPTER THREE

TYPES OF TEACHER PLANNING

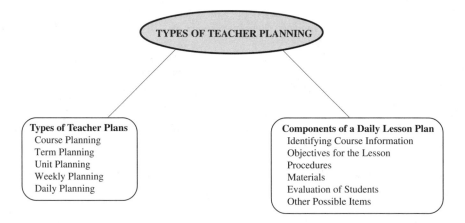

OBJECTIVES

This chapter provides information that will help you to:

1. Describe ways that yearly, term, unit, weekly, and daily plans contribute to the planning process.

2. Describe the reasons for planning, the resources and factors to consider, the steps in the planning process, and the products for yearly, term, unit, weekly, and daily planning.

3. Identify the components of a daily lesson plan.

4. Prepare instructional objectives.

5. Select a format for your weekly plans and your daily lesson plans.

**PRAXIS/Principles of Learning
and Teaching/Pathwise**

The following principles are relevant to content in
this chapter:

1. Creating or selecting teaching methods, learning
   activities, and instructional materials or other resources that are appropriate for the students and
   that are aligned with the goals of the lesson   (A4)

2. Creating or selecting evaluation strategies that are
   appropriate for the students and that are aligned
   with the goals of the lesson   (A5)

INTASC

The following INTASC standard is relevant to content in this chapter:

1. The teacher plans instruction based on knowledge
   of subject matter, students, the community, and
   curriculum goals.   (Standard 7)

Comprehensive planning is needed for effective teaching in all grade levels. When making plans for instruction, teachers typically think of the big picture first—the entire course. Then, their planning is broken down into successively smaller subparts—into each marking term, each unit, each week, and finally each lesson.

When preparing a daily lesson plan, you need to make decisions about the instructional objectives, the standards that students are to meet, the activities and procedures that are designed to help students meet the objectives, instructional materials and resources, the means of evaluating students, and other related issues. Furthermore, you will need to select a format for your weekly and daily plans that is functional for you.

TYPES OF TEACHER PLANS

Planning is a critical function to ensure student learning, and you will likely plan for two reasons. First, the planning process helps you organize the curriculum and address the complex classroom variables that are constantly blending during a typical day as you make instructional decisions. These are variables such as available time, appropriate teaching strategies, available materials, and the level of student need or motivation. Second, the planning process provides you with a sense of direction and a feeling of confidence and security.

Experienced teachers develop written plans for the course, term, unit, week, and day (Clark & Yinger, 1979; Clark & Peterson, 1986). See Figure 3.1 for an illustration showing plans of different duration. Plans for an entire course are more general than plans for each particular lesson. But course plans serve as a framework for term plans, just as term plans serve as a framework for unit plans. Thus, you will likely refer to earlier general plans as you proceed to more specific plans for each unit, week, and lesson. Teacher plans are more

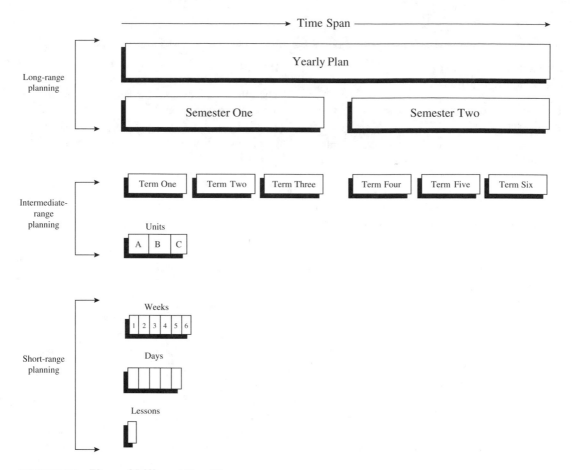

FIGURE 3.1   Plans of Different Durations

specific at the unit and daily levels, and teachers tend to deviate less from unit and daily plans than from course or term plans. In addition, most teachers give equal importance to the planning they do mentally and to their written plans (Earle, 1996).

To more fully understand these characteristics, each type of planning can be examined from four perspectives: (1) its goal or purpose, (2) sources of information, (3) its form or structure, and (4) the criteria for judging its effectiveness (Yinger, 1980). Table 3.1 represents Yinger's ideas and our own, and it outlines these dimensions for yearly (course), term, unit, weekly, and daily planning. Yinger uses the term *yearly planning* to describe course planning, even though some courses may be only a semester long or shorter.

Course Planning

A *course* is a complete sequence of instruction that includes a major division of the subject matter. Courses in middle schools, junior high schools, and high schools vary in length. Some

TABLE 3.1 Types of Teacher Planning

	GOALS OF PLANNING	SOURCES OF INFORMATION	FORM OF THE PLAN	CRITERIA FOR JUDGING THE EFFECTIVENESS OF PLANNING
Yearly planning	1. Establish yearlong general content (framed by standards and district curriculum objectives) 2. Establish basic curriculum sequence 3. Order and reserve resource materials	1. Students (general information about numbers and returning students) 2. Curriculum guidelines (district objectives) 3. Resource availability 4. Personal experience with specific curricula and materials	1. General outline listing basic content and possible ideas in each subject matter area	1. Comprehensiveness of plans 2. Fit with own goals, district objectives, and learners
Term planning	1. Spell out details of content to be covered in next school term 2. Establish weekly schedules that conform to the goals and emphases for the term	1. Direct contact with students 2. Time constraints set by school schedule 3. Availability of resources	1. Elaboration of outline constructed for yearly planning 2. A weekly schedule outline specifying activities and times	1. Outlines: comprehensiveness, completeness, and specificity of elaborations 2. Schedule: comprehensiveness and fit with goals for term, balance 3. Fit with goals for term 4. Fit with learners
Unit planning	1. Develop a sequence of well-organized learning experiences 2. Present comprehensive, integrated, and meaningful content at an appropriate level	1. Students' abilities, interests, etc. 2. Materials, length of lessons, set-up time 3. District objectives 4. Facilities available for activities	1. List of outlines of activities and content 2. Lists of sequenced activities 3. Notes in plan book	1. Organization, sequence balance, and flow of outlines 2. Fit with yearly and term goals 3. Fit with anticipated student interest and involvement
Weekly planning	1. Lay out the week's activities within the framework of the weekly schedule 2. Adjust schedule for interruptions and special needs 3. Maintain continuity and regularity of activities	1. Student performance in preceding days and weeks 2. Scheduled school interruptions (e.g., assemblies, holidays) 3. Continued availability of materials, aids, and other resources	1. Activity names and times entered into a plan book 2. Day divided into four instructional blocks punctuated by A.M. recess, lunch, and P.M. recess	1. Completeness of plans 2. Degree to which weekly schedule has been followed 3. Flexibility of plans allows for special time constraints or interruptions 4. Fit with goals, learners

(continued)

TABLE 3.1 CONTINUED

	GOALS OF PLANNING	SOURCES OF INFORMATION	FORM OF THE PLAN	CRITERIA FOR JUDGING THE EFFECTIVENESS OF PLANNING
Daily planning	1. Set up and arrange classroom for next day 2. Specify activity components not yet decided on 3. Fit daily schedule to last-minute intrusions 4. Prepare students for day's activities	1. Instructions in materials to be used 2. Set-up time required for activities 3. Assessment of class disposition at start of day 4. Continued interest, involvement, and enthusiasm	1. Schedule for day written on chalkboard and discussed with students 2. Preparation and arrangement of materials and facilities in the room	1. Completion of last-minute preparations and decisions about content, materials, etc. 2. Involvement, enthusiasm, and interest communicated by students

courses, such as required courses in English, social studies, or mathematics, may run the entire school year. Other courses are completed within a semester, a trimester, or a quarter.

Course planning involves organizing and scheduling the content to be taught during the time allotted for the course, whether that time is for a year, semester, trimester, or quarter. School districts break up the school year in various ways and have the courses completed within these time frames. When the school year is broken up into two parts, each part is called a semester. When the school year is broken up into three parts, each part is called a trimester. When the school year is broken up into four parts, each part is called a quarter.

Reasons for Course Planning.   There are several reasons for planning for an entire course (Brown, 1988).

- To become familiar with the content to be taught.
- To determine the sequence in which the content will be taught.
- To incorporate any changes in materials, textbooks, or content that may have been made since the last time you taught a particular topic.
- To develop a rough schedule of when various topics will be taught during the course.
- To make additions, deletions, and adaptations to the curriculum, taking into account your own particular circumstances and the needs of your students.
- To plan classroom routines.

Resources and Factors for Course Planning.   There are several resources that could be useful when preparing course plans. If available, the curriculum guide for the course may include objectives, an outline of content, and a proposed timetable for the amount of time to spend on each unit. The textbook for the course and the accompanying teacher's edition, if one is available, provide information about goals and content. The school calendar also needs to be taken into account when planning for the course because it indicates the vacation days, holidays, and other days that school is not in session as well as the grading-term weeks and other special events.

TEACHERS IN ACTION

COURSE PLANNING

Teresa Pierrie, high school English teacher, Raleigh, North Carolina

When I start to plan for the school year, I plan backwards going from the whole curriculum back to the small parts. I begin by deciding on the focus that I want the year to have. Do I want to teach from a thematic unit or a chronological approach, or is there a way for me to use both? I then look at the major divisions within the curriculum and determine what material must be addressed and how much time each unit will take.

Next, I look at the calendar and break the school year into semesters and then quarters. I decide where I need to be at the end of each quarter so that I can include all the required topics in the year. Finally, I come to the individual weeks and assign units to each week based on the number of days I think I need for each topic.

If you have taught the course before, the unit file folders that you have prepared are commonly full of useful information and materials that can aid in course planning. These unit file folders often include lecture notes, handouts, worksheets, audiovisual aids, quizzes, tests, lists of guest speakers, and other resources used in previous years (Brown, 1988). Teachers usually keep a unit file folder for each unit they teach for the course. Thus, the folders can be a rich resource when planning for a course.

In addition, the successes or failures that you had in previous instruction of the course will undoubtedly affect your course-planning decisions. As you can see, experienced teachers have an advantage over inexperienced teachers because they have more information to draw upon about the curriculum and instruction. Classroom management, motivational factors, and student interest and ability also are taken into account when planning for the course.

Steps in Course Planning.   There are several steps to course planning that can lead to useful results (e.g., Callahan, Clark, & Kellough, 2002).

1. Determine the course goals (to indicate what you plan for students to learn from the course) and the principal supporting objectives.
2. Decide on course content that is related to the course goals. This includes selecting the topics to be studied, arranging them into an appropriate sequence, and deciding how much emphasis to place on each topic.
3. Decide how much time to spend on each topic.
4. In view of the goals and topics you selected, determine your approach in the course, including basic strategies, major assignments, texts, and so on. A course syllabus is one of the products of this step.
5. Make plans to order special supplies, books, videotapes, computer software, or other materials, and also to arrange for special speakers or for collaborative planning when conducting term, unit, or weekly planning.
6. Determine procedures for evaluating student attainment of course objectives.

The Products of Course Planning.   Course planning commonly takes the form of a general outline of content with specific ideas noted within the outline concerning course content, methods, and evaluation. Other accompanying materials are also produced as a result of course planning. You could keep these materials in separate notebooks for each course or subject area that you teach. When you prepare your plans for the term, unit, and week, you will likely need to refer to these materials.

1. *A list of course goals.*   Using the steps in course planning as a guide, a list of course goals would be the first product you would prepare. You may determine these goals after careful review and consideration of the goals that are in the curriculum guide, the teacher's edition of the textbook, state department of education guidelines, and other sources.

2. *An outline of course content.*   For many teachers, this outline is a listing of the various units within a course and the chapter numbers and titles within each unit. This outline of units, in fact, may be the same as what is in the textbook that you use, or you might decide to change the sequence of the units.

3. *Notations for time to be spent on each unit.* Using that content outline as a base, you would then indicate how much time you plan to spend on each particular unit. For example, you could make notations in your outline that the first unit, consisting of four chapters, will be covered from the start of the school year to the middle of October. Similar notations would be made for each unit.

4. *A course syllabus.* This is the printed material that you would give your students concerning general information about the course, the course description, materials required, instructional approaches and activities to be used, course requirements and evaluation procedures, policies on various issues, and an outline of course content. It is especially important that you decide about course requirements and evaluation procedures before the course begins and include detailed information about these issues in the syllabus so students are well informed.

5. *Notes about ordering supplies and other instructional resources.* You may immediately need to order special supplies, books, videotapes, computer software, or other materials, or you might make notes to yourself to order these items at a later point in the course. Similarly, you might need to arrange for special speakers or for collaborative planning at that time, or you could make notes to yourself to do this at a later point closer to the time the unit will actually be conducted.

Term Planning

A *term* is the amount of time the school district designates for the length of a marking period (typically 8 to 10 weeks) for report cards. *Term planning* involves the preparation of more detailed outlines of the content to be covered within a marking period or term. They are elaborations of course-planning outlines and indicate which units will be covered during that term. Term plans help you arrange for handling specific issues related to the curriculum and instruction of each unit; they will be useful resources when preparing your unit plans.

Term plans are commonly broken down into weeks, with an outline indicating instructional activities and materials to be included each week. The balance of content, goals, and time are important considerations when preparing term plans. Curriculum guides may include a recommended number of weeks to cover each part of the content outline. This is very helpful, especially for beginning teachers, when making decisions about the pace of content coverage.

Unit Planning

A *unit* is a major subdivision of a course involving planned instruction about some central theme, topic, issue, or problem for a period of several days to a maximum of three weeks. Essentially, *unit planning* involves developing a sequence of daily plans that addresses the topic of the unit in a cohesive way. Unit planning is considered by many teachers to be the most important phase of planning.

Unit plans have more detail than term plans and are often linked directly to major themes or concepts within the curriculum (e.g., exploration in social studies, fractions in mathematics, poetry in English, nutrition in science). A unit plan should provide increased organization and ensure that the material presented is accurate, thorough, and comprehensive.

Reasons for Unit Planning.   There are several reasons for unit planning (Muth & Alvermann, 1999). First, planning for units allows you to organize and sequence a related body of material into a series of lesson plans. Next, unit planning allows you to decide on the specific activities that you will use to teach the content. Finally, unit planning helps you gather and make the materials that are necessary for the various activities throughout the unit.

Teachers usually begin planning their units several weeks before they intend to teach them. In this way, you have sufficient time to develop your plans and take any needed actions resulting from your plans prior to the first lesson of the unit. For example, you may need to schedule a field trip, arrange for a guest speaker, develop a cooperative learning activity, or prepare handouts some time in advance of the first lesson.

Resources and Factors in Unit Planning.   When planning a unit, you will likely use some of the same materials used in course planning, such as unit file folders, the curriculum guide, the textbook, and calendar. At this point, you need to give special attention to planning and selecting instructional resources. You might need to order or schedule certain videotapes, films, or guest speakers. Or you might need to prepare various instructional materials. In addition, you will likely take into account your previous experiences with the unit, student interest, and other issues when planning a unit.

Steps in Unit Planning.   After selecting the unit topic, there are several steps that are commonly taken when planning a unit.

1. *Select the overall goals and the more specific objectives for the unit.* Since a unit involves a central theme or topic, one or more overall goals are appropriate. Each goal then would have several related, specific objectives.

In unit plans, make plans to teach the course content at an appropriate level of complexity for the students. The appropriate level of complexity is considered in terms of the ability of students to (a) understand the material in its present form, and (b) build on their understanding for future learning. If you expect students to apply a concept, then teach them to apply it, not to just comprehend or define it. For example, if you want to teach students to write paragraphs, you are better off having them write topic sentences and receive feedback as a warm-up activity rather than having them memorize the definition of a topic sentence and recite it.

2. *State the rationale for the unit.* This step encourages you to be thoughtful and reflective during the planning process and helps link learning experiences to unit goals. This rationale can help connect the unit content to the course as a whole. Also, sharing the rationale for the unit with the students enables them to see the importance of the material in their lives.

3. *Outline or organize the content.* Outlining the content helps you clarify the subject matter and provides organization to the unit. It helps you consider the most appropriate order of the content and examine the interrelationships among the content.

4. *Plan a sequence of daily lessons with appropriate instructional activities.* The lessons throughout the unit should enable your students to reach the goals and objectives of the unit. There are three types of lessons to consider in this sequence (Callahan et al., 2002). There should be some *introductory lessons* that identify the reasons for studying this unit, provide for preassessment and diagnostic activities, set the tone for the lessons to follow, and generally motivate the students. Next, there should be *developmental lessons* that build the learning that makes up the unit objectives and content. Many instructional strategies could be used, including lectures, questions, practice, group and discussion methods, and inquiry and discovery methods (see Chapters 6, 7, and 8). Finally, there should be *culminating lessons* that tie together what has been learned in the developmental lessons. These may include review lessons, student reports, and some type of student evaluation such as a test.

■ ■ ■ ■ ■ ■

CLASSROOM DECISIONS

Effective units include introductory, developmental, and culminating lessons. Assume that you are planning a three-week unit on the countries in South America and that you want to include information on cultural, economic, political, geographical, and historical issues. What might you plan for your introductory, developmental, and culminating lessons in this unit?

5. *Plan and prepare for ways that students will be evaluated.* Student learning can be assessed in a variety of ways including tests, observation tools, work samples, logs, portfolios, and other approaches (see Chapter 12). Any assignments or other requirements should be included in the course syllabus.

6. *Gather and prepare the materials needed for instruction.* You may need to gather and prepare many materials for the unit. Materials to be prepared for students may include handouts, study guides, bibliographies, project guideline sheets, books and resource materials for the students, and various supplies and equipment. In addition, you may need to gather and prepare materials for yourself that will help you prepare for instruction or that you will use during instruction. These may include transparencies, notes, resources, texts, posters, maps, computer programs, or other items.

The Products of Unit Planning.   Unit planning will likely result in several products. First, there will be a list of goals and objectives for the unit, a statement of the rationale for the unit, and an outline of unit content. Next, there will be a written sequence of daily lessons with appropriate instructional activities. The daily lesson plans that you prepare later will have more details than the brief descriptions of the lesson plans that are within the unit plan. Further, the materials needed for instruction will be prepared and gathered (e.g., handouts, study guides, various supplies). In addition, the materials needed for student evaluation will be prepared (e.g., worksheets, tests). Finally, the material that you need for yourself for instruction will be gathered and prepared (e.g., transparencies, posters, notes).

Strategies Leading to Successful Implementation of Unit Plans.   It is one thing to successfully plan a unit by choosing objectives or standards, selecting content and materials, and sequencing lessons. Yet it is another thing to actually incorporate learning strategies that help students to learn (Marzano, Pickering, & Pollock, 2001). Some strategies that can be used to successfully implement your unit plans include the following:

1. Set clear learning goals for students, and let them personalize and record their own learning goals.
2. Provide students with corrective feedback and the criteria used in grading to help them to assess their own progress. Ask students to reflect on their own learning, effort, and achievement. Celebrate meaningful progress.
3. Provide an environment in which students are expected to articulate what they know about topics in the unit. Help students to link the information that they know to the new information that they will be learning. Have students keep notes on what they are learning.
4. Vary instructional strategies and have students work both individually and as members of collaborative groups.
5. Assign homework that allows students to practice, review, and apply what they have learned. Then provide feedback on their performance.
6. Involve students in long-term projects.
7. Ask students to represent what they have learned in paragraph form and by drawing figures, comparison charts, and outlines.
8. Provide clear assessment of student progress concerning the learning objectives and standards and have students compare these assessments to their own self-assessments using the same rubric or criteria. Ask students what they have learned about the content and themselves as learners.

The topic of how to assess students will be covered in detail in Chapter 12, but the following example is included here to illustrate the concept of providing students with corrective feedback and the criteria used for grading. By making the grading criteria clear to students prior to beginning a unit, students can begin assessing their own progress and take ownership and responsibility for their own learning. Table 3.2 shows a set of criteria that

TABLE 3.2   Criteria for Assessing Student Writing

ORGANIZATION	MECHANICS	EDITING	CREATIVITY
Uses clear organizational structure Arranges information, facts, and examples effectively Uses headings and formatting to aid organization Provides closure	Uses language appropriate to the audience Demonstrates strong control of grammar, paragraph structure, punctuation, sentence construction, spelling, and usage	Includes all pertinent information Excludes unsuitable information Clarifies difficult points	Creates a clear point of view Recognizes complexity in issues Makes a case based on facts Provides support for statements with clear information and evidence

These sample criteria could be used to create a rubric to assess student writing.

could be used to assess student writing. These criteria could be the basis for creating a rubric on this assignment.

Weekly Planning

Weekly planning involves laying out the week's activities within the framework of the daily schedule throughout the week. While the degree of detail that teachers write in weekly plans varies, weekly plans for each class period may include a list of the instructional objectives, the instructional activities, resources and materials (e.g., the page numbers in the

---

SPOTLIGHT ON TECHNOLOGY

RESOURCES ON THE WEB

As a teacher, you will always be looking for new ideas for lessons and unit plans and also for sources that your students can use for papers and projects. An excellent source for you is Navigator. This Web site was originally developed to be used by the newsroom of the *New York Times* to seek and check information on the Web. As a beginning teacher, you may have similar needs. In addition, there are Navigator Web sites for teachers, students, and parents. The Navigator address is http://www.nytimes.com/learning/general/navigator/index.html.

Although this site starts off with a comprehensive list of search engines, it goes far beyond to provide information on government, references, and much more. A few examples are listed next to whet your appetite.

Search Engines

- *Google.* A helpful search engine
- *Alta Vista.* Offers efficient Web search; its no-frills text search loads faster
- *Yahoo.* Subject guide and free-text searching of the World Wide Web
- *Ask Jeeves.* Searching with a human touch

Government Information

- FedWorld Information Services: Comprehensive guide to government databases
- The White House
- The House of Representatives
- The Senate
- The Supreme Court
- State and local government Web sites from Piper Resources
- *Statesearch.* State-level information on a variety of topics
- *Thomas.* The Library of Congress information service

Reference Desk

- *Research It.* All-in-one reference desk: dictionary, quotes, translators, more
- *LibrarySpot.* Extensive guide to online reference works
- *Information Please Almanac.* Almanac, dictionary, and the full *Columbia Encyclopedia*
- *Biography.com.* Offers brief, cross-referenced biographies of more than 25,000 notables
- *C.I.A. World Factbook*
- *Library of Congress,* including Marvel and Locis
- *The World Wide Web Virtual Library*
- *National Geographic's Map Machine*

textbook, the title of the videotape), and student assignments. Many school districts require beginning teachers to submit weekly lesson plans to the principal for review, sometimes several days before instruction is to begin.

Consider student performance during the preceding weeks as you identify content to be covered and determine the pace of instruction. Identify what you expect the students to complete and how you will evaluate student progress. Interruptions and any special events (e.g., field trips, assemblies, holidays) should be noted in the weekly plans. The completeness of the plans and mesh of activities with goals are important considerations in weekly plans.

Using a Plan Book for Weekly Plans. A *plan book* is used to display weekly plans in a brief way, commonly on a two-page grid format. In commercially prepared plan books, the days of the week are often labeled on the top of the grid and the class period or subject area is labeled on the left of the grid. Consequently, there is only about a 1½- by 1½-inch box to write the planning notes for each class period to be taught in that week. A sample plan book format for weekly plans is displayed in Figure 3.2. This sample format indicates the plans in the order of the class periods for each day throughout the week.

School districts often provide teachers with commercially prepared plan books to display their weekly plans. Due to the limited amount of space in the boxes of the plan books, you might prefer to develop your own format in a separate notebook. Regardless of the format that you use, it is important to prepare the weekly plans and write them in a plan book for your own use, for review by your school administrator, and for use by a substitute teacher in case you are absent.

It is possible that you will teach several subjects and will need to prepare plans for each subject. For example, you might have two classes of algebra, two classes of geometry, and one class of trigonometry. If you use the format shown in Figure 3.3, you will need one page of that format for each subject area that you teach. You may prefer this format because it provides more space for your plans as compared to the format shown in Figure 3.2.

TEACHERS IN ACTION

UNIT PLANNING

Diane Low, junior high English teacher, Lawrence, Kansas

As I set up my units, there are four basic considerations. First, I decide what is most important and give that the most time. Since I emphasize written analysis of literature, which is a new skill for the students, the first unit on short stories takes longer than others. Second, I consider school breaks. For example, I finish *Great Expectations* before the December holiday break instead of having to finish the last part after a two-week recess.

Third, I consider ways to coordinate the content with other courses. For example, when the civics classes are studying the court system, my English class reads *Twelve Angry Men*. This means preplanning with other teachers. Last, I consider the attention span of students at various times of the year. For example, ninth graders are notorious for wanting to be out of school in May. Therefore, we read Greek mythology, which keeps the attention of even my most reluctant learners.

FIGURE 3.2 Sample Plan Book Format for Weekly Plans: Version A

PERIOD SUBJECT GRADE	TEACHER _____ ROOM NO. _____ WEEK OF _____				
	MONDAY	**TUESDAY**	**WEDNESDAY**	**THURSDAY**	**FRIDAY**

Daily Planning

A *lesson* is a subdivision of a unit, usually taught in a single class period or, on occasion, two or three successive periods. *Daily planning* involves preparing notes about objectives, materials, activities, evaluation, and other information for a lesson for a particular day, but in more detail than in the weekly plan.

Reasons for Daily Planning.   As discussed more thoroughly in the last chapter, there are a number of reasons for planning, and many of these reasons apply specifically to preparing written daily lesson plans. Written daily plans help you clarify the instructional objectives of a particular lesson, precisely identify the content, determine the instructional activities and the specific means about how the activities will be conducted, and arrange for appropriate evaluation of student learning.

Written daily plans give you a sense of direction and a feeling of confidence and security about what you are doing. They help you organize, sequence, and become familiar with the lesson's content. The preparation of the plans also sparks your preparation or collection of the necessary instructional materials needed for the lesson.

The content area you teach may also affect your consideration of factors you believe are important to planning and implementing a successful lesson. For example, in a study of beginning mathematics and social studies teachers (Grant, 1996), the mathematics teachers

FIGURE 3.3   Sample Plan Book Format for Weekly Plans: Version B

TEACHER _____   CLASS PERIOD(S) _____

WEEK OF _____   GRADE LEVEL AND COURSE TITLE _____

ROOM NUMBER _____   UNIT TOPIC _____

DAY	DATE	OBJECTIVES	PROCEDURES	MATERIALS	ASSIGNMENT	COMMENTS
MONDAY						
TUESDAY						
WEDNESDAY						
THURSDAY						
FRIDAY						

focused on difficulties and successes they had as learners and thus focused their planning on "How do I get students to learn mathematics?" However, the social studies teachers focused on whether they found lessons to be boring or interesting and thus centered their planning on "What do I teach kids?" During the planning process, consider your prior experience as a learner, your knowledge of the content, and your knowledge of how students learn the subject you will teach.

How Detailed?   The degree of detail that teachers include in daily lesson plans varies considerably. Experienced teachers prepare their weekly plans in their plan book and may not prepare any additional, detailed plans for each particular lesson. Therefore, an experienced teacher may write the objective(s) that they want students to achieve, the content standard that students will be working on, and some short notations about activities and materials. From these short notes, the experienced teacher knows exactly how to conduct the lesson, whereas a novice teacher may need to write out an explicit step-by-step outline that includes the following:

- *Objectives/standards:* What will your students know and be able to do as a result of this lesson? Which national or state content standards are targeted in this lesson?
- *Instructional materials and resources:* What materials, texts, manipulatives, or resources will you need for this lesson? What technological resources will you need?
- *Learner factors:* How does this lesson accommodate different developmental levels of students? How does this lesson accommodate individual differences in approaches to learning, create connections between subject matter and student experiences, and/or include provisions for students with particular learning differences or needs?
- *Environment factors:* What student groups will be used? What changes will you need to make in the classroom arrangement due to the instructional strategy that you are using?
- *Assessment activities:* How will you determine what the students know and are able to do during and as a result of the lesson? (Is there a direct relationship with the objectives and the content standards that students are asked to meet?)

Lesson Plan Formats.   Throughout your teacher education program, but especially during student teaching, you will be expected to prepare a detailed lesson plan for each lesson that you teach. The main purpose of this activity is to ensure that you have a clear representation of how you expect the lesson to progress. This outline can be invaluable as you reflect on the success of the lesson relative to both student performance and your ability to implement a plan successfully. If the lesson is not as successful as you would like, a detailed plan can help you to decide if the problem was in the plan or its implementation. As a beginning teacher, it is wise to continue writing lesson plans. As you become more experienced, you may find that you do not have to write such detailed descriptions of your lesson plans.

No single lesson plan format is used by all teachers, nor is there a list of universally adopted components of a lesson plan. As a result, you need to decide on the type of information that you would like to include in your lesson plans and then display this information in a format that suits your needs and preferences. Two sample lesson plan formats are displayed in Figures 3.4 and 3.5.

In the sample formats, some common categories of information are included in each. You may want to adapt these formats or use a different layout that is better suited to your specific philosophy, your teacher education program, or the content area that you teach. For example, if you have lessons in which you pose a number of questions to students, you might want to adapt the layout of Figure 3.5 by adding an extra column to the right side of the procedures list to show the main questions that you plan to ask during the lesson.

In any case, you will need to create a format for the lessons that you develop. You will probably create a master format on your computer so that you can simply copy the file and type the detailed information about the lesson that you are working on. In this way, you have a computer file for each lesson, making it easier to read, print, and modify the next time that you teach the lesson. It is helpful to keep lessons filed or organized by unit topic.

FIGURE 3.4   Sample Lesson Plan Format: Version A

TEACHER _____   DATE _____

TITLE OF LESSON _____   GRADE LEVEL _____

CLASS _____   UNIT TOPIC _____

OBJECTIVES AND STANDARDS What will your students know and be able to do as a result of this lesson? Which standards are targeted with this lesson?	
INSTRUCTIONAL MATERIALS AND RESOURCES What materials, texts, etc., will you need for this lesson? What technological resources (if any) will you need?	
LEARNER FACTORS How does this lesson accommodate different developmental levels of students? How does this lesson accommodate individual differences in approaches to learning, create connections between subject matter and student experiences, and/or include provisions for students with particular learning differences or needs?	
ENVIRONMENT FACTORS What student groups will be used? What changes will you need to make in the classroom due to instruction, materials, etc.?	
ASSESSMENT ACTIVITIES How will you determine what the students know and are able to do during and as a result of the lesson?	
LESSON PLAN OUTLINE[a] Introductory activities Developmental activities Closing activities	

[a]In this section you give an overview of the lesson introduction, development, and closing activities. These form the outline for a detailed lesson plan in which activities and tasks are fully described.

See University of Rhode Island School of Education Portfolio Project for additional examples and sample unit and lesson plans. http://www.efolio.uri.edu/portfolio/SOE/home.

FIGURE 3.5   Sample Lesson Plan Format: Version B

TEACHER _____   GRADE LEVEL _____

ROOM NUMBER _____   COURSE TITLE _____

CLASS PERIOD(S) _____   UNIT TOPIC _____

DATE _____   LESSON TOPIC _____

OBJECTIVES/STANDARDS	PROCEDURES (AND THE NUMBER OF MINUTES)
A.	A-1
	A-2
	A-3
B.	B-1
	B-2
	B-3
C.	C-1
	C-2
	C-3

Instruction Materials and Resources

Evaluation of Students

Assignment

Comments about the Lesson, and Ideas for Revision

Lesson planning for experienced teachers is usually a mental activity (e.g., Morine-Dershimer, 1979). Instead of writing down their plans, experienced teachers create mental pictures of lesson plans that usually guide their classroom instruction. Therefore, they may not need any more written details than what they wrote in their weekly plan book. Even though experienced teachers tend not to write detailed lesson plans, many of them report that this type of planning served as an important foundation for them as beginning teachers (Clark & Peterson, 1986).

Beginning teachers generally benefit from writing down detailed, well-organized lesson plans and from the experience of conducting these lessons. As you become more experienced, you may be able to write your plans in less detail, knowing that in your mind you have made decisions about some parts that are not written in detail.

CLASSROOM DECISIONS

It is recommended that beginning teachers write detailed lesson plans. How detailed do you think your lesson plans need to be? In addition to listing the introductory, developmental, and culminating activities, would you also include key questions that you would ask, notes about the content, or reminders about certain explanations? What else might you need to include to be sure that you are prepared and confident about the lesson that you are planning?

Parts of an Effective Lesson.   Take into account the three parts of an effective lesson as you make planning decisions about the content and sequence of events within the lesson. Many planning experts recommend that each lesson have introductory, developmental, and closing activities. Some additional considerations in managing lesson delivery are addressed in Chapter 9.

1. *Introductory activities.* These activities are designed to introduce the content to the students, capture student attention and interest, and set the stage for the developmental activities that follow. As discussed more thoroughly in Chapter 5, it is important to have activities at the start of the lesson to capture the interest of the students as a means to motivate them to learn that particular content. Introductory activities serve these purposes.

This introductory overview of the lesson helps students understand what they will be studying, how the lesson is related to previous lessons, and how the lesson fits into the larger framework of the course content. This brief introduction about the lesson's objectives and about your expectations of the students is very important. Telling students in advance what they are going to learn, what the key points will be, and what the students should know by the end of the lesson has been positively related to student achievement (Berliner, 1987).

2. *Developmental activities.* These activities address the content and are the vehicles for student learning. As discussed in Chapters 6, 7, and 8, there are many instructional strategies to use, including lectures, questions, practice, group and discussion methods, and inquiry and discovery approaches. Furthermore, there are various ways to group the students for instruction, including whole-group instruction, small-group instruction, and independent work.

The instructional strategies selected must help students be successful in meeting the instructional objectives for the lesson. It is often helpful to plan for the sequential use of several different types of instructional strategies during a lesson to add instructional variety, to take into account the students' attention spans, and to accommodate the students' different learning styles.

For example, a lesson in a tenth grade literature class might begin with a brief lecture about the parts of a short story. Next, the class may view a videotape about short stories, and then work in pairs to analyze and identify the parts of a particular short story they recently read as a class assignment. The class might end with a whole-class discussion about these issues and perhaps a listing on the board of the key concepts. This lesson has four major segments with each part requiring a different type of activity and student role in the activity.

3. *Closing activities.* These are activities that are designed to provide a summary of the lesson's content and to allow the students time to prepare to leave the classroom. Effective teachers plan to stop the developmental part of the lesson a few minutes before the end of the class period to provide sufficient time for the content closing and the procedural closing of a lesson (Muth & Alvermann, 1999).

The *content closing* of a lesson includes a summary of the main points in the lesson. This helps reinforce the content that was covered in the lesson and helps students see how the content fits with the context of the other information in the unit and the course. The *procedural closing* of a lesson involves actions that help students get ready to move on to the next subject or class at the appropriate time. Students might use the time during the procedural closing to write down the homework assignment, to put away materials and supplies, turn in papers, and get ready to leave the classroom.

While introductory, developmental, and closing activities are considered by many educators to be important parts of any lesson, there are some additional views about the key parts of a lesson, such as those offered by Barak Rosenshine and Madeline Hunter. Their ideas will be covered more fully in Chapter 9; a brief review of their recommendations is provided here.

Based on the review of research studies, Rosenshine (1987) proposed that lessons which are teacher-directed include review of content previously covered, presentation of new content, guided practice by students, corrections and feedback, and independent practice. In addition, weekly and monthly reviews should be scheduled.

Again with a teacher-directed instructional approach, Hunter (1984) proposed that lessons include an anticipatory set to focus student attention on what will be covered, a statement of the purposes and objectives of the lesson, the instructional input, modeling, monitoring to check for understanding, guided practice, and independent practice.

Making Ongoing Changes. You may have three classes of world history and prepare only one daily lesson that would be used for each class. Yet no two classes are the same; each has its own characteristics that will likely affect how you actually go about instruction. In one class, for example, you might have some students who have traveled to a country that you are covering in the lesson, and you might want to draw upon these particular students during the lesson. Another class may work better with cooperative learning activities. Consequently, even before instruction begins, you may modify your daily lesson somewhat after taking into account the unique characteristics of each class.

In another case during actual instruction, you might find that the lesson is not working out in the way that you had planned. Students may have difficulty grasping the concepts, they may have little interest in the topic, or participation may not be what you expected. For these and other reasons, you might find that you need to alter the lesson during instruction. You might decide to alter the approach of an activity to have students work in pairs instead of individually, or you might shorten one activity and add in something entirely different. If things do not work as you had planned, you should change the type of activity or the manner of delivery in some way.

For these and other reasons, you might need to make ongoing changes in your lessons. It is useful to make additional notes on your lesson plans about the changes that you made. In this way, these annotated lesson plans can be a rich source of information when you make plans for the next time you teach the lesson.

Tips for Daily Planning. As you become more experienced at daily planning, you will automatically take into account a number of factors as you design each lesson. As a starting point, several tips are offered here as you prepare your daily lesson plans.

1. Keep all your notes and daily plans for a unit in your unit file folder as a resource the next time you teach that material.
2. Have some additional, backup plans if something unexpected happens, such as a guest speaker not arriving in time or the videotape machine not working.

TEACHERS IN ACTION

CHANGING YOUR DAILY LESSON PLAN

Edward Gamble, third grade teacher, Jamestown, Rhode Island

Sometimes even the best prepared plans for a day may have to be changed because an educational opportunity may arise which needs to be seized. This happened last week in my classroom. I had my morning planned with my usual reading period, but we had a special assembly which was a sheep shearing demonstration.

The assembly was fantastic! Two people from a nearby farm sheared a sheep, carded and spun the wool, and discussed raising sheep. Another woman used a loom to demonstrate how the yarn is woven. They had brought five sheep with them, including two lambs.

I thought to myself, "Why should I stop this excitement when I get back to class?" I started to think of new vocabulary words, new concepts, and hands-on experiences. I first jotted down some terms the farmers had used: ewes, rams, mutton, lambs, carding, and wool. I then thought of some questions that the students could answer: How do you shear a sheep? What do you call a male and a female sheep? And other questions.

When we got back to class, we discussed what we had learned. I wrote some of the words the farmers had used on one chalkboard and questions I had come up with on another board. Then I had the class answer these questions in complete sentences. They really did a good job answering these questions.

I initially had not planned on following up on the content of the assembly. But, I got some of the best discussion and work during that week because I was willing to change my plans when I felt it was called for.

3. Seek help from other teachers when planning, since they can be a rich source of ideas and support.
4. Have the lesson's objectives tie in directly to the unit and course goals.
5. Be sure that each instructional activity addresses a lesson objective.
6. Plan for a variety of instructional activities within each lesson as well as varied use of instructional media.
7. Build motivational strategies into the lesson.
8. Arrange for a suitable amount of time for each instructional activity.

COMPONENTS OF A DAILY LESSON PLAN

Written lesson plans might be displayed in various formats, but regardless of the format, the plans typically have the following information: identifying course information, objectives of the lesson, procedures, materials, and evaluation. You may want to add some categories of information or modify these components in some way. Some alternative formats for displaying this information in written lesson plans are provided later in this chapter.

Identifying Course Information

Certain information about the course, subject, and lesson is needed at the top of each lesson plan. This information can include the name of the teacher, the course title, the grade level, the room number, the name of the unit, the topic of that particular lesson, and the date of the lesson. Certainly, you would know this information, but anyone else reading your lesson plans would need it. Substitute teachers, for example, would need that information in order to use the appropriate lesson plan that you briefly described in your weekly plans. Your principal or members of your planning team also would need to see that information on the plan sheet.

Objectives for the Lesson

Each lesson will have one or more objectives. An *objective* is a statement of the intended learning outcomes. Objectives commonly describe what the student will be able to do when instruction has been completed.

Stating Objectives.   As suggested by Mager (1997), each *performance objective* should include (a) an *action statement* identifying the action that the teacher expects the student to perform (e.g., Write an essay describing the process of selection of members of the House of Representatives); (b) a *conditions statement* identifying the conditions under which the action occurs (e.g., using information found in the textbook); and (c) a *criterion statement* identifying the criteria or level of performance expected of the student (e.g., all five major steps central to the election process listed in the text must be present).

Placing each of these parts together, we have a complete performance objective: "Write an essay describing the process of selection of members of the House of Representatives (ACTION), incorporating the five major steps central to the election process (CRITERION) listed in the textbook (CONDITION)."

Here's another example: "After practicing the concept during class in small work groups (CONDITION), the student will underline the key information needed to solve each of 10 word problems (ACTION) with 80 percent accuracy (CRITERION)." It is useful to examine each part of the performance objective in more detail.

Action Statements.   The action statement in a performance objective is always stated in terms of what the student is expected to know or do. This central action or performance by the student is observable by the teacher, and through observation or assessment of the performance, the teacher knows whether the student has learned the content or skill under study. To select a particular behavior, analyze the goals of the course, the content and materials available for teaching, the learning task prepared for students, and the skills or knowledge you hope they will retain for future use in school or work environments. After reflecting on these issues, identify an action verb. This action verb describes the student behavior you will observe as the student successfully completes the learning task.

Performance objectives are intended to give students clear statements about what they are to do or complete in the learning situation. Often, when first thinking about what students should be able to know and do, words open to many interpretations come to mind (e.g., to know, understand, appreciate, enjoy, or believe). Instead, words open to limited interpretations are desired (e.g., to write, recite, identify, differentiate, contrast, list, or compare). For example, it is very appropriate to have student appreciation of literature as an instructional goal, but that is an abstract goal. Thus, you should write performance objectives in observable terms rather than with abstract terms open to many interpretations. Action verbs need to be selected which are specific and which clarify what is expected of students.

Conditions Statements.   Another important part of a performance objective is the statement of conditions or circumstances under which the students are to perform the task or assignment given to them by the teacher. These conditions or circumstances may include (a) materials given to students (e.g., with a calculator, without using the text), (b) time limits for the completion of the task (e.g., in 15 minutes, in a two-week period of time), and (c) the location for the task to be performed (e.g., at the student's desk, in small groups, in the library).

For example, if students are asked to list the states which border their own state, it matters a great deal whether or not they can use a map to answer the question or if they are expected to respond from memory. In another example, you might ask, "What rights does the first amendment to the Constitution of the United States of America give to the citizens of this country?" It is important for students to know if they should turn to the Bill of Rights in their textbooks or if they are to respond from memory, and the performance objective should be written accordingly. Students also should have the opportunity to master content in the form that will be asked on the test. If the textbook is not to be used during the test, students should be made aware before the day of the exam.

Criterion Statements.   The third component of a behavioral objective is the standard by which students' successful completion of the objective is measured. This level, sometimes referred to as the standard of performance, sets the level of acceptable performance for the objective. Some examples of criterion statements include:

- Five out of five parts of the definition
- 80 percent of the given problems will be answered correctly

- Write a topic sentence and at least three supporting sentences
- With 90 percent accuracy

While this level of performance is often thought of as the minimum level of acceptable performance, it should *not* be thought of only in terms of the traditional grading scale: A = 90 or above, B = 80 through 89, C = 70 through 79, D = 65 through 69, and F = 64 and below. Instead, you may want your students to master a given objective at a higher rate than simply a grade of D. The belief that students need higher than minimal levels of competence can be based on any number of related factors.

For example, the material may have been covered in the past, but it is essential for students to be confident in their understandings since the material is a building block to new concepts or skills. Material of this type is often referred to as *prerequisite information* or information which is essential or required for successful completion of the next or related learning task. Without near complete understanding of this information, the student has little chance of successfully mastering the new concept or skill and subsequent, related skills. Many teachers like to give students a pretest before a unit to make sure student needs are served by the objectives.

An example of this type of knowledge might be the multiplication tables for fifth graders. They should have mastered this information in earlier grades and, because it will be built upon extensively during completion of more complex multiplication activities and word problems, the knowledge is practiced and assessed again. For content that would be called prerequisite information, teachers may set a minimum level of competence of 95 or 100 percent.

■ ■ ■ ■ ■ ▬▬▬▬▬▬▬▬▬▬▬▬▬▬▬▬▬▬▬▬▬▬▬▬▬▬▬▬

CLASSROOM DECISIONS

Lesson plan objectives should include the criterion or standard by which the student's completion of the objective will be measured. If you were a physical education teacher and the lesson concerned effective passing in basketball, what kind of criterion statements would be appropriate? How might you take into account the various levels of student experience in basketball and their overall physical coordination?

Learning Domains.   One way of translating goals into learning objectives and performance objectives is to categorize the desired outcomes into a classification system. A *taxonomy* is a classification system that enables educators to precisely organize learning objectives in an effort to achieve specific outcomes (Bloom, 1984). Bloom's taxonomy of objectives is hierarchical, and there is a relationship among the levels of the classification system. Thus, the higher levels of a taxonomy are more complex than the lower levels, and each of the lower levels is built upon to form the next higher level.

Bloom's classification system has three *learning domains,* which are categories for organizing the logically related purposes of the learning objectives. The three learning domains are (a) cognitive, which refers to mental or intellectual thinking skills and abilities; (b) affective, which classifies student attitudes toward learning; and (c) psychomotor, which involves physical movement and related skills. Each of these areas has a classification system to aid in the process of describing and designing the learning activities. Perhaps as much as

80 percent of what is learned is in the cognitive domain, with the balance in the other two domains.

Carefully consider the performance objectives when preparing lesson plans, because the objective will dictate the nature of the content to be taught. Furthermore, if you want to have students achieve a particular learning objective at a particular level of understanding, then you should assess the student only for that level.

The objective selected should guide your selection and presentation of content. For example, if students are expected to describe the reasons for Columbus' voyage, then more than dates and a calendar of events need to be presented. Also, the test over this material should be in line with the objective and content covered (i.e., test questions should deal with the reasons for the voyage if the objectives and content were about reasons for the voyage). In short, a taxonomy allows the cross checking of objectives, instructional processes, and evaluation instruments to ensure that content is taught, practiced by students, and evaluated at the same level of complexity.

Teachers often select several objectives for a lesson, and information about the cognitive complexity of an objective can help you decide on appropriate teaching strategies to help students achieve these objectives. In this regard, you can use question prompts as a strategy to encourage higher-order thinking by students. For example, after reading from a text or source material, you could ask students to provide information on who, what, when, where, and why? From this simple technique, students can also be taught to use a list of question stems to form higher-level questions about the material they are studying (King, 1990). The following are examples:

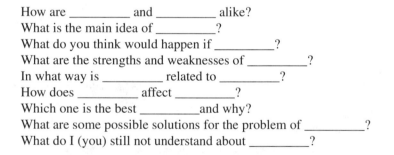

How are _____ and _____ alike?
What is the main idea of _____?
What do you think would happen if _____?
What are the strengths and weaknesses of _____?
In what way is _____ related to _____?
How does _____ affect _____?
Which one is the best _____and why?
What are some possible solutions for the problem of _____?
What do I (you) still not understand about _____?

Prompts such as these help students develop the skills necessary to think at higher cognitive levels. However, students will need to practice higher-level thinking and receive feedback on their performance if they are to master the ability and habit of mind to think consistently at higher cognitive levels. Your modeling and thinking aloud can be important first steps in this process. As students gain skills, they can take increasing responsibility for designing the prompts they use to promote their thinking. When students have difficulty, you can help them by asking questions, but the goal is for students to become independent learners (Rosenshine & Meister, 1995).

Cognitive Domain.   The classification system most often used for the *cognitive domain* is Bloom's taxonomy of educational objectives (Bloom, 1984). Using Bloom's taxonomy, there are six levels of the cognitive domain dealing with mental or intellectual thinking skills and abilities. Descriptions of each level are presented here along with sample objectives that teachers might write for daily lesson plans. The sample objectives do not include conditions and the intended degree of success; these would be added by the teacher.

1. *Knowledge.* Included at this level are objectives related to (a) knowledge of specifics such as terminology and facts; (b) knowledge of ways and means of dealing with specifics such as conventions, trends and sequences, classifications and categories, criteria, and methodologies; and (c) knowledge of universals and abstractions such as principles, generations, theories, and structures. Examples include:
   - The student will be able to identify the capitals of each state.
   - The student will be able to write the formula for sulfuric acid.
   - The student will be able to list the principal parts of a speech.
   - The student will be able to state the quadratic formula.
2. *Comprehension.* Objectives at this level include (a) translation, (b) interpretation, and (c) extrapolation of materials. Examples include:
   - The student will be able to identify transitive verbs.
   - The student will be able to describe photosynthesis in his or her own words.
   - The student will be able to interpret the symbols on a weather map.
   - The student will be able to interpret the quadratic formula.
3. *Application.* Objectives at this level are related to the use of abstractions in particular situations. Examples include:
   - The student will be able to compute miles per gallon for an auto trip.
   - The student will be able to predict the effects of combining certain paint colors.
   - The student will be able to apply the formula to determine the area of a triangle.
   - The student will be able to use the quadratic formula.
4. *Analysis.* This includes objectives related to breaking a whole into parts and distinguishing (a) elements, (b) relationships, and (c) organizational principles. Examples include:
   - The student will be able to identify bias in a news story.
   - The student will be able to identify relevant data in a report on a consumer product.
   - The student will be able to point out the effects of public opinion in the election of political candidates.
   - The student will be able to explain why the quadratic formula may give imaginary answers.
5. *Synthesis.* This includes objectives related to putting parts together in a new form, such as (a) a unique communication, (b) a plan of operation, and (c) a set of abstract relations. Examples include:
   - The student will be able to design a plan for completing a class project.
   - The student will be able to write an acceptable term paper.
   - The student will be able to design an experiment for testing a hypothesis.
   - The student will be able to graph a quadratic equation.
6. *Evaluation.* This is the highest level of complexity and includes objectives related to judging in terms of (a) internal evidence or logical consistency, and (b) external evidence or consistency with facts developed elsewhere. Examples include:
   - The student will be able to determine which writing project meets the stated criteria.
   - The student will be able to discriminate which conclusions are supported by evidence.

- The student will be able to appraise fallacies in an argument.
- The student will be able to explain the relationship between the graph and the results of the quadratic formula.

With these six levels of the cognitive domain, you will be able to more precisely state the performance objectives in the daily lesson plans. Illustrative verbs for the cognitive domain are listed in Table 3.3 for general instructional objectives that might be in unit plans and for specific learning objectives that might be used in daily lesson plans.

Affective Domain.   The taxonomy for the *affective domain* deals with students' attitudes, values, and emotions. While schools focus heavily on the cognitive domain, students' attitudes about learning and the content are equally important to their long-term success in school. To aid the task of classification of these attitudes, values, and emotions related to schooling, the affective taxonomy was developed by David Krathwohl and colleagues (Anderson & Krathwohl, 2001).

While the cognitive and the affective taxonomies are discussed as separate entities, it is impossible to separate how students think about a learning activity and how they feel about it. The cognitive taxonomy and the affective taxonomy are interrelated, if not completely parallel in their structure. For example, students' ability to gain knowledge is dependent on their willingness to "receive" information. Thus, you might include instructional objectives in the affective domain as a means to enhance student learning in the cognitive domain.

Using the structure set up by Krathwohl and colleagues, there are five levels of the affective taxonomy. Descriptions of each level are presented along with sample objectives for each. The sample objectives do not include conditions and the intended degree of success; you would add these.

1. *Receiving.* This objective is indicative of the learner's sensitivity to the existence of stimuli and includes (a) awareness, (b) willingness to receive, and (c) selected attention. Examples include:
   - The student pays close attention to directions for an activity.
   - The student shows awareness of the importance of fire safety practices.
   - The student listens closely to classroom presentations.
2. *Responding.* This includes active attention to stimuli, such as (a) acquiescence, (b) willing responses, and (c) feelings of satisfaction. Examples include:
   - The student completes assigned homework.
   - The student volunteers for special tasks.
   - The student finds pleasure in reading.
3. *Valuing.* Included in this objective are beliefs and attitudes of worth in the form of (a) acceptance, (b) preference, and (c) commitment. Examples include:
   - The student recognizes the value of freedom of speech.
   - The student expresses an appreciation for the role of science in everyday life.
   - The student shows concern for language by trying to speak and write precisely.
4. *Organization.* This level of internalization involves (a) conceptualization of values and (b) organization of a value system. Examples include:
   - The student forms judgments about proper behavior in school.

TABLE 3.3   Cognitive Domain: Illustrative Objectives and Verbs

LEVEL OF THE DOMAIN	ILLUSTRATIVE GENERAL INSTRUCTIONAL OBJECTIVES	ILLUSTRATIVE VERBS FOR STATING SPECIFIC LEARNING OUTCOMES
Knowledge	Knows common terms Knows specific facts Knows methods and procedures Knows basic concepts Knows principles	Defines, describes, identifies, labels, lists, matches, names, outlines, reproduces, selects, states
Comprehension	Understands facts and principles Interprets verbal material Interprets charts and graphs Translates verbal material to mathematical formulas Estimates future consequences implied in data Justifies methods and procedures	Converts, defends, distinguishes, estimates, explains, extends, generalizes, gives examples, infers, paraphrases, predicts, rewrites, summarizes
Application	Applies concepts and principles to new situations Applies laws and theories to practical situations Solves mathematical problems Constructs charts and graphs Demonstrates correct usage of a method or procedure	Changes, computes, demonstrates, discovers, manipulates, modifies, operates, predicts, prepares, produces, relates, shows, solves, uses
Analysis	Recognizes unstated assumptions Recognizes logical fallacies in reasoning Distinguishes between facts and inferences Evaluates the relevancy of data Analyzes the organizational structure of a work (art, music, writing)	Breaks down, diagrams, differentiates, discriminates, distinguishes, identifies, illustrates, infers, outlines, points out, relates, selects, separates, subdivides
Synthesis	Writes a well-organized theme Gives a well-organized speech Writes a creative short story (or poem, or music) Proposes a plan for an experiment Integrates learning from different areas into a plan for solving a problem Formulates a new scheme for classifying objects (or events, or ideas)	Categorizes, combines, compiles, composes, creates, devises, designs, explains, generates, modifies, organizes, plans, rearranges, reconstructs, relates, reorganizes, revises, rewrites, summarizes, tells, writes
Evaluation	Judges the logical consistency of written material Judges the adequacy with which conclusions are supported by data Judges the value of a work (art, music, writing) by use of internal criteria Judges the value of a work (art, music, writing) by use of external standards of excellence	Appraises, compares, concludes, contrasts, criticizes, describes, discriminates, explains, justifies, interprets, relates, summarizes, supports

Adapted and reprinted with permission of Prentice Hall, Inc. from *How to Write and Use Instructional Objectives,* Sixth Edition, by Norman E. Gronlund. Copyright © 2000 by Prentice Hall, Inc. Page 113.

- The student decides what values are most important to him or her.
- The student forms a judgment about his or her life work based on abilities, interests, and beliefs.

5. *Characterization.* This is the highest level of internalization; it includes behavior related to (a) a generalized set of values and (b) a characterization or philosophy of life. Examples include:
   - The student regularly cooperates in class and group activities.
   - The student tries to solve problems objectively.
   - The student works independently and diligently.

Illustrative verbs for the affective domain are listed in Table 3.4 for general instructional objectives and for specific learning objectives.

Psychomotor Domain. The *psychomotor domain* is primarily concerned with the development of movement and coordination, ranging from reflex to creative movement. This domain receives vastly different levels of interest depending on the subject area being taught. The psychomotor domain is especially important in physical education, vocational education, music education, and early childhood education.

In physical education, students may be expected to learn to throw, catch, swim various strokes, or hit a golf ball. All these tasks require psychomotor skills, as does learning to type, playing a musical instrument, drilling a hole, or sketching a picture. Cognitive and affective goals are also present in each of these examples—understanding, knowledge, and positive attitudes are important in all learning.

Although a number of authors have attempted to clarify the elements of the psychomotor domain, Harrow (1972) has presented perhaps the most comprehensive system or classification, and her classification system is described here. It has several levels ranging from simple reflex movements to highly complex integrated movement. Descriptions of each level are presented along with sample objectives for each. The sample objectives do not include conditions and the intended degree of success; you would add these.

1. *Reflex movements.* These objectives include (a) segmental reflexes (involving one spinal segment) and (b) intersegmental reflexes (involving more than one spinal segment). Examples include:
   - The student will blink when something comes at their face.
   - The student will contract a muscle.
2. *Fundamental movements.* Included in these objectives are behaviors related to (a) walking, (b) running, (c) jumping, (d) pushing, (e) pulling, and (f) manipulating. Examples include:
   - The student will run a 100-yard dash.
   - The student will perform push-ups.
3. *Perceptual abilities.* These objectives include (a) kinesthetic, (b) visual, (c) auditory, (d) tactile, and (e) coordination abilities. Examples include:
   - The student will distinguish distant and close sounds.
   - The student will distinguish smooth and rough surfaces.

TABLE 3.4   Affective Domain: Illustrative Objectives and Verbs

LEVEL OF THE DOMAIN	ILLUSTRATIVE GENERAL INSTRUCTIONAL OBJECTIVES	ILLUSTRATIVE VERBS FOR STATING SPECIFIC LEARNING OUTCOMES
Receiving	Listens attentively Shows awareness of the importance of learning Shows sensitivity to human needs and social problems Accepts differences of race and culture Attends closely to the classroom activities	Asks, chooses, describes, follows, gives, holds, identifies, locates, names, points to, selects, sits erect, replies, uses
Responding	Completes assigned homework Obeys school rules Participates in class discussion Completes laboratory work Volunteers for special tasks Shows interest in subject Enjoys helping others	Answers, assists, complies, conforms, discusses, greets, helps, labels, performs, practices, presents, reads, recites, reports, selects, tells, writes
Valuing	Demonstrates belief in the democratic process Appreciates good literature (art or music) Appreciates the role of science (or other subjects) in everyday life Shows concern for the welfare of others Demonstrates problem-solving attitude Demonstrates commitment to social improvement	Completes, describes, differentiates, explains, follows, forms, initiates, invites, joins, justifies, proposes, reads, reports, selects, shares, studies, works
Organization	Recognizes the need for balance between freedom and responsibility in a democracy Recognizes the role of systematic planning in solving problems Accepts responsibility for his or her own behavior Understands and accepts his or her own strengths and limitations Formulates a life plan in harmony with his or her abilities, interests, and beliefs	Adheres, alters, arranges, combines, compares, completes, defends, explains, generalizes, identifies, integrates, modifies, orders, organizes, prepares, relates, synthesizes
Characterization of a value or a value complex	Displays safety consciousness Demonstrates self-reliance working independently Practices cooperation in group activities Uses objective approach in problem solving Demonstrates industry, punctuality, and self-discipline Maintains good health habits	Acts, discriminates, displays, influences, listens, modifies, performs, practices, proposes, qualifies, questions, revises, serves, solves, uses, verifies

4. *Physical abilities.* Included at this level are objectives related to (a) endurance, (b) strength, (c) flexibility, (d) agility, (e) reaction-response time, and (f) dexterity. Examples include:
   - The student will be able to run four laps around the playing field without stopping.
   - The student will be able to complete ten sit-ups.
5. *Skilled movements.* This includes objectives concerning (a) games, (b) sports, (c) dances, and (d) the arts. Examples include:
   - The student will be able to accurately serve a volleyball.
   - The student will be able to play the piano.
6. *Nondiscursive communication.* This level includes objectives related to expressive movement through (a) posture, (b) gestures, (c) facial expressions, and (d) creative movements. Examples include:
   - The student will act a part in a play.
   - The student will create interpretative dance steps to music.

Illustrative verbs for the psychomotor domain are listed in Table 3.5 for general instructional objectives and for specific learning objectives.

Procedures

When selecting instructional procedures, you should consider the parts of an effective lesson discussed earlier and place your procedures within that framework: introductory activities, developmental activities, and closing activities (including both the content closing and the procedural closing). It is often useful to indicate an approximate amount of time each activity will take so that you can better gauge what can be completed within the class period. Furthermore, your decisions will likely focus on selecting the activities, sequencing the activities, and grouping students for the activities within that lesson framework.

When you select instructional activities, many factors need to be considered: student characteristics, the nature of the instructional activities themselves, the instructional setting and physical environment, your knowledge and skills, the complexity of the task, the degree of student engagement, the amount of time required, and others.

When deciding how to sequence the activities, you should consider two guidelines (Muth & Alvermann, 1999). First, your activities should lead students from simple to complex and from concrete to abstract. Second, in general, students should not be asked to do something new and difficult for the first time on their own.

There are a number of ways to group students for instruction (see Chapter 6). Briefly, you might choose whole-group instruction, small-group instruction (including cooperative learning and peer tutoring), or independent work. You will have to decide what type of grouping best helps students meet the objectives of the lesson. Your decision could be affected by your desire to vary your instructional delivery over time.

Materials

Your lesson plan should include a listing of materials you will need during instruction of that lesson, including items such as textbooks, additional resource books, handouts, film-

TABLE 3.5   Psychomotor Domain: Illustrative Objectives and Verbs

LEVEL OF THE DOMAIN	ILLUSTRATIVE GENERAL INSTRUCTIONAL OBJECTIVES	ILLUSTRATIVE VERBS FOR STATING SPECIFIC LEARNING OUTCOMES
1. Reflex movements	Responds to some stimulus (are involuntary movements)	Blinks, ducks
2. Fundamental movements	Builds upon reflex movements (are more complex movements)	Walks, runs, jumps, pushes, pulls, manipulates, reaches, grasps, crawls
3. Perceptual abilities	Combines cognitive and physical abilities Discriminates by touch, body awareness balance, and hand-eye coordination	Distinguishes, discriminates, coordinates
4. Physical abilities	Meets the demands of complex sustained movement	Expresses endurance, strength, flexibility, agility, or dexterity
5. Skilled movements	Performs skillfully in games, sports, dances, and the arts (addresses levels of proficiency: beginner, intermediate, advanced, highly skilled)	Serves, plays, dances, draws
6. Nondiscursive	Demonstrates expressive and interpretive movements through posture, gestures, facial expressions, and creative movements	Moves, dances, expresses, gestures

Adapted from *A Taxonomy of the Psychomotor Domain: A Guide for Developing Behavioral Objectives* by A. J. Harrow. Copyright © 1972 by Longman Publishing Group. Reprinted with permission.

strips, videotapes, audiotapes, audiovisual equipment, maps, pictures, posters, globes, charts, supplies, laboratory equipment, bulletin boards, or other items. Before making final decisions in your lesson plan, check to be sure the items that you are thinking about will be available on the day and time of the class. For example, you might want to have a demonstration with a computer and a program related to your subject area, but the computer might already be reserved for the day that you were planning the lesson.

Evaluation of Students

At some point, you need to evaluate whether your students have achieved the goals of the unit and the objectives of each lesson. However, you do not have to give a test or quiz in each class period. Instead, you may formally evaluate your students periodically. It is important, however, to check for student understanding in each lesson as you proceed through it.

Your evaluation during a lesson might simply include checking for comprehension by questions or activities in which the students are quizzed about the content of the lesson. Student responses will give you important feedback about student mastery of the content, and will help you decide whether to continue with your lesson plan or perhaps reteach some part of the lesson that students had difficulty with. Review questions at the start of a lesson also provide a gauge concerning student understanding.

CLASSROOM DECISIONS

Students' understanding and performance can be evaluated in various ways, both formally and informally. If you were teaching an art lesson on depth and perspective in drawings, how might you evaluate your students' understanding of these concepts other than by a test? How might your approach be different if this were a more advanced class?

Other Possible Items

The items discussed so far are common elements of a lesson plan. You might also want to include information about the following items on your lesson plan sheets.

1. *Rationale for the lesson.* Some teachers prefer to include the rationale for why the lesson is important. In this way, you can identify and clarify the value of the lesson and convey this rationale to the students.

2. *An outline of the subject matter.* Some teachers prefer to attach an outline of the subject matter to be covered in the lesson to the lesson plan sheet. In this way, all important information is together.

3. *A list of key points.* Sometimes there is a key point that you want to emphasize in a lesson. By having a spot on your lesson plan sheet, you are able to clarify that point for yourself and then convey it to students during the lesson.

4. *The assignment of homework or other requirements.* You may prefer to include a spot in your lesson plan sheet to list any assignment given to students.

5. *A timetable.* Some lesson plan sheets include a column on one side for you to indicate the approximate amount of time each activity will take. As an alternative, you might simply indicate this estimate of the number of minutes next to the activity description in the plan.

6. *Special notes or reminders.* You may have special announcements that you want to make to students on a particular day, such as information about special projects, reminders about an upcoming due date for a project, additional information about an assignment, or other information.

7. *Evaluation of the lesson.* This space is reserved for you to make notes about the lesson after instruction has taken place. For example, one activity might have required more time than you originally planned, or would have worked better with fewer students in each group. Or you could make notes about the quality of a videotape you used. In this way, you will have a written record about your experiences with the lesson. When you begin your planning for the next time you teach this les-

son, you can read these notes and comments and make any needed changes to improve it.

KEY TERMS

Action statement
Affective domain
Closing activities
Cognitive domain
Conditions statement
Content closing
Course
Course planning
Criterion statement
Culminating lessons

Daily planning
Developmental activities
Developmental lessons
Introductory activities
Introductory lessons
Learning domain
Lesson
Objective
Performance objective
Plan book

Procedural closing
Psychomotor domain
Taxonomy
Term
Term planning
Unit
Unit planning
Weekly planning

MAJOR CONCEPTS

1. The planning process helps you organize the curriculum and address complex classroom variables, and also provides you with a sense of direction and a feeling of confidence and security.

2. Plans need to be written for each course and for each marking period, unit, week, and lesson within each course.

3. Course planning involves organizing and scheduling the content to be taught during the time allotted for the course, whether that time is for a year, semester, trimester, or quarter. Course planning commonly takes the form of a general outline of content with specific ideas noted within the outline concerning course content, methods, and evaluation.

4. Term planning involves the preparation of more detailed outlines of the content to be covered within a marking period.

5. Unit planning involves developing a sequence of daily plans that addresses the topic of the unit in a cohesive way.

6. Weekly planning involves laying out the week's activities within the framework of the daily schedule throughout the week. A plan book is used to display your plans in a brief way.

7. Daily planning involves preparing notes about objectives, materials, activities, evaluation, and other information for a lesson for a particular day, but in more detail than in the weekly plan.

8. Performance objectives include (a) an action statement identifying the action that the teacher expects the student to perform; (b) a conditions statement identifying the conditions under which the action occurs; and (c) a criterion statement identifying the criteria or level of performance expected of the student.

9. Learning objectives can be written in three learning domains: (a) cognitive, which refers to mental or intellectual thinking skills, (b) affective, which classifies student attitudes toward learning, and (c) psychomotor, which involves physical movement and related skills.

10. When planning for instructional activities and procedures, select introductory, developmental, and closing activities within the lesson.

11. You need to decide what type of information you would like in your lesson plans and then display that information in a format that suits your needs and preferences.

DISCUSSION/REFLECTIVE QUESTIONS

1. Why is the preparation of a series of daily lesson plans not sufficient when planning for an entire course?

2. What are the benefits of unit planning? What might be some consequences if you did not conduct unit planning?

3. Identify several ways that you might conduct the content closing of a lesson to provide for a summary of the main concepts covered in the lesson.

4. What is the rationale for novice teachers to prepare detailed lesson plans?

5. Should all objectives that you write be at the upper three levels of the cognitive domain? Why or why not?

SUGGESTED ACTIVITIES

For Clinical Settings

1. Obtain a textbook for a course that you might teach. Select a unit within the text and outline the introductory, developmental, and culminating lessons that you would include in the unit.

2. Write at least five performance objectives concerning content in this chapter representing different levels of the cognitive domain. Also consider if objectives in the affective and psychomotor domains are appropriate for this chapter.

3. After considering the information that you want to include in your weekly plans, design a weekly plan format that you would like to use.

4. After considering the information that you want to include in your daily lesson plans, design a lesson plan format that you would like to use.

For Field Settings

1. Examine the curriculum guide for one course and compare it to the textbook that is used. In what ways would the curriculum guide help you in your planning?

2. Ask one or more teachers to describe how they prepare their yearly, unit, weekly, and daily plans.

3. Ask several teachers to look at their weekly plans. Ask the teachers to describe how they prepared those weekly plans and to identify factors they took into account when planning.

4. Ask several teachers about changes they make in their weekly plans once the school week begins. What causes them to change their plans? In what ways do they change their plans?

USEFUL RESOURCES

Gronlund, N. E. (2000). *How to write and use instructional objectives* (6th ed.). Upper Saddle River, NJ: Prentice Hall.

A thorough, practical guide that examines how to prepare instructional objectives in each learning domain. Considers performance objectives. Includes many examples and summary charts.

WEB SITES

- Site offers formats for daily, weekly and long range planning
  http://intranet.cps.k12.il.us/Lessons/LessonPlanning/

- Great site with lesson planning ideas and links
  http://www.adprima.com/lesson.htm

- Lesson plans by content area

  http://www.iglou.com/wcet/edtech/currlink/lesson.htm

- Lesson plans page

  http://www.lessonplanspage.com/edu.htm

- More lesson plans

  http://www.lessonplanz.com

- Education World® - Lesson Planning - Best of 1998

  http://www.education-world.com/best_of/1998/articles_lesson.shtml

- The *New York Times* Learning Network is a free service for students in grades 3 to 12 and their teachers and parents. The site is updated Monday through Friday throughout the year.

  http://Nytimes.com/learning/

- Navigator is the home page used by the newsroom of the *New York Times* for searching the Web. Its primary intent is to give reporters and editors a solid starting point for a wide range of journalistic functions without forcing all of them to spend time wandering around blindly to find a useful set of links of their own. Its secondary purpose is to show people that there's a lot of fun and useful stuff going on out there.

  http://Nytimes.com/learning/general/navigator/index.html

- The GatewaySM Collections List

  http://www.thegateway.org/collections.html

- Discovery Channel School

  http://school.discovery.com/teachers/

CHAPTER FOUR

THE INCLUSIVE AND MULTICULTURAL CLASSROOM

THE INCLUSIVE AND
MULTICULTURAL CLASSROOM

Sources of Student Diversity
 Cognitive Area
 Affective Area
 Physical Area
 Learning Styles
 Creative Potential
 Gender
 Language
 Cultural Diversity
 Disabilities
 Students at Risk
 Socioeconomic Status

Creating an Inclusive, Multicultural Classroom
 Create a Supportive, Caring Environment
 Offer a Responsive Curriculum
 Vary Your Instruction
 Provide Assistance When Needed

OBJECTIVES

This chapter provides information that will help you to:

1. Describe multiple ways in which diversity is exhibited in student characteristics.

2. Select instructional approaches and ways to interact with students that take into account their characteristics to promote student learning.

3. Create a supportive, caring classroom.

4. Offer a responsive curriculum and vary your instruction with student characteristics in mind.

**PRAXIS/Principles of Learning
and Teaching/Pathwise**

The following principles are relevant to content in this chapter:

1. Becoming familiar with relevant aspects of students' background knowledge and experiences   (A1)

2. Creating or selecting teaching methods, learning activities, and instructional materials or other resources that are appropriate for the students and that are aligned with the goals of the lesson   (A4)

3. Creating a climate that promotes fairness   (B1)

4. Establishing and maintaining rapport with students   (B2)

INTASC

The following INTASC standards are relevant to content in this chapter:

1. The teacher understands how students differ in their approaches to learning and creates instructional opportunities that are adapted to diverse learners.   (Standard 3)

2. The teacher plans instruction based on knowledge of subject matter, students, the community, and curriculum goals.   (Standard 7)

Just think about the diversity apparent in a typical urban classroom. There may be a wide range of student cognitive and physical abilities. Students may have different degrees of English proficiency, and some may have a disabling condition such as a hearing disorder. A wide range of ethnic characteristics may be evident, and various socioeconomic levels are likely to be represented. The students may prefer to learn in different ways, such as in pairs, small groups, or independently. Some may prefer written work; others may learn best when performing an activity.

People differ in countless ways, and it is helpful to examine variables that account for human differences. *Variables* include human characteristics that differ or vary from one person to the next. For example, height, weight, and measured intelligence are variables. Gender, race, socioeconomic status, and age also are variables. Less observable but equally important variables include self-esteem, confidence, anxiety, and learning style.

These examples are just a few of the human and environmental variables that create a wide range of individual differences and needs in classrooms. Individual differences need to be taken into account when instructional methods and procedures are selected for classroom management and discipline. What are the sources of student diversity? How can our understanding of these student characteristics help teachers to create an inclusive, multicultural classroom? These issues are explored in this chapter.

SOURCES OF STUDENT DIVERSITY

Individual differences abound, and adapting instruction to student differences is one of the most challenging aspects of teaching. The first step in planning to address the diversity of students is to recognize those differences. This section explores differences in cognitive, affective, and physical areas; differences due to gender, ethnicity, learning style, language, or creative potential; differences due to exceptionalities and at-risk characteristics; and others. In the classroom, students rarely fall cleanly into one category or another and may exhibit characteristics from several categories.

Cognitive Area

Cognitive activity includes information processing, problem solving, using mental strategies for tasks, and continuous learning. Children in a classroom will differ in their cognitive abilities to perform these tasks. Thus, there may be a range of low academic ability to high academic ability students in a classroom. *Intelligence* involves the capacity to apprehend facts and their relations and to reason about them; it is an indicator of cognitive ability. Two of the most prominent contemporary researchers in intelligence are Howard Gardner and Robert Sternberg.

Gardner (1985) believes that all people have multiple intelligences. He identified seven independent intelligences: linguistic, musical, logical–mathematical, spatial, bodily kinesthetic, interpersonal, and intrapersonal. Later, he added an eighth one on naturalistic characteristics. According to this theory, a person may be gifted in any one of the intelligences without being exceptional in the others. Gardner proposes more adjustment of curriculum and instruction to individuals' combinations of aptitudes. His vision of appropriate education is clear: Do not expect each student to have the same interests and abilities or to learn in the same ways. Furthermore, do not expect everyone to learn everything, for there is simply too much to learn.

Sternberg (1988) calls for greater understanding of what people do when they solve problems so they can be helped to behave in more intelligent ways. He believes that intelligent people use the environment to accomplish goals by adapting to it, changing it, or selecting out of it.

The work of Gardner, Sternberg, and other cognitive psychologists provides ideas for teachers when selecting instructional techniques. When considering the cognitive differences of your students, you should:

1. Expect students to be different.
2. Spend the time and effort to look for potential.
3. Realize that student needs are not only in deficit areas. Development of potential is a need, too.
4. Be familiar with past records of achievement.
5. Be aware of previous experiences that have shaped a student's way of thinking.
6. Challenge students with varied assignments, and note the results.
7. Use a variety of ways of grading and evaluating.
8. Keep changing the conditions for learning to bring out hidden potential.
9. Challenge students occasionally beyond what is expected.
10. Look for something unique that each can do.

There are many useful resource guides about addressing the diversity of students by applying the multiple intelligences to lesson activities (e.g., Lazear, 1991; Chapman, 1993; Fogarty, 1997; Campbell et al., 1999).

TEACHERS IN ACTION

CONSIDER GARDNER'S MULTIPLE INTELLIGENCES WHEN PLANNING

Patricia Vandelinder, former middle school social studies teacher, now an educational consultant, Detroit, Michigan

I have found that students learn at different rates and in different ways. One way to deal with the different learning styles is to create lessons around Gardner's eight intelligences. Besides the two primary intelligences—verbal/linguistic and mathematical/logical—instructional lessons can be designed around the other intelligences to meet the needs of the majority of the students.

In a social studies lesson on current events, for example, students could be asked to illustrate the main events in the news article as a way to relate to the visual/spatial intelligence. Students can role-play the situation, debate it with other students, or write reflectively about how they would feel if the article was about them. The eight intelligences offer many ways that students can learn and teachers can teach.

Struggling Learners.   A student who is considered a *struggling learner* cannot learn at an average rate from the instructional resources, texts, workbooks, and materials that are designated for the majority of students in the classroom (Bloom, 1982). These students often have limited attention spans and deficiencies in basic skills such as reading, writing, and mathematics. They need frequent feedback, corrective instruction, special instructional pacing, instructional variety, and perhaps modified materials.

For the struggling learners in your class, you should (a) frequently vary your instructional technique; (b) develop lessons around students' interests, needs, and experiences; (c) provide for an encouraging, supportive environment; (d) use cooperative learning and peer tutors for students needing remediation; (e) provide study aids; (f) teach content in small sequential steps with frequent checks for comprehension; (g) use individualized materials and individualized instruction whenever possible; (h) use audio and visual materials for instruction; and (i) take steps to develop each student's self-concept (e.g., assign a task where the student can showcase a particular skill).

Gifted or Talented Learners.   *Gifted or talented learners* are those with above average abilities, and they need special instructional consideration. Unfortunately, some teachers do not challenge high-ability students, and these students just "mark time" in school. Unchallenged, they may develop poor attention and study habits, negative attitudes toward school and learning, and waste academic learning time. This problem is illustrated in Figure 4.1, which reproduces a real note that a middle school teacher received concerning the need to challenge the class.

For these students, you should (a) not require that they repeat material they already have mastered; (b) present instruction at a flexible pace, allowing those who are able to progress at a productive rate; (c) condense curriculum by removing unneeded assignments to make time for extending activities; (d) encourage students to be self-directing

FIGURE 4.1   A Petition to Be Challenged

The petition provided here is real. It was handed to the middle school math teacher by an identified gifted student who had become frustrated with his math class. The student attended a large middle school in a small city in the Midwest. Twenty other students also signed the petition before it was given to the teacher.

WANTED: WORK

I, as a concerned and bored student, am protesting against you underestimating our abilities. I'm sorry to say that I'm writing this in class, but what we do in here is really not worth working on. Review, review, that's all we do. This class is no challenge. If I've learned anything in this class, it would be boredom. I want work. We want work. I have no intention to do anything in this class except twiddle my thumbs. I've found no enjoyment in sitting here listening to my teacher repeat things I've learned in the fifth grade. I'm sure others feel the way I do. Please, we want a challenge.

Sincerely,

Bob

---

and self-evaluating in their work; (e) use grading procedures that do not discourage students from intellectual risk-taking or penalize them for choosing complex learning activities; (f) provide resources beyond basal textbooks; (g) provide horizontal and vertical curriculum enrichment; (h) encourage supplementary reading and writing; and (i) encourage the development of hobbies and interests.

Affective Area

Education in the *affective area* focuses on feelings and attitudes. Emotional growth is not easy to facilitate, but sometimes the feelings students have about their skills or the subject are at least as important as the information they learn (Slavin, 2000). Self-esteem, time management, confidence, and self-direction are typical affective education goals. While affective goals have played a secondary role to cognitive goals in school, they should be given an important place when planning and carrying out instruction. Love of learning, confidence in learning, and cooperative attitudes are important objectives that teachers should have for students (Slavin, 2000). You may find a range of affective characteristics exhibited in the classroom, from low to high self-esteem, confidence, cooperation, self-direction, and the like.

To encourage affective development, you should:

1. Identify students by name as early as possible.
2. Accept the student as he or she is, for each has interesting, valuable qualities.
3. Be aware of previous experiences that have helped shape the student's feelings.

4. Observe students; notice moods and reactions from day to day.
5. Make observations over a period of time, noting trends.
6. Observe changes, or stability, under different conditions.

Physical Area

Perhaps the best place to observe the wide range of physical differences among students is the hallway of any junior high or middle school. Tall and short, skinny and heavy, muscular and frail, dark and fair, active and quiet, describe just a few of the extremes one can see there. Physical (psychomotor) differences among students have sometimes been overlooked by teachers who are not involved in physical education (Woolfolk, 2001). *Psychomotor skills* involve gross motor skills and fine motor skills, such as dribbling a basketball or drawing a fine line. These skills are integral parts of most learning activities. Indeed, psychomotor and affective objectives often overlap.

Physical demands upon learning are obvious in areas of handwriting, industrial arts, sewing, typing, art, and driver education. However, they must not be minimized in less obvious areas such as science labs, computer classes, speech and drama, and music. Vision and hearing deficiencies also contribute to individual differences. You should recognize the importance of physical skills to the total learning program and explore the possibilities for including psychomotor development activities in classroom objectives. You should:

1. Remember that students come in many different sizes, shapes, colors, and physical states.
2. Be aware of previous experiences that have shaped physical performance and self-expression.
3. Know what the normal physical pattern is for each age level and note any extreme variations.
4. Provide materials for manipulation and observe carefully to see what skills emerge, or are lacking.
5. Observe student responses to different environmental factors and different kinds of physical activities.
6. Give students a chance to express themselves physically.

Learning Styles

A *learning style* is an individual's preferences for the conditions of the learning process that can affect one's learning (Woolfolk, 2001), including *where, when,* and *how* learning takes place, and *with what* materials. These styles may play an integral role in determining how the student perceives the learning environment and responds to it. Therefore, knowledge about learning styles could allow teachers to provide options in the classroom that would enhance students' learning. Theories and research studies about learning styles are tentative and ongoing, but several promising areas of instructional assistance have emerged. These include cognitive style, brain hemisphericity, and sensory modalities.

Cognitive Style.   *Cognitive style* should be considered in planning. Cognitive style refers to the way people process information and use strategies in responding to tasks. Conceptual tempo and field-dependence/field-independence are two categories of cognitive style that educators may consider when planning instruction.

First, *conceptual tempo* deals with students being impulsive or reflective when selecting from two or more alternatives. For example, impulsive students look at alternatives only briefly and select one quickly. They may make many errors because they do not take time to consider all the alternatives. However, not all cognitively impulsive students are fast *and* inaccurate. On the other hand, reflective students deliberate among the alternatives and respond more slowly.

Second, *field-dependence/field-independence* (sometimes referred to as global/analytic style) deals with the extent to which individuals can overcome effects of distracting background elements (the field) when trying to differentiate among relevant aspects of a particular situation.

You could expect field-dependent students to be more people-oriented, to work best in groups, and to prefer subjects such as history and literature. Field-independent students would prefer science, problem-solving tasks, and instructional approaches requiring little social interaction (Slavin, 2000). Field-dependent students respond more to verbal praise and extrinsic motivation, while field-independent students tend to pursue their own goals and respond best to intrinsic motivation (Good & Brophy, 1995).

Brain Hemisphericity. *Brain hemisphericity* is another aspect of student preferences for learning environments. The two halves of the brain appear to serve different functions even though they are connected by a complex network which orchestrates their teamwork. Each side is dominant in certain respects. Left-brain dominant people tend to be more analytical in their orientation, being generally logical, concrete, and sequential. Right-brained domi-

TEACHERS IN ACTION

LEARNING STYLES

Loraine Chapman, instructional technology training, Tucson, Arizona

Shortly after I began teaching, I noticed that students react differently to learning tasks. For example, Kelly stated that unless she can hear the words she reads, she has difficulty comprehending. Delila needs complete silence when she reads and will even put her fingers in her ears when reading to make it quieter. When given the option, some students always select a partner for work, while others work alone.

After gathering more information about learning styles, I began to incorporate that information into my lesson plans and developed strategies to take into account the various cognitive learning styles of my students. For example, sometimes I let students choose from a list of activities that all fulfill the lesson's objectives, but each activity involves a different type of learning experience reflecting the various learning styles.

I also believe that students need to learn to stretch and use all learning styles. So within a class, or over a few days or a week, tasks using all learning styles will be incorporated into the lessons, and each student must complete each activity, no matter what the learning style.

nant people tend to be more visually and spatially oriented and more wholistic in their thinking.

Teacher presentations focusing on left-hemisphere activity include lecture, discussion, giving verbal clues, explaining rules, and asking yes–no and either–or questions in content areas. Useful materials include texts, word lists, workbook exercises, readings, and drill tapes. To develop left-hemisphere functions, teachers should (a) introduce and teach some material in the linear mode, (b) sequence the learning for meaning and retention, (c) conduct question-and-answer periods, (d) emphasize the meaning of words and sentences, and (e) increase student proficiency with information processing skills such as note-taking, memorization, and recall.

Teacher presentations featuring right hemisphere activity involve demonstration, experiences, open-ended questions, giving nonverbal clues, manipulations, and divergent thinking activity. Useful materials for these activities include flash cards, maps, films, audiotapes for main ideas, drawings, and manipulatives. To develop right-hemisphere functions, teachers should (a) encourage intuitive thinking and "guess-timating," (b) allow for testing of ideas and principles, (c) introduce some material in the visual/spatial mode, (d) use some nonsequential modes for instruction, and (e) integrate techniques from art, music, and physical education into social science, science, and language arts disciplines.

Sensory Modality.   Sensory modality is a third factor in students' preferences for a learning environment. A *sensory modality* is a system of interacting with the environment through one or more of the basic senses: sight, hearing, touch, smell, or taste. The most important sensory modalities for teachers are the visual, auditory, and kinesthetic modes. Information to be learned is first received through one of the senses. The information is either forgotten after a few seconds or, after initial processing, is placed in short-term or long-term memory. Learning may be enhanced when the information is received through a preferred sensory modality. Use a variety of instructional approaches that enable the students to receive the content through one or more of the basic senses.

Creative Potential

Creativity is defined by Torrance and Sisk (1997) as the process of creating ideas or hypotheses concerning these ideas, testing the hypotheses, modifying and retesting the hypotheses, and communicating the results. Highly creative individuals sometimes demonstrate characteristics that are not always liked by others, such as independence of thought and judgment, courage of convictions, skepticism toward the voice of authority, and displays of nonconformity.

Creative students process information differently and react to the world in ways unlike their peers. Teachers and parents say they want creative children, but too often set up constraints to prevent a truly creative child from "getting out of hand." Highly creative children tend to be estranged from their peers and misunderstood by their teachers who reward students that exhibit conforming behavior. Too many teachers suppress individualism and creativity. You might show examples of work done by former students which reflect creativity. This leads to a discussion of the value of creativity and can encourage creative potential.

SPOTLIGHT ON TECHNOLOGY

THE CONCRETE–ABSTRACT CONTINUUM

Instructional or audiovisual materials vary in the way that they realistically represent the content, and this variation can be viewed on a continuum. On one end of the *concrete–abstract continuum* are concrete, real, direct experiences with the content (such as manipulating actual materials), whereas the other end of the continuum includes instructional materials that are more abstract, even using symbols, diagrams, and words.

Students vary in the way that they are able to learn from abstract symbols and experiences. With content new to students, learning is facilitated if instruction follows a sequence (a) from direct experience, (b) through representations of actual experiences (as in films and pictures), and (c) then to symbolic representations of experiences. It is often a mistake to begin with abstract or symbolic instructional materials. Concrete experiences facilitate learning and the acquisition, retention, and usability of abstract symbols. Instructional media, therefore, provide the necessary concrete experiences and also help students to integrate prior experiences.

Time is also a factor in the use of this continuum. In general, real, concrete experiences take more instructional time; abstract materials and experiences take less time (if the students are ready for such experiences). For example, it takes more time to take part in contrived experiences (e.g.,

models, labs, simulations) or dramatized experiences (e.g., plays, role playing) than it does to present the same information in a motion picture, a recording, or a series of visual or verbal symbols.

Consider whether the particular nature of the direct experiences is worth the extra time that they take. Of course, you also must consider whether the learning experience is appropriate to the experiential background of the students. Take into account the learning styles and grade level of the students. Generally, younger students need more concrete experiences, whereas older students can handle more abstract experiences. As a general rule, use many direct, concrete experiences to ensure student learning, but go as high as you can on the abstraction continuum so that you can be the most time efficient.

1. If you were teaching a science unit on rocks and minerals, what types of instructional materials and media might you use to illustrate the various points on the concrete–abstract continuum? Select a different unit topic and do the same thing.
2. When considering the concrete–abstract continuum, how might your selection of media accommodate different learning styles?

You can nurture creativity by learning about creative personalities and developing ability for divergent production. In this regard, you should:

1. Listen for creative (unconventional) responses.
2. Reward creative responses by asking students to elaborate upon those ideas.
3. Provide some learning activities in which students may be creative, not conforming.
4. Allow some work to be open ended, perhaps messy, and ungraded, to encourage exploration, guessing, and playing with the material.
5. Set up flexible learning environments in which students are free to make choices and pursue areas of personal interest.

Gender

The difference in learning between males and females is hard for psychologists and educators to understand. Researchers acknowledge that many descriptions of *gender difference* reflect social and political influences and previous experiences. At the same time, a strong case has been made for differences in neurological makeup between the sexes that lead them to think and learn differently.

Good and Brophy (1995) believe that gender roles in which children are socialized will interact with the student roles stressed in schools to create gender differences for children in school. They also believe that these roles influence how teachers respond to boys and to girls. Research suggests that boys are more active and assertive in class, so you should avoid self-defeating patterns of interaction with low-achieving, disruptive boys. You should guard against reinforcing obedience and conformity in girls, and work toward developing their intellectual assertiveness and efforts to achieve.

Current data on scholastic achievement of males and females fail to confirm some of the traditional assumptions about gender differences. Strategies can be followed that address gender issues and reduce gender bias (Grossman & Grossman, 1994).

In addressing gender differences in your classroom, you should:

1. Remember that differences between boys and girls are not absolute, but a matter of degree.
2. Take care to provide equal opportunities for each sex; for example, encourage girls to explore math and science areas, and promote artistic sensitivity in boys.
3. Recognize that knowing a student's gender is just one way of knowing about that student.
4. Encourage students of each gender to test the limits of learning and achievement.
5. Find ways of rearranging children for greater interaction and less gender-based distinction during learning activities.
6. Monitor your own teaching behaviors, and ask others to observe your sensitivity about sex bias in responding to students, giving instructions and assistance, leading discussions, encouraging students, or dealing with misbehaviors.

Language

Some students come from homes where English is not the primary language, or it is not spoken at all. They may have limited proficiency in English. In descending order, Spanish, French, German, Italian, and Chinese are the top five languages spoken at home other than English. This fact has a bearing on teachers' decisions about management and work.

Three types of *bilingual education programs* are available to help children with limited proficiency in English (Romero et al., 1987): (a) *transition* programs, which help students move into English as quickly as possible; (b) *maintenance* programs, where both languages are maintained; and (c) *enrichment* programs, where English-speaking students learn the language of the minority and language-minority students learn English.

To address language differences, you should (a) learn about the student's previous educational experiences, language ability, and achievement levels; (b) use alternative means of presenting material (e.g., tactile, visual, kinesthetic); (c) learn about the student's culture and be alert to cultural differences; (d) have the student work with someone who is bilingual with the same language; (e) use instructional materials that are at the proper reading level and include photos, illustrations, and content that will interest the student; and (f) share information from the student's culture and other cultures represented by your students.

CLASSROOM DECISIONS

Your students may represent several languages. Suppose that you had three students who spoke Spanish with limited English, two students who spoke Chinese with limited English, and one student who spoke Vietnamese with limited English. How might you need to vary your instruction to deal with language barriers? How might you have other students assist? What are the implications for your actions on maintaining order?

Cultural Diversity

Several approaches can be taken to examine individual differences created by cultural diversity. The emerging concepts of cultural pluralism and respect for cultural identity in the United States are replacing "melting pot" connotations with a "salad bowl" concept. *Cultural diversity* is reflected in the wide variety of values, beliefs, attitudes, and rules that define regional, ethnic, religious, or other culture groups. Minority populations wish their cultures to be recognized as unique and preserved for their children. The message from all cultural groups to schools is clear—make sure that each student from every cultural group succeeds in school.

Each cultural group teaches its members certain lessons about living. Differences exist among cultures in the way members of the culture conduct interpersonal relationships, arrive on time, use body language, cooperate with group members, and accept directions from authority figures. You need to treat each student as an individual first because that student is the product of many influences. Many resources are available concerning cultural diversity (e.g., Banks, 2002; Gollnick & Chinn, 2002). As you consider individual differences produced by cultural diversity, you should:

1. Examine your own values and beliefs for evidences of bias and stereotyping.
2. Read materials written by and about members of many culture groups.
3. Invite members of varied cultural groups to discuss the values and important beliefs within their culture, while remembering not to form perceptions based on one member of a particular group. Wide variances exist in every group.
4. Regard students as individuals first, with membership in a culture group as only one factor in understanding that individual.
5. Learn something about students' family and community relationships.
6. Consider nonstandard English and native languages as basic languages for students from culturally diverse populations, to support gradual but necessary instruction in the majority language.

7. Allow students to work in cross-cultural teams and facilitate cooperation while noting qualities and talents that emerge.
8. Use sociograms and other peer ratings to determine cross-cultural awareness and acceptance. A *sociogram* is a diagram that is created to show which students are interacting with which other students.
9. Introduce global education content and materials into lessons.
10. Infuse the curriculum with regular emphasis on other cultures, not just one unit a year, or a few isolated and stereotyped activities.
11. Take care not to assume that culturally diverse groups are deprived groups.
12. Select classroom routines that do not conflict with any cultural values.

Disabilities

Exceptional students include those with conditions considered disabilities. More than 10 percent of students in the United States are identified as having disabling conditions which justify placement in a special education program (Turnbull et al., 2002). This figure increases to 15 percent when gifted children are counted as special education students. Categories for special education services include learning disabilities, speech or language impairment, mental retardation, emotional disturbance, other health impairment, multiple handicaps, hearing impairment, orthopedic impairment, visual impairment, and deafness or blindness.

The Individuals with Disabilities Education Act (IDEA) committed the nation to a policy of mainstreaming students who have handicapping conditions by placing them in the least restrictive environment in which they can function successfully while having their special needs met. The degree to which they are treated differently is to be minimized. The *least restrictive environment* means that students with special needs are placed in special settings only if necessary and only for as long as necessary; the regular classroom is the preferred, least restrictive placement.

When considering the instructional needs of students with disabilities, you should:

1. Concentrate on student strengths, capitalizing on those strengths to overcome or circumvent deficits (e.g., Consider allowing some work to be done orally if the student has limited writing skills.).

TEACHERS IN ACTION

GET TO KNOW YOUR STUDENTS

Steffanie Ogg, high school teacher, St. Paul, Minnesota

The number one tip for classroom management is to know your students. Let them know who you are and that you enjoy their company. You can find at least one good thing about every student, even if it is just "I like your shoes." Make the rounds, try to say at least one nice thing to each student each day. Sure, this isn't going to handle any major classroom management crises, but it will help to create a community in which students know that you want what is best for them.

2. Read about successful children and adults who have surmounted disabilities.
3. Communicate often with special education teachers and collaborate with them in providing appropriate programs for exceptional students' needs.
4. Hold appropriate expectations for exceptional students. Teachers sometimes expect too much; however, an even more debilitating practice for some students is to expect too little.
5. Model appropriate attitudes and behaviors for nonhandicapped students toward those with disabilities.

Students at Risk

Other environmental and personal influences may converge to place a student at risk. *Students at risk* are children and adolescents who are not able to acquire and/or use the skills necessary to develop their potential and become productive members of society (Dunn & Dunn, 1992b). Conditions at home, support from the community, and personal and cultural background all affect student attitudes, behaviors, and propensity to profit from school experiences. Students potentially at risk include children who face adverse conditions beyond their control, those who do not speak English as a first language, talented but unchallenged students, those with special problems, and many others. At-risk students often have academic difficulties and thus may be low achievers.

TEACHERS IN ACTION

STUDENTS WITH LEARNING DISABILITIES IN THE REGULAR CLASSROOM

Linda Innes, seventh grade language arts teacher, Kansas City, Missouri

I teach one class that is labeled a class-within-a-class, which means that students identified as being learning disabled (LD) are placed in the same class with regular middle school students. To help meet state standards required for LD students, the learning disability teacher co-teaches the class with me. To meet the students' needs in this class, I do several things to be very clear and specific when teaching or giving directions.

First, I give directions in various ways. I have two or three other students repeat the directions I just gave. Also, it is helpful to have the students write down the directions, especially for homework.

Second, I give instruction thoroughly and slowly. When the students are taking notes, I speak in a slower manner, write out the notes word for word on the overhead projector, repeat what I have written and spoken several times, and monitor the room and the notes of the students to make sure that they are getting them copied down correctly. There are times when I or the LD teacher actually write the notes for some of the students or provide a photocopy due to the severe writing handicaps or slow processing skills.

Third, I place each LD student next to an academically strong student who can provide help whenever necessary. I have found that the stronger students benefit as well as the LD students. LD students get the personalized attention they require, and the regular student has the opportunity to explain the information and in the process learn it more thoroughly.

Students who are classified as at risk may include youth in poverty, youth in stress, youth without a home, abused and neglected youth, academically disadvantaged youth, youth from dysfunctional families, youth with eating disorders, chemically abusive youth, sexually active youth, homosexual youth, youth with sexually transmitted diseases, pregnant youth and young parents, delinquent youth, youth in gangs, dropouts, suicidal youth, youth members of Satanic cults, overemployed youth, mentally ill youth, disabled and handicapped youth, and lonely and disengaged youth (Redick & Vail, 1991).

These youth have some common characteristics. All the following traits need not be present for a student to be identified as at risk. Based on a review of research and experience (Bhaerman & Kopp, 1988; Lehr & Harris, 1988), youth at risk tend to exhibit the following characteristics: academic difficulties, lack of structure (disorganized), inattentiveness, distractibility, short attention span, low self-esteem, health problems, excessive absenteeism and truancy, dependence, narrow range of interest, lack of social skills, inability to face pressure, fear of failure (feels threatened by learning), and lack of motivation.

A study of successful teachers of low achieving students revealed a number of skills/competencies that can help at-risk students (Lehr & Harris, 1988). The skills/competencies fell into five major areas: personal skills/competencies, professional skills/competencies, materials, methods, and learning environment. Over half of the teachers in the study listed the following skills/competencies needed to teach low-achieving, at-risk students:

1. Using a variety of techniques and methods
2. Reteaching and giving students time to practice the skill
3. Being positive
4. Being patient
5. Being caring, concerned, empathetic, loving, respecting, and humanistic
6. Setting realistic goals and objectives (high expectations)
7. Being an effective communicator with students and parents
8. Being a firm, consistent, and fair classroom manager
9. Using a wide range and variety of materials

Socioeconomic Status

Socioeconomic status (SES) is a measure of a family's relative position in a community, determined by a combination of parents' income, occupation, and level of education. There are many relationships between SES and school preformance (Woolfolk, 2001). SES is linked to intelligence, achievement test scores, grades, truancy, and dropout and suspension rates. The dropout rate for children from poor families is twice that of the general population; for the poorest children, the rate exceeds 50 percent (Catterall & Cota-Robles, 1988).

Taking these factors into account, you should (a) capitalize on students' interests; (b) make course content meaningful to the students and discuss the practical value of the material; (c) make directions clear and specific; (d) arrange to have each student experience some success; (e) be sure that expectations for work are realistic; and (f) include a variety of instructional approaches, such as provisions for movement and group work.

CREATING AN INCLUSIVE, MULTICULTURAL CLASSROOM

Understanding the sources of student diversity is not enough. You must use this information as the basis of many classroom decisions when creating a positive learning environment, selecting a responsive curriculum, determining instructional strategies, and providing assistance.

Create a Supportive, Caring Environment

How students feel about the classroom can make a big difference in the way that they participate. Your attitude toward the students and the curriculum can influence these student feelings. In an effort to create a supportive, caring environment, you can translate your attitude into the following actions.

1. *Celebrate diversity.* Student diversity exists in many ways, as reviewed earlier in this chapter. Students don't want to be criticized because they have some characteristic that is different from others. Through your actions, recognize that each student contributes to the rich variety of ideas and actions in the classroom. Show that you appreciate and value the diversity that is reflected in the students in the classroom. In turn, students will feel appreciated, rather than feeling different, and this will make them feel more comfortable in the classroom.

2. *Have high expectations for students and believe that all students can succeed.* Teachers may sometimes consider certain sources of student diversity—cognitive ability, language, disabilities, socioeconomic status, for example—as having a negative effect on student performance. Thus, teachers may lower expectations and adjust the content and activities accordingly. However, this is a disservice to the students when they are not given the opportunity to address meaningful and challenging content and to develop their knowledge and skills. It is important to hold high expectations for all students and to believe that all students can succeed. Students appreciate the challenge and will find the classroom more stimulating and worthwhile as compared to a classroom with lowered expectations.

3. *Give encouragement to all students.* Students who perform well academically often receive words of praise, reinforcement, and encouragement from teachers. There may be many students in a classroom who do not perform at the highest academic levels, but they would appreciate encouraging statements as well. Encouraging words and guiding suggestions will help all students to feel that they are being supported in their efforts.

4. *Respond to all students enthusiastically.* When students see that their teacher is welcoming and enthusiastic about each student, they feel more comfortable in the classroom and more willing to participate fully. Warm greetings when students enter the classroom, conversations with individual students, and positive reactions when students contribute to classroom discussion are just a few ways that enthusiasm might be expressed. The main thing is that each student needs to feel valued and that each see this through enthusiastic teacher responses.

5. *Show students that you care about them.* When students know that you care for them and that you are looking out for them, it makes all the difference in the world. Students then feel valued, regardless of their characteristics, and are more likely to actively participate in the classroom. Even when the teacher needs to deal with a student concerning a problem, the student recognizes that the teacher's actions are well intended.

Offer a Responsive Curriculum

Students feel that they are valued when the curriculum is fair and relevant and when the content and curriculum materials reflect the diversity of learners in the classroom.

1. *Use a fair and relevant curriculum.* Teachers can make decisions to ensure that the curriculum is inclusive, relevant, and free of bias. Using the district-approved curriculum guide as a starting point, teachers can select appropriate instructional content to demonstrate that their students are valued as people and that they offer a challenging, culturally relevant curriculum. This content may involve integrating subject areas from diverse traditions, and the content may even arise out of students' own questions so that they can construct their own meaning.

2. *Consider differentiating curriculum materials.* Curriculum materials must also reflect the diversity of learners in the classroom. Books and other instructional materials should be free of bias, and they should provide the voices and perspectives of diverse people.

Once appropriate curriculum materials are selected, teachers may allow students options in the use of these materials. Learning activity packets, task cards, and learning contracts are examples of *differentiated materials* that address individual differences by providing curriculum options. Learning centers, for example, include differentiated materials with several kinds and levels of goals and activities. Centers, packets, and cards can be made for a particular student's needs and then stored until another student has need of them. When prepared properly, the materials will accommodate different rates of learning and different cognitive styles.

CREATING A LEARNING COMMUNITY

ADDRESSING TEACHER AND STUDENT CULTURAL DIFFERENCES

Many classrooms have students from a variety of ethnic and cultural backgrounds. It is possible that you will feel disconnected from your students because you have a different ethnicity or different cultural background from them. This could be a source of discomfort or tension in the classroom.

1. What could you do so that both you and your students feel comfortable with one another?

2. What could you do so that the different backgrounds do not contribute to misunderstandings and off-task behavior?
3. What could you do to help to develop a learning community with all students?

Although used more often at the elementary level, differentiated materials can also be used at the middle, junior high, and high school levels with careful explanation, monitoring, and evaluation. Ample time must be allowed for follow-up of the activity and evaluation of the learning.

The use of differentiated materials requires good classroom management and generally calls for tolerance of some movement and noise, particularly with learning centers. If students are not monitored, they could practice and learn the wrong thing.

When using differentiated materials, you should:

- Identify the objectives to be accomplished by the materials.
- Plan and construct (or purchase) the materials with care.
- Structure a record-keeping system to monitor student progress.
- Orient students to the materials.
- Schedule ample time for follow-up and evaluation.

CLASSROOM DECISIONS

Differentiated materials can be used to meet the instructional objectives. If you teach a lesson on soil erosion, how can you vary your instructional materials to accommodate individual differences? How can you relate this topic to students' lives and make it interesting? How might students' individual differences affect your planning decisions?

Vary Your Instruction

To meet the needs of diverse students, instruction cannot be one-dimensional. A variety of instructional approaches is needed to challenge all students and to meet their instructional needs. Several ways to vary your instruction are highlighted here.

1. *Challenge students' thinking and abilities.* Students have various learning styles, and they may learn best with their preferred learning style. However, should teachers always try to match student preferences and instructional methods? Probably not. Sprinthall and colleagues (1998) point out that you should (a) start where the learner is (i.e., in concert with the pupil's level of development), (b) then begin to mismatch (i.e., use a different approach than what the student prefers) by shifting to a slightly more complex level of teaching to help the student to develop in many areas, and (c) have faith that students have an intrinsic drive to learn. These practices complement the recommendations of Vygotsky, Kohlberg, and others to nudge students beyond comfort zones of learning into just enough cognitive dissonance to facilitate growth.

2. *Group students for instruction.* Grouping makes differentiation of instruction more efficient and practical. When each group is challenged and stimulated appropriately, students are motivated to work harder. Differentiated materials can be used more easily. On the other hand, labeling can be stigmatizing if grouping is based on variables such as ability or achievement. Grouping too much and changing groups too infrequently can obstruct student integration and cooperation.

With the proper planning, structure, and supervision, grouping is a useful way to provide for individual differences. When using grouping arrangements, you should:

- Re-form groups often on the basis of students' current performance.
- Make liberal use of activities that mix group members frequently.
- Adjust the pace and level of work for each group to maximize achievement. Avoid having expectations that are too low for low groups. Students tend to live up or down to teachers' expectations.
- Provide opportunities for gifted students to work with peers of their own level by arranging cross-age, between-school, or community-based experiences.
- Groups are composed of individuals, so remember that all do not have to do the same things at the same time in the same way. Retain individuality within the group.
- Form groups with care, giving attention to culture and gender.
- Structure the experience and supervise the students' actions.
- Prepare students with the necessary skills for being effective group members, such as listening, helping, cooperating, and seeking assistance.
- Adjust methods when necessary. For example, expect to cover less content when using cooperative learning techniques and supplement with reading assignments, handouts, or homework.

3. *Consider differentiated assignments. Alternative or differentiated assignments* can be provided by altering the length, difficulty, or time span of the assignment. Alternative assignments generally require alternative evaluation procedures.

Enrichment activities qualify as alternative assignments when directed toward the individual student's needs. There are three types of enrichment activities. First, relevant enrichment provides experiences that address the student's strengths, interests, or deficit areas. Second, cultural enrichment might be pleasurable and productive for the student even if not particularly relevant to his or her needs. An example would be an interdisciplinary study or a global-awareness topic. Third, irrelevant enrichment might provide extra activity in a content area without really addressing student needs.

4. *Consider individualized study. Individualized study* can be implemented through learning contracts or independent studies as a means to address individual needs. Such plans are most effective when developed by the student with your assistance. Individualized study facilitates mastery of both content and processes. Not only can the student master a subject, but he or she can also master goal setting, time management, use of resources, self-direction, and self-assessment of achievement. Independent study is ideal for accommodating student learning styles. Individual ability is nurtured, and students often learn more than the project required.

Independent study encourages creativity and develops problem-solving skills. It can be used in any school setting and all curricular areas. Most importantly, this method of learning approximates the way that the student should continue to learn when no longer a student in school.

This method requires varied, plentiful resources, and it may not provide enough social interaction. The student may spend too long on the study, and parents may complain that nothing is being accomplished.

When considering individualized study, you should:

- Include the student in all phases of planning, studying, and evaluating.
- Encourage the student to ask higher-order questions (analysis, synthesis, evaluation) as study goals.
- Encourage the student to develop a product as an outcome of the study.
- Provide the student with an opportunity to share the product with an interested audience.
- Emphasize learner responsibility and accountability.

5. *Have students participate in all class activities.* Regardless of the source of their diversity, all students like to participate in class activities such as discussions, projects, group activities, or computer-based endeavors. They enjoy the opportunity for involvement and interaction, and they seek the challenge. These activities also provide an opportunity for individual expression and serve as a vehicle for recognition and appreciation.

6. *Give opportunities for students to try different types of activities.* Although certain class activities and instructional strategies may seem well suited for a particular student, it is important to involve the student in many different types of activities in an effort to challenge the student and the student's thinking and understanding.

TEACHERS IN ACTION

INDIVIDUALIZED STUDY

John Wolters, sixth grade teacher, Manhattan, Kansas

Getting away from dependence on the textbook is one way I've learned to provide for individual differences within my classroom. I decided to approach the unit on Mexico from an independent study format, allowing each student to choose the focus of his or her own study of this country. We began as a class by listing as many possible topics as we could. Then we listed resources that were available for our use. Each student was then free to choose his or her own topic(s) to study, learn the information, and present the content to the class.

One of my students, Steve, read between 75 and 100 pages of information, made a time line, drew three maps and a sketch book of Aztec people, and participated in a three-person panel discussion comparing the Aztecs, Incas, and Mayas. Not bad for a student who had finished only one book so far that school year, who struggled to keep on task during social studies discussions and work time, and who had a track record of turning in about 50 percent of his work.

What was the difference this time? Steve felt like he was in charge, and he thrived on this feeling. No one was telling him to answer the questions on page 232, to outline pages 56 to 60, or to be ready for the test on Thursday. Steve tasted success once he got into this project.

This format for covering material does not work in all subject areas all the time. It does, however, allow the students to choose topics relevant to their personal interest and create finished products that reflect their abilities. All this results in increased motivation, creativity, and pride in the job completed.

7. *Use authentic and culturally relevant pedagogies.* Each instructional strategy has particular strengths, and some of the strengths may match up well with students with particular needs. Direct instruction, for example, has been used effectively in teaching basic skills to students with special needs. Cooperative learning has been shown to be effective in urban classrooms with diverse student populations and in positively changing the attitudes of nondisabled students toward their peers who have disabilities.

Instructional approaches should be selected that develop classrooms that are multicultural and inclusive. Techniques can be used to anchor instruction in students' prior knowledge and help them to learn the new content. Instructional approaches can be selected that are seen by the student to be realistic and culturally relevant.

8. *Use authentic and fair assessment strategies.* Some students demonstrate their learning better through certain types of assessment. Since there are many types of students in classrooms, a variety of methods for evaluating student learning should be used. Using a variety of approaches, such as written or oral tests, reports or projects, interviews, portfolios, writing samples, and observations, will circumvent bias. In addition, evaluation of student learning should be at several levels: recall, comprehension, application, analysis, synthesis, and evaluation.

Provide Assistance When Needed

Many classrooms include students who could benefit from special assistance in their learning. When creating an inclusive, multicultural classroom, these students must not be overlooked, because they may not advance in their learning without such assistance.

1. *Provide special individualized assistance to all students.* Teachers often provide individualized assistance to students who have difficulty learning. This assistance can make a big difference in helping students to overcome hurdles and can lead to better understanding. However, other students can benefit from this type of assistance as well. By providing assistance to all types of diverse learners, teachers express their interest in the student, provide support for student learning, and have the opportunity to challenge the learners in new directions.

2. *Work with students with special needs.* As a first step, teachers need to know district policies concerning students with special needs and what their responsibilities are for referrals, screening, and the preparation of individualized educational plans (IEP). Learning materials and activities can be prepared commensurate with the abilities of students with special needs. Positive expectations for student performance are a means to promote student learning.

KEY TERMS

Affective area	Cognitive style	Exceptional students
Alternative or differentiated assignments	Conceptual tempo	Field dependence/independence
	Concrete–abstract continuum	Gender difference
Bilingual education programs	Creativity	Gifted or talented learners
Brain hemisphericity	Cultural diversity	Individualized study
Cognitive activity	Differentiated materials	Intelligence

Learning style
Least restrictive environment
Psychomotor skills

Sensory modality
Socioeconomic status
Sociogram

Struggling learner
Students at risk
Variables

MAJOR CONCEPTS

1. Individual differences need to be taken into account when instructional methods are selected and procedures are determined for classroom management.

2. Cognitive, affective, and physical differences are only part of the array of variables that accounts for student diversity.

3. Diversity can be due to influences of learning style, creative potential, gender, language, and cultural diversity.

4. Diversity can be affected by disabilities, conditions placing the student at risk, and socioeconomic factors.

5. Information about the sources of student diversity can be used as the basis of classroom decisions to create a supportive, caring learning environment.

6. Curriculum content and materials should reflect the diversity of learners in the classroom.

7. A variety of instruction approaches is needed to challenge all students and to meet their instructional needs.

DISCUSSION/REFLECTIVE QUESTIONS

1. What types of student diversity were evident in classrooms in your own K–12 schooling experience? In what ways did your teachers take these student characteristics into account in the selection of content and the use of instructional approaches?

2. Are you enthusiastic or skeptical about the relevance of learning style theory and brain hemisphere research for classroom instruction? Why?

3. What are some challenges that you might experience in dealing with students with limited English proficiency? What could you do to overcome these challenges to promote student learning?

4. How might you recognize and celebrate the diversity of students in your own classroom and even use this information to enhance instruction?

5. How might you determine whether you are using authentic and fair assessment strategies when evaluating student learning?

6. Should you have different expectations and evaluation standards to reflect the diverse students in your classroom? Why or why not?

SUGGESTED ACTIVITIES

For Clinical Settings

1. Make a list of 10 or more questions that you would like to ask an effective teacher about addressing the diversity of students.

2. Analyze textbooks and instructional materials in your major teaching area(s) and grade level for ways in which they address individual differences and provide for individual needs.

3. Select a unit that you might teach, and identify specific ways that you could offer a responsive curriculum and also vary your instruction over a two-week unit when taking student diversity into account.

For Field Settings

1. Using the categories of differences addressed in this chapter as a guide, ask several teachers to describe individual differences that they notice in their students. How do the teachers take these differences into account?

2. Ask several teachers about difficulties that they have experienced when trying to provide for individual differences in the classroom. What could be done to help to overcome these difficulties?

USEFUL RESOURCES

Gollnick, D. M., & Chinn, P. C. (2002). *Multicultural education in a pluralistic society* (6th ed.). Upper Saddle River, NJ: Merrill/Prentice Hall.

Examines differences in students based on class, ethnicity and race, gender, exceptionality, religion, language, and age. Considers ways that education can be multicultural.

Marshall, P. L. (2002). *Cultural diversity in our schools.* Belmont, CA: Wadsworth/Thomson Learning.

Examines diversity in schools. Thorough descriptions of African American, Asian Pacific American, Hispanic American, Native American, and white American students. Considers implications for teaching strategies and effective teaching.

Tomlinson, C. A. (1999). *The differentiated classroom: Responding to the needs of all learners.* Alexandria, VA: Association for Supervision and Curriculum Development.

Describes ways that teachers can differentiate content, process, and product according to the student's readiness, interests, and learning profile.

WEB SITES

- African and African American history and culture: a very useful site.

  http://www.africana.com

- Clearinghouse for multicultural/bilingual education

  http://www.Weber.edu/MBE/htmls/mbe.html

- Equity and cultural diversity

  http://eric-Web.tc.columbia.edu/equity

- Resources on multicultural education

  http://www.nwrel.org/comm/topics/multicultural.html

- ESL lesson plans and resources

  http://www.csun.edu/~hcedu013/eslplans.html

- Links to information on learning styles and multiple intelligences

  http://falcon.jmu.edu/~ramseyil/learningstyles.htm

- National Women's History Project

  http://www.nwhp.org/

- Women in American History: from *Encyclopedia Britannica,* provides histories and lesson plans.

  http://women.eb.com/women/ind_womenweb.html

- Council for Exceptional Children

  http://www.cec.sped.org/

- Special Education Resources from the Curry School of Education at the University of Virginia

  http://curry.edschool.virginia.edu/go/cise/ose/resources

- Special education resources on the Internet; extensive resource featuring numerous links and information on many types of exceptionalities

  http://seriweb.com/

CHAPTER FIVE

MOTIVATING STUDENTS FOR A LEARNING COMMUNITY

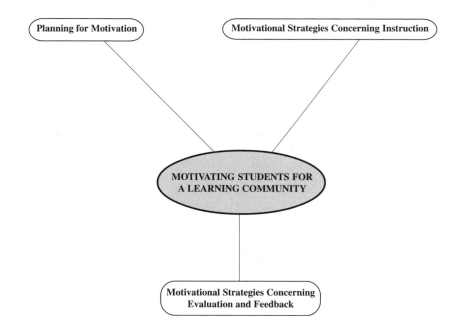

OBJECTIVES

This chapter provides information that will help you to:

1. Adopt a comprehensive approach when incorporating motivational strategies in all levels of instructional planning.

2. Apply motivational strategies in instruction through the instructional strategies that you se-

lect, the tasks that you ask students to complete, and the way that you interact with students during lessons.

3. Apply motivational strategies in the ways that you evaluate students and provide recognition.

PRAXIS/Principles of Learning and Teaching/Pathwise

The following principles are relevant to content in this chapter:

1. Communicating challenging learning expectations to each student   (B3)

2. Making learning goals and instructional procedures clear to students   (C1)

3. Encouraging students to extend their thinking   (C3)

4. Monitoring students' understanding of content through a variety of means, providing feedback to students to assist learning, and adjusting learning activities as the situation demands   (C4)

INTASC

The following INTASC standards are relevant to content in this chapter:

1. The teacher understands and uses a variety of instructional strategies to encourage students' development of critical thinking, problem solving, and performance skills.   (Standard 4)

2. The teacher uses an understanding of individual and group motivation and behavior to create a learning environment and encourages positive social interaction, active engagement in learning, and self-motivation.   (Standard 5)

3. The teacher uses knowledge of effective verbal, nonverbal, and media communication techniques to foster active inquiry, collaboration, and supportive interaction in the classroom.   (Standard 6)

4. The teacher understands and uses formal and informal assessment strategies to evaluate and ensure the continuous intellectual, social, and physical development of the learner.   (Standard 8)

Imagine that one of your students doesn't seem interested in the subject matter of your course. The student exerts minimal effort on classroom activities, seatwork, projects, homework, and tests. The student gets off-task easily, bothers other students, and disturbs classroom order. It may be that there are many students like this in your classroom, and you are searching for ways to get these students interested and engaged in the lesson.

This is where motivation ties in. If you can motivate students, they are more likely to participate in activities and less likely to get off-task and contribute to disorder. An effective classroom manager deliberately plans for ways to motivate students.

Motivation is one important part of effective classroom management. However, it involves more than simply praising a student. Student motivation will be affected by your selection of instructional content, the instructional strategies, the tasks that you ask the students to complete, the way you provide feedback, the means of assessment, and other issues.

Many educators use the word *motivation* to describe those processes that can arouse and initiate student behavior, give direction and purpose to behavior, help behavior to persist, and help the student to choose a particular behavior. Of course, teachers are interested in a particular kind of motivation in their students—the motivation to learn. Teachers who ask questions such as "How can I help my students get started?" or "What can I do to keep them going?" are dealing with issues of motivation.

Keller (1983) suggested that there are four dimensions of motivation: interest, relevance, expectancy, and satisfaction. *Interest* refers to whether the student's curiosity is aroused and sustained over time. *Relevance* refers to whether the students see instruction as satisfying personal needs or goals. Keller maintained that motivation increases when students perceive that a learning activity will satisfy basic motives, such as needs for achievement, power, or affiliation. *Expectancy* refers to whether students have a sense that they can be successful in the lesson through their personal control. *Satisfaction* refers to the student's intrinsic motivations and their responses to extrinsic rewards.

PLANNING FOR MOTIVATION

Before examining specific motivational strategies, it is important to consider three aspects of planning for motivation (Burden, 2000).

1. *Develop a comprehensive approach to motivation.* The message about motivation from research and best practice is clear—develop a comprehensive approach to motivate students to learn, instead of looking at one or two classroom variables in isolation. Much of the information about motivation addresses important topics, such as needs, satisfactions, authority, and recognition. These issues should not be considered in isolation, and the ways that teachers address these issues show up in their decisions about instructional tasks, evaluation, recognition, and other areas.

2. *Adjust motivational strategies to your instructional situation.* Motivational strategies discussed in this chapter come from research and best practice, and thus they provide a framework for classroom decisions. However, it is likely that you will need to evaluate your own situation—grade level, subject area, student characteristics—to determine which strategies are most appropriate in your context. Some strategies might need to be modified to work successfully in your classroom. Some strategies might be used a great deal, while others might not be used at all. Your professional assessment of your situation will guide the selection and use of the motivational strategies.

3. *Build motivational issues into all levels of your instructional planning.* Your instructional planning actually includes many time frames: the course, the semester, the marking period, each unit, each week, and each lesson.

As you consider how to incorporate the motivation concept of relevance, for example, into your instruction, you would think about ways to apply that concept in each time frame listed here. How might you help students to see the relevance of the entire course, and how might that be reflected in your course syllabus and introduction to the course? How might you highlight the relevance of the content during each marking period and each unit? Similarly, students would appreciate seeing the relevance of the content that is covered in each week and each lesson.

You need to think globally to help students to see the big picture, as well as the importance of each smaller piece of content. Your long-range planning should take the topic of relevance into account, and the relevance should be apparent in each unit and lesson. Therefore, your planning for motivation needs to be conducted for all levels of planning.

TEACHERS IN ACTION

PLANNING FOR MOTIVATION AND OPPORTUNITIES TO LEARN

Janet Roesner, elementary school mentor teacher, Baltimore, Maryland

It is important to identify the learning goals and the indicators of learning for each unit; this provides a clear focus when planning the unit. Next, a teacher needs to determine the skills and type of thinking that the students will need to be successful in the lesson. These acquired skills then become strategies for success and can be applied to all areas of learning.

One important question to ask when planning a unit is "How will this learning be meaningful?" Making meaningful connections to the students'

background knowledge, experiences, and interests is key to motivating the learners. Giving students opportunities to decide on real-life assessments that are clearly related to the learning goals is very motivating. In this way, interest peaks, application of knowledge soars, and students succeed.

Each lesson in a unit must make meaningful connections to the learning goal. In this way, students begin to learn for understanding, rather than for just completing the work.

MOTIVATIONAL STRATEGIES CONCERNING INSTRUCTION

The instructional strategies that you use, the tasks that you ask the students to complete, and the way that you interact with students during instruction all influence students' motivation to learn. As you prepare your plans, try to incorporate the following 12 motivational strategies into your instruction.

Capture Student Interest in the Subject Matter

One of the first tasks in motivating students to learn is to arouse their curiosity and sustain this interest over time (Keller, 1983). Useful techniques for capturing student interest address the inner need to know or to satisfy curiosity; thus the techniques are intrinsically satisfying. Try to incorporate the approaches described next, especially at the start of the lessons. These approaches are especially useful when introducing new material. Teachers need to model interest in the subject matter.

■ *Take time to understand what students perceive as important and interesting.* To capture student interest in the subject matter, it is useful to first recognize what the students' interests are. Listen to your students. You can then adapt the content and select instructional activities that address these interests.

You can identify these interests through various approaches. As you near the start of a new unit, you might briefly describe to the students what issues and activities you are currently planning. They might then be asked to indicate topics or activities that they are especially interested in and to offer additional suggestions. This interaction could be in the form of an informal discussion.

You may prefer to draw a web of these issues on the chalkboard. To do so, write the main topic in the center of a circle; then draw lines out from the circle and write the related issue on each line. As additional lines are drawn to represent the related topics, the diagram will look like a spider's web. Still more connecting lines may be drawn.

Another way to identify student interests is through a questionnaire about the unit topics and proposed activities. You may also devise your own ways to gather this student input. The key thing is to identify student interests in the subject matter and the possible instructional strategies and take them into account in your planning decisions. With this information, you will be able to make better decisions to capture student attention throughout all sessions.

CLASSROOM DECISIONS

In an effort to capture student interest in the subject matter, it is helpful to take student interests into account when making planning decisions about content, instructional strategies, and performance requirements. How would you gather information from your students to determine their interests? How might your approaches be different for students at other grades? What approaches could you use that do not rely on reading and writing? What approaches involve student interaction to identify the interests?

■ *Select topics and tasks that interest students.* Whenever possible, incorporate into the lesson topics that the students will find enjoyable and exciting. Relating some current event is often a useful way to connect student interests. When considering tasks for a lesson, choose one that enables students to select and explore their interests in the topic while achieving the lesson objective. Students often appreciate a choice of tasks that relate to their preferred learning style.

■ *Set the stage at the start of the lesson.* You can set the stage for learning by providing a brief, initial activity at the beginning of the lesson that is used to induce students to a state of wanting to learn. This is sometimes referred to as a *set induction*. This activity helps to establish the context for the learning that is to follow and helps students to engage in the learning. Set induction helps students to see what the topic of the lesson is in a way that is related to their own interests and their own lives.

For example, a health lesson on the topic of first aid might begin with the reading of a newspaper report about a recent fire or accident. After reading the article, you could ask the students what they would do if they were the first ones to arrive after the accident. A number of ideas are likely to be generated in this discussion. Then you could bring that opening discussion to a close by saying that today's lesson will be about this exact topic—what type of first aid to administer for various conditions. Then you would move into the first part of the lesson. This set induction activity helps to create interest in the lesson in a way that students can relate to their own lives.

Effective set induction activities should get students interested in what is to be taught during the lesson, must be connected to the content of the lesson that is to follow, must help students to understand the material, and should be related to the students' lives or to a previous lesson.

■ *State learning objectives and expectations at the start of the lesson.* Students need to know exactly what they are supposed to do, how they will be evaluated, and what the consequences of success will be. Avoid confusion by clearly communicating learning objectives and expectations. At the start of a class, for example, you might list the five main issues to be considered in the next unit and explain that today's lesson deals with the first issue. In this way, the students have a conceptual picture in which to organize the content.

Your description of learning objectives and expectations also serves as an advance organizer for the students so that they understand what will happen in class. This introduction should also include a description of the value of the subject matter to be examined and the related tasks. In this way, students can better appreciate the material and have a reason to be motivated. Advance organizers help students by focusing their attention on the subject being considered, informing them where the lesson is going, relating new material to content already understood, and providing structure for the subsequent lesson.

■ *Use questions and activities to capture student interest in the subject matter.* As part of the advance organizer or soon after the beginning of a lesson, stimulate curiosity by posing interesting questions or problems. Students will feel the need to resolve an ambiguity or obtain more information about a topic. For example, you might ask students to speculate or make predictions about what they will be learning or raise questions that successful completion of the activity will enable them to answer. Hook the students with key questions. In the study of presidents, for example, you might ask, "What are the characteristics of effective leaders?"

You may use these questions and activities as a means to induce curiosity or suspense. Divergent questions that allow several possible acceptable answers are useful (e.g., what do you think the author was trying to express in the first eight lines of this poem?). Provide opportunities for students to express opinions or make other responses about the subject matter.

■ *Introduce the course and each topic in an interesting, informative, and challenging way.* When introducing the course and each topic, highlight the tasks to be accomplished, pique the students' interest, challenge their views, and even hint at inconsistencies to be resolved. The enthusiasm and interest in the subject that you express will carry over to the students.

Highlight the Relevance of the Subject Matter

Another important motivational task is to help the student to understand that the subject matter is related to their personal needs or goals (Keller, 1983). Actions taken to achieve this purpose can also arouse student curiosity and sustain this interest over time. You might take the following actions as a means of highlighting the relevance of the subject matter.

■ *Select meaningful learning objectives and activities.* Students will be motivated to learn only if they see the relevance of their learning. Select academic objectives that include some knowledge or skill that is clearly worth learning, either in its own right or as a step to some greater objective. Avoid planning continued practice on skills that have already been mastered, memorizing lists for no good reason, looking up and copying definitions of terms that are never meaningfully used, and other activities that do not directly relate to the learning objective.

■ *Directly address the importance of each new topic examined.* Students are more likely to appreciate the relevance of the subject matter if you discuss the ways that it would be useful to them, both in school and outside. They need to see the connections between the concepts and the real world. Discuss the reason why the learning objective is important—in its own right or as a step to additional, useful objectives. Relate the subject matter to today's situation and everyday life. Call students' attention to the usefulness to their outside lives of the knowledge and skills taught in schools.

You could have your students think about the topics or activities in relation to their own interests. This helps students to understand that motivation to learn must come from within, that it is a property of the learner, rather than a task to be learned. You might ask them, for example, to identify questions about the topic that they would like to have answered.

■ *Adapt instruction to students' knowledge, understanding, and personal experience.* The content will be more relevant to the students if you relate it to the students' personal experiences and needs and to prior knowledge. You might begin a lesson on geography by listing several state or national parks and asking students if they have visited them. You then could ask why people are interested in visiting these parks. The mountains, lakes, or other geographical features often make these parks appealing. Through this discussion, students will see the importance of the content and will more likely become actively engaged in the lesson.

■ *Have students use what they have previously learned.* Another way to demonstrate the relevance of the subject matter is to have students use what they previously learned. This may be easy to do, since one learning objective often provides the foundation for the next. For example, when discussing the reasons for the Civil War, you could ask the students if their earlier study of the U.S. Constitution and the Bill of Rights point to the reasons.

TEACHERS IN ACTION

ADAPT INSTRUCTION TO STUDENTS' PERSONAL EXPERIENCE

Ruth Criner, first grade teacher, Houston, Texas

Students are motivated to write when they know the purpose of the writing or if the topic is one of their choice. I try to plan lessons around topics that interest my students, but there are times when I totally ignore my lesson plans, usually because a student or the class has brought up a topic of interest that is relevant at the time.

One day, Andrew walked in slowly. His eyes were red, and it was obvious that he had been crying. After a brief discussion with him, I learned that his mom had been rushed to the hospital the night before. "Her gall bladder was hurting." His classmates and I listened as Andrew talked about the incident. During the discussion, the students asked,

"What's a gall bladder?" and "Will Andrew's mom be okay?" Andrew suggested that she might feel better if we all made get well cards for her.

Although we usually spend the first 30 minutes of the morning writing in our journals, we spent the morning researching the gall bladder and writing get well wishes to Andrew's mom. We used the Internet, encyclopedia, dictionary, and anatomy charts to find out more about the gall bladder. We used the information to draw pictures and write the letters.

The students were researching and writing on a topic that was relevant to them. The students put their hearts into their efforts and, at the end, Andrew had a backpack full of get well wishes for his mom.

In this way, you reinforce the previous learning and highlight the importance of each learning objective. You demonstrate to the students that each learning objective will have some subsequent use. Whenever possible, call for previously acquired facts and concepts.

■ *Illustrate the subject matter with anecdotes and concrete examples to show relevance.* Students may find little meaning in definitions, principles, or other general or abstract content unless the material can be made more concrete or visual. Promote personal identification with the content by relating experiences or telling anecdotes illustrating how the content applies to the lives of particular individuals. An initial lesson on fractions, for example, might include a discussion of how the students divide a pizza at home. This helps students to see application of the content in the real world.

Vary Your Instructional Strategies Throughout the Lesson to Maintain Interest

Students often become bored if they are asked to do the same thing throughout the lesson. Student interest is maintained and even heightened if you vary your instructional approach throughout the lesson.

■ *Use several instructional approaches throughout the lesson.* After capturing student interest at the start of a lesson, maintain interest by using varied approaches, such as lectures, demonstrations, recitations, practice and drills, reviews, panels and debates, group projects, inquiry approaches, discovery learning and problem solving, role playing and simulation, gaming, and computer-assisted instruction. These varied approaches help to provide links to the students' learning style preferences.

As effective as a strategy may be, students will lose interest if it is used too often or too routinely. Vary your strategies over time and try not to use the same one throughout an entire class period. Try to make sure that something about each task is new to the students, or at least different from what they have been doing. Call attention to the new element, whether it be new content, media involved, or the type of responses required.

■ *Use games, simulations, or other fun features.* Activities that students find entertaining and fun can be used to capture their attention in the subject matter. Students find these intrinsically satisfying. An instructional game is an activity in which students follow prescribed rules unlike those of reality as they strive to attain a challenging goal. Games can be used to help students to learn facts and evaluate choices. Many games can be used as a drill-and-practice method of learning.

An instructional simulation re-creates or represents an actual event or situation that causes the student to act, react, and make decisions. Simulations provide a framework for using the discovery method, the inquiry approach, experiential learning, and inductive approaches to instruction. Simulations help students to practice decision making, make choices, receive results, and evaluate decisions.

Games, simulations, and other activities with fun features motivate students, promote interaction, present relevant aspects of real-life situations, and make possible direct involvement in the learning process. Games and simulations are commercially available, with many now designed for use on computers. You can also devise your own games and simulations for use in the classroom.

■ *Occasionally do the unexpected.* Another way to maintain student interest and to get their attention is by doing something unexpected. Note what usually goes on and then do the opposite. If you normally have a reserved presentation style, occasionally include some dramatic elements. Instead of preparing a worksheet for the class, have the students prepare it. If your discussions in social studies have been about the effects of certain events on the United States, focus your discussion on the effects on your community. An occasional departure from what the students have come to expect adds some fun and novelty to your instruction and helps to maintain student interest. You might even change some of your classroom routines to add some variation.

Plan for Active Student Involvement

Rather than passively writing notes and preparing worksheets, students appreciate the opportunity to be more actively involved. As you consider ways to arrange for this student involvement, take into account the students' learning and cognitive styles.

■ *Try to make study of the subject matter as active, investigative, adventurous, and social as possible.* Students will find the subject matter more intrinsically interesting if they are actively involved in the lesson. You can capture their interest in the lesson if the activities that you select have built-in appeal. The students' first learning experience with a new topic should incorporate these characteristics. Whenever possible, provide opportunities for students to physically move and be active.

Students might manipulate objects at their desks or move around the room for an activity. They might be allowed to investigate topics through activities that are part of an ac-

■ ■ ■ ■ ■

MODIFICATIONS FOR DIVERSE CLASSROOMS

INSTRUCTIONAL VARIETY TO REACH ALL STUDENTS

Your students are likely to express differences due to their academic ability, learning styles, creative potential, gender, language, cultural diversity, and other factors. As a result, certain instructional strategies may work with some students but not others. To reach all students, you must vary your instructional strategies throughout your lesson and also over the course of several days in a unit.

But which instructional strategies should you use and how do you know which will help you to reach all students? Your own professional insights will provide some guidance, but talking to other teachers and your own students will likely provide many useful ideas about various instructional approaches that will reach all students.

1. What questions might you ask other teachers at your grade level or in your subject area to gain insights into instructional strategies that reach all students?
2. It is often helpful to discuss this issue with the students themselves and gather input from them. How might you gather ideas from your students about instructional strategies that they like and that aid in their learning?

TEACHERS IN ACTION

ACTIVE STUDENT INVOLVEMENT

Mike Edmondson, high school chemistry and physics teacher, Columbus, Georgia

Students learn best when they are actively involved in the learning process, so I plan a variety of ways to get students engaged in my chemistry and physics classes, including some offbeat activities.

I have had my classes identify and research ecological issues and then debate them in front of audiences and even write editorials for the local newspaper. My chemistry students have designed a mural-sized periodic table and various wall murals on other topics. They have used computer software to study the content, designed crossword puzzles about course content, written essays for science contests, and even participated in a cooking contest in which students designed and cooked their own recipes and then related the processes to chemistry.

My physics students have used toys to explain physical principles, built kites to study aerodynamics, and designed and built mobiles based on physics principles. We visited a large community theater to study how pulleys and counterweights are used to move sets and scenery. After reading about quantum theory, students presented skits in groups to illustrate the fundamental principles. We have used electric trains to determine velocity and acceleration, and we include art and music in the design of many projects. In addition, the students have served as tutors in elementary classrooms.

tivity center or through cooperative learning tasks. Students might conduct a debate concerning a controversial issue, prepare a product as a result of a group project, or conduct a survey in the class or beyond the classroom. In addition to independent work, students need opportunities for social interaction through pairing or small groups.

■ *Vary the type of involvement when considering the students' learning and cognitive styles.* Information about multiple intelligences and brain hemisphericity can be used to plan various types of student involvement. Gardner (1985) believes that all people have *multiple intelligences.* He identified seven independent intelligences: linguistic, musical, logical–mathematical, spatial, bodily kinesthetic, interpersonal, and intrapersonal. In an effort to address the various intelligences of your students, you might plan for some activities that involve movement, student discussion, outlining, charting, organizing, and so on. A number of good sources are available offering suggestions for ways to incorporate the multiple intelligences into your teaching (e.g., Lazear, 1991; Chapman, 1993; Fogarty, 1997; Campbell, Campbell, & Dickinson, 1999).

Brain hemisphericity is another aspect to consider when planning for student involvement. Research on the human brain indicates that there are hemisphere-specific skills. The left side of the brain helps people to be more analytical in their orientation and to deal with facts in a logical, concrete, and sequential manner. The right side of the brain helps people to be more wholistic in their thinking and to use their visual and spatial skills when learning. As you plan for student involvement, incorporate tasks that require skills from both sides of the brain in an effort to maintain student interest and involvement.

Recognize that students' learning and cognitive styles determine their level of comfort and challenge in learning tasks. Students need times when they are comfortable with the tasks, but also times when they are challenged by strategies outside their preferred learning or cognitive styles. You might allow students to choose from a menu of activities, for example, but also have them complete certain activities.

Select Strategies That Capture Students' Curiosity

If students are curious about the content, they are more likely to be interested in participating in the lesson. You can capture students' curiosity in the various ways outlined here.

■ *Select tasks that capitalize on the arousal value of suspense, discovery, curiosity, exploration, and fantasy.* Stimuli that are novel, surprising, complex, incongruous, or ambiguous help to lead to cognitive arousal. When their curiosity is aroused, students are motivated to find ways to understand the novel stimulus. This is especially important at the start of a learning experience when you are trying to capture students' attention.

Curiosity can be aroused through (a) surprise; (b) doubt, or conflict between belief and disbelief; (c) perplexity, or uncertainty; (d) bafflement, or facing conflicting demands, (e) contradiction, and (f) fantasy (Lepper & Hodell, 1989). With these strategies, a conceptual conflict is aroused. The motivation lasts until the conflict is resolved or until the students give up. If they cannot resolve the conflict, they will become bored or frustrated, so the activity should lead to resolution of the conflict to capture and maintain student interest.

Let's look at some examples of how these strategies might be used.

1. *Surprise* could result when an activity leads to an unexpected ending, for example, a ball passing through a metal ring when cold, but not passing through after being heated.
2. *Doubt* could be created when students are asked if the interior angles of a triangle always total 180 degrees.
3. *Perplexity or uncertainty* could be created when a number of possible solutions to an issue are available, but none seems absolutely right. Creative problem-solving activities can address issues of uncertainty.
4. *Bafflement* occurs when there does not seem to be a reasonable solution to an issue.
5. *Contradiction* occurs when the solution is the opposite of a general principle or common sense. Contradiction can be introduced in science with the use of discrepant events, such as a long needle being pushed through a balloon and the balloon not breaking.
6. *Fantasy* can be created by using an imaginary situation as the context for the activity. In a writing activity, for example, you might turn the lights out in the room, describe a cave that the students might be exploring, and then have the students write a creative story about their imagined trip in the cave.

■ *Use anecdotes or other devices to include a personal, emotional element into the content.* When students feel that they have some personal or emotional connection to the content, their curiosity and interest will be enhanced. Therefore, try to link to students'

TEACHERS IN ACTION

HOOKING STUDENTS ON CONFUSION

Nancy Kawecki Nega, middle school science teacher, Elmhurst, Illinois

One of the best ways to interest students in a topic is to introduce the topic in a way that confuses or astounds them. Using a demonstration of a discrepant event is sure to capture and hold student interest. Making the demonstration interactive and involving as many students as possible increases the chances of success.

For example, when introducing the idea of air pressure, I use a two-liter plastic bottle. I pour a small amount of very warm water into it, swirl it around, pour it out, and immediately cap the bottle. I set the bottle where the whole class can see it and then continue talking. Within a few minutes, the class notices that the bottle has started to cave in. I have them write in their notebooks what they observe and what they think is causing it. Soon the bottle is completely caved in. They are in awe of what they see and can understand the idea of a higher pressure being "stronger" than a lower pressure. Demonstrations like this make an impression on the students, raise their curiosity, and start the investigation of a topic in a positive, interesting, and challenging way.

---

emotions and personal experiences whenever possible. When examining civil rights, for example, you might ask your students if they have experienced any situation where they have been treated unfairly due to gender, ethnicity, or other factor. In this way, students have an emotional connection to the content.

Select Strategies and Present Material with an Appropriate Degree of Challenge and Difficulty

Students are motivated when the learning tasks are challenging and interesting. You should monitor the difficulty of the learning tasks, break down difficult tasks into smaller parts, and select higher-level outcomes whenever possible.

■ *Assign moderately difficult tasks that can be completed with reasonable effort.* Students lose interest rapidly if they are not able to succeed because the work is too hard or if they are able to succeed too easily when the work is not challenging enough. Activities should be at a moderate level of difficulty to maintain student interest and involvement.

Assessments conducted before instruction determine what your students already know and thus help you to decide on the appropriate degree of difficulty for the work at hand. Also, carefully observe students at work to see if there is an appropriate level of difficulty.

You might provide students with a menu of tasks to be completed in a unit: some tasks might be required, and some may be optional. The optional list should include some moderately difficult and some challenging tasks, allowing students to choose those that are moderately challenging to them.

■ *Divide difficult tasks into smaller parts that are achievable without requiring excessive effort.* When difficult content or tasks are scheduled, break the activities down into smaller parts so that each part is challenging yet manageable for students to complete. Once each part is completed, the students can look back with pride at their accomplishments with difficult content.

■ *Focus on higher-order learning outcomes.* Higher-level outcomes are often more intrinsically challenging and interesting to students. The lower levels of the cognitive domain include knowledge, comprehension, and application, and important curricular content is addressed at these levels.

The higher levels of the cognitive domain include analysis, synthesis, and evaluation. These levels require students to do something with the knowledge—to differentiate, relate, categorize, explain, reorganize, appraise, compare, justify, and so on. These higher-level outcomes often involve a higher level of difficulty and require students to be engaged in a variety of learning activities that would be seen as interesting and challenging.

■ *Monitor the level of difficulty of assignments and tests.* Students' expectations for success erode quickly when teachers repeatedly give assignments and tests that are very difficult. Continuously check to see that your assignments and tests are at a reasonable level of difficulty and that students have a good opportunity to be successful. Also, help your students to learn from their errors. You could retest students to the point where they reach mastery.

Group Students for Tasks

Arranging for various ways to group students can have a positive effect on student motivation. Grouping students promotes cooperation and teamwork.

■ *Plan to use a variety of individual, cooperative, and competitive activities.* The way that you group students will be affected by the types of activities that you want your students to complete. Interest is maintained when there is variety in the way that the learning activities are structured. Some activities, such as seatwork, may be completed individually. Other projects can be completed in cooperative learning groups with four to six students in each group.

Competitive activities also can be used to provide excitement and rewards. Students can compete either as individuals or as teams, depending on the game or competition used. Team approaches may be more desirable, because they can be structured so that students cooperate with members of their team. Make use of group competitive situations that stress fun rather than winning.

■ *Promote cooperation and teamwork.* To satisfy students' needs for affiliation, provide opportunities for no-risk, cooperative interaction. As you form groups, take into account such factors as the size of the group, the ability of group members, and gender and ethnic composition. Cooperative learning activities enable students to work together, thus minimizing individual fears of failure and competition among students. Each student in a group, however, must be held accountable for his or her contribution to the group. This could be achieved by participation points or other approaches.

TEACHERS IN ACTION

GROUPING STUDENTS IN A JIGSAW ACTIVITY

Alicia Ruppersberger, middle school teacher, Towson, Maryland

I like to use student-centered activities that actively engage students in the learning process. One type of strategy is the jigsaw (Aronson & Patnoe, 1997). In this activity, students are assigned to groups and given individual and group assignments. They work independently or with members from other teams to share and teach the new knowledge with their teammates. I am able to assess the students by observing whether the students are using knowledge in a meaningful way, staying on task, and/or using critical or creative thinking skills and strategies. Cooperation, organization, and communication skills can also be observed.

Aronson, E., & Patnoe, S. (1997). *The Jigsaw Classroom: Building Cooperation in the Classroom.* New York: Longman.

Design the Lesson to Promote Student Success

Motivation to learn is enhanced when students are interested in the subject matter and expect to be successful (Keller, 1983). The lesson should be designed to accomplish these ends. The following techniques are intended to achieve these purposes through both intrinsic and extrinsic motivation.

■ *Design activities that lead to student success.* Students are motivated to learn when they expect to be successful. Therefore, make sure that they fairly consistently achieve success at their early level of understanding, and then help them to move ahead in small steps, preparing them for each step so that they can adjust to the new step without confusion or frustration. Pace students through activities as briskly as possible while thoroughly preparing them for new activities.

■ *Adapt the tasks to match the motivational needs of the students.* Individual differences in ability, background, and attitudes toward school and specific subjects should be considered as you make decisions about motivational strategies. Some students need more structure than others. Other students need more reinforcement and praise. Some students are more motivated to learn than others. You will need to select motivational strategies that are most effective for your students and adjust the frequency and intensity of their use depending on individual needs.

■ *Communicate desirable expectations and attributes.* If you treat your students as if they already are eager learners, they are more likely to become eager learners. Let them know that you expect them to be curious, to want to learn facts and understand principles, to master skills, and to recognize what they are learning as meaningful and applicable to their everyday lives. Encourage questions and inquiry. Through these means, you communicate desirable expectations and attributes.

■ *Establish a supportive environment.* Be encouraging and patient in an effort to make students comfortable about learning activities and to support their learning efforts. Establish a businesslike yet relaxed and supportive classroom atmosphere. Reinforce students' involvement with the subject matter and eliminate any unpleasant consequences. Organize and manage your classroom to establish an effective learning environment.

CLASSROOM DECISIONS

Students have safety needs that should be taken into account when planning the beginning of a lesson. One aspect of safety is not fearing to try new things and being willing to participate in class activities. Students need to feel secure that they will not be criticized for a wrong answer or for sharing information in class. What specific actions could you take to ensure student safety in these ways? How could safety be provided in practice activities or group discussions?

■ *Use familiar material for initial examples, but provide unique and unexpected contexts when applying concepts and principles.* When you want to build interest, involve the familiar. For applications once learning has been achieved, however, it is unique and unexpected examples that keep interest high and help students to transfer what they have learned. For example, when teaching students about the classification system for plants and animals, you might begin by classifying different kinds of dogs to illustrate classification. You could then have them develop a classification system for music sold on compact disks at a local music store or for DVDs rented at a video store.

■ *Minimize performance anxiety.* To motivate students to learn, they need to believe that they will be successful in their efforts. If you establish situations that cause tension, pressure, and anxiety, your students will likely choose safety and remain uninvolved for fear of failure. On the other hand, if you minimize risks and make learning seem exciting and worthwhile, most students will join in.

One way to reduce anxiety is to make clear the separations between instruction or practice activities designed to promote learning and tests designed to evaluate student performance. Most classroom activities should be structured as learning experiences rather than tests. You might say, for example, "Let's assess our progress and learn from our mistakes."

To encourage participation, make it clear that students will not be graded on their questions or comments during recitation. Don't impose conditions or restrictions on assignments, homework, or projects that might get in the way of students giving their whole effort. For example, requiring all papers to be typed perfectly with no typing or formatting errors may seem to be a barrier to some students.

Allow Students Some Control over the Lessons

Allowing students some control over the lessons helps them to develop responsibility and independence. It also provides students with opportunities to develop self-management skills and to feel like they have some authority in the instructional situation. To the extent possible, allow students choices concerning instruction, but be sure to monitor their choices so that the students are still able to be successful.

TEACHERS IN ACTION

APPOINTMENT CLOCKS FOR NO-RISK COOPERATION

Deleen Baker, K–6 reading specialist, Oregon City, Oregon

Compared to primary grade students, I find that intermediate grade students are less likely to share their knowledge and learning with peers due to concerns about being ridiculed if they make errors. As a result, I have used "Appointment Clocks" as a means to group students for no-risk cooperation in learning activities.

Before a lesson begins, I direct all students to draw a clock and to place the times for 12, 3, 6, and 9 on their clock. After setting the scene for the lesson, students are instructed to move quietly around the room and make appointments with four students (one at each of the times that they placed on their clock) and to record on their clock sheet what their appointment hopes to learn in the lesson that is to follow.

After the lesson is presented, I use the Appointment Clock as a way to check for understanding. I ask the students to meet with their 6:00 appointment, for example, to compare two characters in a poem we just read, to list the three main points in the lesson, or to do some task designed to summarize and analyze the lesson.

Even students who are shy to speak in front of the class work well with the Appointment Clock sessions. Those who are reluctant learners are motivated to listen and complete the tasks assigned so that they can successfully contribute to the meetings.

Danielle is a very shy and reserved student who has difficulty expressing her thoughts in front of a group. With the Appointment Clock, she has gained confidence and feels that she is helping her partners. I have also found this approach to be effective in working with English as second language students. Through Appointment Clocks, students are motivated to learn and work cooperatively, and I receive the assessment of student understanding.

■ *Promote feelings of control by allowing students a voice in decision making.* To the extent possible, allow students a degree of control over their learning. Students who feel that they can control the situation for learning (where, when, how) and the outcomes for learning (seeking the level that they want to achieve) are more intrinsically motivated (Lepper & Hodell, 1989). This will help students to feel that they can be successful in their learning.

Depending on your situation, the range of choices that you give students may be limited or broad. The degree of control that you permit will be affected by the students' age and maturity, among other factors. Students appreciate even a limited degree of choice. For example, you might let students select the instructional activities from a menu of choices, the order in which they must be completed, when they are due, or how they should be completed. Then students are more likely to have expectations for success.

■ *Monitor the difficulty of the goals and tasks that students choose for themselves.* When choices are available, students should be counseled to select moderately difficult goals that they can reasonably expect to achieve. If they do not establish suitable goals, you can help them to determine what to do to achieve such goals. When you include help sessions, study sheets, review sessions, or even training on study skills, students are more likely to feel that even moderately difficult goals can be achieved.

At times you may need to prepare a contract to address the learning needs of individual students. The parents, the student, and possibly others may be involved in the preparation of this learning contract. Even in these cases, it is important to monitor the difficulty of the goals and tasks and to make adjustments as the need warrants.

Express Interest in the Content and Project Enthusiasm

To be motivated to learn, students need to be interested in the subject matter and see its relevance (Keller, 1983). By expressing interest in the content yourself and projecting enthusiasm, you address these motivational issues.

■ *Model interest and enthusiasm in the topic and in learning.* Let your students see that you value learning as a rewarding, self-actualizing activity that produces personal satisfaction and enriches your life. Furthermore, share your thinking about learning and provide examples for its application. In this way, students see how an educated person uses information in everyday life. For example, a social studies teacher might relate how her understanding of community, state, and national events helped her to make informed decisions when voting on candidates during political elections. If you display a scholarly attitude while teaching and seem genuinely interested in achieving understanding, then your students are more likely to display these values.

■ *Project enthusiasm.* Everything that you say should communicate in both tone and manner that the subject matter is important. If you model appropriate attitudes and beliefs about topics and assignments, the students will pick up on these cues. Use timing, nonverbal expressions and gestures, and cuing and other verbal techniques to project a level of intensity and enthusiasm that tells the students that the material is important and deserves close attention.

■ ■ ■ ■ ■

CLASSROOM DECISIONS

Students often like a teacher to be animated and exciting. But having a high degree of enthusiasm all the time may present some problems. What might these problems be? Exhibiting a low degree of enthusiasm all the time also may be a problem. How can you determine what is an appropriate degree of enthusiasm to use? How might your approach to displaying your enthusiasm be different in fourth grade, ninth grade, or twelfth grade?

■ *Introduce tasks in a positive, enthusiastic manner.* It is especially important to be positive and enthusiastic when introducing tasks that you expect students to complete. Introducing new tasks involves actions such as providing clear directions, discussing the importance of the material, going over examples, and responding to student questions. Your positive manner will likely affect the attitude that your students carry as they complete the tasks.

■ *Expect interest, not boredom, from the students.* If you think that the students will find the material boring, then students typically react with indifference and boredom. However, if you treat students as active, motivated learners who care about their learning and who are trying to understand, then positive motivation is much more likely to occur. Students will typically rise to the expectations of their instructor.

Provide Opportunities to Learn

Higher levels of student motivation to learn occur in classrooms where teachers not only go over the material, but also take specific actions to provide students with opportunities to learn (Blumenfeld et al., 1992). These actions include the following:

■ *Focus lessons around mid-level concepts that are substantive but not overwhelming to students.* Mid-level concepts are likely to be challenging but achievable. New material is presented, and most students should be able to successfully learn it.

■ *Make the main ideas evident in presentations, demonstrations, discussions, and assignments.* Obscure facts and insignificant information are not emphasized. Instead, make the main concepts apparent in every aspect of the lesson—in the introduction at the start of the lesson, the notes and instructional materials, the assignments, and the evaluation.

■ *Present concrete illustrations of the content, and relate unfamiliar information to your students' personal knowledge.* When new content is introduced, specific examples should be provided to enhance student learning. Especially in cases where students may be totally unfamiliar with the content, it is useful to relate the content to some aspect of the students' personal experiences. For example, when considering the types of cadence in several lines of poetry, you might provide an example of the cadence in a popular song that the students know.

■ *Make explicit connections between new information and content that students have learned previously, and point out relationships among new ideas by stressing similarities and differences.* By deliberately referring back to related content previously covered, you repeat and reinforce some of the content, which will enhance understanding. You also can show how the content previously covered and the new content are connected. In a U.S. history class, for example, you might refer back to the causes of World War I when examining the causes of World War II. In doing so, you can show any similarities and differences. Students are likely to leave with a better understanding of both wars.

■ *Elaborate extensively on textbook readings, rather than allowing the book to carry the lesson.* By supplementing the textbook, you can bring in contemporary information, real-life examples, and unique extra resources that enrich your students' understanding of the textbook content. Furthermore, your elaborations and supplements make the class more interesting to the students.

■ *Guide students' thinking when posing high-level questions.* High-level questions may require students to analyze, synthesize, and evaluate the content in some meaningful way, and some students may have difficulty with this. You may need to guide your students' thinking by carefully sequencing the questions so that the students are better able to answer correctly. Or you may need to provide clues or some type of assistance when dealing with high-level questions.

■ *Ask students to summarize, make comparisons between related concepts, and apply the information that they are learning.* After learning new content, it is important to provide an opportunity for the students to summarize and process their learning in some way before moving ahead with new material. This summary helps students to organize their learning and demonstrate their understanding. Advance organizers used earlier in the lesson may help students to understand the concepts and apply the information.

Support Students' Attempts to Understand

Higher levels of student motivation to learn occur in classrooms where teachers take extra steps to support students' attempts to understand the material, see Table 5.1 (Blumenfeld et al., 1992). These actions include the following:

■ *Model thinking and problem solving, and work with students to solve problems when the students have difficulty* (instead of just providing the correct answers). Make deliberate efforts to help students to understand. You might describe how you organize and remember the content in *your* mind. You might suggest various types of memory strategies for the students. When students have difficulty, guide them through the problem so that they will know how to deal with it the next time. You could think "out loud" as you demonstrate to students how they might approach an issue or problem.

Modeling opportunities arise whenever an academic activity calls for use of some cognitive process or strategy. For example, you can model for them how to conduct an experiment, identify the main ideas in paragraphs, develop a plan for writing a composition, or deduce applications of a general principle to specific situations.

■ *Keep the procedures in instructional tasks simple.* Sometimes the procedures used in instructional tasks get in the way of student learning. To overcome this problem, keep the procedures as simple as possible. To help students with the procedures, you could demonstrate the procedures, highlight problems, provide examples, or allow for sufficient time for work completion.

■ *Encourage collaborative efforts by requiring all students to make contributions to the group.* Students may better understand the content when interacting with other students in some way about the content. Provide opportunities for students to work together to share and process the content.

MOTIVATIONAL STRATEGIES CONCERNING EVALUATION AND FEEDBACK

The way that you evaluate student performance and provide recognition influences students' motivation to learn. Consider the following seven motivational strategies as they relate to assessment and recognition.

TABLE 5.1   Motivational Strategies Concerning Instruction

1. *Capture Student Interest in the Subject Matter*
   a. Take time to understand what students perceive as important and interesting.
   b. Select topics and tasks that interest students.
   c. Set the stage at the start of the lesson.
   d. State learning objectives and expectations at the start of the lesson.
   e. Use questions and activities to capture student interest in the subject matter.
   f. Introduce the course and each topic in an interesting, informative, and challenging way.

2. *Highlight the Relevance of the Subject Matter*
   a. Select meaningful learning objectives and activities.
   b. Directly address the importance of each new topic examined.
   c. Adapt instruction to students' knowledge, understanding, and personal experience.
   d. Have students use what they have previously learned.
   e. Illustrate the subject matter with anecdotes and concrete examples to show relevance.

3. *Vary Your Instructional Strategies Throughout the Lesson to Maintain Interest*
   a. Use several instructional approaches throughout the lesson.
   b. Use games, simulations, or other fun features.
   c. Occasionally do the unexpected.

4. *Plan for Active Student Involvement*
   a. Try to make study of the subject matter as active, investigative, adventurous, and social as possible.
   b. Vary the type of involvement when considering the students' learning and cognitive styles.

5. *Select Strategies That Capture Students' Curiosity*
   a. Select tasks that capitalize on the arousal value of suspense, discovery, curiosity, exploration, and fantasy.
   b. Use anecdotes or other devices to include a personal, emotional element into the content.

6. *Select Strategies and Present Material with an Appropriate Degree of Challenge and Difficulty*
   a. Assign moderately difficult tasks that can be completed with reasonable effort.
   b. Divide difficult tasks into smaller parts that are achievable without requiring excessive effort.
   c. Focus on higher-order learning outcomes.
   d. Monitor the level of difficulty of assignments and tests.

7. *Group Students for Tasks*
   a. Plan to use a variety of individual, cooperative, and competitive activities.
   b. Promote cooperation and teamwork.

8. *Design the Lesson to Promote Student Success*
   a. Design activities that lead to student success.
   b. Adapt the tasks to match the motivational needs of the students.
   c. Communicate desirable expectations and attributes.
   d. Establish a supportive environment.
   e. Use familiar material for initial examples, but provide unique and unexpected contexts when applying concepts and principles.
   f. Minimize performance anxiety.

9. *Allow Students Some Control over the Lessons*
   a. Promote feelings of control by allowing students a voice in decision making.
   b. Monitor the difficulty of the goals and tasks that students choose for themselves.

(continued)

TABLE 5.1   CONTINUED

10. *Express Interest in the Content and Project Enthusiasm*
    a. Model interest and enthusiasm in the topic and in learning.
    b. Project enthusiasm.
    c. Introduce tasks in a positive, enthusiastic manner.
    d. Expect interest, not boredom, from the students.

11. *Provide Opportunities to Learn*
    a. Focus lessons around mid-level concepts that are substantive but not overwhelming to students.
    b. Make the main ideas evident in presentations, demonstrations, discussions, and assignments.
    c. Present concrete illustrations of the content, and relate unfamiliar information to your students' personal knowledge.
    d. Make explicit connections between new information and content that students have learned previously, and point out relationships among new ideas by stressing similarities and differences.
    e. Elaborate extensively on textbook readings, rather than allowing the book to carry the lesson.
    f. Guide students' thinking when posing high-level questions.
    g. Ask students to summarize, make comparisons between related concepts, and apply the information that they are learning.

12. *Support Students' Attempts to Understand*
    a. Model thinking and problem solving, and work with students to solve problems when the students have difficulty.
    b. Keep the procedures in instructional tasks simple.
    c. Encourage collaborative efforts by requiring all students to make contributions to the group.

Source: Burden, P. R. (2000). *Powerful classroom management strategies: Motivating students to learn.* Thousand Oaks, CA: Corwin Press. Pages 72–74. Reprinted by permission of Corwin Press, Inc.

Establish Evaluation Expectations and Criteria

Student learning can be fostered when the evaluation expectations and criteria are consistent with motivational principles (Ames, 1992; Blumenfeld, Puro, & Mergendoller, 1992; Stipek, 2002). The evaluation and reward system should focus on effort, improvement, and mastery. Factors that students have control over should be emphasized, and competition should be minimized.

■ *Develop an evaluation system that focuses on effort, individual improvement, and mastery, rather than on work completion, getting the right answer, or comparisons to others.* In an evaluation with these focal points, learning goals will be fostered and student attention will be directed to their own achievement.

■ *Make rewards contingent on effort, improvement, and good performance.* If your evaluation system focuses on effort, improvement, and good performance, then any rewards provided students should be contingent on these features. Recognize that there is a range of ability levels in the classroom and all students should be expected to demonstrate good performance for their ability, even high-ability students.

■ *Avoid norm-referenced grading systems.* When teachers grade on a curve, they ensure that some students will have a failing grade. This grading system reinforces negative expectations, promotes competition among students, and limits the number of students who receive positive reinforcement. Criterion-referenced grading systems are preferred.

■ *Describe evaluations as feedback to show how well students are doing.* Consistent with the focus of your evaluation system, students need to see that feedback given to them will serve as feedback on their performance. Any feedback needs to be balanced, specific, and given in a timely way. Some teachers use a three-to-one rule: three positive statements to one negative statement when giving feedback.

■ *Emphasize the factors that students have control over as affecting their performance.* Factors that students have control over include effort, note taking, persistence, preparation, and other issues. Minimize reference to uncontrollable factors such as mood, luck, ease or difficulty of the unit, poor test items, or other factors.

■ *Minimize the use of competition and comparisons to others when evaluating students.* Competition can be used to prompt students to apply more effort, but it has drawbacks. Competition focuses students' attention on winning, often at the expense of valuing the new content being addressed. Failure in a competitive situation also undermines self-esteem and prompts students to blame their failure on lack of ability, rather than on lack of effort. To avoid these difficulties, minimize your use of competition and stress the cooperative nature of learning.

■ *If competition is used, make sure that all students have an equal chance of winning.* Don't use the highest score as the only criterion when determining the winner in any classroom competition. Depending on the activity, your winning criterion might focus on the most creative, most unusual, most insightful, or most decorative or on a host of other possibilities.

■ *Avoid unnecessary differential treatment of high and low achievers.* Criteria and feedback to students should be consistent whether the students are high or low achievers. Teachers sometimes expect less of low achievers and then provide positive statements when their performance is not necessarily praiseworthy.

Select Procedures for Monitoring and Judging

Student motivation to learn can be enhanced by taking intrinsic motivation and learning goals into account when selecting procedures for monitoring and judging student performance (Ames, 1992; Stipek, 2002). To be satisfied about their work, students need to receive feedback about their progress.

■ *Use several approaches to evaluation to give students information about their accomplishments.* Rather than relying on one means of evaluating students, use several

■ ■ ■ ■ ■ ■

CREATING A LEARNING COMMUNITY

ESTABLISHING YOUR EVALUATION SYSTEM AND EXPECTATIONS

The evaluation and reward system should focus on effort, improvement, and mastery. Factors that students have control over should be emphasized, and competition should be minimized. If you build these features into your evaluation and feedback system, they will help to create a learning community in which students have a positive focus on evaluation, feedback, and their own development. You will be better able to develop a successful evaluation plan if you break down your decision making into components.

1. In what ways can you have your evaluation system focus on effort, individual improvement, and mastery?
2. How can you make rewards contingent on effort, improvement, and good performance?
3. How can you emphasize factors that students have control over (such as effort, note taking, persistence, preparation) concerning their performance?

approaches to provide students information about their performance. Tests, homework, projects, drill and practice, recitation, boardwork, and seatwork often measure different types of knowledge and skills. Multiple approaches provide students with a broader base of information, as well as providing several means for students to demonstrate their knowledge and skills.

In addition, active response opportunities can occur through projects, experiments, role plays, simulations, or other creative applications of what has been learned. Students also like activities that allow them to create a finished product. All these activities offer opportunities for students to work and respond to instructional stimuli, and they give you opportunities to provide feedback about the students' work.

■ *Provide frequent opportunities for students to respond and to receive feedback about their academic work.* Frequent feedback is needed throughout the grading period to provide students with reinforcement about their successes and to indicate areas that need improvement. This helps students to feel satisfied about their work, and it can be a tool to fuel extra effort and commitment in the event of dissatisfaction.

Give many short tests rather than a few major tests. This gives students more opportunities to correct poor performance. Students should realize that a single poor performance will not do irreversible damage to their grades. Preparing for a short evaluation is also more manageable for students. Since students need frequent feedback, plan to use several evaluation approaches for students to demonstrate their competence.

■ *Provide immediate feedback about student performance whenever possible.* Students also need to receive immediate feedback that can be used to guide subsequent responses. Drill, recitation, boardwork, and seatwork can be used to provide immediate feedback. For example, you might have five students at a time work on math problems at the chalkboard while you and the rest of the class watch them. You then could offer the students feedback about their work and discuss how to overcome the difficulties that they had in ar riving at a solution. Students profit from this feedback, which guides them in solving future problems.

■ *Limit practices that focus students' attention on extrinsic reasons for engaging in tasks* (e.g., close monitoring, deadlines, threats of punishment, competition). While it may be necessary to closely monitor student progress and have deadlines, students' attention should be directed to their own progress and mastery of the content, rather than to the extrinsic reasons for completing the tasks.

■ *Make evaluation private, not public.* Evaluation information is personal and should be given privately to the student. If this information were made public, students would feel that it is a competitive situation, which you do not want to emphasize.

Decide When to Give Feedback and Rewards

Students need to reach a point of satisfaction for what they are doing and what they are achieving (Keller, 1983). This satisfaction is the result of their intrinsic motivations about what they are doing as well as their responses to extrinsic rewards. You can help students to be satisfied by providing feedback and rewards for their performance.

■ *Give some rewards early in the learning experience.* By providing some type of reward early in the learning experience, students will likely put forth more effort to receive additional rewards. The reward may simply be praise or an opportunity for a special activity. Ultimately, students will feel satisfied, which is a motivator to learn.

TEACHERS IN ACTION

GIVING IMMEDIATE FEEDBACK WITH A STAMP

Leslie Seff, high school English teacher, Baltimore, Maryland

Many high school teachers underestimate the value of simple, external reinforcing techniques. I use a Koala Bear stamp to encourage correctness, on-task behavior, and excellence. In our study of *Macbeth,* for example, we worked on paraphrasing skills. At the end of Act III, I wanted students to make a connection between the animal imagery in the play and the plot. The students were asked to paraphrase two quotes with snake images. As they worked, I circulated around the room with the stamp. I defined the criteria for the stamp in this case as a precise, accurate paraphrase.

I gave students feedback by pointing out parts of the paraphrase that were not quite on the mark, and students had to go back and rework their answers. Eventually, I gave a limited number of stamps to the most accurate answers. Everyone in the class who completed the assignment on time and with correct answers on their papers would get full credit. Koala Bear stamps were used in this case as bonus points. Everyone wants to be recognized for a good job, and immediate recognition such as that given with the Koala Bear stamp is a powerful tool in inspiring students to make the extra effort.

Select easy tasks in the early steps of the learning activity. This offers you opportunities to deliver praise and rewards, which in turn help to influence subsequent student behavior. Every student should be able to receive some type of positive reinforcement early in the lesson. For example, you might select fairly simple sentence translations in the first part of a French class, but then gradually lead to more difficult translations later in the class. This gives you an opportunity to reward and reinforce students at an early point.

■ *Use motivating feedback following correct responses to maintain the quantity of student performance.* Students need to receive the satisfaction of receiving recognition for their successful performance, and this extrinsically reinforces students for their actions. Students are then more likely to continue performing the instructional tasks.

■ *Provide corrective feedback when it will be immediately useful to improve the quality of performance.* This corrective feedback can be given just before the next opportunity to practice. In this way, students receive feedback before they are expected to perform the next activity. If students have been making errors in math class, for example, you can give corrective suggestions to students just before they begin working on sample problems in class.

Select the Types of Feedback and Rewards

Feedback and rewards for students come in various forms. Praise, informative feedback, and rewards are satisfying to students and affect the quantity and quality of student performance

■ *Use verbal praise and informative feedback.* Rather than using threats or close monitoring, intrinsic satisfaction with instruction can be enhanced with verbal praise and other types of informative feedback. In this way, students receive satisfaction for the progress that they have made. However, too much verbal praise may become ineffective. Specific praise statements should focus on the student's behavior.

■ *Offer rewards as incentives, but only when necessary.* Rewards motivate many students to put forth effort, especially if they are offered in advance as incentives for reaching a certain level of performance. To ensure that rewards act as incentives for everyone and not just those of high ability, see that all students have reasonable opportunities to receive rewards.

When students receive consequences that they value, they become satisfied with themselves. This helps to motivate students to continue working in ways that lead to success. Rewards can be delivered in various ways, including (a) grades; (b) spoken and written praise; (c) activity rewards and special privileges (opportunities to play games, use special equipment, or engage in special activities); (d) symbolic rewards (honor roll, posting good papers); (e) material rewards (prizes, trinkets); and (f) teacher rewards (opportunities to do things with the teacher). Be cautious about relying too heavily on extrinsic rewards since this may become counterproductive.

■ *Make rewards contingent on mastery or a performance level that each student can achieve with effort.* Through this approach, students receive positive information about competence, and it is intrinsically satisfying that they have reached the mastery level.

■ *Provide substantive, informative evaluation that is based on mastery, rather than on social norms.* Feedback about performance is intrinsically satisfying for students. In contrast, feedback about how the student performed in relation to other students may promote feelings of competition, which is not as satisfying.

Help Students to Feel Satisfied with Their Learning Outcomes

An important part of motivating students to learn is to enable students to feel satisfied with their learning outcomes. This can be done by drawing attention to successes that they have experienced and by helping students recognize their efforts and improvements over time.

■ *Draw attention to the successes that students have achieved.* Displays and announcements about the work of individual students or groups will draw attention to the successes that students have experienced. In addition, you can make statements about class progress toward achieving the goals and about their overall performance.

■ *Help students to attribute achievement to effort.* For students to obtain feelings of satisfaction about their academic work, they must actually be successful in various ways. Success doesn't just happen—students must put forth effort. They need to see that their effort is related to their achievements and their feelings of success.

You can help students to recognize that achievement is related to effort by drawing attention to the effort that they exert in certain tasks. For example, when a student has achieved a better report card grade, you could say, "Gina, coming in for extra help and putting in extra study time really paid off during this grading period. You raised your grade by 14 points. Congratulations!"

Statements drawing attention to effort can also be made during single class sessions. In an art class, you might say, "Reggie, your careful application of the water colors has helped you show realistic images." The student is reinforced for specific actions and effort and is likely to continue these same actions.

■ *Help students to recognize that knowledge and skill development are incremental.* Students may not see that each small step that they take helps them to become more knowledgeable and skilled. If they recognize the importance of each small step, they will realize that their learning is incremental, and they will have more feelings of success and satisfaction.

To help students to recognize this, show how their understanding of each part of the subject matter contributes to their understanding of the whole. For example, when teaching students how to do a layup in basketball, help them to recognize and practice each important part of the actions—dribbling, dribbling while running, raising the proper foot and arm when releasing the ball, and so on. Students realize that their skill development is incremental, and they can feel satisfaction as they successfully perform each step of the process. Even reading a novel to elementary students one chapter a day shows students that information is incremental.

Use Mistakes and Redoing Work as Learning Opportunities

Students need to see that their errors are a normal part of learning and that they can improve their thinking and understanding by examining their errors (Ames, 1992; Blumenfeld et al., 1992; Stipek, 2002). You can provide opportunities for students to improve their academic work and to redo assignments as a way to motivate students to learn and to foster learning goals as seen in Table 5.2.

■ *Treat errors and mistakes as a normal part of learning.* Your response to student errors and mistakes can set the tone for the students. If you treat mistakes as a normal part of learning and see them as a way to improve understanding, then students will likely adopt the same perspective. This takes the pressure off students, and it reinforces the concept that learning is incremental.

■ *Use mistakes as a way to help students to check their thinking.* Instead of just seeing how many questions they got wrong, students should be given the opportunity to examine their mistakes and to identify the errors in their understanding. This process will help to lead to improved student learning.

■ *Provide opportunities for improvement or for redoing assignments.* After examining their mistakes, students should have opportunities to correct them and to improve their performance. In this way, student learning is fostered. You may provide students with the chance to redo assignments or retake quizzes as a means to promote understanding. You might ask students to show something that they learned from an error, perhaps through a reflection sheet.

Press Students to Think

Students need feedback to help to improve their thinking and understanding of the content. You can press students to think during the lessons through your feedback and expectations for lesson participation. Blumenfeld et al. (1992) offer the following ways to press students to think.

■ *Require students to explain and justify their answers.* Teachers ask many questions for students to answer during instruction. Rather than accepting a brief answer to a question, you can ask students to explain their reasoning for their answers and to justify their answers. In addition, you might ask higher-order questions that require students to apply, analyze, synthesize, or evaluate the concepts, rather than asking only questions that require students to repeat the facts.

■ *Prompt, reframe the question, or break it into smaller parts when students are unsure, and probe students when their understanding is unclear.* Many adjustments in your lesson delivery may be needed depending on the students' ability to understand the content. If students seem to be unsure in their understanding, you may need to provide prompts or clues, reframe the question, or present it in a different way. Especially if the content is complex, you

TABLE 5.2 Motivational Strategies Concerning Evaluation and Recognition

1. *Establish Evaluation Expectations and Criteria*
   a. Develop an evaluation system that focuses on effort, individual improvement, and mastery, rather than on work completion, getting the right answer, or comparisons to others.
   b. Make rewards contingent on effort, improvement, and good performance.
   c. Avoid norm-referenced grading systems.
   d. Describe evaluations as feedback to show how well students are doing.
   e. Emphasize the factors that students have control over as affecting their performance.
   f. Minimize the use of competition and comparisons to others when evaluating students.
   g. If competition is used, make sure that all students have an equal chance of winning.
   h. Avoid unnecessary differential treatment of high and low achievers.

2. *Select Procedures for Monitoring and Judging*
   a. Use several approaches to evaluation to give students information about their accomplishments.
   b. Provide frequent opportunities for students to respond and to receive feedback about their academic work.
   c. Provide immediate feedback about student performance whenever possible.
   d. Limit practices that focus students' attention on extrinsic reasons for engaging in tasks (e.g., close monitoring, deadlines, threats of punishment, competition).
   e. Make evaluation private, not public.

3. *Decide When to Give Feedback and Rewards*
   a. Give some rewards early in the learning experience.
   b. Use motivating feedback following correct responses to maintain the quantity of student performance.
   c. Provide corrective feedback when it will be immediately useful to improve the quality of performance.

4. *Select the Types of Feedback and Rewards*
   a. Use verbal praise and informative feedback.
   b. Offer rewards as incentives, but only when necessary.
   c. Make rewards contingent on mastery or a performance level that each student can achieve with effort.
   d. Provide substantive, informative evaluation that is based on mastery rather than on social norms.

5. *Help Students to Feel Satisfied with Their Learning Outcomes*
   a. Draw attention to the successes that students have achieved.
   b. Help students to attribute achievement to effort.
   c. Help students to recognize that knowledge and skill development are incremental.

6. *Use Mistakes and Redoing Work as Learning Opportunities*
   a. Treat errors and mistakes as a normal part of learning.
   b. Use mistakes as a way to help students to check their thinking.
   c. Provide opportunities for improvement or for redoing assignments.

7. *Press Students to Think*
   a. Require students to explain and justify their answers.
   b. Prompt, reframe the question, or break it into smaller parts when students are unsure, and probe students when their understanding is unclear.
   c. Monitor for comprehension rather than procedural correctness during activities.
   d. Encourage responses from all students.
   e. Supplement short-answer assignments in commercial workbooks with questions that require higher levels of student thinking.

Source: Burden, P. R. (2000). *Powerful classroom management strategies: Motivating students to learn.* Thousand Oaks, CA: Corwin Press. Pages 88–89. Reprinted by permission of Corwin Press, Inc.

may need to break it down into smaller parts to facilitate student understanding. When student understanding is unclear, it is best to probe their understanding with questions to be sure that they understand or to identify the areas that they do not understand.

■ *Monitor for comprehension rather than procedural correctness during activities.* Rather than have a work orientation in your classroom, have a learning orientation by which you focus on student understanding. Less importance should be placed on whether students followed the project procedures precisely, and more importance should be placed on whether students understand the content for which the project was designed.

■ *Encourage responses from all students.* Rather than allowing a small number of students to dominate the lessons, try to actively involve all students in the lesson. This could be done by asking students to vote on issues, to compare their responses, or to debate the merits of the issue under consideration. These and other approaches encourage active participation in the lesson and promote student thinking.

■ *Supplement short-answer assignments in commercial workbooks with questions that require higher levels of student thinking.* Teachers often use worksheets from commercial workbooks for student seatwork or homework. The questions in these worksheets, however, often require the students to report back facts. As a result, it is important to supplement commercial worksheets with questions that require higher levels of student thinking that involve application, analysis, synthesis, or evaluation of the concepts.

KEY TERMS

Brain hemisphericity	Interest	Relevance
Curiosity	Motivation	Satisfaction
Expectancy	Multiple intelligences	Set induction

MAJOR CONCEPTS

1. Motivation describes those processes that can arouse and initiate student behavior, give direction and purpose to behavior, help behavior to persist, and help the student to choose a particular behavior.

2. There are four dimensions of motivation: interest, relevance, expectancy, and satisfaction.

3. A comprehensive approach to motivate students to learn is needed because classroom factors are mutually dependent on each other and interact with each other.

4. Planning for motivation needs to be conducted for all levels of planning (the course, the semester, the marking period, each unit, each week, and each lesson).

5. The instructional strategies that you use, the tasks that you ask the students to complete, and the way that you interact with students during instruction all influence students' motivation to learn.

6. The way that you evaluate student performance and provide recognition influences students' motivation to learn.

DISCUSSION/REFLECTIVE QUESTIONS

1. Based on your schooling and through your experiences in classrooms, what types of intrinsic and extrinsic motivation did you find most effective?

2. What are the merits and disadvantages of offering students choices in instructional tasks and requirements?

3. What are some factors to consider when determining the degree of control that you will give your students in decision making about content, activities, and assignments?

4. What are the merits and problems of using games and simulations as a motivational strategy?

5. Describe several ways that review can be conducted at the end of a lesson to give students a sense of competence about what they have just learned.

6. How might you adapt evaluation and recognition for a student with low abilities without lowering your standards?

SUGGESTED ACTIVITIES

For Clinical Settings

1. Examine lesson plans that you previously prepared and critique them in relation to the motivational strategies concerning instruction listed in Table 5.1.

2. Select a unit in a subject area of your choice. Describe the ways that you could highlight the relevance of this subject matter for your students throughout the unit and in each lesson.

3. Critique your system of evaluation and recognition in relation to the motivational strategies in Table 5.2. How might your system be changed to enhance students' motivation to learn?

For Field Settings

1. Ask several teachers how they introduce learning objectives to the students and provide advance organizers.

2. Talk with other teachers at your grade level or in your subject area to see how they motivate students or how they apply the motivational strategies in Tables 5.1 and 5.2.

USEFUL RESOURCES

Brophy, J. E. (1998). *Motivating students to learn.* New York: McGraw-Hill.

A scholarly review of many principles to motivate students. Includes a review of the literature and offers guidance for classroom application of the motivational concepts.

Burden, P. R. (2000). *Powerful classroom management strategies: Motivating students to learn.* Thousand Oaks, CA: Corwin Press.

Provides a practical framework for decision making to motivate students. Includes content on motivating hard-to-reach students and on incorporating motivational planning into instruction and assessment.

Mendler, A. N. (2000). *Motivating students who don't care.* Bloomington, IN: National Educational Service.

This brief guidebook offers suggestions for addressing effort, hope, power, relationships, and enthusiasm to motivate students.

WEB SITES

- Clearinghouse on Educational Management, College of Education, University of Oregon (the first site is for general information; the second Web site has specific information on motivating students)

  http://eric.uoregon.edu/

  http://eric.uoregon.edu/hot_topics/index.html#student_motivation

- Hints on motivating students from the Teaching Effectiveness Program—Academic Learning Services, University of Oregon

  http://darkwing.uoregon.edu/~tep/tshooting/motivating.html

- ERIC Center on Reading, English and Communication at Indiana University has bibliographies on topics on which they receive frequent inquiries (the first site is the general Web site; the second is the site for specific information on motivation).

  http://www.indiana.edu/~eric_rec/

  http://www.indiana.edu/~eric_rec/ieo/bibs/motgen.html

- Student achievement and student motivation

  http://ericcass.uncg.edu/virtuallib/achievement/motivation.html

CHAPTER SIX

DIFFERENTIATING YOUR INSTRUCTION

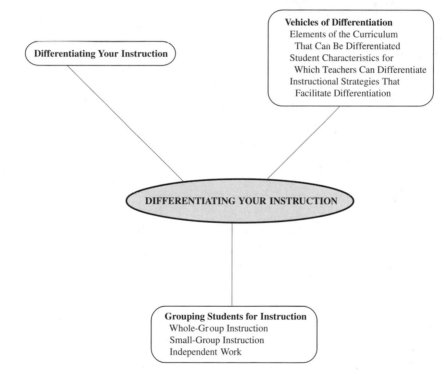

Differentiating Your Instruction

Vehicles of Differentiation
Elements of the Curriculum
That Can Be Differentiated
Student Characteristics for
Which Teachers Can Differentiate
Instructional Strategies That
Facilitate Differentiation

DIFFERENTIATING YOUR INSTRUCTION

Grouping Students for Instruction
Whole-Group Instruction
Small-Group Instruction
Independent Work

OBJECTIVES

This chapter provides information that will help you to:

1. Describe the reasons for differentiating instruction in the classroom.

2. Identify ways that the curriculum could be differentiated for students.

3. Identify ways to differentiate based on student characteristics.

4. Describe the range of instructional strategies available for use in the classroom.

5. Determine ways to group your students for instruction.

PRAXIS/Principles of Learning and Teaching/Pathwise

The following principles are relevant to content in this chapter:

1. Becoming familiar with relevant aspects of students' background knowledge and experiences   (A1)

2. Demonstrating an understanding of the connections between the content that was learned previously, the current content, and the content that will be learned in the future   (A3)

3. Creating or selecting teaching methods, learning activities, and instructional materials or other resources that are appropriate for the students and that are aligned with the goals of the lesson   (A4)

4. Communicating challenging learning expectations to each student   (B3)

INTASC

The following INTASC standards are relevant to content in this chapter:

1. The teacher understands the central concepts, tools of inquiry, and structures of the discipline(s) that he or she teaches and can create learning experiences that make these aspects of subject matter meaningful for students.   (Standard 1)

2. The teacher understands how children learn and develop and can provide learning opportunities that support their intellectual, social, and personal development.   (Standard 2)

3. The teacher understands how students differ in their approaches to learning and creates instructional opportunities that are adapted to diverse learners.   (Standard 3)

4. The teacher understands and uses a variety of instructional strategies to encourage students' development of critical thinking, problem solving, and performance skills.   (Standard 4)

5. The teacher plans instruction based on knowledge of subject matter, students, the community, and curriculum goals.   (Standard 7)

Have you ever been a student in a classroom where the teacher used the same instructional strategy most of the time? Or where the teacher didn't seem to adjust the content or activities based on the background knowledge and skills of the students? Or where the teacher did not vary the way that the students were grouped for instruction? Or where the teacher asked all students to complete the same evaluation products?

What were your reactions to these experiences? Did you feel challenged to learn as much as you could have? Did you feel excited about attending and participating in that class? Do you feel that you were able to demonstrate your learning in the best possible way?

These issues are at the heart of differentiating your instruction. All too often, students complain that teachers do not take their characteristics into account and thus teach in the same way for every student. In these classrooms, there is little flexibility in the content, instructional activities and strategies, and assessment approaches. Students may not receive instruction in the way that they best learn and thus may not learn the material very well and then score low on classroom assessments.

Instead, teachers can differentiate their instruction to meet the needs of the learners in the classroom. *Differentiation* is simply attending to the learning needs of a particular student or group of students, rather than the more typical pattern of teaching the class as though all individuals in it were basically alike (Tomlinson, 2000). This chapter examines the concept of differentiation and the various ways that you can differentiate your own classroom.

DIFFERENTIATING YOUR INSTRUCTION

Differentiating your instruction means that a teacher recognizes student academic differences and modifies classroom instruction in order to help each student to reach his or her academic potential (Tomlinson, 1999). Students come to school with varying levels of readiness to learn, different ways in which they learn best, and a wide range of interests. Teachers take these factors into account when designing instruction. With differentiated instruction, all students are challenged without excessive stress, and each student is helped to grow academically.

Differentiation of instruction is a teacher's response to learner's needs guided by general principles of differentiation, such as respectful tasks, flexible grouping, and ongoing assessment and adjustment.

This is the heart of differentiation: teachers can adapt one or more of the curricular elements (the content, the learning process, and the products that students prepare) based on student characteristics (readiness, interests, and learning profiles) at any point in a lesson or unit using a range of instructional and management strategies (Tomlinson, 1999). However, you do not need to differentiate all elements in all possible ways. Modify a curricular element only when you see a student need and are convinced that modification increases the likelihood of student learning. Details about these factors are discussed later in this chapter.

Several principles guide differentiation (Tomlinson & Allan, 2000). Understanding and adhering to these principles facilitate the work of the teacher and the success of the learner in a responsive classroom.

1. *A differentiated classroom is flexible.* Teachers and students understand that time, materials, modes of teaching, ways of grouping students, ways of expressing learning, ways of assessing learning, and other classroom elements can be used in a variety of ways to promote individual and whole-class success.

2. *Differentiation of instruction stems from effective and ongoing assessment of learner needs.* In a differentiated classroom, student differences are expected and thus serve as a basis for instructional planning. A tight bond should exist between assessment and instruction. Assessment information about students serves as the basis for selecting content and strategies to reach all students.

3. *Flexible grouping helps to ensure student access to a wide variety of learning opportunities and working arrangements.* In a flexibly grouped classroom, a teacher plans student working arrangements that vary widely and purposefully over a relatively short period of time. This may include whole-class, small-group, and individual studies.

Students may work in groups based on their readiness to address the academic content. However, mixed readiness groups can be beneficial. Students also may be grouped based on their interests in the content and activities. Finally, students who have similar learning styles or patterns may be grouped together to facilitate learning. At other times, groups with students of varied learning styles are preferred.

4. *All students consistently work with "respectful" activities and learning arrangements.* This principle provides that each student must have tasks that are equally interesting and equally engaging and that provide equal access to essential understanding and skills. In differentiated classrooms, each child must feel challenged most of the time. In doing so, students grapple with the information or skills, leading to understanding and preparation to move to the next learning stage.

5. *Students and teachers are collaborators in learning.* In differentiated classrooms, teachers study their students and continually involve them in decision making about the classroom. Teachers diagnose and prescribe for learning needs, facilitate learning, and craft effective curriculum. Students are critical partners in classroom success by sharing information about their readiness, interests, and learning preferences and by participating in decision making.

VEHICLES OF DIFFERENTIATION

How might teachers differentiate their instruction? As Table 6.1 indicates, differentiation can take place when planning, grouping students, using instructional activities and materials, identifying assignments, and determining the assessments to use. The discussion of the vehicles of differentiation is organized in three areas: the curriculum, student characteristics, and instructional strategies.

Elements of the Curriculum That Can Be Differentiated

The curriculum can be differentiated in three ways: (1) the content—the curriculum and the materials and approaches used for students to learn the content, (2) the process—the instructional activities or approaches used to help students to learn the curriculum, and (3) the products—the assessment vehicles through which students demonstrate what they have learned.

Content.   *Content* includes the knowledge, skills, and attitudes related to the subject and the materials and mechanisms through which learning is accomplished. In practice, many districts have curriculum guides outlining objectives and content that are expected for all students at a particular grade level or subject area. So there may not be much variation in

TABLE 6.1   What a Differentiated Classroom Looks Like

Planning should:
- Be based on understanding student characteristics and needs.
- Be based on ongoing, diagnostic assessments to make instruction more responsive to students.
- Be based on an understanding of student readiness, interest, and learning profiles.
- Include students working with the teacher to establish whole-class and individual learning goals.

Grouping of students should:
- Include many types of groupings (whole class, small group, independent).
- Allow for flexible groups.

Instructional activities should:
- Permit multiple approaches to the content, activities, and products demonstrating student learning.
- Guide students in making interest-based learning choices.
- Permit many learning profile options.
- Use time flexibly based on student needs.
- Permit students to share multiple perspectives on ideas and events.
- Encourage students to be more self-reliant learners.
- Support students helping other students and the teacher to solve problems.
- Foster the students' responsibility for their own learning.

Materials should:
- Be many and varied, including instructional technology.

Assignments should:
- Vary in content, based on student need.
- Vary in difficulty, based on student readiness.
- Allow for choice based on student interests and strengths.
- Vary in time allotted.
- Contain directions that are clear and direct enough for students to understand.
- Provide a mechanism for students to get help when the teacher is busy with other students.

Assessments should:
- Be used to guide initial planning.
- Be conducted throughout instruction of a unit to guide teacher decisions when making adjustments for the students.
- Be conducted in multiple ways.
- Define excellence in large measure as individual growth from a starting point.

the content to be taught, but there could be differentiation in the materials used in instruction (Gregory & Chapman, 2002).

Some ways that a teacher might differentiate access to the content include (Tomlinson & Allan, 2000; Tomlinson, 2001) the following:

- Use math manipulatives for some, but not all, learners to help students to understand a new idea.
- Use texts or novels at more than one reading level.
- Present instruction through both whole-to-part and part-to-whole approaches.

- Use texts, computer programs, videos, and other media as a way of conveying key concepts to varied learners.
- Focus on teaching the concepts and principles, rather than on all the minute facts about the issues.
- Have advanced students work on special, in-depth projects, while the other students work on the general lessons.
- Use varied text and resource materials.
- Prepare learning contracts with individual students to enable differentiation.
- When reteaching is necessary, alter the content and delivery based on student readiness, interests, or learning profile.
- Provide various types of support for learning, such as using study buddies, note-taking organizers, or highlighted printed materials.

Process. *Process* includes the instructional activities or approaches used to help students to learn the curriculum. Process is how the student comes to make sense of and understand the key facts, concepts, generalizations, and skills of the subject. An effective activity involves students using an essential skill to understand an essential idea, and the activity is clearly focused on the learning goal.

Some ways that a teacher might differentiate process or activities include (Tomlinson, 1999; Wormeli, 2001) the following:

- Provide options at differing levels of difficulty or options based on differing student interests.
- Give students choices about how they express what they learn in a project (e.g., create a newspaper article report, display key issues in some type of graphic organizer).
- Differ the amounts of teacher and student support for a task.

Products. *Products* are the vehicles through which students demonstrate what they have learned. Products can also be differentiated, and they may include actual physical products

CREATING A LEARNING COMMUNITY

STUDENT INPUT ABOUT INSTRUCTIONAL ACTIVITIES

When creating a learning community, student input into decision making is often sought. Information and guidance that students may offer about instructional activities will help the teacher to make better decisions about ways to differentiate instruction. For example, students might prefer to have options for the types of activities that they are asked to complete for a unit. Also, students might prefer having the choices of instructional activities be at different levels of difficulty, with different ways to report on their activities.

1. How might you gather information from your students about their preferences for the types of activities to be used in a unit?
2. How will you gauge the levels of difficulty that should be built into the various activities that you develop?
3. How might you arrange for various ways to provide student and teacher support for students needing assistance?

(e.g., portfolios, reports, diagrams, or paper-and-pencil tests) that students prepare, as well as student performances designed to demonstrate a particular skill. Performance-based assessment, including student products and performances, is discussed more thoroughly in Chapter 12.

A good product causes students to rethink what they have learned, apply what they can do, extend their understanding and skill, and become involved in both critical and creative thinking.

Examples of ways to differentiate products include the following:

- Allow students to help to design products around essential learning goals.
- Provide product assignments of varying degrees of difficulty to match student readiness.
- Use a wide variety of assessments.
- Work with students to develop rubrics that allow for demonstration of both whole-class and individual goals.
- Provide or encourage the use of varied types of resources in preparing products.

Particular attention often needs to be given to *struggling learners* so that they have challenging products to create and the support systems that lead to success. Here are some suggestions (Tomlinson, 2001):

- Be sure product assignments for learners require them to apply and extend essential understandings and skills for the unit or other product span.
- Use product formats that allow students to express themselves in ways other than written language alone.
- Give product assignments in smaller increments, allowing students to complete one portion of a product before introducing another.
- Think about putting directions on audio- or videotape so that students can revisit explanations as needed.
- Prepare, or help students to prepare, time lines for product work so that tasks seem manageable and comfortably structured.
- Provide miniworkshops on particular skills, such as note-taking, conducting interviews, and various study skills.
- Support students as they try to find various resources for their products or performances.
- Provide templates or organizers that guide students through each step of doing research.
- Occasionally review with the students the reasons for preparing the products to consider the big picture.
- With challenging tasks, help to set up groups so that students can work together.
- Work with students to emphasize particular parts of the rubrics that reflect their individual needs.
- Help students to analyze sample products from prior years so that they develop an awareness of what is expected.
- Provide time, materials, and partnerships at school for students who do not have resources and support at home for project completion.
- When students speak a primary language other than English, be sure that the student has access to information in his first language.

Advanced learners need to be stretched in their learning as they prepare products. To do so, here are some suggestions (Tomlinson, 2001):

- Structure product assignments for advanced learners so that they are stretched forward in a number of ways.
- Consider having advanced learners study the key issues or questions across time periods, disciplines, or cultures.
- As much as possible, include advanced-level research and information.
- Consider using mentors who are at an advanced level to guide the work of advanced learners to new levels.
- Consider letting advanced students begin their projects earlier than other students if the complexity of their products warrants it.
- Let each advanced learner help you to develop criteria for expert-level content and production.

Student Characteristics for Which Teachers Can Differentiate

Students vary in at least three ways that make modifying instruction a wise strategy for teachers. Students differ (1) in their readiness to work with a particular idea or skill at a given time, (2) in the topics that they find interesting, and (3) in learning profiles that may be shaped by gender, culture, learning style, or intelligence preference.

Readiness.   *Readiness* is a student's entry point into a particular content or skill. To differentiate in response to student readiness, teachers can construct tasks or provide learning choices at different levels of difficulty.

TEACHERS IN ACTION

LET YOUR STUDENTS SELECT THE TEST FORMAT

Steffanie Ogg, high school teacher, St. Paul, Minnesota

One way that I accommodate various student learning styles is to offer students a choice of test formats. I usually offer my tests in three formats: multiple choice, short essay (or fill-in-the-blank), and matching questions. The student can then select the test format that he or she prefers. The test questions are similar, but the way that the student needs to respond to the questions addresses various ways that students learn and retain information.

I knew that this was a good idea when I heard the students say, "I want to do the matching test; that is a breeze." But another student will say the same thing about one of the other test formats.

At first, creating different versions of a test may be more work for the teacher, but it is worth it when you have greater student success. In fact, some textbook companies provide computer programs with premade tests in different formats.

I also provide students with a little orientation about how to take different types of tests. This includes teaching a simple testing strategy and giving a few practice problems. The results have been great.

Students with *less-developed readiness* may need (Tomlinson, 1999) the following:

- Someone to help them to identify and make up gaps in their learning so that they can move ahead
- More opportunities for direct instruction or practice
- Activities or products that are more structured or concrete, with fewer steps, closer to their own experiences, and calling on simpler reading skills
- A more deliberate pace of learning

Advanced students may need (Tomlinson, 1999) these opportunities:

- To skip practice with previously mastered skills and understandings
- Activities and products that are quite complex, open ended, abstract, and multifaceted, drawing on advanced reading materials
- A brisk pace of work, or perhaps a slower pace to allow for greater depth of exploration of a topic

Some *general strategies* to adjust for readiness include these:

- Adjust the degree of difficulty of a task to provide an appropriate level of challenge.
- Make the task more or less familiar based on the proficiency of the learner's experiences or skills for the task.
- Add or remove teacher or peer coaching, use of manipulatives, or presence or absence of models for a task. This varies the degree of structure and support being provided.
- Vary direct instruction by small-group need.

When planning lessons, you should give consideration to various dimensions of the content and the learning tasks as they relate to readiness. For example, simple concepts should be taught before students are ready for complex concepts. Drawing on Tomlinson (2001), several dimensions of the content and learning tasks are outlined in Table 6.2.

TABLE 6.2   Readiness for Content and Activities

Your instructional content and activities may be seen on a continuum of simple to complex. Students often need to start on the left side of this continuum and then move to the right as they are ready.

LIMITED READINESS FOR CONTENT OR ACTIVITIES	READY FOR ADVANCED CONTENT OR ACTIVITIES
You can use:	*You can use:*
Simple content or activities	Complex content or activities
Single facet	Multiple facets
Concrete ideas	Abstract ideas
More structured	Less structured
Less independence	More independence
Slow pace	Quick pace

Interest.   *Interest* refers to a student's affinity, curiosity, or passion for a particular topic or skill. To differentiate in response to student interest, a teacher aligns key skills and material for understanding from a curriculum segment with topics or pursuits that intrigue students. Some ways to differentiate in response to student interest include the following:

- Provide broad access to a wide variety of materials and technology.
- Give students a choice of tasks and products, including student-designed options.
- Provide a variety of avenues for student exploration of a topic or expression of learning.
- Encourage investigation or application of key concepts and principles in student interest areas.

Learning Profiles.   *Learning profile* refers to the ways in which we learn best as individuals. It may be shaped by intelligence preferences, gender, culture, or learning style. Integrating issues related to learning styles and multiple intelligences provides additional guidance for ways to differentiate instruction (Silver, Strong, & Perini, 2000).

Some ways that teachers can differentiate in response to student learning profiles include the following:

- Create a learning environment with flexible spaces and learning options.
- Present information through auditory, visual, and kinesthetic modes.
- Encourage students to explore information and ideas through auditory, visual, and kinesthetic modes.
- Allow students to work alone or with peers.
- Ensure a choice of competitive, cooperative, and independent experiences.

Instructional Strategies That Facilitate Differentiation

Here you are, starting to plan a new unit in your science class and you just can't imagine how your students will learn all that information about the human circulatory system. Essentially, you need to select instructional strategies for each lesson that will be the vehicles for students to learn the material.

An *instructional strategy* is a method for delivering instruction that is intended to help students to achieve the learning objective. Strategies range from being very explicit and teacher directed to being less explicit and student centered.

As you plan for instruction, consider instructional strategies that are most suited to help to achieve the objectives of the lessons. A wide range of possible strategies exists. Some strategies are teacher directed, such as lectures, recitations, questions, and practice. Others are more interactive, such as various group and discussion methods. Still other strategies are more student directed; these often emphasize inquiry and discovery.

Predominant instructional strategies are displayed in Figure 6.1 within four categories on a continuum ranging from teacher-centered, more explicit methods to student-centered, less explicit methods.

- *Direct instructional approaches* are those in which teachers tell the students the concept or skill to be learned and then lead students through most of the instructional activities designed to lead to student learning.

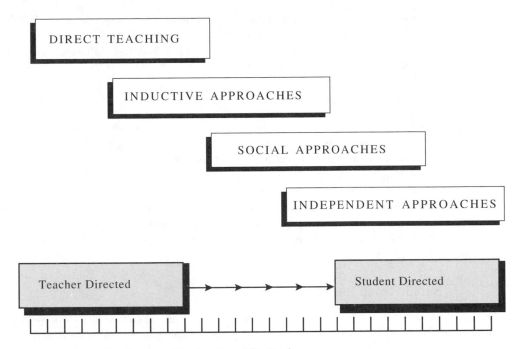

FIGURE 6.1   A Continuum of Instructional Strategies

- *Inductive instructional approaches* are those that involve some type of exploratory activity helping to lead students to discover a concept or generalization. Teachers employ several strategies to help students to attain the concepts.
- *Social instructional approaches* have students working together in various ways to gather, process, and learn the information or skills. Teachers act as a facilitator rather than the information provider.
- *Independent instructional approaches* allow students to pursue content independently with less teacher direction than other lessons. Students sometimes are permitted to pursue their own interests.

Specific types of instructional strategies within these four categories are outlined in Table 6.3. All these instructional strategies are discussed in more detail in Chapters 7 and 8. When deciding on a particular teaching strategy for a lesson, weigh the advantages and disadvantages of the various strategies along with the objectives of the intended lesson. Effective teachers use many different strategies throughout a unit and the school year as a means to differentiate their instruction and be more responsive to student needs.

GROUPING STUDENTS FOR INSTRUCTION

In addition to selecting instructional strategies, you need to consider the type of student grouping that is most appropriate for the instructional strategies and instructional objectives.

It is important to focus on a group as a collection of individuals who learn. Within groups, individual students observe, listen, respond, take turns, rebut, mediate, demonstrate, play, and think. Instructional groups can be large or small. Whole-group, small-group, and independent work are options to consider.

Whole-Group Instruction

In *whole-group instruction,* the entire class is taught as a group. You can use a variety of the instructional strategies previously discussed in this chapter. In the large group, you could (a) lecture, demonstrate, and explain a topic, (b) ask and answer a question in front of the entire class, (c) provide the same recitation, practice, and drill exercises for the entire class, (d) work on the same problems, and (e) use the same materials. Although instruction is directed to the whole group, you can still ask specific students to answer questions, monitor specific students as they work on assigned activities, and work with students on an individual basis. Even with whole-group instruction, give consideration to the individual differences of students.

Small-Group Instruction

Sometimes instructional objectives can be better met when students work in small groups; this is *small-group instruction.* Small groups enable students to be more actively engaged in learning and teachers to monitor student progress better.

Groups of four students often work well. In a group of more than six, generally not everyone will actively participate. Many teachers find that they can use small-group and individualized techniques with larger classes by dividing into groups, committees, or teams and changing the arrangements frequently. Small groups can be used in all grade levels and subjects.

TABLE 6.3   Types of Instructional Strategies

The strategies are listed here in four categories, starting with the most teacher directed and moving to the most student directed.

DIRECT APPROACHES	SOCIAL APPROACHES
Direct instruction	Discussions
Presentations	Cooperative learning
Demonstrations	Panels and debates
Questions	Role playing, Simulations, and Games
Recitations	
Practice and drills	**INDEPENDENT APPROACHES**
Reviews	Learning centers or stations
Guided practice and homework	Contracts and independent work
INDUCTIVE APPROACHES	
Concept attainment approaches	
Inquiry lessons	
Projects, reports, and problems	

Small groups can be formed based on issues such as student ability, interest, skill, viewpoint, activity, or integration (Cohen, 1994). Also, groupings could be done arbitrarily. Three common types of groupings are cooperative learning groups, ability groups, and peer tutoring.

Cooperative Learning Groups.   *Cooperative learning* refers to a variety of teaching methods in which students work in small groups to help one another to learn academic content (Slavin, 2000). One approach is with the use of student team learning methods for which there are team goals, and success is achieved if all team members learn the objectives being taught. Other types of cooperative learning groups include group investigations, jigsaw activities, and complex instruction. All these approaches are discussed more fully in Chapter 8.

As you consider ways to differentiate your instruction, cooperative learning groups serve as an important means to provide instructional variety for your students while relating to various learning styles and student learning preferences. These groups also provide the opportunity to differentiate the content and tasks to meet the diversity of student interests and skills.

Ability Groups.   *Ability grouping* involves the clustering of students who are judged to be similar in their academic ability into classes for instruction. There are two common types of ability grouping: between-class grouping and within-class grouping.

Between-class grouping involves having separate classes for students of different abilities. When reporting research on between-class ability grouping, Slavin (2000) notes that grouping arrangements made on the basis of standardized test scores are not effective in reducing the range of differences that affect the specific class. In addition, the quality of instruction often is lower in lower-track classes, and students feel stigmatized by their

■ ■ ■ ■ ■ ■

MODIFICATIONS FOR DIVERSE CLASSROOMS

DIVERSE STUDENTS IN COOPERATIVE LEARNING GROUPS

Cooperative learning groups offer students an opportunity to work together on a particular project. Students work with each other and support each other as they take actions to complete the group tasks. However, students vary in their content background, their preferences for the learning tasks, their skills in working with other group members, and many other factors. Teachers often give careful thought about the ways that they will select group members.

1. When selecting students for cooperative learning groups in your classroom, will you try to create groups with common skills and interests or will you create groups with varied skills and interests? How did you make this decision? How will students benefit from this decision?

2. Let's say that for a particular cooperative learning group project you want to create groups with common characteristics. What characteristic(s) would you select to create these homogeneous groups?

3. If you had a classroom with much cultural diversity, how might this affect the ways that you arrange for and conduct the cooperative learning groups?

assignments to low tracks. They may become delinquent and truant and may eventually drop out of school. The disadvantages of between-class ability grouping suggest that it be avoided when possible (Oakes, 1990). Instead, you might consider within-class ability grouping for a short time, as well as individualized instruction techniques.

Within-class grouping involves creating subgroups within a class, with each subgroup being fairly homogeneous in terms of ability. A small number is better than a large number of groups. In this way, group assignments can be flexible, role models for low achievers are available, teacher morale is higher, and the stigmatizing effect is minimized (Slavin, 2000).

Within one classroom, you may group students for various activities or subjects. For example, middle and secondary teachers may use ability groups for only part of a class period and use whole-group activities or other approaches for the rest of the class time. You may group students to work on selected projects or activities.

However, you should use ability grouping, especially between-class grouping, with caution and seriously consider whether it is in the best interest of all students. Research into the effects of ability grouping has not demonstrated increased student achievement in the lower or middle tracks compared to heterogeneously mixed or whole-group instruction. In fact, Oakes (1990) reported fewer opportunities with ability grouping for students who exhibit patterns of low achievement and minimal participation in science and mathematics. Teachers of low-ability classes seem to have lower expectations of the students than teachers of classes at other tracks. Researchers have questioned if this is related to teachers' decreased expectations for lower-tracked students (Slavin, 2000). Dividing students into ability groups within one classroom for reading and mathematics is a common practice.

Peer Tutoring.   *Peer tutoring* involves students teaching students. The two types of peer tutoring are (1) cross-age tutoring, by which older students work with younger students, and (2) peer tutoring, by which students within the same class work together. There are several advantages of peer tutoring (Johnson & Johnson, 1999): (a) peer tutors are often effective in

TEACHERS IN ACTION

PEER TUTORING

Alan Drake, high school English and literature teacher, Gillette, Wyoming

My class uses peer tutoring in two ways, and the classroom seating facilitates this by having an inner and an outer horseshoe of seats. The first type of peer tutoring is what I call a study buddy. Two students who sit next to each other in our horseshoe seating arrangement collaborate in ACT review, rehearse prior to a discussion, edit pieces of writing, and do other cooperative tasks.

The second type of peer tutoring occurs when two study buddy groups (i.e., four adjacent students in the horseshoe seating) form a peer revision group. After doing some writing, one student reads his or her writing while the other three group members listen. Then the members respond in any of these ways: What did they like about the writing? What didn't they understand? What would they do differently if it were their writing? These groups provide invaluable benefit by providing considerable response to each student about his or her writing.

teaching students who do not respond well to adults; (b) peer tutoring can develop a bond of friendship between the tutor and tutee, which is important for integrating slow learners into the group; (c) peer tutoring allows the teacher to teach a large group of students, but still gives slow learners the individual attention that they need; (d) tutors benefit by learning to teach; and (e) peer tutoring happens spontaneously under cooperative conditions, so the teacher does not have to organize and manage it in a formal, continuing way.

Peer tutoring can be used at all grade levels. Before having students work in pairs, clarify the purposes of the tutoring, obtain necessary materials, and provide an appropriate area where the students can work without disturbing other students. In addition, provide some guidance for the students in ways to work and study together in their peer tutoring arrangement.

CLASSROOM DECISIONS

In your class, you have discovered a wide range of academic ability in your students. For part of the class time each week, you would like to use peer tutoring to have the more advanced students work with students needing more assistance. What criteria will you use when making decisions about how to pair the students? What orientation or training is needed for the students in their new role as peer tutors?

Independent Work

Many teachers create opportunities for students to work on tasks of their own choosing, or they assign activities that enable students to work alone; this is *independent work.* Good and Brophy (2000) found that one-third of elementary teachers attempt to individualize instruction, as do one-fifth of secondary teachers.

When assigning independent work, you may have students involved in any of a number of the instructional strategies. Quite often, inquiry and discovery instructional approaches are used, such as computer-assisted instruction, learning centers, learning stations, laboratory, discovery techniques, and others. But not all independent work involves inquiry approaches. Mastery learning is a well-known instructional strategy used for independent work that is very teacher directed.

KEY TERMS

Ability grouping	Independent work	Readiness
Between-class grouping	Inductive instructional approaches	Small-group instruction
Content	Interest	Social instructional approaches
Cooperative learning	Instructional strategy	Whole-group instruction
Differentiation	Learning profile	Within-class grouping
Direct instructional approaches	Peer tutoring	
Independent instructional approaches	Process	
	Products	

MAJOR CONCEPTS

1. Differentiation is simply attending to the learning needs of a particular student or group of students, rather than the more typical pattern of teaching the class as though all individuals in it were basically alike.

2. Teachers can adapt one or more of the curricular elements (the content, the learning process, and the products that students prepare) based on student characteristics (readiness, interests, and learning profiles) at any point in a lesson or unit, using a range of instructional and management strategies.

3. The curriculum can be differentiated in three ways: (1) the content—the curriculum and the materials and approaches used for students to learn the content, (2) the process—the instructional activities or approaches used to help students to learn the curriculum, and (3) the products—the assessment vehicles through which the students demonstrate what they have learned.

4. Students differ (1) in their readiness to work with a particular idea or skill at a given time,

(2) in topics that they find interesting, and (3) in learning profiles that may be shaped by gender, culture, learning style, or intelligence preference.

5. An instructional strategy is a method for delivering instruction that is intended to help students to achieve the learning objective.

6. Your selection of an instructional strategy for a particular lesson is determined by the lesson's content, objectives, student needs and characteristics, and the learning context or environment.

7. There is a continuum of instructional strategies, ranging from teacher-centered, explicit approaches to student-centered, less explicit approaches.

8. Select the type of student grouping that is most appropriate for the instructional strategies and instructional objectives. Whole-group, small-group, and independent work are options to consider.

DISCUSSION/REFLECTIVE QUESTIONS

1. What challenges might teachers face when trying to differentiate the curriculum and the techniques of delivering the content?

2. What have your experiences been when teachers have tried to account for different student readiness (in content background or other factors)?

3. How might you systematically plan to use a variety of instructional strategies as you teach a unit?

4. How might the subject matter affect your selection of the instructional strategy to be used in a lesson? How might the age and maturity of the students affect this decision?

5. What is the rationale for using a variety of whole-group instruction, small-group instruction, and independent work in each unit that you teach?

SUGGESTED ACTIVITIES

For Clinical Settings

1. Examine a unit from a textbook that you might use and identify ways that you might differentiate elements of the curriculum.

2. Select one unit and make a list of ways that you could differentiate your instruction based on the students' varying learning styles.

3. Select one unit and identify ways that you would use cooperative learning groups, peer tutoring, and independent work at various points in the unit.

For Field Settings

1. Ask several teachers how they differentiate the curriculum or their techniques to deliver the curriculum.

2. Talk to several teachers to identify the types of instructional strategies that they use in the classroom. Determine why they selected these various strategies. Ask for recommendations for effective use of these strategies.

3. Ask several teachers how they use whole-group, small-group, and independent work. What recommendations do they offer for effective use of these approaches?

USEFUL RESOURCES

Gregory, G. H., & Chapman, C. (2002). *Differentiated instructional strategies: One size doesn't fit all.* Thousand Oaks, CA: Corwin Press.

> Offers a thorough, yet practical review of differentiation issues, including creating a climate for learning, knowing and assessing the learner, grouping, instructional strategies, and curricular approaches for differentiating classrooms.

Johnson, D. W., & Johnson, R. T. (1999). *Learning together and alone: Cooperative, competitive, and individualistic learning* (5th ed.). Boston: Allyn and Bacon.

> Thoroughly examines the goals and elements of cooperative, competitive, and individualistic approaches to learning. Well written and organized to facilitate application.

Tomlinson, C. A. (2001). *How to differentiate instruction in mixed-ability classrooms* (2nd ed.). Alexandria, VA: Association for Supervision and Curriculum Development.

> Discusses the concept of differentiating instruction and the justification for this approach. Explains ways to differentiate instruction through the curriculum, instructional strategies, and adjustments based on student characteristics.

WEB SITES

- Adapted and condensed from the 1999 ASCD book The Differentiated Classroom: Responding to the Needs of All Learners by Carol Ann Tomlinson.

  http://www.ascd.org/readingroom/cupdate/2000/1win.html

- Differentiating Curriculum for Gifted Students. ERIC Digest #E510.

  http://www.ed.gov/databases/ERIC_Digests/ed342175.html

- Differentiating Instruction for Advanced Learners in the Mixed-Ability Middle School Classroom

  http://www.kidsource.com/kidsource/content/diff_instruction.html

- Differentiated Curriculum: A Successful Experience. (From Learning Network, an international media company—Pearson plc).

  http://www.teachervision.com/lesson-plans/lesson-4627.html

- The Association for Supervision and Curriculum Development (ASCD) has a Web site on many educational topics, including differentiated instruction and curriculum. Use the Reading Room search feature to find materials on differentiated instruction and related topics.

  http://www.ascd.org/readingroom.html

- How to Differentiate Instruction in Mixed-Ability Classrooms

  http://www.ascd.org/readingroom/books/tomlin95book.html#chap1

- The Role of the Teacher in a Differentiated Classroom

  http://www.ascd.org/readingroom/books/tomlin95book.html#chap3

- Allentown Schools Web page (full text articles and ideas on lesson development)

  http://www.allentownsd.org/Differentiated Instruction.htm

CHAPTER SEVEN

DIRECT INSTRUCTIONAL STRATEGIES

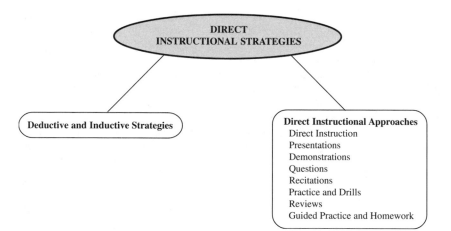

OBJECTIVES

This chapter provides information that will help you to:

1. Identify the characteristics of deductive and inductive teaching strategies.

2. Describe features of direct instruction.

3. Identify guidelines for the effective use of presentations, questions, and recitations.

4. Describe effective techniques when using practice, drills, reviews, guided practice, and homework.

**PRAXIS/Principles of Learning
and Teaching/Pathwise**

The following principles are relevant to content in
this chapter:

1. Becoming familiar with relevant aspects of students'
   background knowledge and experiences   (A1)

2. Demonstrating an understanding of the connections between the content that was learned previously, the current content, and the content that
   remains to be learned in the future   (A3)

3. Creating or selecting teaching methods, learning
   activities, and instructional materials or other resources that are appropriate for the students and
   that are aligned with the goals of the lesson   (A4)

4. Communicating challenging learning expectations to each student   (B3)

INTASC

The following INTASC standards are relevant to
content in this chapter:

1. The teacher understands the central concepts,
   tools of inquiry, and structures of the discipline(s)

that he or she teaches and can create learning experiences that make these aspects of subject
matter meaningful for students.   (Standard 1)

2. The teacher understands how children learn and
   develop and can provide learning opportunities
   that support their intellectual, social, and personal
   development.   (Standard 2)

3. The teacher understands how students differ in
   their approaches to learning and creates instructional opportunities that are adapted to diverse
   learners.   (Standard 3)

4. The teacher understands and uses a variety of instructional strategies to encourage students' development of critical thinking, problem solving,
   and performance skills.   (Standard 4)

5. The teacher plans instruction based on knowledge
   of subject matter, students, the community, and
   curriculum goals.   (Standard 7)

Now that you see the need for differentiating your instruction, you need to examine the
various specific instructional strategies. First, it is useful to consider the ways that deductive and inductive strategies can be used to aid in your instructional differentiation. Then
the chapter describes a number of direct, teacher-centered instructional approaches.

DEDUCTIVE AND INDUCTIVE STRATEGIES

Students learn in various ways, and you should vary your use of instructional strategies so
that you can relate to their learning styles and needs. One way to vary instruction is to use
deductive and inductive instructional strategies. Deductive strategies are more direct and
straightforward and lend themselves to direct instructional approaches, whereas inductive
strategies are intended to tap into the interests and thinking abilities of the students. Let's
look at some examples.

  Deductive strategies are instructional approaches that start with a known principle
and then attention moves to the unknown. *Inductive strategies* are instructional approaches
that start with an unknown principle and then attention moves to a known. The differences

in these strategies can be illustrated in the way that a teacher might teach the concept of a topic sentence.

A teacher using a deductive approach might give students the following definition of a topic sentence: "A topic sentence is usually the first sentence in a paragraph or composition. This sentence provides the reader with a sense of the writer's purpose. The rest of the paragraph contains specific details related to this purpose."

With this deductive approach, the teacher next might give students some examples of topic sentences and finish the lesson by having students write their own topic sentences. The teacher could then review these sentences and give feedback on the students' performance. The strengths of the deductive strategy are the directness and specific focus of the teaching strategy and the tight linkage between the teacher's examples and the task required of students. The lesson began with known principles (i.e., what is a topic sentence) and then led to examples of this principle. It was a fairly direct, straightforward way of addressing the lesson objective.

In contrast, a teacher using an inductive approach might give students sample paragraphs with the topic sentence underlined. With this strategy, the teacher would not tell students at the start that they are studying topic sentences, nor would the teacher provide a definition of a topic sentence. Instead, students would study the paragraphs and answer questions posed by the teacher. For example, the teacher might ask, "What do the underlined sentences in these paragraphs have in common?" And after receiving a series of answers, the teacher may ask a second question: "Can anyone provide a name for the underlined sentences?" From these two questions, many ideas might be generated.

The teacher would need to focus students' comments toward the concept of topic sentences, while also being aware that students may introduce other interesting concepts. By asking, "What do the sentences have in common?" the teacher anticipates that students will give the attributes or characteristics of topic sentences: (1) they are the first sentence in the paragraph, and (2) they seem to tell what the paragraph will be about. Thus, this inductive lesson used examples and questions that helped students to recognize the fundamental principle of topic sentences. This inductive approach is more indirect, but it can be very effective because students interact with the content to make meaning.

Sometimes you may want to have fairly direct presentation of the content and thus would use deductive teaching approaches. Other times, you may want to start out with examples and then lead to the main concept through the use of inductive approaches. This chapter discusses a variety of indirect instructional approaches, many of which lend themselves to inductive strategies. It also examines direct instructional approaches, those that are often teacher directed in a whole-class format. Deductive teaching strategies can be used effectively to promote student learning.

DIRECT INSTRUCTIONAL APPROACHES

As demonstrated in Chapter 6, there are many ways to differentiate your instruction. Table 6.3 displayed a continuum of instructional strategies going from direct, teacher-centered approaches at one end to indirect, student-centered approaches at the other end. This chapter examines many of the direct, teacher-centered approaches, including direct instruction, presentations, demonstrations, questions, and several other directed strategies.

Direct Instruction

Direct teaching strategies are instructional approaches in which the teacher structures lessons in a straightforward, sequential manner. The teacher is clearly in control of the content or skill to be learned and the pace and rhythm of the lesson. Generally, direct strategies allow the teacher to introduce new skills or concepts in a relatively short period of time. Direct instructional strategies are academically focused, with the teacher clearly stating the goals for the lesson to the students. The teacher closely monitors student understanding and provides feedback to students on their performance.

Direct instruction has four key components:

1. Clear determination and articulation of goals.
2. Teacher-directed instruction.
3. Careful monitoring of students' outcomes.
4. Consistent use of effective classroom organization and management methods.

Direct instruction is effective because it is based on behavioralistic learning principles, such as obtaining students' attention, reinforcing correct responses, providing corrective feedback, and practicing correct responses. It also tends to increase the academic learning time, or the amount of instructional time during which students are attending to the task and performing at a high success rate. Many studies have found that students learn basic skills more rapidly when they receive a greater portion of their instruction directly from the teacher.

Two well-known direct instruction approaches are examined in the next sections: (1) explicit teaching proposed by Barak Rosenshine, and (2) Instructional Theory Into Practice (ITIP) proposed by Madeline Hunter.

Explicit Teaching.   *Explicit teaching* calls for the teacher to gain student attention, reinforce correct responses, provide feedback to students on their progress, and increase the amount of time that students spend actively engaged in learning course content. Its objective

TEACHERS IN ACTION

USING DIRECT INSTRUCTION

Stacie Mitchell, fourth grade teacher, Davenport, Iowa

Direct instruction is an important method for delivering broad lessons to a large group of students. I often use direct instruction to model math problems to my whole class before giving them an assignment that they work on independently. I have found that fourth-graders are able to follow a lesson and ask appropriate questions, learning from each other during the discussion.

Some students have difficulty with whole-class direct instruction and then need additional, individual assistance to complete the assignments. I think that it is important to teach the students how to follow a whole-group lesson so that they can be introduced to the content. In this way, they should be better prepared to complete the assignments individually without the need for excessive assistance.

is to teach skills and help students to master a body of knowledge. Rosenshine (1987) believes this strategy to be most effective in the "teaching of mathematical procedures and computations, reading decoding, explicit reading procedures (such as distinguishing fact from opinion), science facts and concepts and rules, and foreign language vocabulary and grammar" (p. 75).

Ten general principles apply when developing an explicit teaching lesson (Rosenshine, 1987, p. 76):

1. Begin a lesson with a short statement of goals.
2. Begin a lesson with a short review of previous, prerequisite learning.
3. Present new material in small steps, with student practice after each step.
4. Give clear and detailed instructions and explanations.
5. Provide a high level of active practice for all students.
6. Ask many questions, check for student understanding, and obtain responses from all students.
7. Guide students during initial practice.
8. Provide systematic feedback and corrections.
9. Provide explicit instruction and practice for seatwork exercises and, when necessary, monitor students during seatwork.
10. Continue practice until students are independent and confident.

Based on studies of explicit teaching, Rosenshine (1987) identified six *teaching functions.*

1. *Daily review.* The purpose of daily review is to determine if the students have obtained the necessary prerequisite knowledge or skills for the lesson. Typically, an effective teacher will begin the lesson by reviewing previously covered material, correcting homework, or reviewing prior knowledge relevant to the day's lesson.

■ ■ ■ ■ ■

CLASSROOM DECISIONS

Let's say that you are teaching an art lesson concerning painting styles (e.g., impressionistic, modern). As part of your daily review, you want to know if the students can identify the names of the various styles, representative painters, and the characteristics of each style. What strategies might you use to conduct your daily review as a means to confirm that students know this material, which was covered during the previous three class sessions?

2. *Presenting new material.* Research indicates that effective teachers spend more time presenting new material and guiding practice than do less effective teachers (Good & Grouws, 1979; Evertson et al., 1980). To begin a lesson, effective teachers capture the students' attention by explaining the learning objectives to be covered during the lesson. In this way, students are able to better focus on the lesson's purpose without being distracted by extraneous material.

After the lesson's introduction, effective teachers continue by teaching one point at a time. Each point consists of a short presentation utilizing many examples. The examples provide concrete experiences or knowledge by which the students can process the new material. It is important that these presentations be clear and concise. The clarity of the presentation avoids any misunderstanding by the students. As the lesson progresses, effective teachers periodically assess student understanding of the material. They may assess the students by asking them questions or by having them summarize the main points of the lesson up to that point.

Based on his review of experimental and correlational research, Rosenshine (1987) lists the following suggestions for an effective presentation:

- Organize material so that one point can be mastered before the next point needs to be introduced.
- State lesson goals.
- Give step-by-step directions.
- Focus on one thought at a time, completing one point and checking for understanding before proceeding to the next.
- Model behaviors by going through the directions.

It is important to realize that presenting too much material to your students can often leave them confused. Thus, it is better to proceed in small steps, pausing periodically to assess student achievement.

3. *Conducting guided practice.* The purpose of guided practice is to supervise the students' initial practice of a skill and to provide the reinforcement necessary to progress new learning from short-term into long-term memory. Little research exists concerning the appropriate length of the presentation prior to the guided practice. But shorter segments of presentation appear to be more effective with less able students or with new material.

Students participate actively during guided practice by working problems or answering teacher questions. A number of studies indicate that teachers who are more effective in obtaining student achievement ask a large number of questions (Wilen, 1991). Effective teachers typically ask questions that require specific answers or that call for an explanation of how an answer was found.

The frequency of guided practice is an important variable in the success rate of students learning new material. Continually reinforcing new material helps students to retrieve the information from long-term memory. In addition to the frequency of guided practice, the percentage of correct student responses is also significant. Rosenshine (1987) reports that the most effective teachers appear to have a 75 to 80 percent success rate during guided practice, suggesting that effective teachers combine success and challenge.

4. *Provide feedback and correctives.* During guided practice, it is important to give process feedback to the students. Process feedback provides the student with an additional explanation that is sometimes needed when the student is correct but hesitant about how he or she arrived at the answer (Good & Grouws, 1979). For example, you might say, "Yes, the answer is correct…" and then proceed to explain the process for arriving at the correct answer.

When a student has made an error, it is inappropriate to simply provide the correct answer. This does not provide you with an opportunity to determine how the student made the incorrect response and robs the student of a learning opportunity. Rather, when a student has made an error, it is appropriate to simplify the question and to then probe for the correct answer. Often this is done by providing clues or reteaching the material. It is important that errors not go uncorrected.

5. *Conduct independent practice.* After conducting guided practice, it is important to have the student do independent practice. Independent practice provides the additional review and reinforcement necessary to become fluent in a particular skill. Independent practice differs from guided practice in that you do not provide the cues that you gave during guided practice. The independent practice should involve identical material as that covered during guided practice. It is appropriate for you to cover the material before the students take it home.

Researchers have discovered that students are more engaged during seatwork when teachers spend more time circulating around the room and supervising and monitoring their work (Fisher et al., 1978). They also reported that effective teachers provide sufficient and clear explanations prior to the independent practice.

6. *Weekly and monthly review.* Much of the previous discussion about the teaching functions has suggested frequent review and reinforcement of new material for the students. Good and Grouws (1979) recommend that teachers review the previous week's work every Monday and the previous month's work every fourth Monday.

The Hunter Model.   Instructional Theory into Practice (ITIP) is a method for planning and implementing instruction developed by Madeline Hunter (1976, 1981, 1984, 1994). ITIP is essentially a lesson design process that considers relevant factors in making instructional decisions. Furthermore, it is a teacher-directed approach to instruction.

According to Hunter, three categories are basic to lesson design. First, teachers decide what content to teach within the context of the grade level, student ability, and the lesson rationale. Next, teachers must decide what students will do to learn and to demonstrate that they have learned. Finally, teachers must decide which research-based teaching behaviors will most effectively promote learning.

Hunter is perhaps best known for her seven elements of a lesson (see Table 7.1, which is adapted from Hunter, 1984). To implement the three categories mentioned previously, Hunter maintains that the seven elements be used. Hunter asserts that these seven elements should be considered in planning a lesson and then included or excluded for a reason. Each lesson does not need every element, nor are they steps that necessarily are taken in sequence. When used as intended to select objectives and to plan instruction, ITIP is a useful tool. This is no surprise, since ITIP contains elements that educators have long associated with effective teaching and learning.

Hunter's ITIP has been widely adopted and adapted by many school districts. Unfortunately, problems arise when the model is used beyond its intended purpose. ITIP is intended to serve as a planning tool, but many districts inappropriately view the model as a solution to instructional problems if all teachers use the seven elements. Hunter has maintained that they are not steps, but they are sometimes used this way. Some districts even evaluate teachers on how well they demonstrate ITIP principles. The problem lies in using ITIP as a teaching checklist instead of a planning tool.

Presentations

A *presentation* is an informative talk that a more knowledgeable person makes to less knowledgeable persons. There may be little or no student participation by questioning or

TABLE 7.1   Hunter's Elements of Lesson Design

1. *Anticipatory Set*
   a. Focus the students' attention on content to be learned.
   b. Provide tie with prior learnings if appropriate.
   c. Develop readiness for learning.

2. *The Objective and Its Purpose:* Learners usually should know what they will be learning and why it is important to them.

3. *Instructional Input*
   a. Present material in achievable steps.
   b. Present varied and specific examples.

4. *Modeling*
   a. Visual or kinesthetic input accompanied by verbal input.
   b. Criteria for a correct performance are known.

5. *Monitoring to Check for Understanding*
   a. Sampling: Question whole group and take responses from individuals.
   b. Signaled responses.
   c. Private response: Written or whispered to teacher.

6. *Guided Practice:* The initial practice stage in which the response of the learner must be monitored by the teacher to make certain that it is accurate.

7. *Independent Practice:* The student can perform the task without major errors, discomfort, or confusion and with a minimum of teacher supervision.

Adapted with permission from the author. Hunter, M. (1984) Knowing, teaching, and supervising. In P. L. Hosford (ed.), *Using what we know about teaching* (pp. 169–192). Alexandria, VA: Association for Supervision and Curriculum Development. Reprinted with permission of the Association for Supervision and Curriculum Development. Copyright 1984 by the Association for Supervision and Curriculum Development. All rights reserved.

discussion. Presentations can be used to disseminate information in a short time, to explain difficult ideas, to stimulate student desire to learn, to present information in a certain way or adapt it to a particular group, or to introduce or explain learning tasks.

Presentations should not be used when objectives other than knowledge acquisition are sought; the information is complex, abstract, or detailed; learner participation is important; higher cognitive learning is sought; or students are below average in ability (Gage & Berliner, 1998). Presentations often do not actively engage students in learning, permit passive learning, and generally do not provide the teacher with opportunities to check student understanding.

You should thoroughly plan and prepare presentations, know the content like an expert, limit the length of the presentation to the tolerance levels of the particular age group, present in a way that is interesting to students, provide appropriate levels of structure and sequence, maintain flexibility, provide organizers, use the presentation in combination with other methods, use instructional media and materials, summarize the content, and provide follow-up activities.

Good and Brophy (1997) suggest that the attention span of students needs to be taken into consideration when preparing a presentation. Certainly, the age and maturity level of the students need to be taken into account. Few students can sustain their interest when a teacher talks for over 20 minutes. After presenting for a short time, you could add variety by asking a series of questions that would be the focus of large-group or small-group discussions. Then you could return to the presentation. It is useful to alternate class time with various presentation techniques that require active involvement by students. Some teachers minimize presentations and use more interactive discussion; they often teach by asking questions.

Based on a review of the research, Rosenshine and Stevens (1986) describe several useful aspects of clear presentations: (a) clearly state goals and main points, (b) provide step-by-step presentations, (c) use specific and concrete procedures, and (d) check for students' understanding. In addition, teaching behaviors such as clarity, enthusiasm, and smooth transitions are all necessary for the presentation if the students are to be motivated and learn the material. Some teachers like to provide students with a note-taking outline to help students to follow the lecture and fill in selected information.

Take these guidelines into account as you plan for and conduct presentations:

1. Present the lesson objectives to the students.
2. Use an advance organizer to introduce the topic and capture the students' interest.
3. Present the information in an organized, step-by-step manner.
4. Expect student interaction in the form of questions and comments.
5. Move from general to specific ideas and information.
6. Use a graphic organizer (see Figure 7.1) or other aides to promote learning.
7. Use good explanations and examples.
8. Encourage students to reflect on and apply what they have learned.
9. Check for student understanding.

Demonstrations

A demonstration is similar to a lecture in its direct communication of information from teacher to students. A *demonstration* involves a visual presentation to examine processes,

---

TEACHERS IN ACTION

STUDENT PRESENTATIONS WITH COMPUTERS

Tina Cross, high school science teacher, Columbus, Georgia

Students tend to be adept with technology, and they are eager to demonstrate their expertise. When we study the organelles of the cell, I assign one organelle to a small group of students. These students prepare five power point slides on each organelle. I create several small groups in a similar way.

To prepare their slides, the students use the textbook, print sources, and the Internet. Graphics are encouraged, and the final slide must feature questions on the material presented. The grading rubric provides the highest scores for incorporating music and animations.

Once the presentations from each small group are prepared, then presentations from all the student groups are merged into one complete presentation. In doing so, some students work on the timings, transformations, the end of the unit test, and other features. These features are then added to the merged presentation, and then it is burned into a compact disk. Each student receives a copy of the CD, and we make them available for other teachers to use in their classrooms.

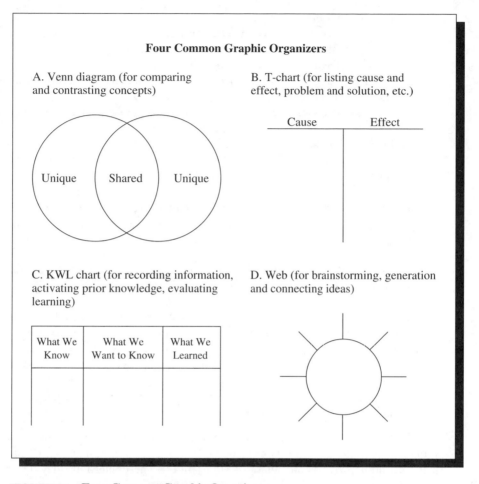

FIGURE 7.1   Four Common Graphic Organizers

information, and ideas. The demonstration allows students to see the teacher as an active learner and a model. It allows for students to observe real things and how they work. There may be pure demonstrations, demonstrations with commentary, or participative demonstrations with students. In many cases, a teacher demonstrates a certain action or activity prior to having the students perform the activity individually, such as the teacher locating certain points on a map before students are asked to do so. For many students, this teacher demonstration provides a model of the actions and establishes expectations.

Demonstrations can be used to illustrate points or procedures efficiently, stimulate interest in a particular topic, provide a model for teaching specific skills, and provide a change of pace. To carry out effective demonstrations, consider the following guidelines:

1. Carefully plan the demonstration.
2. Break down complex procedures into separate components that can be adequately demonstrated.

3. Practice the demonstration.
4. Develop an outline to guide the demonstration.
5. Make sure that everyone can see the demonstration.
6. Introduce the demonstration to focus attention.
7. Describe the procedure at the same time that you demonstrate it. Repeat as needed.
8. Ask and encourage questions.
9. Permit students to practice the procedure if they are expected to use the procedure.
10. Provide individual corrective feedback.
11. Plan a follow-up to the demonstration.

Questions

Questioning is a critical instructional tool, but there are many facets to successful questioning. Guidance about questioning falls into two categories: the kinds of questions and questioning techniques.

Kinds of Questions.   When using questions, consider the level of question, the use of convergent and divergent questions, and the type of question.

1. *Questions for the learning domains.* Most questions focus on the cognitive domain, as discussed in Chapter 3. Questions can be developed for each level of the cognitive domain (see Table 3.3): knowledge, comprehension, application, analysis, synthesis, and evaluation. The first three levels are considered to require low-level questions because they emphasize primarily the recall and moderate use of the information. The upper three levels of the cognitive domain require high-level questions that go beyond memory and partial recall; they deal with abstract and complex thinking.

2. *Divergent and convergent questions.* Two types of answers might be required from questions. *Convergent questions* tend to have one correct or best answer (What is the capital of Illinois? Who is the author of *Moby Dick*?). These questions may be phrased to require either low- or high-level thinking. *Divergent questions* are often open ended and usually have many appropriate but different answers (Why is it important that we continue to explore space? What would be a good title for this story?).

3. *Types of questions.* There are different types of questions for different purposes.

- *Focusing questions* are used to focus students' attention on the day's lesson or on material being discussed. They may be used to determine what students have learned, to motivate and arouse students, interest at the start of or during a lesson, or to check for understanding during or at the close of a lesson (Moore, 2001). You may need to prompt students when asking questions.
- *Prompting questions* include hints and clues to aid students in answering questions or to assist them in correcting an initial response. A prompting question is usually a rewording of the original question with clues or hints included.
- *Probing questions.* Sometimes, a student may not answer the question completely. In this case, you may stay with the same student by asking one or more probing questions that are intended to seek clarification and to guide students to more complete

---

TEACHERS IN ACTION

USING WAIT TIME WHEN QUESTIONING

Susan Bosco, fourth grade teacher, East Greenwich, Rhode Island

I made the decision to practice wait time during a social studies lesson. Wait time is the amount of time that a teacher waits between asking a question and calling on students. I realize that I have not always practiced enough wait time. Therefore, I asked some higher-order questions and waited a while before calling on students. Wondrous things happened!

In a review of a unit entitled "The Northeastern States," by my asking complex questions and waiting for responses, I had students talking to each other about the questions. Also, a greater number of students were willing to answer questions. By waiting for a longer time after asking my questions, students were able to think about the material more completely, and I had better answers and more involvement by students.

---

answers (What do you mean by that? Could you explain that more fully? What are your reasons for that?).

Questioning Techniques.   Once instruction begins, you need to use effective questioning techniques to get the desired results. You will need to consider a number of factors when selecting questions. Based on a research review, Wilen (1991) outlined fundamental questioning techniques (see Table 7.2). In addition, use the following questioning technique guidelines.

   1. *Use random selection when calling on students.* Calling on students in a prearranged format often leads to boredom and disruptive behavior for those who have already answered a question. Calling on students at random helps to keep them more attentive. Teachers tend to call on higher-achieving students rather than their lower-achieving peers. However, you should call on students at all achievement levels. In addition, it is important to create an environment that encourages success for everyone. You will want to ask the lower-achieving students questions that allow them to be successful.

   2. *Use variety and unpredictability in asking questions.* Students should know that they may be called on at any time, regardless of what has gone on before. You need to be cautious about using predictable patterns, such as calling only on students who raise their hands, always calling on someone in the first row first (or another particular area), taking questions in the same order as in the textbook, and not questioning a student again after he or she has answered one question.

   3. *Ask the question before calling on a particular student.* Asking the question before calling on someone allows all students more time to consider the question and a possible answer, creates greater interest, and increases attentive behavior. If one student is named before asking the question, others may not pay attention to what follows because they realize they will not have to perform.

   4. *Wait at least three to five seconds after asking the question before calling on a student.* After asking a question, the average teacher waits for less than one second before

TABLE 7.2   Questioning Techniques

1. *Plan key questions to provide lesson structure and direction.* Write questions into lesson plans, at least one for each objective, especially higher-level questions necessary to guide discussions. Ask spontaneous questions based on student responses.

2. *Phrase questions clearly and specifically.* Avoid vague or ambiguous questions such as "What did we learn yesterday?" or "What about the heroine of the story?" Ask single questions; avoid run-on questions that lead to student confusion and frustration. Clarity increases the probability of accurate responses.

3. *Adapt questions to student ability level.* This enhances understanding and reduces anxiety. For heterogeneous classes, phrase questions in natural, simple language, adjusting vocabulary and sentence structure to students' language and conceptual levels.

4. *Ask questions logically and sequentially.* Avoid random questions lacking clear focus and intent. Consider students' intellectual ability, prior understanding of content, topic, and lesson objective(s). Asking questions in a planned sequence will enhance student thinking and learning, particularly during discussions.

5. *Ask questions at a variety of levels.* Use knowledge-level questions to determine basic understandings and diagnose potential for higher-level thinking. Higher-level questions provide students opportunities to use knowledge and engage in critical and creative thinking.

6. *Follow up student responses.* Develop a response repertoire that encourages students to clarify initial responses, expand their responses, lift thought to higher levels, and support a point of view or opinion. For example, "How would you clarify that further?" "How can you defend your position?"

7. *Give students time to think when responding.* Increase wait time after asking a question to three to five seconds to increase the frequency and duration of student responses and to encourage higher-level thinking. Insisting on instantaneous responses, particularly during discussions, significantly decreases the probability of meaningful interaction with and among students.

8. *Use questions that encourage wide student participation.* Distribute questions to involve the majority of students in learning activities. For example, call on nonvolunteers, using discretion regarding the difficulty level of questions. Be alert for reticent students' verbal and nonverbal cues, such as perplexed looks or partially raised hands. Encourage student-to-student interaction. Use circular or semicircular seating to create an environment conducive to participation, particularly during discussions.

9. *Encourage student questions.* This promotes active participation. Student questions at higher cognitive levels stimulate higher levels of thought, essential for inquiry. Give students opportunities to formulate questions and carry out follow-up investigations of interest.

Source: Wilen, W. W. (1991). *Questioning skills, for teachers* (3rd ed.). Washington, DC: National Education Association. Pages 10–11. Reprinted with permission.

calling on a student or answering the question herself. This short amount of time may be fine when using a lower-order question that deals with recall. However, one second or even three seconds do not provide the student with enough time to reflect on a complex question and formulate an appropriate answer.

While five seconds does not seem like a long time, research indicates that many possible benefits can be gained from waiting that amount of time. Increasing your wait time to five seconds can result in an increase in the length of students' responses, the number of unsolicited but appropriate responses, children's confidence, the number of students' questions, lower-achieving students' contributions, students' proposals, the variety of students' responses, and also increased evidence to support answers (Tobin, 1987).

5. *Have students respond to classmates' answers.* It is important that all students attend to their classmates' responses to the teacher's questions. This can be accomplished by occasionally asking other students to comment on another's answer. After one student finishes giving reasons for the United States to maintain membership in the United Nations, for example, you might ask others if they agree with that answer or if they might elaborate on these reasons. This strategy not only results in increased attentiveness, but also encourages additional student–student interaction.

6. *Do not consistently repeat student answers.* Teachers do this for a variety of reasons, but most commonly it is done to make sure that all students hear the answer. Although the motive for this behavior is meant to be positive, it often results in students believing that they do not need to listen to their fellow students' answers and that the individual answering the question does not need to speak loudly.

7. *Ask questions that relate to students' own lives or similar situations.* Students will find learning more meaningful when it can be related to their own lives and interests. Useful questions might include "Have you ever felt this way?" "Do you believe it is right to…?" or "How would your parents feel about this?"

8. *Vary the type of questions being asked.* Questions might be convergent (leading to a single correct answer: "What is the capital of Florida?") or divergent (there may be a number of possible answers: "What are the consequences of sex role stereotyping in K–12 textbooks?"). In addition, questions should be asked at various levels of the cognitive domain.

TEACHERS IN ACTION

ENLIVEN CLASS DISCUSSIONS WITH STUDENT-GENERATED QUESTIONS

Lorene Reid, middle school language arts teacher, St. Louis, Missouri

The best thing I ever did to improve class discussions was to use a strategy called Reciprocal Questions. I first give my students time in class to read a chapter or two of a novel that we are reading together. After 20 minutes of reading, we start our discussion of the reading. But before I ask the students any questions, we begin the discussion by students asking *me* questions about what we had just silently read.

When I first started doing this, students asked nit-picky questions like "how many baseball cards did the main character collect?" I had to admit many times that I didn't know the answers to their "tricky" questions. Then they had to show me where the answer was located in the text. The students were delighted when they thought they tricked me, but the novelty of that wore off as time passed.

Soon their questions became more sophisticated as they tried to really understand the text. They became more involved in the discussions of the book and often couldn't wait to get a turn to ask me a question. Formulating these questions caused them to really focus on the text. This lead to rich discussions of the content and has helped to enliven class discussions.

Recitations

A *recitation* involves a teacher asking students a series of relatively short answer questions to determine if students remember or understand previously covered content. You might use recitations as a means to diagnose student progress. The typical interaction pattern is teacher question, student response, and teacher reaction. Questions often deal with who, what, where, and when. Recitation is highly structured, with the teacher clearly in control of directing the learning. In fact, Roby (1987) referred to recitation as a "quiz show," because students try to discover the right answers to topic-oriented teacher questions. It is important to direct questions to both volunteering and nonvolunteering students.

Teachers usually ask "known" information questions during recitations. Thus, you ask questions to find out if the student knows the answer, not to get information (Dillon, 1988). Recitation is frequently used in middle and secondary schools. It has flexible use because it can be tailored to the amount of time and the number of students. Gage and Berliner (1998) noted that the most common uses of recitation are in review, introduction of new material, checking answers, practice, and checking understanding of materials and ideas.

Practice and Drills

Practice involves going over material just learned. Practice is intended to consolidate, clarify, and emphasize what the student has already learned. Practice sessions are more meaningful when spread out over time (not just the day before a test), when conducted in context, when whole issues are examined rather than parts, and when used in different activities.

Drill involves repeating information on a particular topic until it is firmly established in the students' minds. It is used for learning that needs to be habitualized or to be retained a long time (e.g., the times tables). Many teachers find that drill works best at a certain point in the lesson, such as at the beginning of class.

Practice and drills involve repetition that is intended to help students to better understand and recall the information. They are useful in developing speed and accuracy in the recall of facts, generalizations, and concepts. They could be used, for example, when learning certain information, such as dates and events in history, chemical symbols, or translations in foreign language. Practice and drills help the long-term retention of facts.

Reviews

A *review* is an opportunity for students to look at a topic another time. A review differs from practice and drill in that it does not require drill techniques. It does involve reteaching and is intended to reinforce previously learned material and to sometimes give new meaning to the material. Reviews can be in the form of summaries at the end of a lesson or a unit, or at the end of a term; quiz games; outlines; discussions; questioning session; and other approaches.

Daily reviews at the start of a class help you to determine if your students have the necessary prerequisite knowledge or skills for the lesson. Weekly and monthly reviews help to check student understanding, ensure that the necessary prior skills are adequately learned, and also check on the teacher's pace (Rosenshine & Stevens, 1986).

CREATING A LEARNING COMMUNITY

PROVIDING NONTHREATENING PRACTICE AND REVIEWS

A learning community is a classroom designed to help all students to feel safe, respected, and valued in order to learn new skills. Anxiety, discomfort, and fear are incompatible with the learning process. Key characteristics of learning communities are security, open communication, mutual liking, shared goals or objectives, and connectedness and trust.

The very nature of practice and review sessions might make students feel pressured. If they are not performing well, they may be uneasy about disclosing answers in an open review or practice session. They may feel embarrassed if they give wrong answers.

1. What could you do when designing practice sessions in your classroom so that students would feel secure and part of the learning community?
2. How might you arrange for small-group practice and review sessions to create a supportive environment?

Guided Practice and Homework

Another teacher-directed instructional approach is the use of techniques through which the students use and practice the knowledge and skills being addressed in class. The use of guided practice in class and homework are the two most common techniques.

TEACHERS IN ACTION

USING A GAME FORMAT FOR REVIEW

Daniel Larsen, high school social studies and government teacher, Lincolnshire, Illinois

With games, reviewing an assignment or material for the next test doesn't need to be dull. Students like games, and I do, too. One of my favorite games is Chalk-Talk.

Chalk-Talk begins with one student and one piece of chalk. This student must respond to something I have written on the board, such as "The Legislative Branch." After writing a related concept or fact, the student gives the chalk to another student who has not had a turn. In a class of 30 students, this gets interesting after the first 15 or so. Through this approach, you get 30 review items on the board, and each student watches intently to know who has gone up and who has not.

What happens if the chalk is given to someone who already has gone up? This is where the fun begins. Usually, the penalty is that the student must make an animal noise or celebrity impersonation. Even with high school seniors, this is a riot.

After round 1, we play round 2 in which each student selects one item that has been put up on the board and talks about it. One by one, each of the 30 comments already on the board from the first round is explained, reviewed, and practiced. Again, students choose who is to go next, making sure that they select a person who has not already gone up in this new round. Games like Chalk-Talk have made my teaching more fun and effective.

Guided Practice.   Although teachers commonly use seatwork for guided practice, there are additional approaches such as teacher-led practice and student cooperative practice.

Seatwork.   *Seatwork* involves students working on in-class assignments, often independently. Students in grades 1 through 7 spend more time working alone on seatwork than on any other activity, approximately 50 to 75 percent of their time (Rosenshine & Stevens, 1986). Therefore, it is important to learn how to maintain student engagement during seatwork.

Successful independent practice requires both adequate preparation of the students and effective teacher management of the activity. In addition to the guidelines described previously for identifying and introducing assignments, the following suggestions from the research are ways to improve student engagement during seatwork (Rosenshine & Stevens, 1986).

1. Circulate around the classroom during seatwork, actively explaining, observing, asking questions, and giving feedback.
2. Have short contact with individual students (i.e., 30 seconds or less).
3. For difficult material in whole-class instruction, have a number of segments of instruction and seatwork during a single class period.
4. Arrange seats to facilitate monitoring the students (i.e., face both small-group and independently working students).
5. Establish a routine to use during seatwork activity that prescribes what students will do, how they will get help, and what they will do when they have completed the exercises. (p. 388)

CLASSROOM DECISIONS

You often plan time at the end of math class for students to work on problems independently while you monitor the students and provide assistance. What routines would you establish for students during this seatwork? How might you use peer tutoring as part of this seatwork time?

Teacher-led Practice.   *Teacher-led practice* is often in the form of repetition drills and question and answer sessions. Drill is the intensive repetition of content to ensure swift, accurate responses. It is intended to establish associations that are available without "thinking through" each time that the associations are needed. Drill is useful for skill learning and intellectual skills; it is not effective on complex principles and appreciations.

Student Cooperative Practice.   Another type of in-class supervised study is *student cooperative practice* in which students help each other during seatwork. In some cases, the students in the groups prepare a common product, such as an answer to a drill sheet, and in other situations the students study cooperatively to prepare for competition that takes place after the seatwork. Research using these procedures usually shows that students who do seatwork under these conditions achieve more than students who are in regular settings (Rosenshine & Stevens, 1986).

Homework.   *Homework* is study that students do when they are not under the direct supervision of their teachers, such as study at home, in the library, or in study hall. Homework does not include (a) in-school guided study, (b) home study courses delivered through the mail, television, or on audio- or videotape, or (c) extracurricular activities such as sports teams and clubs (Cooper, 1989, 2001).

There are four types of homework assignments: (1) practice, to help students to master specific skills and to reinforce material presented in class; (2) preparation, to prepare students for upcoming lessons; (3) extension, to go beyond the information obtained in the classroom and to transfer new skills and ideas to new situations; and (4) creative, to offer students the opportunity to think critically and engage in problem-solving activities. Many teachers assign only practice and preparation assignments, but extension and creative assignments can also be used. Homework should engage students in meaningful rather than repetitive experiences.

Use these guidelines as you make decisions about homework for your students.

1. *Recognize that homework serves different purposes at different grade levels.* For younger students, homework should be used to foster positive attitudes toward school and better academic-related behaviors and character traits, not to improve subject matter achievement measurably. As students grow older, the function of homework should change toward facilitating the acquisition of knowledge in specific topics.

2. *Have a mixture of mandatory and voluntary homework.* Some homework should be mandatory at each grade level. A mixture of mandatory and voluntary assignments may be most beneficial to students. Voluntary assignments are probably most helpful for producing intrinsic motivation.

3. *Use homework to address topics previously covered, those covered on the day of the assignment, and those yet to be covered.* In this way, students are reinforced for topics previously covered, address topics covered on the day of the assignment, and are familiarized with topics soon to be covered.

4. *Have homework focus on simple skills and material or on the integration of skills already possessed by the student.* Do not use homework to teach complex knowledge and skills. Also be sure that the assignments and directions are very clear since students will be working on the homework independently.

5. *Select an appropriate amount of homework for the grade level.* While much will depend on the individual community, teacher, and student, general guidelines can be offered. After reviewing research on homework, Cooper (2001) made recommendations for the frequency and duration of assignments. Grades 1 to 3 may have one to three mandatory assignments each week, each lasting no more than 15 minutes. Each week, grades 4 to 6 may have two to four mandatory assignments; grades 7 to 9, three to five; and grades 10 to 12, four to five. At all grade levels, additional voluntary assignments may be presented at the discretion of the teacher.

It is important to note that these time recommendations represent the total of all assignments from all subject areas at a given grade level. For example, each teacher of a ninth grade subject should not assign three to five homework assignments of 45 to 75 minutes each week; instead, all the subject areas combined can come up to this time recommendation.

6. *Select a process for providing feedback and grading homework.* Different strategies for providing feedback differ little in their influence. Cooper (2001) suggested that the practice of grading homework be kept to a minimum, especially if the purpose of homework is to foster positive attitudes toward the subject matter (as in the lower grades). He proposed that the purpose of homework should be to diagnose individual learning problems and provide feedback, rather than to test students. You should collect homework, check it for completeness, and give intermittent instructional feedback.

7. *Do not use homework as punishment.* Using homework as punishment conveys an inappropriate message about the value of academic work. If a student misbehaves and punishment is needed, nonacademic consequences should be selected.

8. *Clearly communicate your homework policy to students.* Students need to know the procedures and policy for homework. The importance of doing homework must be carefully explained. Students' motivation for doing homework is enhanced when they recognize the value of it and its place in the academic program.

9. *Show students ways to overcome distractions.* The most prominent disturbances for students studying and doing homework at home are the phone, television, family members, and the radio. You can provide guidance for ways to minimize, overcome, or respond to these distractions. These include selecting a quiet study place and using a regular study time. Some schools provide a study room that students can use after school to do their homework; sometimes students prefer this when they do not have a quiet place to study at home.

10. *Teach homework skills to students.* Students can improve homework skills by establishing appropriate places and times for studying, previewing the material, focusing attention, reading carefully and thinking about the concepts covered, casting what is learned in different forms, self-testing, and taking notes effectively.

KEY TERMS

Convergent questions
Deductive strategies
Demonstration
Direct teaching strategies
Divergent questions
Drill
Explicit teaching

Focusing questions
Homework
Inductive strategies
Practice
Presentation
Probing questions
Prompting questions

Recitation
Review
Seatwork
Student cooperative practice
Teacher-led practice

MAJOR CONCEPTS

1. Deductive strategies are instructional approaches that start with a known principle and then attention moves to the unknown. Inductive strategies are instructional approaches that start with an unknown principle and then attention moves to a known.

2. Direct teaching strategies are instructional approaches in which the teacher structures lessons in a straightforward, sequential manner.

3. There are a number of direct, teacher-centered instructional strategies. These include presentations, demonstrations, questions, recitations, practice and drills, reviews, guided practice, and homework.

DISCUSSION/REFLECTIVE QUESTIONS

1. What are the merits and possible disadvantages of using direct, teacher-centered instructional strategies such as lectures, demonstrations, practice, and reviews?

2. What type of instructional approaches did you prefer as a student? Why?

3. Why might some teachers prefer a direct approach to instruction? Why might some teachers prefer other approaches that are more student centered?

4. What skills does a teacher need to effectively conduct a whole-class discussion?

SUGGESTED ACTIVITIES

For Clinical Settings

1. Select a unit topic and prepare a two-week unit plan that includes several types of direct, teacher-centered strategies throughout the unit.

2. Prepare a description of how you will use seatwork as part of your instructional approach. What types of tasks will you include in seatwork? How often will you require it? Will every item be assessed, and how? What weight will homework carry in the report card grade?

For Field Settings

1. Talk to several teachers to explore how they make presentations. Ask them to offer you guidelines for planning and delivering effective presentations.

2. Talk to several teachers to explore how they use questions during instruction. Ask them for recommendations for the effective use of questions.

USEFUL RESOURCES

Chuska, K. R. (1995). *Improving classroom questions: A teacher's guide to increasing student motivation, participation, and higher-level thinking.* Bloomington, IN: Phi Delta Kappa.

Provides concise, practical guidance for asking better questions, using questions as motivators, designing questions, and using specific questioning strategies.

Cooper, H. M. (2001). *The battle over homework: Common ground for administrators, teachers, and parents* (2nd ed.). Thousand Oaks, CA: Corwin Press.

Provides useful guidance about the purposes and types of homework assignments. Research evidence is reviewed.

Harmin, M. (1994). *Inspiring active learning: A handbook for teachers.* Alexandria, VA: Association for Supervision and Curriculum Development.

Provides very practical suggestions and guidance about selecting and using instructional strategies, organizing the classroom, handling homework and testing, and producing meaningful learning.

Marzano, R. J., Pickering, D. J., & Pollock, J. E. (2001). *Classroom instruction that works: Research-based strategies for increasing student achievement.* Alexandria, VA: Association for Supervision and Curriculum Development.

Identifies instructional strategies that have research support for being successful in promoting student learning. Strategies are reviewed in ten chapters and three additional chapters discuss specific applications.

WEB SITES

- Saskatchewan Education provides leadership in the development and operation of education from kindergarten to grade 12 in the Saskatchewan Province, Canada. This site contains the Evergreen Curriculum, including curriculum guides, bibliographies, foundation documents, World Wide Web resources, and discussion areas. The first site has general information; the second site has good specific information for both direct and indirect instructional strategies.

  http://www.sasked.gov.sk.ca/

  http://www.sasked.gov.sk.ca/docs/physed/physed2030/instruction.html

- Designed for new teachers and education students, this site contains information on lesson planning, teaching methods, home schooling, instructional grouping, teaching and values, classroom management, assertive discipline, study skills, thinking skills, job searching, education reform, discussions, contrary opinions, and a whole lot more. The first address has general information; the second address has information and links about direct instruction.

  http://www.adprima.com/

  http://www.adprima.com/direct.htm

- The National Science Teachers Association provides standards-based units and lessons.

  http://dev.nsta.org/ssc/

CHAPTER EIGHT

INDIRECT INSTRUCTIONAL STRATEGIES

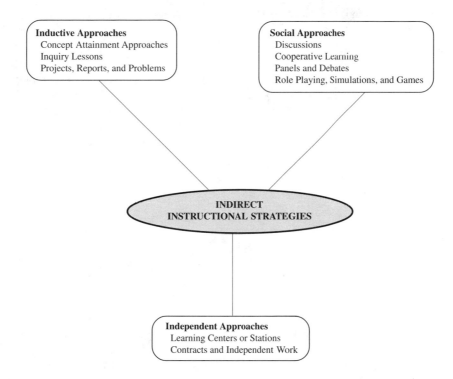

Inductive Approaches
   Concept Attainment Approaches
   Inquiry Lessons
   Projects, Reports, and Problems

Social Approaches
   Discussions
   Cooperative Learning
   Panels and Debates
   Role Playing, Simulations, and Games

INDIRECT INSTRUCTIONAL STRATEGIES

Independent Approaches
   Learning Centers or Stations
   Contracts and Independent Work

O B J E C T I V E S

This chapter provides information that will help you to:

1. Design lessons which involve inductive instructional approaches such as concept attainment, inquiry lessons, and projects and reports.

2. Design lessons during which students work cooperatively in groups.

3. Identify ways to effectively use discussions, panels, debates, and other social instructional approaches.

4. Determine ways to have students learn through independent means with learning centers, contracts, or other approaches.

■ ■ ■ ■ ■

**PRAXIS/Principles of Learning
and Teaching/Pathwise**

The following principles are relevant to content in this chapter:

1. Becoming familiar with relevant aspects of students' background knowledge and experiences   (A1)

2. Demonstrating an understanding of the connections between the content that was learned previously, the current content, and the content that remains to be learned in the future   (A3)

3. Creating or selecting teaching methods, learning activities, and instructional materials or other resources that are appropriate for the students and that are aligned with the goals of the lesson   (A4)

4. Communicating challenging learning expectations to each student   (B3)

INTASC

The following INTASC standards are relevant to content in this chapter:

1. The teacher understands the central concepts, tools of inquiry, and structures of the discipline(s) that he or she teaches and can create learning experiences that make these aspects of subject matter meaningful for students.   (Standard 1)

2. The teacher understands how children learn and develop and can provide learning opportunities that support their intellectual, social, and personal development.   (Standard 2)

3. The teacher understands how students differ in their approaches to learning and creates instructional opportunities that are adapted to diverse learners.   (Standard 3)

4. The teacher understands and uses a variety of instructional strategies to encourage students' development of critical thinking, problem solving, and performance skills.   (Standard 4)

5. The teacher plans instruction based on knowledge of subject matter, students, the community, and curriculum goals.   (Standard 7)

As you consider your students' abilities, interests, and needs, you will want to differentiate your instruction. One way to differentiate is by your selection of instructional approaches. As was discussed in Chapter 6, there is a continuum of instructional approaches to use. At times, you may want to use some of the more direct, teacher-centered instructional approaches discussed in Chapter 7. At other times, you will want to use some strategies that are less direct and more student-centered. A number of these indirect instructional strategies are discussed in this chapter, including inductive approaches, social approaches, and independent approaches.

INDUCTIVE APPROACHES

Inductive instructional approaches often begin with exploratory activities and then lead to students discovering a concept or generalization. There are various ways to use inductive approaches; some have a higher degree of teacher-directed activity and others have students more actively involved in planning and designing their instructional activities. Some of the more common inductive instructional approaches are concept attainment strategies; inquiry lessons; and projects, reports, and problems.

Concept Attainment Approaches

Concepts serve as the building blocks for student higher-level thinking. In general, concepts are main ideas used to help us to categorize and differentiate information. Therefore, when you ask students to place things together or to classify them, you are asking students to use concepts. Robert Gagné (1985) believes being able to label or classify things demonstrates an understanding of concepts and that combinations of concepts can be joined together into rules. He takes this a step further to say that the understanding of concepts and rules is what allows students to problem solve.

Concepts are central to the curriculum in every classroom. Table 8.1 lists a number of common concepts that students are asked to understand in various content areas. As demonstrated in the table, concepts can be simple, such as *verb,* or difficult, such as *evolution.* Many strategies designed to help students to understand concepts call for students to identify similarities and differences. This can be accomplished through a number of research-based methods.

Concept attainment is an instructional strategy in which students are provided both examples and nonexamples of a concept. For instance, you might list a series of words containing some examples of, or attributes of, the concept that you want students to recognize. Table 8.2 shows a list of words, and each word is followed by a yes or a no. The yes answers form the concept under study. Can you guess the concept?

Based on the work of Bruner (1966), Joyce, Weil, and Calhoun (2000) suggest that the following process be used for indirect concept learning:

1. You prepare labeled examples.
2. Students compare attributes of positive and negative examples.
3. Students put forward possible concepts.

TABLE 8.1   Typical Curricular Concepts

LANGUAGE ARTS	SCIENCE	SOCIAL STUDIES	MATHEMATICS
Summarize	Technology	Cities	Congruent
Metaphor	Density	Democracy	Factions
Perspective	Energy	NATO	Patterns
Verb	Motion	Terrorism	Equations
Audience	Evolution	Representative	Estimate
Context	Ecosystems	Manifest destiny	Predict
Theme	Diversity	Power	Triangle
Grammar	Genes	Distribution of wealth	Area
Essay	Cells	Culture	Volume
Point of view	Climate	Citizenship	Relationship

TABLE 8.2   Concept Lesson

Elections	Yes	Volume	No
Snowstorms	No	Closure	No
Right to vote	Yes	Majority decision making	Yes
Osmosis	No		
Participation	Yes	Freedom	Yes

4. Students provide a definition based on the essential attributes of the concept. From the attributes listed in Table 8.2, for example, students might define a democracy as follows: "A country with a government that has been elected freely and equally by all its citizens."
5. Add examples, and call on students to indicate a yes or no descriptor for each label.
6. You confirm student hypotheses, name the concept, and have students come up with a common definition.
7. Students generate examples.
8. Students describe their thought processes and discuss the role of hypotheses and attributes.

A variation of this approach would involve you providing students with a list of examples of countries that practice democracy in the first column and countries that do not in the second column. Since we are discussing indirect models in this chapter, concept-based lessons can take either a direct or indirect form. In using the indirect form, you would not label the columns as democratic or totalitarian countries, but rather you let students reflect on what similarities the words share and have the students respond with concepts that they feel join the examples together.

Concept learning activities can also take a number of other forms. Some of the most productive concept attainment approaches are based on a rich line of research (Marzano, Pickering, & Pollock, 2001) in four key areas: comparisons, classifications, metaphors, and analogies.

Comparisons.   *Comparing* is identifying similarities and differences. The comparison of important characteristics can be used to outline similarities and differences. This can be accomplished by the use of graphic organizers such as *Venn diagrams* or comparison charts. Figure 8.1 represents a concept using a Venn diagram.

Similarities are listed in the intersection between the two circles. Differences are listed in area of the circles that do not intersect. A second method that can be used to represent similarities and differences is a simple matrix. For example, you could have students who are investigating various expeditions throughout history fill out a matrix for the concept of *exploration.* A basic start would be for them to fill in a matrix that compares various explorers based on key concepts, such as personal information, goal for exploration, resources, and accomplishments. Table 8.3 represents a matrix for comparing Neil Armstrong, the first man to walk on the moon, and Richard Byrd, polar explorer. A matrix allows you to design lessons so that your students respond to set categories of information.

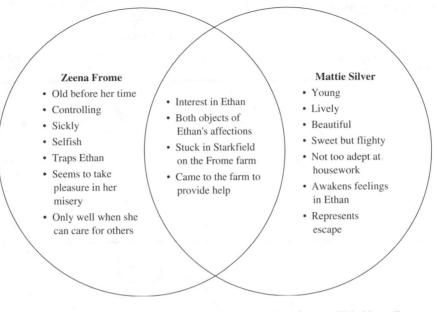

Zeena Frome
- Old before her time
- Controlling
- Sickly
- Selfish
- Traps Ethan
- Seems to take pleasure in her misery
- Only well when she can care for others

- Interest in Ethan
- Both objects of Ethan's affections
- Stuck in Starkfield on the Frome farm
- Came to the farm to provide help

Mattie Silver
- Young
- Lively
- Beautiful
- Sweet but flighty
- Not too adept at housework
- Awakens feelings in Ethan
- Represents escape

FIGURE 8.1   Venn Diagram Comparing Characters in a Story   This Venn diagram compares Zeena and Mattie who are characters in Edith Warton's *Ethan Frome.*

Classifications.   *Classifying* is the grouping of ideas or concepts into categories or groups based on similar characteristics. A useful method for showing the organizational structure of major concepts is by creating concept webs or maps. The Iroquois League of Nations before 1492, for example, could be organized into a web to illustrate the key concepts that represent these native peoples' way of life. A web representing the economy, housing, and social structures of the Iroquois League of Nations is shown in Figure 8.2.

Through organized representation, students can link concepts they already know to new concepts being considered. Students can either be given a web to work with, or they can be asked to produce their own.

Metaphors.   A *metaphor* is a figure of speech, often used in poetry, to make an implicit comparison or connection between two unlike things (e.g., he was a rock through all this; she is a pillar in the community; I have a song in my heart). The two seemingly unrelated things, however, upon examination, share a relationship on an abstract level (e.g., a rock is literally solid and hard to break; on an abstract level, someone is strong and resilient in a difficult situation; and, therefore, on a literal level, some people appear to remain unmoved and stay tough during hard times).

Beyond their role as a figure of speech, metaphors can be used as instructional strategies to help your students to understand abstract patterns and convey the meaning of complex concepts or ideas in simpler terms. To help students learn to identify abstract patterns after reading a novel or a short story, you could guide students through the process of identifying

TABLE 8.3   Comparison Matrix Exploration

COMPARISON (similarities and differences)	CONCEPT TO COMPARE: EXPLORERS		CHARACTERISTICS FOR COMPARISON
	Neil Armstrong	*Richard Byrd*	
Similarities			Personal information
Differences			
Similarities			Goals for exploration
Differences			
Similarities			Resources
Differences			
Similarities			Accomplishment
Differences			

Sample technology resources for student investigation
- Web site for Astronaut Hall of Fame includes biography of Neil Armstrong http://www.astronauts.org/
- This site is dedicated to the stamps, postal history, and heroic explorers of the Polar Regions. Noteworthy data, not limited strictly to philately, but also useful reference material for students researching the history of exploration in the polar latitudes. http://www.south-pole.com/p0000107.htm

Other explorers:
- LITTLE EXPLORERS   A Picture Dictionary. with Links from EnchantedLearning.com. Specific address is for biography of Louise Arner Boyd (1887–1972), known as the "ice woman," she was an American who repeatedly explored and photographed the Arctic Ocean; she was also the first woman to fly over the North Pole. http://www.enchantedlearning.com/explorers/page/b/boyd.shtml
- Web site for *National Geographic* includes story of *Geographic* photographer Barry C. Bishop, one of the first Americans to climb Mount Everest in May 1963. http://www.nationalgeographic.com/explore/classic/

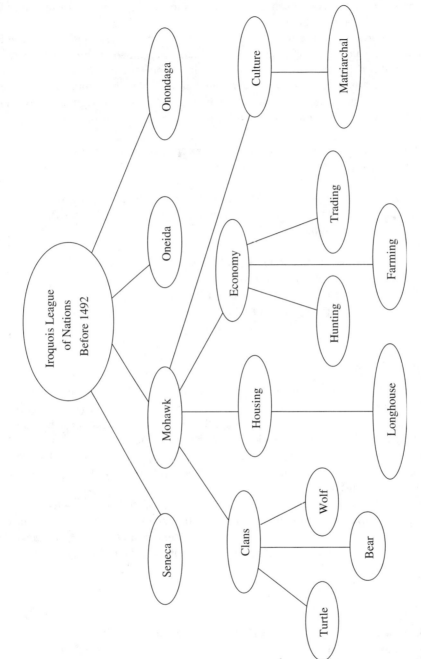

FIGURE 8.2 Concept Web for the Iroquois League of Nations

character traits. You could then ask the students to identify characters from other literature that you have read who also fit this pattern.

Another way to use metaphors in the classroom is to ask students to take the topic that you are studying, talk about it in literal terms, and then create a metaphor, or an abstract method of discussing it. For example, in science you could ask students to create a metaphor for the role that arteries and veins play in the circulatory system. The student could use streets and highways to explain how blood moves through the body. In geology, students could say that Earth's crust is a cake to explain the various layers in its crust.

Analogies. *Analogies* are comparisons between two similar things and are often used to explain something or to make it easier to understand. Analogies are often represented by asking students to identify pairs of concepts. When students can fill in the appropriate word, they demonstrate comprehension of the concept that they are studying. Analogies are represented in the following relationship: A is related to B in the same way that C is related to D. For example:

Bush is to the United States as Putin is to	(Russia)
Galaxy is to Star as Beach is to	(Sand)
Deciduous is to Maple as Evergreen is to	(Pine)
Blood is to Vein as Water is to	(Pipe)
Shakespeare is to Hamlet as J. K. Rowling is to	(Harry Potter)

Inquiry Lessons

Inquiry, discovery, and problem-solving approaches allow students to become involved in the process of discovery by enabling them to collect data and test hypotheses. As such, these approaches are inductive in nature. Teachers guide students as they discover new meanings, practice the skills, and undergo the experiences that will shape their learning. Generally, inquiry, discovery, and problem-solving approaches are student centered and less explicit than direct-teaching approaches. Several common inquiry and discovery approaches are considered here.

Inquiry is an open-ended and creative way of seeking knowledge. One of the strengths of this approach is that both the lesson content and the process of investigation are taught at the same time. The steps of inquiry essentially follow John Dewey's (1910) model of reflective thinking. The common steps include the following:

1. Identify and clarify a problem
2. Form hypotheses
3. Collect data
4. Analyze and interpret the data to test the hypotheses
5. Draw conclusions

Dewey, along with Jean Piaget and Lev Vygotsky, were instrumental in developing a major concept central to understanding the power of inquiry learning. This concept is referred to as constructivism. Through his studies of how children think and develop, Piaget

TEACHERS IN ACTION

STUDENTS AS ACTIVE PARTICIPANTS IN INQUIRY

Leo Harrison, middle school mathematics teacher, Louisville, Kentucky

Teacher-oriented, passive-student approaches to instruction are outdated. Especially in the middle school, we cannot effectively conduct our classes as if students were sponges who sit passively and absorb attentively. I base my approaches on the philosophy that the teacher is a coach of students. Thus, I view the student as having an active role in learning, and I serve as a guide in the pursuit of knowledge. This approach to instruction makes all gained knowledge more valuable, well learned, and better retained.

For students to care, the knowledge must be provocative, valuable, and reality based. Therefore, instruction should have much problem solving, research, and cooperative investigations. This doesn't mean that we eliminate standard lectures or guided practice. In fact, guided practice becomes essential to reinforce learning of useful knowledge. Overall, I have included a variety of instructional approaches in my teaching to help students to learn things that are important to them.

confirmed that children strive to construct understandings of the world in which they live. Vygotsky held that individuals develop intellectually when they confront new and puzzling events that they try to understand by linking this new knowledge to knowledge that they already possess in an effort to create new meanings.

Therefore, a *constructivist approach* involves students constructing meaning out of information that they have been exposed to through active engagement and investigation (Doyle, 1990). Constructivism promotes (a) the student point of view, (b) teacher–student interaction, (c) questioning to promote student thought, and (d) the importance of nurturing student reflection and thought, rather than a primary focus on a single correct answer or product.

A constructivist approach provides students with the opportunity to investigate concepts and assists students in understanding new information by providing an environment of student-based discussion and investigation. You should ensure that your students are challenged by the instructional activities and stimulated by their own questions and the questions that you also might offer. Encourage your students to actively seek understanding and knowledge and to use prior knowledge to help them to understand new material.

Using the process of inquiry also provides opportunities for students to learn and practice skills associated with critical thinking and problem solving. Educators have strongly supported the need to develop higher-order thinking skills. Beyer (1987) proposed a series of critical thinking skills and several practical approaches to teaching these skills sequentially within a K–12 curriculum. The skills include the following:

1. Distinguishing between verifiable faith and value claims
2. Determining the reliability of a claim or source
3. Determining the accuracy of a source
4. Distinguishing between warranted and unwarranted claims

5. Distinguishing between relevant and irrelevant information, claims, or reasons
6. Detecting bias
7. Identifying stated and unstated assumptions
8. Identifying ambiguous or equivocal claims or arguments
9. Recognizing logical inconsistencies in a line of reasoning
10. Determining the strength of an argument

Several approaches to inquiry may be used. *Guided inquiry* involves the teacher providing the data and then questioning the students in order to help them inductively to arrive at an answer, conclusion, generalization, or solution. *Unguided or open-ended inquiry* has the students take more responsibility for examining the data, objects, or events; these investigations are commonly done individually. Guided and unguided inquiry approaches may involve discussion and question sessions, guided or controlled discussions, projects, and research projects.

An inquiry problem-solving lesson typically consists of the following five components:

1. *Students are presented with a problem* that is socially important and personally meaningful to them. The problem should be authentic, one that stimulates and motivates the students by having them seek solutions to meaningful problems that exist in the world. Problems often have an interdisciplinary focus that encourages students to investigate and apply many subjects—science, math, economics, government. A cooperative learning approach, in which students work in pairs or small groups, is often used in an inquiry problem-solving lesson.

2. *Students describe what is creating the problem* or the barriers barring its solution.

3. *Students identify solutions* for overcoming constraints and hypothesize which solution is likely to work. Students should feel free to brainstorm regarding the hypotheses. At this point, there is no right answer, so no hypotheses should be rejected. All hypotheses should be recorded either within individual student groups or as a whole class on the board.

4. *Students gather data to solve the problem and try solutions.* During this stage the students, not the teacher, should do the thinking.

5. *Students analyze the data* and compare the results to the earlier generated hypotheses and decide if they want to test another solution or hypothesis. Students construct exhibits or reports that represent their solutions. These could take many forms, from an experiment in science to a mock debate in social studies (Arends, 2000; Marzano, Pickering, & Pollock, 2001).

Jerome Bruner (1966) maintained that *discovery learning* and *problem solving* are approaches to instruction in which the teacher can create situations where students can learn on their own. Bruner suggests that students learn through their own active involvement with concepts and principles and that they should be encouraged to have experiences and conduct experiments that permit them to discover principles for themselves. Discovery learning has applications in science and related fields.

Discovery learning has several important advantages. First, it arouses students' curiosity and motivates them to continue to work until they find answers. Second, it can teach independent problem-solving skills and may force students to analyze and manipulate information, rather than simply absorb it.

CLASSROOM DECISIONS

In your science class, you want the students to participate in a discovery learning activity concerning the characteristics of various rocks and minerals. You have not had your students do an activity like this before. What preparations would you need to make to ensure the success of this activity? How might your preparations be different if you were to have the students work independently as compared to working in small groups? How might you include the students in your preparations?

Problem solving involves the application of knowledge and skills to achieve certain goals. There are several components for problem-solving skills (Slavin, 2000). First, means–ends analysis is a problem-solving technique that encourages identifying the goals (the ends) of a problem, the current situation, and what needs to be done (the means) to reduce the difference between the two conditions. Second, creative problem solving involves cases for which the answers are not very clear or straightforward. Based on a review of research, Frederiksen (1984) proposed six ways to teach through problem solving: allow time for incubation, suspend judgment, establish appropriate climates, analyze and juxtapose elements, teach the underlying cognitive abilities, and provide practice with feedback.

Projects, Reports, and Problems

Project-based lessons flow naturally in a problem-solving environment. Students often work cither independently or cooperatively on projects related to the objectives of the unit being covered. A *project* is an activity that involves investigation about the facts of a particular issue and the reporting of these facts in various ways. Projects may include research reports, surveys, or case studies that have a particular purpose or objective. Problem-based instruction is essentially a project-based approach. Projects provide students with the opportunity to work somewhat independently from the teacher, have positive academic experiences with their peers, develop independent learning skills, become especially knowledgeable in one area of the subject matter, and develop skill in reporting this knowledge.

The degree of teacher direction can vary with projects. For a given unit, you may ask all students to prepare a report on one particular topic, or you may give a choice of several topics. You may ask students to work independently or in small groups, or you could let each student select the grouping that he or she would prefer. It is often helpful to provide written guidelines and time lines for the outlines, drafts, and completed projects. Criteria for evaluation of the project should be clearly stated.

After receiving initial guidelines, students would decide on the tasks to be done, such as conducting library research or interviewing, and then collecting the information in a cohesive way to report their findings and conclusions that they have drawn. Provide sufficient class time over a number of days to enable students to plan their actions, gather the information, and organize and prepare their report. After providing the initial project guidelines, your role will be to assist, advise, and facilitate student learning.

Creative ways of reporting the findings can generate student interest in this activity. For example, depending on the subject matter, students may want to create a display of their results (pictures, maps, charts, posters, models, exhibits), act out some of their findings (role playing, skits, plays), create a computer-generated report, have a panel discussion of the results (debates, town meeting, panel), prepare written materials (newspapers, duplicated materials, notebooks), or report in a number of unique ways.

SOCIAL APPROACHES

Another indirect, student-oriented approach to instruction involves *social instructional approaches,* which permit students to interact with each other in various ways to help each others' learning. Some common social approaches include discussions, cooperative learning, panels and debates, and role playing, simulations, and games.

Discussions

A group discussion is a powerful indirect instructional strategy since students learn and remember when they participate. No matter what the format of the discussion—whole group, small group, or other opportunities for interaction—students have the opportunity to think out loud about concepts, giving them practice that they can then apply to other

MODIFICATIONS FOR DIVERSE CLASSROOMS

MEETING DIVERSE INTERESTS WITH INTERNET RESOURCES

The Internet is an excellent source of information for you and your students. When projects or assignments permit student selection of the topics, the Internet can be an important way to meet diverse student needs and interests.

Information that in the past was difficult to find or impossible to access is now a few key strokes away using a Web browser. For example, you can assign a project in which students are asked to compare and contrast the inauguration speeches of George W. Bush and Vladimir V. Putin. Information of this type is easily available using search engines such as:

Google: http://www.google.com,
Yahoo: http://www.yahoo.com/,
Lycos: http://www.lycos.com/

Using the same example, the next two Web sites provide the type of information available to students as a result of a search on the Web:

Inauguration speech of president of the Russian Federation—Vladimir V. Putin. http://www.russianembassy.org/RUSSIA/President.HTM

Inauguration speech of President of the United States—George W. Bush http://www.whitehouse.gov/news/inaugural-address.html

concepts. As instructional strategies go, discussions are generally less explicit and less teacher centered than other strategies. The class setting may range from informal to formal, with the teacher having a dominant to nondominant role.

Whole-Class Discussions.   A *discussion* is a conversation among several people having a particular purpose or objective. A *whole-class discussion* involves all students in the class discussing a topic with guidance from the teacher. When conducting a whole-class discussion, you must be able to clearly focus the discussion, keep it on track by refocusing, and encourage all participants to listen carefully to all points of view. Teachers often direct whole-class discussions. Whole-class discussions may go astray when the class drifts from the main objectives of the discussion. Thus, prior to the discussion, it is important to plan key questions to be used so that the discussion is more likely to remain focused on the objectives.

Before beginning a whole-class discussion, make sure that students have an adequate knowledge base about the subject. A discussion cannot take place if students do not know much about the topic. Sometimes a discussion can be used before instruction as a means to generate interest, but the information must still be presented to students at some point.

If used properly, discussions can stimulate critical thinking and encourage average and less able students to engage in the learning process. If used incorrectly, discussions may result in individual students responding to teacher-directed, lower-order questions or

---

TEACHERS IN ACTION

STIMULATING CLASSROOM DISCUSSIONS

Hildie Brooks, seventh and eighth grade health teacher, Manhattan, Kansas

Stimulating a discussion in the classroom is often a challenge for most teachers. The challenge is to include all the students. Many times the same 5 or 6 students enter a discussion and the other 15 to 20 students start to daydream. I have a terrific strategy that encourages all the students to participate in some manner. The form of the discussion is called the *Discussion Continuum,* which is intended to allow students to identify their own opinion by literally standing up for their opinion on the imaginary continuum line from one side of the room to the other side. If students choose to explain the reasons for their own opinion, they simply need to raise their hand. By having the students place themselves on the imaginary line, students are actively participating in the discussion.

I place two signs on opposite ends of the room: one states AGREE and the other states DISAGREE. I explain to the students what a continuum is and emphasize that there are no right or wrong answers, just their opinions. After a statement is read, students move to a point on the continuum that represents their own position on the statement. If a student is uncertain about his or her opinion, agrees with both sides of the issue, or does not choose to share his or her opinion, then, for any of these reasons, the student can stand in the middle of the continuum. Students may change their opinions at any time as they listen to each other. Thus, students may move themselves along the continuum as the discussion progresses.

In the seventh grade drug education curriculum, I use this type of discussion approach when considering issues such as drinking alcohol, legalizing marijuana, and dealing with the rights of nonsmokers. In the eighth grade class, which includes sex education, I use this format when discussing abortion and AIDS. The students enjoy using the Discussion Continuum.

in the mere restatement of ideas espoused by the teacher. If used in this manner, discussions become boring and do not stimulate student thinking.

Discussions can be used to address both cognitive and affective objectives. In the cognitive domain, discussions encourage students to analyze ideas and facts from the lesson and to discover interrelationships between previously taught content. In the affective domain, discussions encourage students to examine their opinions, to interact with and evaluate other students' ideas, and to develop good listening skills. Whatever the objective, discussions must be well planned and key questions must be formulated prior to the lesson.

Take the following guidelines into account when planning and implementing effective discussions (e.g., Borich, 2000; Jacobsen, Eggen, & Kauchak, 2002). These eight guidelines apply to whole-class or small-group discussions, as well as to panels and debates.

1. *Consider the goals of the discussion.* The goals of the lesson should structure the discussion. If the objective is to focus on cognitive development, then questions dealing with concepts and ideas are appropriate. If the discussion is to focus on the affective domain, then questions dealing with values and personal experiences are appropriate.

2. *Consider the experience and development of the students.* Younger and/or inexperienced students may need more direction during the discussion. The directions and questions may need to be more explicit, and the discussion itself may need to be shorter than it might be with an older group of students. As students become more mature and gain experience in discussions, they can take on more direction themselves.

3. *Study the issues.* Be familiar with the issues and/or material to be discussed during the lesson. This may appear too obvious to mention, but too often teachers have not prepared themselves by learning about all the various issues surrounding a topic and thereby allow the discussion to drift during presentation.

4. *Orient the students to the objective of the discussion.* Explaining the objectives of the discussion to the students provides a road map for them and gives students a better idea of what to expect during the lesson.

5. *Provide a supportive classroom environment.* If a classroom discussion is to be successful, students must believe that they can contribute to the discussion without fear of embarrassment or ridicule. The effective teacher creates an environment where all ideas are welcome and where students give and receive constructive criticism in a supportive climate.

6. *Provide new or more accurate information when it may be necessary.* At times, it may be necessary for you to contribute information to the discussion. This allows the discussion to remain focused on the objectives.

7. *Review, summarize, or weave opinions and facts into a meaningful relationship.* At times, restate the major themes emerging from the discussion in order to provide a needed structure to the lesson. This permits the students to see how ideas are interrelated.

8. *Use humor.* Some discussions can cause tension within the class. Depending on the topic, students may not always agree with the opinions of their classmates. Students say something, without realizing it, that might offend another student. You can reduce the tension in the classroom by interspersing humor into the discussion.

Small-Group Discussions. *Small-group discussions* can meet the goal of increased student participation by allowing more students to become involved in the discussion. Groups of four to five students are most appropriate for small-group work. In addition to promoting the higher-level thinking skills, small-group discussions help to promote the development of communication skills, leadership ability, debate, and compromise.

Students involved in small-group discussions often get off-task easily. Careful organization can help these discussions to run more smoothly. There are at least four things that you can do to effectively conduct small-group discussions.

1. Carefully monitor the activity by moving around the room and checking with each group to make sure it remains focused on the discussion's objectives.
2. Make sure that students have enough background knowledge to effectively contribute to the discussion. Thus, small-group discussions should follow a lesson focusing on content and should build on topics previously developed.
3. Plan for relatively short discussions. If you see that the students are interested and are on-task, the discussion can be allowed to continue. If a time limit is specified at the beginning of the lesson, the students are encouraged to remain on-task.
4. Give students precise directions for the activity. If the students realize specifically what they are to do during the discussion, they are more than likely to remain on-task. At the conclusion of the small-group activity, each group should report its results to the class. This can be accomplished by a written report or by having a representative from the group give an oral report to the class.

Cooperative Learning

Cooperative learning involves students working together in small, mixed-ability learning teams to address specific instructional tasks, thus aiding and supporting each other during the learning process. It is a popular instructional approach. The teacher presents the group with a problem to solve or task to perform. Students in the group then work among themselves, help one another, praise and criticize one another's contributions, and often receive a group performance score.

For example, you might divide the class into cooperative groups of four and assign each group to prepare a report on a different country in South America. Within each group, students would agree to take on various responsibilities: leader–organizer, recorder of discussions, timekeeper, or other needed roles. Each group would decide on strategies to divide up the work. For example, who would be responsible for (a) collecting information, (b) organizing the information collected from various group members, (c) preparing the report, and (d) presenting the report to the class as a PowerPoint presentation. You would serve as a resource for the students in each group. Collaborative learning generally occurs in three different ways:

1. Students have specific responsibilities within a larger group task or project.
2. Students work together on a common project or task.
3. Students take responsibility for all group members' learning.

During the last 20 years, cooperative learning has become one of the primary methods of mixed-ability grouping (Johnson, Johnson & Holubec 1994; Slavin, 1995, 2000;

Johnson & Johnson, 1999). Students work in groups of four to six members and cooperate with each other to learn the material. Groups usually are rewarded according to the amount learned, although variations such as Student Teams—Achievement Divisions (STAD) allow for individual gain scores to be a part of the evaluation.

Johnson and Johnson (1999) point out that each lesson in cooperative learning should include five basic elements:

1. *Positive interdependence.* Students must feel that they are responsible for their own learning and that of other members of the group.
2. *Face-to-face interaction.* Students work in groups of three to five and therefore have the opportunity to explain what they are learning to each other.
3. *Individual accountability.* Each student must be held accountable for mastery of the assigned work.
4. *Interpersonal and small-group skills.* Each student must be taught to communicate effectively, maintain respect among group members, and work together to resolve conflicts.
5. *Group processing.* Groups must be assessed to see how well they are working together and how they can improve.

Research indicates that cooperative learning approaches lead to higher academic achievement than strategies that call for students to complete similar tasks as individuals or to compete against each other (Johnson et al., 1981). Cooperative learning has a powerful effect on learning, as measured by its effect size of 0.78 (Marzano, Pickering, & Pollock, 2001). In addition, cooperative learning has been shown to have a positive effect on student attitudes. Students in cooperative learning groups have (a) better interpersonal relationships and (b) more positive attitudes toward subjects studied and the overall classroom experience (Johnson & Johnson, 1999).

CLASSROOM DECISIONS

Studies have shown that the average student in a cooperative learning group scores as much as 28 percentile points higher than the average student working individually (Johnson et al., 1981; Walberg, 1999). Consequently, it makes sense to have students in your classroom work in cooperative learning groups at some time. Before starting, however, it is important to show students how to work together as a supportive group. You should provide clear written directions and opportunities for students to receive feedback on their academic performance and the group's success in working together. What additional orientation or training do you think would enable students to work effectively in cooperative learning groups? How might this orientation be different for second graders as compared to tenth graders? How might you accommodate the different knowledge and skills of the students in their roles within the groups?

Cooperative learning works best with heterogeneous groupings of students. Having students work in groups generally has a positive effect on their achievement when compared to their work as individuals. However, the findings become more complex when we compare the achievement of low-ability students who worked in homogeneous groups to low-ability students who were grouped heterogeneously. Low-ability students actually perform significantly worse when placed in homogeneous groups (Lou et al., 1996).

Through cooperative learning, students understand that they are not only responsible for their own learning but also for the learning of their team members. Cooperative learning approaches are often used to supplement other instructional practices. Research conducted by Lou et al. (1996) reported that cooperative learning works best when used in a weekly, systematic fashion. Those who criticize cooperative learning, however, focus on its misuse and overuse in education. Misuse often comes when tasks are not defined or structured. Overuse often occurs when not enough time is provided for students to complete tasks or independently practice the skills and knowledge that they are attempting to learn (Marzano, Pickering, & Pollock, 2001).

Johnson and Johnson (1999) outline cooperative learning in three different styles: informal groups, formal groups, and base groups.

Informal Groups.   *Informal groups* are short term, often accomplished by asking students to "turn to a neighbor," and used to clarify information, focus students on objectives, or bring about closure on a topic. They usually take place after lectures or other direct-teaching strategies. There are numerous types of informal grouping, but a feature central to all informal groups is that students are encouraged to actively participate and stay engaged by sharing their solutions with others.

All activities start with the teacher asking students a question or giving them a problem to work on. During *Think–Pair–Share,* students initially work independently, but then move to pairs to discuss their answers. To conclude, you would call on students to report. In a *Round Robin* activity, you place students in groups of three or four and have them share their answers with others in their group.

Having a plan for the order in which students present can add interest and organization to the activity. For example, have students report based on their birthdays (starting with September) or on the age of a younger brother or sister—the person with the youngest sibling going first (those with no sibling going last; ties are broken based on shoe size). A *group interview* calls for each student to be interviewed by the two or three people in their group. Selected interviewers can share best ideas. In all these activities, students have opportunities to build both intellectual and social skills by sharing, listening carefully, asking questions, and summarizing.

Formal Groups.   *Formal groups* are carefully designed so that a heterogeneous mix of students works together on specific learning tasks. Several common types of cooperative learning techniques are described in this section. Robert Slavin and his associates developed the first four; these rely on student team learning methods, which include team rewards, individual accountability, and equal opportunities for success (Slavin, 1987, 1991, 1995).

1. *Student Teams—Achievement Divisions* (STAD) involves four-member learning teams that are mixed in performance level, gender, and ethnicity. After the teacher presents a lesson, students work within their teams to make sure that all members have mastered the lesson. Students then individually take a quiz, and their scores are based on the degree to

TEACHERS IN ACTION

TECHNIQUES IN COOPERATIVE LEARNING GROUPS

Kris Walters, high school art teacher, Augusta, Georgia

Methods for grouping students can be part of the fun of cooperative learning. I make a stack of cards by cutting cartoon figures from the comic section of the paper and give each student a card upon entering the room. Then I put all the Snoopys at one table, the Dagwoods at another, and so on. I've used fruit-flavored lollipops, coins from the Mardi Gras, and even just a pile of objects on each table (e.g., paper clips for one group, pencils for another, and so on).

Identifying tasks within the group is another means for making the lesson enjoyable for the stu-dents. The one with the curliest hair is the reporter, the one wearing the most white is the recorder, the one whose birthday is next is the encourager, and the one with the most siblings is the observer. I make a list of these "qualifiers" for assigning tasks so that I can just glance at the list before starting. Other possibilities include the one with the most pets, the one wearing the most jewelry, or the one whose phone number ends with the highest digit. Devising a list in advance makes cooperative activ-ities fun and motivating for the students and easy for the teacher.

which they meet or exceed their earlier performances. These points are then totaled to form team scores. Teams that meet certain criteria may earn certificates or other awards. If stu-dents want their team to earn rewards, they must help their teammates to learn the material. Individual accountability is maintained since the quiz is taken without the help of team-mates. Because team scores are based on each student's improvement, there is equal op-portunity for all students to be successful.

2. *Teams–Games–Tournament* (TGT) uses the same teacher presentations and team-work as in STAD. In TGT, however, students demonstrate individual subject mastery by playing academic games. Students play these games in weekly tournaments in which they compete with members of other teams who have similar past records in the subject. The competition takes place with three students at each tournament table. Since the tables in-clude students of similar ability (i.e., high-achieving students are at the same table), all stu-dents have the opportunity to be successful. High-performing teams earn certificates or other team-based awards. Individual accountability is maintained during competition since teammates cannot help each other.

3. *Team Accelerated Instruction* (TAI) is a combination of individualized instruction and team learning. With TAI, students again work in heterogeneous teams, but they each study individualized academic materials. Teammates check each other's work from answer sheets. Team scores are based on both the average number and the accuracy of units com-pleted by team members each week.

4. *Jigsaw* involves six-member teams working on academic material that has been broken down into sections. Each team member reads his or her section. Then members of different teams who have studied the same sections meet in "expert groups" to discuss their section. Next the students return to their teams and take turns teaching their teammates about their sections. Since the only way that students can learn about sections other than their own is to carefully listen to their teammates, they are motivated to support and show interest in each other's work.

5. *Learning Together* is a cooperative approach in which students are organized into teams that include a cross section of ability levels (Johnson & Johnson, 1999). Each team is given a task or project to complete, and each team member works on a part of the project that is compatible with his or her own interests and abilities. The intent is to maximize strengths of individual students to get a better overall group effect. Each team is responsible for gathering the information and materials needed to complete its assigned task or project. Final assessment is based on the quality of the team's performance. Each student on the team receives the same grade. This encourages students to pool their talents so that each student makes the greatest possible contribution to the effort.

Base Groups. *Base groups* are long-term, heterogeneous groups that stay together across tasks throughout the year. Base groups provide student-to-student support and a sense of routine in the classroom. Students in these groups build long-term relationships and a support system that encourages academic progress. In elementary schools, base groups might meet in the morning and again at the end of the day. Morning tasks might include taking a lunch count, making sure everyone in the group has completed the homework, getting materials ready for the day, and catching up on outside activities. Afternoon meetings would allow groups to make sure that everyone has the correct homework assignment, share insights into the assignments and tasks, and focus on a question that brings closure to the day's activities.

After working with various students in cooperative learning groups, you will gain a sense of how to get the most out of all participants, how much time is needed for groups to complete their work, and how to transition to other activities. You should move around the room as groups work so that you can assess learning and plan follow-up activities.

Panels and Debates

Panels, symposiums, task forces, and debates all involve a group of students becoming informed about a particular topic, presenting information to the class, and interacting in discussion. Each approach has unique characteristics. Panels and debates are designed to help students to understand several points of view related to a topic or issue. They combine prepared activities and statements with the give and take of discussions. They are useful in large-class activities when more informal whole-class or small-group discussions would not be feasible.

A *panel* is a fairly informal setting in which four to six participants with a chairperson discuss a topic among themselves while the rest of the class listens. Later, there is give and take with the class. Each participant makes an opening statement. A round table is an informal version of a panel. A *symposium* is very similar to a panel, but it involves a more formal presentation of information by each panel member. A *task force* is like a panel, but it involves thorough investigation of a particular problem prior to the presentation to the rest of the class about the problem investigated. A *debate* is a formal discussion approach consisting of set speeches by participants of two opposing teams and a rebuttal by each participant. Panels and debates are conducted for the benefit of the whole class, which becomes involved through question and answer sessions upon the panel's completion.

Role Playing, Simulations, and Games

Role playing is a student-directed activity in which students act out or dramatize a particular situation, circumstance, or idea. The teacher structures and facilitates the role playing and conducts the follow-up discussion. The majority of the class will be involved in observing and analyzing the enactments. Role playing can be successfully used at both the middle and secondary levels.

Role playing is particularly useful in helping students to understand the perspectives and feelings of other people concerning a variety of personal and social issues. In addition, role playing can be used to clarify and demonstrate attitudes and concepts, plan and test solutions to problems, help students to prepare for a real situation, and deepen understanding of social situations. Role playing is usually done spontaneously in the classroom with a limited amount of preparation time for students. It provides students with an opportunity to

---

TEACHERS IN ACTION

COMBINING PANELS AND ROLE PLAYING

Deborah Kauffman, high school literature teacher, Glendale, Arizona

I have often used a Meet the Panel format in my British Literature classes. This is loosely based on the *Meet the Press* television show in which one or more people are interviewed. I often use this when we are discussing satire and the Age of Reason. After the students have read Jonathan Swift's essay "A Modest Proposal" and understood its rhetorical implications, I create a panel of students to play certain roles in this *Meet the Press* format. The roles include an Irish-Catholic priest, an Irish mother of ten, an English pub owner, an English butcher, an English noble couple, and others. I then appoint one student to conduct the session like Oprah or Phil Donahue.

Some of the panel members use the essay to generate charts and other aides; some members bring in hors d'oeuvres or come in costume. The audience members, the rest of the class, are required to compose 15 to 20 questions for the panel that relate directly to the essay. Usually a student

volunteers to videotape the activity and we view that at a later time. Sometimes, a class enjoys the efforts of another class more than its own.

Each year, I am impressed by the amount of student engagement in the activity. The students are genuinely motivated to understand Swift's essay and the satire embedded in it. The forms of satire studied in the unit are used by the panel members in their various roles and are often incorporated in questions from the audience.

I have used variations of this activity when I taught difficult historical periods in literature, such as the Middle Ages. I give students library time and identify specific tasks and questions to answer. They must research the characters and the period in which they lived, and then they report back to the class. The Meet the Panel activity or variations of it provide a nice change of pace from usual classroom routines.

express their feelings, develop a better understanding of other people's feelings and perspectives, and demonstrate creativity and imagination.

Role playing can be time consuming, and some students may not take their responsibility seriously. Unless students are well prepared, the role playing may be superficial. Role playing can be boring for students who are watching and are not actively involved in the acting. Furthermore, students may get so consumed with their acting that they miss the point of the lesson. To ensure that these problems don't occur, Joyce, Weil and Calhoun (2000) suggest that a nine-step process be used to maximize students' performance and learning.

1. *Warm up the group.* The warm-up centers on introducing students to the problem and making sure that they comprehend the problem. Next you provide examples of the problem. These examples can come from a variety of sources, including classroom situations (e.g., how to deal with situations that students often face with peers, such as use of cigarettes, alcohol, or drugs or a friend asking to copy homework), or historical problems without an ending or resolution disclosed (e.g., whether the United States should build a coalition, or go it alone, to fight international terrorism after the attacks on the World Trade Center and the Pentagon on September 11, 2001). Examples can come from students' life experiences, films, texts, newspapers, or other source materials. The final phase of the warm-up is for you to ask students questions to make sure that they understand the problem and that they are ready to start predicting various scenarios and outcomes: "What would you do in this situation?" "What are some possible ways this story could end?"

2. *Select the participants.* In this phase you and your students describe the various characters or roles. What are they like? How do events affect different characters in different ways? How might a specific character act? What would they do and say? Students must want to play a particular role. As the teacher, you should ensure that students are well matched to their roles and understand the complexities these roles bring.

3. *Set the stage.* Ask students to outline the scene and set aside a place for the action to take place.

4. *Prepare the observers.* Several students without a role should be asked to act as observers. They should analyze the enactment relative to its realism, logical sequence of effects, and whether the actors covered the full range of their characters' likely feelings and perceptions.

5. *Enact.* The players start to role play, responding to the situation and to each other as realistically as possible. This first enactment should be kept short, and you should stop it when the major points have been made and the purpose of the enactment is clear. You can ask other students to provide a second enactment to fully investigate the issue.

6. *Discuss and evaluate.* You focus the discussion on what motivated the actors and what would be likely to occur should the scene continue. Alternative scenarios should be investigated.

7. *Reenact.* Reenactments can take place to ensure that students have opportunities to bring in new interpretations. Reenactments and discussion should alternate freely. Cause and effect should be investigated. For example, how does a change in one player's interpretation change the behavior of other players?

8. *Discuss and evaluate.* Repeat this step as needed.

9. *Share experiences and generalize.* As the teacher, you should help students to clarify their perceptions and relate the experience to other real-life problems or historical situations.

It is best to begin the use of role playing slowly with much guidance. Plan the roles and the situation carefully so that students know exactly what is expected of them. Since some students may be uncomfortable doing this, do not force them to take on a role. Students not actively involved in the role playing should be involved in some way, such as taking notes on key points. After the role playing, help students to summarize what they learned, express their feelings, and evaluate the roles played out.

Simulations are exercises that place students in situations that model a real-life environment. They require students to assume roles, make decisions, and face consequences. Through the simulated experience, the hope is that students will understand the important factors and how to behave in real situations. Students will also benefit by seeing how others behave in real situations. Although the roles for the students in the simulation are clearly defined, student responses are impromptu.

Many simulations have been commercially prepared and also include an element of competition. As with role playing, the teacher's role is to structure the simulation, introduce it to students, assign student roles, facilitate the actual simulation, and conduct the debriefing session after the simulation has been completed.

SPOTLIGHT ON TECHNOLOGY

SIMULATION COMPUTER SOFTWARE

Many of the newest simulations are run with computer software. Students often work in teams. Two popular simulations are these:

- *Sim City* (http://simcity.ea.com/us/guide/) Sim City is a computer simulation that allows students to create and control an imaginary city. The challenge of this type of simulation is to create a successful city by applying rules on city planning and management dealing with issues such as land value, human factors, disasters, employment levels, crime, and pollution. Students gain understanding of how these factors affect the quality of life in their city. The tools provided include the ability to plan, zone, clear, build, maintain utilities, and balance natural disasters. Success depends on planning and management. A plan can be altruistic or harmful. Students get to see the results of their philosophy and supervision.
- *Civilization* (http://www.civ3.com/) Civilization is a game in which you build your own civilization. You manage growth, military activity, civic development, diplomacy, and scientific research as your civilization grows. Choice is central to this game. For example, you can support cultural activities or military power.

Games are designed to involve students in competition as the primary means to achieve a learning goal. Games can be used to teach a wide variety of skills, including problem solving and decision making (see the section on cooperative learning earlier in this chapter for specific strategies). Of course, you need to select a game to fit the desired objectives. An instructional game has rules, a structure for playing the game, and a method for determining the winners and losers. You structure the setting, facilitate conducting the game, and supervise the students. Educational games can be useful in an interdisciplinary thematic unit.

INDEPENDENT APPROACHES

Independent instructional approaches are those in which students work by themselves on some project or at a learning center or learning station in the classroom. The teacher may be involved in some way in the identification and design of the particular instructional tasks. However, there is often considerable latitude for students with independent instructional approaches.

Learning Centers or Stations

A *learning center* is a designated place within the room where a student goes to pursue either required or optional activities on a given topic. It is a self-contained environment that includes all materials that students will need. Learning centers or learning stations are used to provide enrichment and reinforcement opportunities for students. Learning centers can be used to motivate students and can provide a variety of instructional activities designed to meet the various ability levels and learning styles of the students. Teachers often design and prepare a number of instructional tasks that the student can perform while in the learning center. These tasks typically accommodate a range of academic abilities and a variety of student interests. Students usually are not required to complete all tasks at a center, but may select the ones that they prefer based on their ability, interests, or other factors.

Contracts and Independent Work

Learning contracts provide a structure that allows a student and teacher to agree on a series of tasks to be completed in a given time frame. Many contracts are designed to allow students to work independently through a body of required content or to carry out an individual project. Most contracts entail specific assignments drawn from the regular curriculum and optional activities either drawn from the curriculum or planned around student interest. It is not necessary that all students have learning contracts. Contract activities may be pursued during any independent work time, such as when other students are involved in skills instruction, when other assignments have been completed, or at any other time designated by the teacher as being appropriate for independent work.

KEY TERMS

Analogies	Formal groups	Project
Base groups	Games	Role playing
Classifying	Guided inquiry	Simulations
Comparing	Inductive instructional approaches	Small-group discussion
Concept attainment	Informal groups	Social instructional approaches
Constructivist approach	Inquiry	Symposium
Cooperative learning	Learning center	Task force
Debate	Metaphor	Unguided inquiry
Discovery learning	Panel	Venn diagram
Discussion	Problem solving	Whole-class discussion

MAJOR CONCEPTS

1. Inductive instructional approaches often begin with exploratory activities and then lead to students discovering a concept or generalization. Some inductive approaches have a higher degree of teacher-directed activity, and others have students more actively involved in planning and designing their instructional activities.

2. Examples of inductive instructional approaches include concept attainment strategies, inquiry lessons, and projects, reports, and problems.

3. Social instructional approaches are indirect, student-oriented strategies that permit students to interact with each other in various ways to help each other's learning. Some common social approaches include discussions, cooperative learning, panels and debates, and role playing, simulations, and games.

4. Cooperative learning involves students working together in small, mixed-ability learning teams to address specific instructional tasks while aiding and supporting each other during the learning process.

5. Independent instructional approaches are those in which students work by themselves on some project or at a learning center or learning station in the classroom. The teacher may be involved in some way in the identification and design of the particular instructional tasks, but there is often considerable latitude for students in independent instructional approaches.

DISCUSSION/REFLECTIVE QUESTIONS

1. Why should you be competent in the use of a variety of indirect instructional strategies?

2. Why might some teachers prefer more student-centered approaches?

3. What skills does a teacher need to effectively conduct a whole-class discussion?

4. What are the merits and possible disadvantages of using cooperative learning, inquiry, and concept-based instructional strategies?

5. How might the subject area that you are teaching affect your selection of the instructional strategy to be used in a lesson? How might the age and maturity of the students affect this decision?

SUGGESTED ACTIVITIES

For Clinical Settings

1. Select a unit topic and prepare a two-week unit plan that includes inquiry strategies, cooperative learning, discussion methods, and group activities throughout the unit.

2. Explore computer software and other computer-assisted technology that is available. Evaluate this material and determine how you can use it in your instruction.

3. Prepare a list of guidelines and procedures for how you would use cooperative learning groups, problem solving, and independent work in your classroom.

For Field Settings

1. Talk to several teachers to identify the types of indirect instructional strategies that they use in the classroom. Determine why they selected these various strategies. Ask for recommendations for the effective use of these strategies.

2. Talk to several teachers to explore how they use discussion during instruction. Ask them for recommendations for effectively holding discussions.

3. Examine a school's computer equipment, software, and facilities. What procedures are established for teachers and students to use the computers? How do teachers in the school use computers and related technology to assist instruction?

4. Ask several teachers how they use learning centers, contracts, or various types of independent work. What recommendations do they offer for effective use of these approaches?

USEFUL RESOURCES

Cohen, E. G. (1994). *Designing groupwork: Strategies for the heterogeneous classroom* (2nd ed.). New York: Teachers College Press.

Provides a comprehensive view of all aspects of group work. Examines reasons for group work, planning, preparing students, giving everyone a part, evaluating performance, and group work in bilingual and multiability classrooms.

Johnson, D. W., & Johnson, R. T. (1999). *Learning together and alone: Cooperative, competitive, and individualistic learning* (5th ed.). Boston: Allyn and Bacon.

Thoroughly examines the goals and elements of cooperative, competitive, and individualistic approaches to learning. Well written and organized to facilitate application.

Slavin, R. E. (1995). *Cooperative learning* (2nd ed.). Boston: Allyn and Bacon.

A complete presentation of cooperative learning. Written by one of the national leaders in research on cooperative learning, the book presents a readable, concise guide to research and practice on the subject.

WEB SITES

- Guides from the U.S. Department of Education; this one deals with cooperative learning. (*Hint:* Shorten the address and look up other guides.)

  http://www.ed.gov/pubs/OR/ConsumerGuides/cooplear.html

- Excellent example of project-based learning: An Oral History of Rhode Island Women during World War II. Written by students in the Honors English Program at South Kingstown High School, South Kingstown, Rhode Island. Oral history is a unique way to learn about past events and experiences. This method probes memory, evokes emotions and feelings that have long been dormant, and creates a relationship between narrator and interviewer that is often a very special one.

http://www.stg.brown.edu/projects/WWII_Women/tocCS.html

- Inspiration Software®, Inc. is the leading publisher of visual thinking and learning tools for K–12 education. Numerous examples and free downloads that contain a fully functioning version of the software that lets you experience all the features of the real product for 30 days. A terrific program.

http://www.inspiration.com/

- Lengthy explanation of instructional strategies

http://www.sasked.gov.sk.ca/docs/policy/approach/instrapp03.html#methods

- Information about grouping students

http://www.adprima.com/grouping.htm

- Best of Bonk Web Links Cooperative Learning

http://www.indiana.edu/~bobweb/co_hand.html

- A–Z Teacher Stuff Cooperative Learning Resources Page

http://www.atozteacherstuff.com/articles/cooperative.shtml

- The International Association for Study of Cooperation in Education

http://WWW.IASCE.NET

- The Cooperative Learning Center at the University of Minnesota

http://www.clcrc.com/

- Ask ERIC lesson plans, guides, and resources for teachers.

http://www.askeric.org/

- The *New York Times* archive contains hundreds of free lesson plans for grades 6–12. You may perform a keyword search to retrieve a lesson, browse the archive by subject, or scroll down the page to view the most recently published lessons. Includes academic content standard taught through the lessons.

http://Nytimes.com/learning/teachers/lessons/archive.html

Education World®-Lesson Planning

http://www.education-world.com/a_lesson/

- Links to resources for daily lesson planning

http://www.proteacher.com/020001.shtml

CHAPTER NINE

MANAGING LESSON DELIVERY

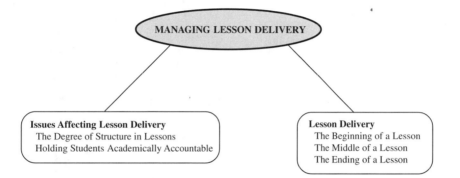

OBJECTIVES

This chapter provides information that will help you to:

1. Select ways to structure lessons and group students.

2. Identify ways to hold students academically accountable.

3. Identify ways to handle administrative actions that are commonly taken at the start of a lesson.

4. Identify actions that can be used at the start of a lesson to capture student interest and focus attention on the learning objectives.

5. Identify teacher actions that contribute to effective group management during the middle part of a lesson.

6. Identify actions which teachers take at the end of a lesson to provide for lesson summary and enable students to prepare to leave.

PRAXIS/Principles of Learning and Teaching/Pathwise

The following principles are relevant to content in this chapter:

1. Making learning goals and instructional procedures clear to students   (C1)

2. Monitoring students' understanding of content through a variety of means, providing feedback to students to assist learning, and adjusting learning activities as the situation demands   (C4)

3. Using instructional time effectively   (C5)

INTASC

The following INTASC standards are relevant to content in this chapter:

1. The teacher uses an understanding of individual and group motivation and behavior to create a learning environment and encourages positive social interaction, active engagement in learning, and self-motivation.   (Standard 5)

2. The teacher uses knowledge of effective verbal, nonverbal, and media communication techniques to foster active inquiry, collaboration, and supportive interaction in the classroom.   (Standard 6)

When planning for a vacation trip, you often need to plan ahead. Do you want to stay in one place and relax, or do you want to visit a number of areas? Would you like to schedule several events for each day, or would you like to leave the daily schedule very open? What type of accommodations would you like?

To ensure an enjoyable vacation, you need to give these questions attention. Similarly, you need to give advance thought to the type of classroom that you would like to have. How structured do you want your classroom and lessons? How do you want to group your students for instruction? How will you hold the students academically accountable? How will you handle various aspects of lesson delivery? These issues will be explored in this chapter. How you attend to these issues will make a difference in managing instruction and student behavior.

ISSUES AFFECTING LESSON DELIVERY

Preparing daily lesson plans is a vital task for effective classroom management and discipline because effective, engaging lessons can keep students on task and can minimize misbehavior. You need to consider the degree of structure that will occur in each lesson. Also, students are more likely to stay on-task and be engaged in instruction when they know that they will be held *academically accountable.*

The Degree of Structure in Lessons

Many instructional strategies can be used, ranging from teacher-centered, explicit approaches to the presentation of content to student-centered, less explicit approaches. *Teacher-centered approaches* include lectures, demonstrations, questions, recitations, practice and drills, and reviews. *Student-centered approaches* include inquiry approaches, discovery learning and problem solving, role playing and simulation, gaming, laboratory activities, computer-assisted instruction, and learning or activity centers. Various types of grouping and discussion methods may be student or teacher directed, depending on how they are used. Teacher-centered approaches are often more structured than student-centered approaches. As a result, the management issues will vary depending on the approach used.

When deciding on your instructional strategy, you need to weigh the advantages and disadvantages of the various strategies along with the lesson objectives. Effective teachers use several strategies, ranging from teacher-directed to student-directed. The lesson objectives may determine what type of approach is most appropriate. Some content may lend itself to inquiry and discovery techniques, whereas other content may be better handled with direct instruction. Over time, students should be given the opportunity to learn through a variety of instructional strategies.

Holding Students Academically Accountable

Procedures to help manage student work must also be selected. *Academic accountability* means that the students must complete certain activities related to the instructional objectives. Teacher responsibilities for holding students academically accountable are displayed in Table 9.1, some of which are adapted from Emmer et al. (2000), Evertson et al. (2000), and Jones and Jones (2001).

Consider the following guidelines when holding students academically accountable:

■ *Determine a system of grading* (e.g., letter grades or numerical grades, and measures for nonachievement outcomes). This decision might have been made for you by the school district as reflected in the report-card format. Use a variety of evaluation measures (e.g., tests, written or oral reports, homework, ratings, projects) throughout the marking period and describe the grading system to the students.

■ ■ ■ ■ ■

CLASSROOM DECISIONS

Effective teachers hold students academically accountable in many ways. Assume that you require your tenth-grade English students to complete three tests, seven homework assignments, and two cooperative projects for the report-card marking period. What provisions would you have for absent students and make-up work? How do these provisions hold students academically accountable?

■ *Make decisions about assignments.* This includes deciding on where and how you will post assignments, as well as the requirements and criteria for grading. Students should understand that completed assignments are part of the grading system.

■ *Decide on work and completion requirements.* Students need to have guidelines or work requirements for the various assignments. Details about due dates, late work, and missed assignments due to absence should be explained. The relevant procedures will help students understand expectations held of them and should minimize questions on a case-by-case basis.

TABLE 9.1   Holding Students Academically Accountable

Consider your grade level and subject area as you make decisions on the following issues in an effort to hold students academically accountable.

1. The Grading System
   a. Select a grading system
   b. Select types of evaluation measures
   c. Determine how grades will be assigned
   d. Address nonachievement outcomes
   e. Communicate the grading system to students
   f. Design a gradebook
   g. Report grades and communicate to parents

2. Assignments
   a. Post assignments
   b. State requirements and grading criteria for assignments
   c. Long-term assignments

3. Work and Completion Requirements
   a. Identify work requirements
      (1) Use of pencil or pen
      (2) Headings on papers
      (3) Writing on the back of the paper
      (4) Neatness and legibility guidelines
   b. Identify completion requirements
      (1) Due dates
      (2) Late work
      (3) Incomplete work
      (4) Missed work
   c. Make provisions for absent students and make-up work
      (1) Have an assignment list or folder
      (2) Identify a due date
      (3) Select a place to pick up and drop off absent assignments
      (4) Provide a regular time to assist students with make-up work

4. Monitoring Progress and Completion of Assignments
   a. Determine when and how to monitor in-class assignments
   b. Determine when and how to monitor longer assignments, projects, or works in progress
   c. Determine when and how to monitor in-class oral participation or performance
   d. Determine which activities will receive a grade and which will be used only for formative feedback for the student
   e. Select checking procedures that will be used in class
      (1) Students exchanging papers
      (2) Marking and grading papers
      (3) Turning in papers

5. Providing Feedback
   a. Decide what kind of feedback will be provided to students, and when it will be provided
   b. Determine what records students will keep concerning their progress
   c. Select incentives and rewards
   d. Record scores in the grade book
   e. Post selected student work

■ *Monitor student progress and completion of the assignments.* You may want to use some in-class activities as formative exercises for students but not count performance on these in your grading. The activities may be written, oral, or performance demonstrations. Student progress should be monitored. In many cases, the entire class is at work on the designated activity; this enables you to walk around and observe each student carefully to see how the student is progressing.

■ *Provide students with feedback about their progress.* Feedback of in-class activities may take the form of statements to the individuals or to the class. Students may exchange papers to evaluate progress on formative exercises. Papers or projects that are to be part of the report-card grade should be collected, graded, and returned promptly. In this way, students receive regular feedback about their progress throughout the marking period. Computer programs available for maintaining a gradebook can easily generate progress reports for both students and teacher.

LESSON DELIVERY

You've finished your planning. You've selected the instructional strategies. You've prepared and gathered the instructional materials. Now it is the day of your lesson. You're all ready to begin, but wait. You also must recognize that you can take certain actions during your instruction that will have an effect on maintaining order in the classroom and on achieving the lesson objectives.

TEACHERS IN ACTION

PROMOTING STUDENT ACCOUNTABILITY BY POSTING A WEEKLY AGENDA

James Roussin, grades 7–12 English and literature teacher, Big Lake, Minnesota

I have found that it is important for students to be aware of the classroom agenda for the week so they can take appropriate actions to prepare for tests or turn in assignments. I post a weekly agenda on the blackboard every Monday morning. I have found this to be extremely useful. In this way, students have a clear idea of what the week will look like and what is expected of them. This weekly agenda also helps if students are absent; they just need to look at the board to see what was missed.

If we cannot get to everything that has been scheduled in the weekly agenda, I collaborate with the class to determine what should be deleted or extended; this allows the students to feel like they are part of the overall planning in the class.

I use various colors on the weekly agenda to emphasize the particular assignments the students will be responsible for. For example, I write in a test with red chalk, a reading assignment in green, and a daily writing assignment in blue. The same colors are used throughout the school year.

The best part of this agenda is that it keeps me organized for the week. I can glance at the board and it will reveal to me if I have a variety of different activities for the lessons that week. One primary "learning goal" is also listed for each day, and this helps me and the students know what is essential in the lesson for that day.

There are a number of actions that you can take at certain points in a lesson to effectively manage the group, maintain order and control, and fulfill various administrative and academic objectives. If these actions are not handled appropriately, students may be more inclined to be off-task and possibly misbehave. As a result, it is important to examine these lesson delivery tasks from the perspective of management and order in the classroom.

The Beginning of a Lesson

A successful lesson beginning can greatly contribute to a meaningful learning experience for students. The beginning of a lesson should be designed to capture the students' attention and focus their attention on the learning objectives to be addressed during the lesson. An effective beginning can increase a student's ability to focus on the objectives.

Actions you take at the start of a lesson help establish an atmosphere in which students have the "motivation to learn" (Brophy, 1998). *Motivation to learn* draws on the meaningfulness, value, and benefits of the academic task to the learner. For example, math problems may be developed which relate to student interests such as selling products for a youth-group fund raiser. Thus, the focus is on learning rather than on merely performing. Often students can be motivated at the beginning of a lesson by emphasizing the purpose of the task or the fact that students will be interested in the task.

Prior to beginning the substance of a lesson, take attendance and solicit attention. At the beginning of the lesson, your actions include providing daily review, providing a set induction, introducing lesson objectives, distributing materials, and giving clear, focused directions.

Taking Attendance.   Elementary teachers in self-contained classrooms commonly take attendance first thing in the morning, whereas secondary teachers take attendance at the start of each class. Tardiness also must be noted, and teachers need to follow school policies when recording and responding to tardy students. It is helpful not to hold up the beginning of class to take attendance. You could plan an opening activity for students to do while you take attendance. Some teachers have the first daily activity posted on the board for the students to do while attendance is taken. Have a seating chart for each class; a substitute teacher would find this especially useful.

Soliciting Attention.   Students should understand that they are expected to give full attention to lessons at all times. A lesson should not begin until you gain their full attention. There should be a predictable, standard signal that tells the class "We are now ready to begin the lesson." The type of signal will vary with teacher preferences. For example, you could raise your hand, ring chimes or a bell, stand in a certain location, or make a statement. After giving the signal, pause briefly to allow it to take effect. Then when you have attention, move quickly into the lesson.

There are a number of ways to solicit attention at the beginning of a lesson. These approaches are designed to secure the students' attention and reduce distractions that might occur at the beginning of a lesson (Jones & Jones, 2001).

1. *Select a cue for getting students' attention.* Students often need a consistent cue to focus their attention. These cues may include a special phrase chosen by the class to indicate that you want immediate attention, or they may include a nonverbal cue such as closing the door at the beginning of class.

TEACHERS IN ACTION

TAKING ATTENDANCE AND OPENING ACTIVITIES

Carolyn Steinbrink, middle school American history teacher, Shenandoah, Iowa

I like the class to begin the second the bell rings. This is difficult because there are a dozen little chores that need to be done before actual teaching begins. Attendance must be taken and recorded, make-up work needs to be assigned, and other forms may need to be filled out. While all of this is being done, the students may become chaotic.

To avoid confusion while I take care of the attendance and other items, I have the students review yesterday's learnings. The best approach I have found involves the use of the overhead projector to display directions for a three-minute task using the objectives from yesterday's lesson. Students may be asked to do a quick bit of writing, discuss a question with a partner and be ready to report, take a short 3–5 point quiz, or any of a variety of review techniques.

Stacie Mitchell, fourth grade teacher, Davenport, Iowa

I have a Welcome Board in my fourth grade classroom, and each day it contains a greeting such as "Compliment someone today." It also gives the students directions on how to begin the day, such as "get a white board out for mental math practice" and "have your reading materials ready." As students enter the room each morning, they read the Welcome Board and begin working on the assigned task. This gives me the opportunity to greet the students personally and take attendance while they begin the day.

I also have an Agenda Board that displays our agenda for the day. Students enjoy knowing what we will be doing for the day, and they often comment on the activities that are listed. It also teaches them flexibility since the schedule sometimes changes when teachable moments occur!

2. *Do not begin until everyone is paying attention.* It is important that no lesson begin until all students are paying attention to the teacher. Teachers who begin lessons without the attention of all their students spend much more time repeating directions. Also, a teacher who begins a lesson in such a fashion is a poor role model since it indicates that it is all right to talk while others are talking. Teachers sometimes just stand silent, waiting—students soon get the message.

3. *Remove distractions.* Some students cannot screen out distracting stimuli. You can help remove distractions by closing the door, having the students remove unnecessary materials from the tops of their desks, adjusting the blinds, or taking other appropriate actions.

CLASSROOM DECISIONS

Various approaches can be used to get the attention of students at the start of class. Identify several cues that rely on light, sound, or movement to give the signal. How might your cues differ for various grade levels?

Providing Daily Review.   A lesson can start with a brief review of previously covered material, correction of homework, and review of prior knowledge that is relevant to the day's lesson. The purpose of daily review is to determine if the students have obtained the necessary prerequisite knowledge or skills for the lesson. This review may last from three to eight minutes, and the length will vary according to the attention span of the learners and the nature of the content. Daily review is especially useful for teaching material that will be used in subsequent learning. Examples include math facts, math computation and factoring, grammar, chemical equations, and reading sight words.

You can conduct a daily review at the beginning of a lesson (a) to provide additional practice and overlearning for previously learned material, and (b) to allow the teacher to provide corrections and reteaching in areas where students are having difficulty. Vary the methods for reviewing material. Checking homework at the start of class is one form of review. Game formats, such as a trivia game, can be used as a means for review. You can conduct review through discussion, demonstration, questioning, written summaries, short quizzes, individualized approaches, and other methods of instruction (Rosenshine & Stevens, 1986). During reviews, students might answer questions at the chalkboard, in small groups, or as a whole class.

■ ■ ■ ■ ■

CLASSROOM DECISIONS

From your schooling experiences, what approaches to review did you find the most successful? How might you provide different approaches for review in your classroom? What are the merits of this variety?

The following approaches can be used for review in a daily lesson (Rosenshine & Stevens, 1986):

- Ask questions about concepts or skills taught in the previous lesson.
- Give a short quiz at the beginning of class on material from previous lessons or the homework assignment.
- Have students correct each other's homework papers or quizzes.
- Have students meet in small groups (2 to 4 students per group) to review homework.
- Have students prepare questions about previous lessons or homework and ask them to each other, or have the teacher ask them to the class.
- Have students prepare a written summary of the previous lesson.
- Have students ask the teacher about problems on homework and the teacher reviews, reteaches, or provides additional practice. (p. 381)

In addition to daily review, the learning of new material is also enhanced by weekly and monthly reviews. Weekly reviews may occur each Monday, and monthly reviews every fourth Monday. These reviews provide additional teacher checking for student understanding, insure that the necessary prior skills are adequately learned, and also check on the teacher's pace (Rosenshine & Stevens, 1986).

TEACHERS IN ACTION

REVIEWING

Fred Dahm, high school social studies teacher, Wisconsin Rapids, Wisconsin

Too often students see reviewing as a dull but necessary chore. But it can be much more. At the end of each lesson, I assign a different student the responsibility of preparing a 5- to 10-minute review of that content for class the next day. This review can take several forms—a discussion of major points, a listing of the material covered, a game, or a crossword puzzle. The possibilities are endless.

At the beginning of the semester, I also assign pairs of students to a particular unit that we will cover to write a two- or three-page newspaper that would serve as part of the review for that unit. Students can select a title and logo for the newspaper. The articles might include a list of materials covered, related materials available in the library, important points of each lesson, political cartoons, an editorial, a crossword puzzle, and jokes. Each item in the newspaper must be related to the unit content. The student editors then distribute the paper to classmates to begin the review session.

Establishing Set.   *Set induction* is the initial activity at the beginning of the lesson that is used to induce students to a state of wanting to learn. This activity helps establish the context for the learning that is to follow and helps students engage in the learning. Typically, the set is brief, lasting only long enough to develop student readiness to accomplish the lessons objective. Set induction helps students see what the topic of the lesson is in a way that is related to their own interests and their own lives. Madeline Hunter (1994) used the term *anticipatory set* to describe this concept, pointing out that the activity is intended to develop a mental readiness (or "set") for the lesson.

For example, a health lesson on the topic of first aid might begin with the reading of a newspaper report about a recent fire or accident. After reading the article, you could ask the students what they would do if they were the first ones to arrive after the accident. A number of ideas are likely to be generated in this discussion. Then you could bring that opening discussion to a close by saying that today's lesson will be about that exact topic— what type of first aid to administer for various conditions. Then you would move into the first part of the lesson. This set induction activity helps create interest in the lesson in a way that students could relate to their own lives.

Effective set induction activities should meet several criteria:

1. *Get the student interested in what is to be taught during the lesson.* This is referred to as an initiating activity. For example, you might begin a lesson on creative writing by turning off the lights in the room and explaining to the students that you will take them on an adventure to a distant planet. As the room remains dark, they are to imagine their trip into outer space.

2. *The set induction activity must be connected to the lesson.* An activity that is designed to get the students' attention but is not connected to the lesson does not meet this criteria.

3. *Students must understand the material and/or activity.* The information contained in the initiating activity must be stated in a clear manner so that the students will not only understand the activity but also know how it is connected to later content. Later, the set induction activity can be referred to while teaching the lesson.

4. *The set induction and the content of the lesson should be related to the students' lives or a previous lesson.* Students will be more interested in a lesson if they can relate the material to their own lives. For example, a lesson at the secondary level in measurement can include measuring ingredients to bake a cake or some other practical application. At the elementary level, a lesson in division can be related to determining baseball batting averages. Also, you can reduce anxiety by relating the lesson to material already learned by the students.

All four criteria must be present in order for the set induction to be effective. It would be unwise for a teacher to begin any lesson without giving some thought and planning to an effective set induction activity. A good beginning sets the tone for the remainder of the lesson.

Introducing Lesson Objectives.   At the start of a lesson, you should clearly describe its purpose. In addition, it is helpful to discuss the activities and evaluation process; these procedures help reduce student anxiety about the lesson. At the beginning, some teachers will clearly explain the objectives, the activities, and evaluation procedures to be used; others will write these elements on the board for the students or wait for an appropriate point in the lesson, such as after the set induction.

By using set-induction activities and introducing lesson objectives, you provide students with an *advance organizer* that supplies a framework for the new content and helps the students relate it to content they already know. Advance organizers help students by focusing their attention on the subject being considered, informing them where the lesson is going, relating new material to content already understood, and providing structure for the subsequent lesson.

Students learn more, in less time, when they are informed of the lesson objectives (Dubelle, 1986). Furthermore, students are more likely to become involved and derive more satisfaction and enjoyment from an activity that has a definite aim. Roehler, Duffy, and Meloth (1987) reported that after teachers learned to give students specific explanations concerning the purpose of instructional activities, their students demonstrated significantly greater understanding of and appreciation for the purpose of the instruction. Results indicated that students taught by these teachers demonstrated significantly greater understanding of and appreciation for the purpose of the instruction. For example, when teaching students how to use the *Reader's Guide,* you might explain that the guide could be used to locate information for a research paper assigned by another teacher.

Consider the alternative if you do not clearly communicate the learning goals to enable the students to understand the goals. Students may go through the motions of an activity without understanding its purpose or its relationship to other content. Students may be concerned only with completing the assignment, rather than attempting to understand the purposes and objectives behind the assignment. Some students, in fact, may become passive when they see no academic purpose and consider assignments to be busy work with no specific learning objective.

Distributing and Collecting Materials.   You often need to distribute materials to students. Their maturity should be considered when determining the most appropriate time and way to distribute materials. Handouts, maps, or student guides can be distributed at the beginning of class to focus student attention on important material and to avoid disruptions during the lesson. Materials could be handed to students as they enter the room to save time during the lesson. You may prefer to distribute materials at the point in the lesson when the materials are actually needed.

Materials should be strategically located in the classroom to provide easy distribution and to minimize disruptions. For example, resource books that are used often should be located where there is sufficient room when they are needed. Procedures should be established for their distribution. You may have one row at a time get the resource books, have one student in each row get enough copies for that row, have students pick up a copy as soon as they enter the room, or give students copies as they enter the room.

Some materials that are distributed need to be collected later in the lesson, and appropriate ways to collect these materials should be selected. The manner of collecting the materials may be the same as or different from the way they were distributed.

Giving Clear, Focused Directions.   To give clear and focused directions, you first must carefully plan them. Directions are often given at the beginning of a lesson; of course, directions might also be given for activities throughout a lesson.

When *planning for directions,* you should (a) have no more than three student actions that are required for the activity to be described; (b) describe the directions in the order that students will be required to complete the tasks; (c) clarify what type and quality of product is expected; (d) make the description of each step specific and fairly brief; (e) provide written (on the chalkboard, a transparency, or a handout) and oral directions; (f) give the directions just before the activity; and (g) make provisions for assisting students who have difficulty.

TEACHERS IN ACTION

GIVING DIRECTIONS

Ron Butler, high school social studies teacher, Gillette, Wyoming

There are several parts of giving directions for class activities. First, I give detailed, step-by-step descriptions for what I want the students to do. This may include mentioning the pages in the textbook and the specific actions that I want the students to take. Second, I seek feedback from the students to see if they understand the directions. Especially when there are several steps in the directions, I ask a randomly selected student to repeat the directions to ensure that the students hear them again. At any time, I can correct any misunderstandings they have. Third, I screen the steps on the overhead projector so the students can refer to them as they move along.

When actually *giving directions,* you need to (a) get student attention, (b) give the directions, (c) check to see if students understand the directions ("Do you have any questions about what you need to do?"), (d) have the students begin the tasks, and (e) remediate if necessary if one or more students are not following directions. Clearly state what books and materials are needed.

It is often helpful to demonstrate the actions expected of the students by doing one problem or activity together. Students then see what is expected of them before they begin to work independently. Once they begin work, you should walk around to observe them to see if they are following the directions and to be available to answer student questions. If many questions arise, it may be useful to gain everyone's attention for further explanation.

■ ■ ■ ■ ■

CLASSROOM DECISIONS

Before starting a review session, students need directions for what they are to do. What directions would you give your students when having some students complete sample problems at the chalkboard? While others are at the board, what would you have the seated students do? How would you check for student understanding of the directions? How might you reinforce students who follow the directions?

The Middle of a Lesson

A number of teacher behaviors during lesson delivery contribute to effective group management. These include pacing the lesson, providing smooth transitions, avoiding satiation, managing seatwork effectively, having a task orientation, being clear, and exhibiting enthusiasm.

Pacing the Lesson.   *Pacing* is the speed at which the lesson proceeds. It is the rhythm, the ebb and flow, of a lesson. Effective pacing is neither too slow nor too fast. Adjustments in the pace of the lesson are made as needed. To effectively pace a lesson, you should not dwell too long on directions, distribute papers in a timely and efficient manner, and move from one activity to another smoothly and without interruption. Classrooms that lack effective pacing will drag at times or will move along at a pace where the students are unable to grasp the material. However, you should recognize it takes more time for students to mentally and physically transition from one activity to another than it does the teacher.

The following guidelines can be followed to effectively pace a lesson (Good & Brophy, 2000; Jones & Jones, 2001):

1. *Develop awareness of your own teaching tempo.* As you gain more experience in the classroom, you will be more aware of your own personal pace in the classroom. A good means of determining your pace is to audiotape or videotape your performance. In this way, you are able to determine how fast you talk, how you move around the classroom, or how much wait time you provide your students.

2. *Watch for nonverbal cues indicating that students are becoming puzzled or bored.* Monitor student attentiveness and then modify the pacing of the lesson as needed. If high-achieving students are looking puzzled, they and perhaps most of the class may be lost. The content may be too complex or being covered too quickly. A good indication that your pacing is too slow is if students are becoming restless and inattentive—looking out the window or fiddling with materials on their desks.

Savage (1999) recommends that teachers choose a pace that is appropriate for about 75 percent of the class. While this pace may be a bit slow for some learners, it will keep the lesson moving along and provide success for a majority of the students. You might select several students to notice on a regular basis throughout the lesson as indicators of your pacing.

3. *Break activities up into short segments.* Many teachers go through an entire activity before beginning discussion or review. However, it is more effective to break the activities up into shorter segments and to ask questions or review these shorter segments rather than the entire activity.

4. *Provide short breaks for lessons that last longer than 30 minutes.* Long lessons can cause inattentiveness and disruptive behavior. A three- to five-minute break can allow the students to return fresh to the activity. These breaks can be short games related to the activity or a stand-up-and-stretch break. A brief activity where students can get up to mingle can provide this break.

5. *Vary style as well as the content of the instruction.* Students often become restless with only a single instructional approach. A lesson plan that incorporates several instructional strategies will result in better attentiveness.

6. *Avoid interrupting the flow of the lesson with numerous stops and starts. Jerkiness* is a term that refers to behaviors that interfere with the smooth flow of the lesson. This occurs when the teacher (a) interrupts an ongoing activity without warning and gives directions to begin another activity, (b) leaves one activity dangling in midair, begins another, only to return to the first, or (c) leaves one activity for another and never returns to the first activity. In such instances, students never experience closure to the activities they were engaged in prior to the switch. Sudden reversals of activities tend to leave students flustered over not completing the previous activity and unprepared to begin the new activity.

7. *Avoid slowdowns that interfere with the pace of the lesson. Slowdowns,* or delays in the momentum or pace of a class, can occur due to overdwelling or fragmentation. *Overdwelling* occurs when teachers spend too much time on directions or explanations. Overdwelling also occurs when the teacher becomes so enthralled with the details of the lesson or a prop that is being used for a demonstration that the students lose sight of the main idea. For example, an English teacher may get so carried away describing the details of an author's life that the students barely have time to read the author's works. Another example is the science teacher who gets carried away describing the laboratory equipment so that the students have little time to conduct any experiments.

Fragmentation is another form of slowdown in which the teacher divides the lesson into such minute fragments that some of the students are left waiting and become bored. For example, the directions for an experiment may be broken down into such minute, simple parts that the students feel belittled by the teacher, or an activity is done by one row of students at a time, leaving many students waiting.

8. *Provide a summary at the end of a lesson segment.* Rather than plan for a single summary at the end of a lesson, it might help the pacing of the lesson to summarize after each main point or activity. For example, students might be asked to write a one-sentence summary of each scene as the play is read orally.

Providing Smooth Transitions.   *Transitions* are movements from one activity to another. A smooth transition allows one activity to flow into another without any breaks in the delivery of the lesson (Doyle, 1984; Smith, 1984). Transitions that are not smooth create gaps in the delivery of the lesson.

Transition time can occur when (a) students remain at their seats and change from one subject to another, (b) students move from their seats to an activity in another part of the classroom, (c) students move from somewhere else in the classroom back to their seats, (d) students leave the classroom to go outside or to another part of the school building, or (e) students come back into the classroom from outside or another part of the building.

Disorder and misbehavior can arise during transition times. Arlin (1979) reported that there was almost twice as much disruption during transitions (including hitting, yelling, and other inappropriate actions) as during nontransition time. There are several reasons why transitions can be problematic (Gump, 1987). First, you may have difficulty getting the students to finish an activity, especially if they are deeply engaged in it. Second, transitions are more loosely structured than instructional activities, and there typically is more freedom to socialize and move around the room. Third, students may "save up" problems or tensions and deal with them during the transition time. For example, a student may ask to use the restroom, complain to you about another student, or ask permission to get something from a locker. Finally, there may be delays in getting students started in the new activity.

MODIFICATIONS FOR DIVERSE CLASSROOMS

PACING LESSONS TO ACCOMMODATE ALL LEARNERS

Pacing is the speed at which the lesson proceeds. Although students vary in the amount of time that they need to process new information and skills, in lessons involving whole-class instruction you will need to make decisions about how quickly you want to move ahead to the next point in the lesson. The time that students need will be affected by cognitive skills, learning styles, language, and other factors. Some students will want to move ahead more quickly, others will want more time. Dealing with this issue is a struggle that all teachers confront.

Your number one concern should be about student learning.

1. If there is a great deal of diversity in your classroom causing considerable variation in the amount of time needed to learn the content, how might you adjust your selection of instructional strategies? Might you also group your students in some ways to facilitate learning? How will these decisions affect the pacing of lessons?

2. In lessons involving whole-class instruction, how might you make provisions for the various time needs of the students?

To reduce the potential for disorder during transitions, you should prepare students for upcoming transitions, establish efficient transition routines, and clearly define the boundaries of lessons. Jones and Jones (2001) offer several suggestions for effective transitions:

1. *Arrange the classroom for efficient movement.* Arrange the classroom so that you and the students can move freely without disturbing those who are working.

2. *Create and post a daily schedule and discuss any changes each morning.* Posting a daily schedule will aid in the elimination of confusion in the students.

3. *Have material ready for the next lesson.* Teachers need to prepare and gather materials for the next lesson to ensure that class time is not taken and that activities flow smoothly.

4. *Do not relinquish students' attention until you have given clear instructions for the following activity.* All too often, teachers allow the class to become disruptive while they pause between activities or lessons to prepare for the next lesson. It requires considerable time and energy to regain the students' attention.

5. *Do not do tasks that can be done by students.* Have students take responsibility for their own preparations for the next class session. This will enable you to monitor student actions.

6. *Move around the room and attend to individual needs.* By moving around the room, you are able to notice any minor disturbances that might expand into major problems.

7. *Provide students with simple, step-by-step directions.* Clearly state exactly what you want your students to do during the time given for the transition.

8. *Remind students of key procedures associated with the upcoming lesson.* Reviewing standard procedures and discussing unique procedures for an upcoming activity helps promote smooth transitions because students know what is expected of them.

9. *Develop transition activities.* After lunch or physical education, for example, students are excited and may not be ready for quieter work. As a result, you could choose structured transition activities to prepare the student for the next class session. These might include reading to students, discussing the daily schedule, having students write in a journal, or some type of activity that may not necessarily deal with the content of the next class session. After this transition time, students will likely be more ready to begin the next class session.

CLASSROOM DECISIONS

Assume that you have planned a lesson in which the students, in sequence, view a videotape, have small-group discussions about the videotape, and then individually outline some content and answer some questions from the textbook. What arrangements would you need to make to ensure smooth transitions throughout the lesson? How might the directions that you determine for the lesson take into account the need for smooth transitions?

Avoiding Satiation.   *Satiation* means that students have had enough of something, and this may lead to boredom, restlessness, and off-task behavior. For example, students may enjoy seeing a videotape, writing a creative story, or working in pairs on a project. When these activities are used too often or for too much time, however, students will start to lose interest, become bored, and will likely get off-task. You need to guard against planning activities that will lead to satiation.

There are three ways to avoid satiation (Kounin, 1970). First, have students experience *progress,* which is the feeling students get when they are steadily moving toward some significant objective. Pacing and group focus help achieve this feeling of progress. Avoid dwelling on one topic too long to promote feelings of progress. Second, provide *variety* as an effective way to avoid satiation. At the same time, classroom routines are necessary to preserve order and organization. You need to sense when enough is enough. Instructional variety helps invite inquisitiveness, excitement, and interest. Third, select an appropriate degree of *challenge* in academic work expected of students. Students do not tire of success if the success is a genuine test of their abilities and culminates in personally relevant accomplishments. When the challenge is sufficient to court and fortify the best efforts of students, satiation is seldom a problem.

Managing Seatwork Effectively.   *Seatwork* involves students working on assignments during class that provide practice or review of previously presented material. Students spend hundreds of hours during a school year doing seatwork privately at their desks. It is imperative that you structure seatwork so that it is done effectively while enabling students to experience a high rate of success.

Guidelines for successfully implementing seatwork in the classroom come from a variety of sources (Rosenshine & Stevens, 1986; Weinstein, 2003; Weinstein & Mignano, 1997; Jones & Jones, 2001). The following recommendations represent a synthesis from these sources:

1. Recognize that seatwork is intended to practice or review previously presented material. It is not suited for students to learn new material.
2. Devote no more time to seatwork than is allocated to content development activities.
3. Give clear instruction—explanations, questions, and feedback—and sufficient practice before the students begin their seatwork. Having to provide lengthy explanations during seatwork is troublesome for both you and the student. In addition to procedural directions, explain why the activities are being done and how to do the seatwork.
4. Work through the first few problems of the seatwork together with the students before having them continue independently. This provides a model for completing the work and provides an opportunity for the students to ask questions for clarification about the content or procedures.
5. Decide if you will allow talking during seatwork. It is often desirable to start out with no talking during seatwork to have students work alone. After a month or two, teachers sometimes allow students to quietly talk with others to seek or provide help. Clarify when quiet talking is allowed.
6. Circulate from student to student during seatwork, actively explaining, observing, asking questions, and giving feedback. Monitoring students to provide this positive and corrective feedback is very important.

TEACHERS IN ACTION

MONITORING DURING SEATWORK

Edward Gamble, third grade teacher, Jamestown, Rhode Island

During seatwork, I used to have students come up to my desk to see me if they had any questions or problems. I discovered that students would line up to see me, and they would talk or misbehave while waiting their turn in line. By staying in my seat, I also realized that I wasn't noticing the other stu-dents very much. As a result, I decided to have everyone stay in their seat during seatwork and raise their hand if they had a question. Overall, this monitoring increased my awareness of what the students were doing and how they were doing.

---

7. Determine how students will seek help from the teacher. When students are working at their seats and need help, ask them to raise their hands. You can then go to them or signal them to come to you at an appropriate time.

8. Determine when students can get out of their seats. To eliminate unnecessary wandering around the room during seatwork, decide when and for what purpose students can get out of their seats. For example, students may get supplies, sharpen pencils, or turn in papers only when necessary.

9. Have short contacts with individual students (i.e., 30 seconds or less).

10. Break seatwork into short segments rather than one long time slot. Rather than having one lengthy presentation of content followed by an extended period of seatwork, break up instruction into a number of segments followed by brief seatwork after each segment.

11. Arrange seats to facilitate monitoring the students (e.g., face both small groups and independently working students).

12. Establish a routine to use during seatwork activity that prescribes what students will do when they have completed the exercises. Students may complete an additional enrichment assignment for extra credit or use the time for free reading or to work on assignments from other classes.

Being Task Oriented.   *Task orientation* has to do with your concern that all relevant material be covered and learned as opposed to your being mired in procedural matters or extraneous material. Task-oriented teachers provide an appropriate amount of time lecturing, asking questions, and engaging the students in activities directly related to the material that is to be learned. Achievement is reported to be higher in classrooms of task-oriented teachers than in classrooms where teachers tend to be off-task.

Task-oriented teachers are goal-oriented, and they plan instructional strategies and activities that support these goals. In addition, task-oriented teachers have a high, but realistic, set of expectations for their students. To be task oriented in the classroom, you should (a) develop unit and lesson plans that reflect the curriculum; (b) handle administrative and clerical interruptions efficiently; (c) stop or prevent misbehavior with a minimum of class disruption; (d) select the most appropriate instructional model for objectives being taught; and (e) establish cycles of review, feedback, and testing (Borich, 2000).

Ensuring Academic Learning Time.   *Academic learning time* is the amount of time students are successfully engaged in learning activities. However, the amount of time that students are actively engaged or on-task can vary greatly across and within classrooms. Low-achieving students often go off-task due to frustrations about not understanding class material. High-achieving students, on the other hand, tend to go off-task after they have completed their assigned work. Therefore, you should ensure that all students are able to be successfully engaged in classroom tasks while also ensuring that high-achieving students are engaged throughout the lesson. Provide feedback and correctives to students who need assistance, and at the same time monitor the rate of students' progress through the lesson.

For new material that students have not yet mastered, expect a lower success rate initially but set a goal of higher success rates as students receive feedback on their performance and gain confidence. As a general rule, students should have a success rate of approximately 80 percent on most initial tasks. The rate of success should be somewhat higher when students are engaged in independent work, such as homework or independent seatwork (Berliner, 1987). The goal is to ensure that students are given meaningful tasks to complete, are given feedback and correctives when needed, and are ultimately able to successfully complete all assigned tasks.

Being Clear.   *Clarity* refers to the precision of your communication to your students regarding the desired behavior. Clarity in teaching helps students understand better, work more accurately, and be more successful. Effective teachers exhibit a high degree of clarity by providing very clear and explicit directions, instructions, questions, and expectations. If you are constantly asked to repeat questions, directions, and explanations, or if your students do not understand your expectations, you are not exhibiting clarity in your instructional behavior.

Clear directions, instructions, and expectations need to be given. Students then know what is expected of them and can act accordingly as they work on classroom activities, assignments, and other tasks. If you are not very clear when giving directions, for example, the student may not complete the assignment in the way you intended, may become confused, and may need additional time and attention to later complete the assignment in the manner intended.

To be clear in the classroom, (a) inform the learners of the objective; (b) provide learners with advance organizers; (c) check for task-relevant prior learning and reteach, if necessary; (d) give directions slowly and distinctly; (e) know the ability levels of students and teach to those levels; (f) use examples, illustrations, and demonstrations to explain and clarify; and (g) provide a review or summary at the end of each lesson (Borich, 2000).

Exhibiting Enthusiasm.   *Enthusiasm* is an expression of excitement and intensity. It is quite obvious that a teacher who is enthusiastic and vibrant is more entertaining to observe than an unenthusiastic teacher. However, teacher enthusiasm has also been related to higher student achievement (Good & Brophy, 2000). Enthusiasm has two important dimensions: interest and involvement with the subject matter, and vigor and physical dynamism. Enthusiastic teachers are often described as stimulating, dynamic, expressive, and energetic. Their behavior suggests that they are committed to the students and to the subject matter. While teachers often expect students to be interested in *what* they say, students more often react to *how* enthusiastically it is said.

Enthusiasm can be conveyed in a variety of ways. These include the use of animated gestures, eye contact, voice inflection, and movement around the room. A teacher who is enthusiastic in the classroom often manages to develop enthusiastic students. Constant, highly enthusiastic actions are not necessary and, in fact, may be counterproductive. Instead, a variety of enthusiastic actions, ranging from low to high degrees of enthusiasm, is appropriate.

The Ending of a Lesson

As stated earlier, an effective lesson has three important sections: a beginning, a middle, and an end. All three sections must be planned and implemented effectively if a lesson is to be successful. Simply ending a lesson when the bell rings or when you have covered the planned material is not appropriate. In such cases, students are not given the opportunity to place the lesson in a context with other related lessons or are not permitted to ask questions that might clarify a misunderstood point from the lesson. Providing a summary is imperative for a successful lesson. Furthermore, students need time at the end of the lesson to get ready to leave the classroom.

Providing Closure to Part of a Lesson.   *Closure* refers to actions or statements that are designed to bring a lesson presentation to an appropriate conclusion (Shostak, 1999). There are three major purposes for closure.

1. *Draw attention to the end of a lesson segment or the lesson itself.* Often students need to be cued that they have arrived at an important segment of the lesson or that it is time to wrap things up. They might be cued with a statement that it is time to summarize key concepts.

2. *Help organize student learning.* It is the teacher's responsibility to relate the many pieces of the lesson to the whole. Some students are able to do this by themselves while

---

TEACHERS IN ACTION

INCLUDE IMPROVISATION IN YOUR LESSONS

Steffanie Ogg, high school teacher, St. Paul, Minnesota

Improvisations, especially in history, are helpful. Students really enjoy the lessons when I dress up and act like someone we are studying. It is amazing how much wearing a K-Mart vest to class to discuss employment skills will do for students' interest and discussion.

Once, while teaching United States history, I was trying to get students to understand aspects of the Revolutionary War and Valley Forge. I opened all the windows in the classroom (it was winter) and brought down the fans. If the students remembered nothing else, they will remember that it was cold during this particular time.

others need the teacher's assistance. To accomplish this purpose, you might provide a diagram, illustration, outline, or other type of summary which indicates how all the content of the lesson is related.

3. *Consolidate or reinforce the major points.* You might emphasize or highlight certain concepts at this point. The major objective is to help the student retain the information presented in the lesson for future use.

Closure is important because students instinctively structure information into patterns that make sense to them. If a learning experience is left with some uncertainties, students may draw inaccurate conclusions as they create their own patterns of understanding from the material, thus detracting from future learning. The second and third purposes involve summarizing, which is addressed later. The time at the end of a lesson segment or the lesson itself can be used to make homework assignments. Between lesson segments, students may be given five to ten minutes to start the homework assignment while you move around the room to answer questions which might arise.

CLASSROOM DECISIONS

Let's assume that you are teaching a history lesson in which a series of significant dates and related events have been discussed. How might you bring closure to this part of the lesson in a way that helps students see how all the dates and events are related? How might you involve students in this closure? How might you take into account students' varied learning styles?

Summarizing the Lesson.   Providing a *summary* of the main points of a lesson can help students gain a better idea of the content or to clarify any misunderstandings. You should plan to stop the lesson several minutes before the bell rings to begin the summation. Make sure that you have the attention of all students before the summary begins. You should avoid merely reiterating the content covered during the lesson. Ask several questions that encourage the students to relate key aspects of the lesson or to evaluate key points. Also, you can ask students for their opinions about what they believe are the key points of the lesson.

To add interest and variety, vary the way that the lesson summary is conducted. Some days may involve simply a series of questions for students. On other days, you may ask several students to go to the chalkboard to solve a problem and discuss the thought process involved. A game format could be used as a means of summary, such as questions out of a hat or a "Trivial Pursuit" type of approach. Several creative approaches could offer the desired variety lesson summaries.

The summary should be used to determine if the students have grasped the main ideas of the lesson (Rosenshine & Stevens, 1986). For example, your summary might discover that several students do not understand the key concepts of a math lesson. It would be foolish to teach the next math lesson as though students understand the concept. There-

---

SPOTLIGHT ON TECHNOLOGY

USING MEDIA TO SUMMARIZE LESSONS AND ASSESS STUDENT LEARNING

At the end of a lesson, you need to provide a summary of the main points of the lesson. Many teachers also use this time as an opportunity to informally assess student learning. To do so, you could use some type of instructional media to summarize the lesson and assess student learning. In addition, some teachers like to get feedback from students at the end of a lesson about the effectiveness of the instructional strategies or the instructional media that was used. These questions can guide your thinking as you address these issues.

1. How can technology be used to determine the degree of student learning that has occurred?
2. How can technology be used to generate teacher and student feedback?
3. In what ways can technology be used to measure the effectiveness, efficiency, and appeal of the implemented instructional materials?

---

fore, you can use the information gathered during the summary to adjust the next day's lesson plan.

Getting Ready to Leave.   At the end of the lesson, middle, junior high, or senior high school students usually need to leave the classroom and go to their next class. The bell will ring at the end of the class period, and the students will have just a few minutes to get to their next class in another room in the building.

You should plan to complete all instruction and lesson summary by the end of the class period so that students are not delayed in moving to the next class. You should not teach right up to the bell, because time needs to be allowed for several other events. First, you must allow time for students to return any books, supplies, or materials to the appropriate locations.

Also, students need time to throw away any scrap paper and to straighten up the classroom. They need time to put away their own books, papers, pencils, or other materials before leaving. You may plan to reserve from 1 to 4 minutes at the end of a lesson to allow sufficient time for these final actions to be completed before the bell rings. Students then should be dismissed on time. You need to schedule this time when planning lessons.

KEY TERMS

Academic accountability	Fragmentation	Set induction
Academic learning time	Jerkiness	Slowdowns
Advance organizer	Motivation to learn	Student-centered approaches
Anticipatory set	Overdwelling	Summary
Clarity	Pacing	Task orientation
Closure	Satiation	Teacher-centered approaches
Enthusiasm	Seatwork	Transitions

MAJOR CONCEPTS

1. The degree of structure in the lesson needs to be taken into account when managing instruction and promoting appropriate behavior.

2. Students are more likely to stay on-task when they are held academically accountable for their work.

3. When beginning a lesson, teachers need to take attendance, solicit attention, provide daily review, provide a set induction, introduce lesson objectives, distribute materials, and give clear, focused directions.

4. When conducting the body of a lesson, effective teachers pace the lesson, provide smooth transitions, avoid satiation, manage seatwork effectively, have a task orientation, are clear, and exhibit enthusiasm.

5. An effective teacher ends a lesson with a summary of important concepts covered in the lesson and allows students time to get ready to leave the room after the lesson.

DISCUSSION/REFLECTIVE QUESTIONS

1. In what ways might the selection of the various accountability procedures be affected by differences in grade level and subject areas?

2. From your own school experiences, what approaches to review did you find the most successful? What are the merits of using different approaches for review?

3. What are some factors that teachers might take into account when deciding on a particular approach to distribute materials to students?

4. Identify situations during a lesson where transitions are needed. How can a teacher ensure smooth transitions at these points?

5. Recall several examples when your teachers were not clear in providing directions, instructions, or expectations. What effect did this lack of clarity have on you as a student?

6. What are some ways that a summary of a lesson could be provided either by the teacher or the students?

SUGGESTED ACTIVITIES

For Clinical Settings

1. List a number of ways that you could conduct daily and weekly reviews.

2. Prepare guidelines for yourself for the selection of seatwork tasks and the assigning and monitoring of seatwork.

3. List a number of approaches that you could use to summarize a lesson. Some of the techniques could be directed by you and some could involve students in an active way.

For Field Settings

1. Talk to teachers about how they hold students academically accountable for each area in Table 9.1.

2. Talk with two or more teachers to determine the ways that they begin and end a lesson.

3. Observe teachers to identify how they handle transitions from one activity or event to another. Talk with these teachers to identify issues that they consider when handling transitions.

USEFUL RESOURCES

Good, T., & Brophy, J. (2000). *Looking into classrooms* (8th ed.). New York: Longman.

Includes thorough review of many aspects of teaching including classroom life, expectations, management, motivation, groupings, and instructional approaches.

WEB SITES

- This collection contains more than 1,100 unique lesson plans written and submitted to AskERIC by teachers from all over the United States.

  http://www.askeric.org/Virtual/Lessons/

- Tons of information and links to a host of classroom topics

  www.awesomelibrary.org/teacher.html

- Google.com and other search engines. You can use a search engine to explore any topic in this chapter.

  http://google.com

http://yahoo.com
http://excite.com
http://search.netscape.com
http://altavista.com
http://askjeeves.com

CHAPTER TEN

CLASSROOM MANAGEMENT

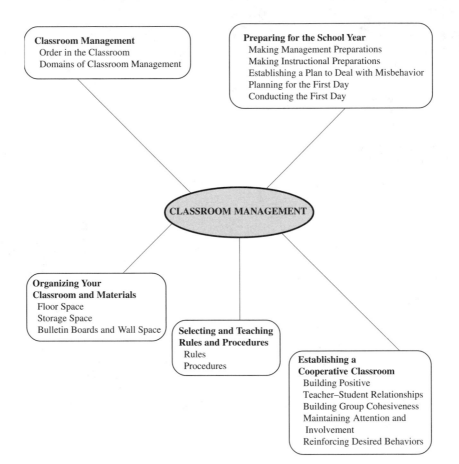

Classroom Management
  Order in the Classroom
  Domains of Classroom Management

Preparing for the School Year
  Making Management Preparations
  Making Instructional Preparations
  Establishing a Plan to Deal with Misbehavior
  Planning for the First Day
  Conducting the First Day

CLASSROOM MANAGEMENT

**Organizing Your
Classroom and Materials**
  Floor Space
  Storage Space
  Bulletin Boards and Wall Space

**Selecting and Teaching
Rules and Procedures**
  Rules
  Procedures

**Establishing a
Cooperative Classroom**
  Building Positive
  Teacher–Student Relationships
  Building Group Cohesiveness
  Maintaining Attention and
  Involvement
  Reinforcing Desired Behaviors

OBJECTIVES

This chapter provides information that will help you to:

1. Describe the role of classroom management in creating a learning community.

2. Determine what constitutes order in the classroom.

3. Identify the domains of responsibility for classroom management and discipline.

4. Identify ways to prepare for the school year.

5. Describe ways to organize your classroom and materials.

6. Select and teach classroom rules and procedures.

7. Identify ways to establish a cooperative classroom.

**PRAXIS/Principles of Learning
and Teaching/Pathwise**

The following principles are relevant to content in this chapter:

1. Creating a climate that promotes fairness   (B1)

2. Establishing and maintaining rapport with students   (B2)

3. Establishing and maintaining consistent standards of classroom behavior   (B4)

4. Making the physical environment as safe and conducive to learning as possible   (B5)

INTASC

The following INTASC standards are relevant to content in this chapter:

1. The teacher uses an understanding of individual and group motivation and behavior to create a learning environment and encourages positive social interaction, active engagement in learning, and self-motivation.   (Standard 5)

2. The teacher uses knowledge of effective verbal, nonverbal, and media communication techniques to foster active inquiry, collaboration, and supportive interaction in the classroom.   (Standard 6)

What do award-winning teachers do that make them so popular and successful? Do they jazz up the curriculum in some way? Do they use especially creative instructional approaches? Do they warm up to the students as if they were their own children? Do they add some magic or sparkle to the classroom experience? The answer is probably a little of each of these suggestions. But it likely goes deeper than that.

Successful teachers are often very effective managers of the classroom environment. They create a positive learning community where students are actively involved in their own learning and the management of the classroom. They organize the physical environment, manage student behavior, create a respectful environment, facilitate instruction, promote safety and wellness, and interact with others when needed. All these issues relate to classroom management. The main objective is to create a positive learning community and then to take steps to maintain this positive environment by guiding and correcting student behavior.

Problems with student misbehavior are minimized in a learning community where students are actively involved in their classroom and instruction. A learning community is designed to help all students to feel safe, respected, and valued in order to learn new skills. Successful classrooms are those in which students feel supported in their learning and are willing to take risks, challenged to become fully human with one another, and open to new possibilities. Many aspects of classroom management help to promote learning communities.

CLASSROOM MANAGEMENT

Classroom management involves teacher actions to create a learning environment that encourages positive social interaction, active engagement in learning, and self-motivation. Several key questions come to mind about classroom management. How can the physical environment be organized? How can the school year begin effectively? What rules and procedures are appropriate? How can students be held academically accountable? How can appropriate behavior be encouraged and supported? How might order be restored if there are disruptions? How can class time and instruction be managed effectively? How can the safety of students be assured? All these issues are part of classroom management. Before discussing the areas of responsibility in classroom management, the issue of order in the classroom is examined.

Order in the Classroom

A learning community needs to have order for students to be successful. *Order* means that students are following the actions necessary for a particular classroom event to be successful; students are focused on the instructional tasks and are not misbehaving. Establishing and maintaining order are an important part of classroom management.

It is useful to distinguish the difference between off-task behavior and misbehavior. *Off-task behavior* includes student actions that are not focused on the instructional activities, yet would not be considered to be disruptive or be defined as misbehavior. Off-task behavior includes daydreaming, writing notes or doodling, or not paying attention. *Misbehavior* includes behavior that interferes with your teaching, interferes with the rights of others to learn, is psychologically or physically unsafe, or destroys property (Levin & Nolan, 2000). Classroom order is threatened by misbehavior. *Discipline* is the act of responding to misbehaving students in an effort to restore order.

There are several important issues concerning order:

1. *A minimal level of order is necessary for instruction to occur.* Order can be established for instruction by actions such as selecting rules and procedures, encouraging and reinforcing appropriate behavior, reacting to misbehavior, and managing instructional tasks. With many students off-task, instruction cannot occur.

2. *Student involvement in learning tasks is affected by order in the classroom.* An effective classroom manager places emphasis on managing the group, rather than managing individual students. When there is order in the classroom, individual students can become engaged in the instructional tasks.

3. *Student cooperation is necessary in establishing order.* Order in classrooms is achieved *with* students and depends on their willingness to be part of the sequence of events. Students in a learning community want to cooperate because they see the benefits of doing so.

4. *Expectations for order are affected by a number of classroom variables.* Teacher expectations for order may vary depending on factors such as the type of instructional activities, the maturity level of the students, the time of day, the time in the lesson, and the particular students involved. For example, a teacher may not enforce a certain rule at the end of a class period when students are gathering their books and materials in the same way as when a discussion is underway in the middle of the class period.

CLASSROOM DECISIONS

Teachers often have special procedures and behavioral guidelines for times when students work in small groups or in a lab setting. Suppose that you are dividing your science class into small groups to examine and test a number of rock and mineral samples in various ways? How might your decisions about guidelines to maintain control be affected by the age level and maturity of the students? How might you need to monitor students differently to maintain control in small groups as compared to whole-class instruction?

Domains of Classroom Management

There are several domains of responsibility for classroom management and discipline (see Table 10.1). An effective classroom manager handles the following seven areas of responsibility (Burden, 2003):

1. *Select a philosophical model of classroom management and discipline.* A number of educators have proposed certain models of classroom management and discipline, such as teaching with love and logic, cooperative discipline, discipline with dignity, and assertive discipline. These models reflect various philosophical views of student development, teaching and learning, and classroom management. Viewing these proposed models on a continuum, they range from low teacher control to high teacher control.

These theoretical models are useful to teachers because they offer a basis for analyzing, understanding, and managing student and teacher behavior. With an understanding of these varied theoretical approaches, you can assess your position on these issues and then select a philosophical model that is consistent with your beliefs. The techniques that you use to manage student behavior should be consistent with your beliefs about how students learn and develop.

TABLE 10.1   Domains of Responsibility for Classroom Management and Discipline

Classroom management involves teacher actions to create a learning environment that encourages positive social interaction, active engagement in learning, and self-motivation. An effective classroom manager handles these areas of responsibility:

1. Select a philosophical model of classroom management and discipline.
2. Organize the physical environment.
3. Manage student behavior.
4. Create a respectful, supportive learning environment.
5. Manage and facilitate instruction.
6. Promote classroom safety and wellness.
7. Interact with colleagues, parents, and others to achieve classroom management objectives.

2. *Organize the physical environment.* The way the desks, tables, and other classroom materials are arranged affects instruction and has an influence on order in the classroom. To create an effective learning environment, you will need to organize several aspects of the physical space. First, you will need to arrange the floor space with the placement of student desks, the teacher's desk, bookcases, filing cabinets, tables, and activity centers. Second, you will need to decide how to store a number of materials, including textbooks and resource books, frequently used instructional materials, teacher supplies and instructional materials, equipment, and infrequently used materials. Finally, you will need to decide how to use bulletin boards and wall space. Decisions in all these areas will determine how you will organize the physical environment for teaching and learning.

3. *Manage student behavior.* Guidelines are needed to promote order in the classroom and to provide a conducive learning environment. Rules and procedures support teaching and learning and provide students with clear expectations and well-defined norms. This, in turn, helps to create a safe, secure atmosphere for learning.

Rules are general codes of conduct that are intended to guide individual student behavior in an attempt to promote positive interaction and avoid disruptive behavior. Procedures are approved ways to achieve specific tasks in the classroom, such as handing in completed work or sharpening a pencil.

When misbehavior occurs, teachers need to respond in an effort to get the student back on task and to maintain order in the classroom. A three-step response plan is discussed in Chapter 11, including providing assistance to get the student back on task as the first step, followed by the use of mild responses such as nonverbal and verbal signals, and then ending with moderate responses such as withdrawing privileges or changing the seat assignment. Special approaches are often needed to deal with challenging students.

To establish order, you must teach, demonstrate, establish, and enforce classroom procedures and routines at the start of the year. Successful classroom managers hover over activities at the beginning of the year and usher them along until students have learned the work system.

4. *Create a respectful, supportive learning environment.* There are many facets to creating a favorable learning environment, but it is vital for a positive learning community.

TEACHERS IN ACTION

ESTABLISHING RULES FOR CONTROLLING CONDUCT

Beatrice Gilkes, high school computer science teacher, Washington, D.C.

To help maintain control in the classroom, I ask my students to discuss realistic expectations for all persons in the classroom, including myself, that will help to lead to the students being successful. Next, we discuss and select specific rules of behavior that affect maximum learning success in the classroom. Throughout this discussion, we emphasize three key words: love, respect, and commitment. We then commit ourselves to these rules, and their recommendations for penalties are included in the agreement. Students place this list of rules in their notebooks. This approach to getting a commitment from the students about classroom conduct has been effective for me in 40 years of teaching.

First, teachers can take a number of actions to establish a cooperative, responsible classroom by developing positive teacher–student relationships, promoting students' self-esteem, and building group cohesiveness. These actions will help to create an environment where students feel valued and comfortable, thus setting the stage for teaching and learning. Second, teachers can focus student attention on appropriate classroom behavior by helping students to assume responsibility for their behavior, maintaining student attention and involvement, and reinforcing desired behaviors.

Third, a comprehensive plan can be developed to motivate students to learn, involving decisions about instructional tasks, feedback and evaluation, and academic and behavioral expectations. Finally, teachers can be most effective in creating a respectful, supportive learning environment when they have an understanding of the diverse learners in their classroom.

5. *Manage and facilitate instruction.* Certain factors in a lesson have a bearing on classroom order, and teachers need to take these factors into account when planning lessons. These include decisions about the degree of structure of the lesson, the type of instructional groups to use, and the means of holding the students academically accountable.

There are also certain actions that teachers often take at the beginning, middle, and end of a lesson that affect the order of the classroom. These include actions such as taking attendance, giving directions, distributing materials, handling transitions, summarizing the lesson, and preparing to leave. Collectively, these instructional management skills help to manage and facilitate instruction, while also influencing classroom order.

6. *Promote classroom safety and wellness.* Students need to feel physically and emotionally safe before they can give their full attention to the instructional tasks. Strategies used to manage student behavior, create a supportive classroom, and manage and facilitate instruction all contribute to classroom safety and wellness. In addition, teachers sometimes need to take actions to solve problems and conflicts that threaten classroom order and the learning environment. For this reason, it is helpful to have a set of tools such as dealing with conflict resolution and anger management to solve problems.

Students who are considered difficult or challenging may threaten the sense of safety and wellness in the classroom. Their actions may cause other students to take guarded or even confrontational actions in response to difficult students. For these reasons, teachers need to be prepared to deal with challenging students in constructive ways.

7. *Interact with colleagues, parents, and others to achieve classroom management objectives.* Working with parents is another means to help to maintain order in the classroom. When the parents and teacher communicate and get along together, students will more likely receive the needed guidance and support and will likely have more self-control in the classroom. In addition, teachers may need to consult and interact with colleagues and others when difficulties occur with classroom management and student behavior.

PREPARING FOR THE SCHOOL YEAR

Imagine that you are going to take a two-week vacation to see the numerous state and national parks in southern Utah and northern Arizona. You gather information about the parks and attractions from a variety of sources, and then you start to plan your itinerary.

Next, you make motel reservations and list all the things that you need to take with you, such as hiking shoes, water bottles, sunscreen, sunglasses, camera, and clothing. Before you leave on the trip, you stop your newspaper and mail delivery and make arrangements for your pets for the days that you are gone. All these arrangements, and probably more, are needed to have a fun, trouble-free vacation.

Starting the school year also requires this type of advance planning. Even before school starts, you can make a number of decisions about instructional and management preparations, plans to promote a positive learning climate, plans for the very first day of school, and arrangements for floor space, storage, and other aspects of classroom space. Early planning and decision making on these issues will help to ensure a positive beginning to the school year. Studies on classroom management have verified that the first few days of the school year set the tone for the entire year (Emmer et al., 2000; Evertson et al., 2000).

To prepare, you can make management preparations and instructional preparations, establish a plan for misbehavior, and also plan for the first day of school. When the school year finally begins, there are certain actions that are appropriate during the first day and over the following few days. A number of these issues are addressed in this section. A number of resources provide more details than can be discussed in this chapter. Resources are available for the *elementary* grades (Canter & Associates, 1998; Williamson, 1998; Bosch & Kersey, 2000; Moran et al., 2000; Jonson, 2001; Roberts, 2001), *secondary* grades (Arnold, 2001; Wyatt & White, 2001), and *K–12* grades (Wong & Wong, 1998; Schell & Burden, 2000).

Making Management Preparations

It is important to consider carefully a variety of management issues such as your school environment, room arrangement, materials, rules and procedures, communication with parents, seating arrangements, and other issues. Based on a study of experienced teachers (Schell & Burden, 2000), you could direct your attention to the following classroom management issues.

1. *The school environment.* The first step is to become thoroughly familiar with the total environment before school starts: the room, school, facilities, personnel, services, resources, policies and procedures, other teachers, children, and the community. You will then have more information upon which to make decisions, will probably feel more confident about your job, and will not need to devote time in the first few weeks to gather this information.

2. *Gather support materials.* After examining the curriculum guide and the textbooks, you might have ideas about activities for a certain unit or lesson. Supplementary materials may be needed when the time comes to teach that lesson. This is the time to gather any additional support materials such as games and devices, pictures, cassette tapes, ideas for activities, charts, maps, and graphs. The school may have discretionary funds for their purchase. They may be obtained from school supply catalogs, a local teacher store, or even at garage sales.

3. *Organize materials.* It is useful to set up a filing system for storing district and school communications and other important documents. Papers kept in a filing cabinet include the district's policy handbook; correspondence from the principal, superintendent, or other supervisors; correspondence from professional organizations; lesson plans; and items on curricular content.

Some teachers use file folders. A separate file folder may be created for each course unit to hold pertinent notes and resource materials. Textbooks, resource books, manipulative materials, and other types of instructional supplies and materials also need to be organized and stored.

4. *Classroom procedures.* You can follow various procedures to accomplish specific tasks. Procedures may be identified regarding handing in completed work, sharpening a pencil, using the restroom, or putting away supplies. Before school starts, identify actions or activities requiring procedures that would contribute to a smoothly running classroom, and then decide what those procedures should be.

5. *Classroom helpers.* Teachers call upon students at all grade levels as helpers to perform various classroom tasks. Make a list of tasks that need to be done and then decide which ones students could perform. Give attention to how task assignment will be rotated to give every student an opportunity to help. Roles are often held for one or two weeks before the assignments are rotated. Depending on the grade level and circumstances, some tasks may include students as line leaders, light switcher, pencil sharpener, paper collector, plant waterer, chalkboard eraser, window and blind opener, and supply manager.

6. *Class lists and rosters.* It is useful to plan a means to record whether students have returned their book orders, picture money, field-trip permission forms, and so on. You can prepare a generic class roster listing the students' names in alphabetical order in the left column, with blank columns on the right to check off the action. It is helpful to input the list on a computer program so that an updated sheet can be easily generated when the roster changes.

7. *Home/school communication.* Open communication with parents is vital. Before school starts, many teachers prepare an introductory letter to parents to welcome them and to inform them about the teacher, the curriculum, grading practices and standards, the homework policy, rules and procedures, and so on. This letter can be sent home with the students on the first day of school. Teachers can also make plans for other types of parental communication such as phone calls, progress reports, or a back-to-school night.

8. *Birthdays and other celebrations.* Depending on your grade level, you may want to recognize student birthdays. Most schools have very specific policies for celebrating major holidays, such as Halloween, Christmas, Hanukkah, Martin Luther King Jr. Day, and Easter. Inquire about these policies so you'll understand what is expected.

9. *Distributing textbooks.* Sometime in the first few days of school, you will need to distribute textbooks. You need to obtain the textbooks and prepare an inventory form on which to record each book number, with a space in which to write the student's name.

You need to think about when and how the textbooks will be distributed. Since the first day of school often necessitates many announcements and activities, you might want to wait until the second or third day before distributing textbooks, or distribute them just before they are needed for the first time. Attention might be given to the specific means of distribution. One way is to have students line up one row at a time and go to the table where the books are stacked. When giving the book to the student, you can record the student's name on the inventory form.

10. *Room identification.* On the first day of school, students need to locate your class-room. Especially for students new to the building, it is important to have the room clearly labeled. A poster on the outside doorway should include the room number, the teacher's name, the grade level and/or subject (Room 211, Mr. Wagner, World History). This infor-mation should also be written on the chalkboard so students see that they are in the correct classroom. Some type of welcoming statement should also be placed on the chalkboard, such as "Welcome; I'm glad you're here."

11. *Room arrangement.* Room arrangement is an issue that can be decided before school starts. Take into account the fixed features in the room, instructional materials and supplies, traffic areas, work areas, boundaries for activity areas, visibility to see all stu-dents, and the purposes of various seating arrangements. Determine the arrangement in the classroom for your desk, the students' desks, tables, book shelves, filing cabinets, and other furniture. The room arrangement that you select should be consistent with your in-structional goals and activities. Teacher-led instructional approaches such as presentations and demonstrations require one type of room arrangement, whereas small-group work re-quires a different type of arrangement.

12. *Seat selections and arrangements.* One teacher may prefer to select each student's seat, while another lets the students select their seats. This decision should be made before school starts. In either case, be sure that there are enough seats for the number of students you expect. You might take the age level and maturity of the students into account as you select the manner of assigning seats.

Inspect the seats to be sure they are not damaged and that they are of sizes to accom-modate your students. You might change the seating arrangements during the school year to accommodate work groups, to move students who need close supervision to more acces-sible seats, or simply to provide a change.

13. *Room decoration.* It is important to make your classroom an attractive, comfortable place. Consider having some plants in the classroom, or even an aquarium. Displays of pic-tures, posters, charts, and maps also help cover the walls with informative and appealing materials. Attractive bulletin boards add color. You might prepare one bulletin board list-ing classroom information and use another one to display seasonal items. After school starts, you could have students prepare bulletin boards.

Making Instructional Preparations

Prior to the start of the school year, carefully consider a variety of instructional issues such as long-range plans, supplementary materials, student assessment, a folder for substitute teachers, a syllabus, and so on. Based on a study of experienced teachers (Schell & Bur-den, 2000), you could direct your attention to the following instructional issues.

1. *Long-range plans.* It is helpful to peruse the curriculum guides and other related mate-rials so you can appreciate what should be covered by the end of the school year. Some tenta-tive decisions need to be made for the amount of time to be spent on each particular unit. Some curriculum guides include recommendations for the number of weeks to spend on each unit.

You may want to solicit advice from other teachers, particularly from those who teach your same subject or grade level. To the extent possible, make these rough schedules conform to the school calendar by taking into account grading periods and holidays. Be careful not to overschedule yourself. Leave some time for review near the end of each unit or chapter for reteaching as the situation warrants and for unexpected occurrences such as school closings due to inclement weather.

2. *Supplementary materials.* For each major curricular topic in your rough long-range plans, start an ongoing list of related supplementary materials or activities. It may include field-trip locations, resource people, media, games, assignments, bulletin boards, and additional books.

Inquire about library or media center resources, such as films or videotapes, and order and reserve them. You might prepare other supplementary materials to use during the first few weeks of school.

3. *Skeleton plans.* A *skeleton plan* is a brief overview of intended accomplishments. It often includes a weekly list of expected accomplishments. Skeleton plans include more details than the long-range, yearly plans, but not the detail needed for daily lesson plans. Skeleton plans for the first three or four weeks serve as a guide for preparing the more detailed lesson plans.

4. *Weekly time schedules.* You should establish your weekly schedule before school starts and include a copy in a handy place such as in your lesson plan book. The weekly schedule is often displayed in a chart, with the weekdays listed at the top and the hours listed on the left-hand column. The class schedule for middle and secondary teachers probably will be determined by the principal or others in the school building, and it will show what grade level and subject are taught during each class period.

5. *Daily lesson plans.* After you have completed the skeleton plans for the first three or four weeks, it is time to prepare the daily lesson plans for the first week of school. Lesson-plan formats vary; one that is often used includes boxes for the days of the week and the subjects taught. In these boxes, notes may be included about objectives, a list of topics to be covered or activities to be conducted, materials, and means of assessment. Beginning and probationary teachers are often required to show the principal or assistant principal their weekly lesson plans for the coming week.

Many teachers prefer to begin the school year with an interesting review of the content the students had in the subject area in the previous year. This is a time to consolidate learning and review while giving you opportunities to reinforce subject matter and identify the students' level of understanding.

■ ■ ■ ■ ■

CLASSROOM DECISIONS

When starting the school year, you will need to decide on a format for your lesson plans. What type of information do you need to include in your lesson plans? How will you indicate any modifications needed due to the diversity of your students? How will you make provisions for adding your comments after conducting the lessons to serve as a guide for your next planning for and instruction of the lesson?

6. *Preparing a syllabus.* You need to give students information about each course at the start of the year. You could plan and prepare this information as well as any related materials before school starts. At the middle and secondary levels, teachers often give each student a course syllabus that outlines this introductory information (see Chapter 2).

The *course syllabus* includes the course title, the title of the textbook and any other primary resource materials, a brief course description, a list of course objectives, a content outline, course requirements (e.g., tests, homework, projects), how grades will be calculated (e.g., the points for each requirement and the point total needed for certain grades), a description of the homework policy, the attendance and tardiness policy, and a listing of classroom rules and procedures. Some teachers also include a description of the instructional methods and activities that students are to engage in.

7. *Preparing policy sheets.* The syllabus might include all related classroom policies and procedures, though some teachers do not include these items. (Depending on the grade level and circumstances, some teachers do not provide a course syllabus.) As a result, a teacher might prepare a separate policy sheet for the students. The sheet may state the classroom rules and procedures, the policy for attendance and tardiness, and the like. If a course syllabus is not used, this policy sheet might also state the grading policy.

8. *Tentative student assessment.* It is useful to make an initial assessment of the students' understanding and skills at the start of the school year so you can better recognize the abilities and differences within the class. These assessments could be conducted sometime during the first week of school, but you should think about how to plan for the assessment and then make any necessary arrangements before school starts. Assessment procedures might include worksheets, oral activities, observation checklists, pretests, or review lessons. After conducting these early assessments, you could then record the results on a class roster that was drawn up earlier.

9. *Planning for homework.* Give careful consideration to how you will evaluate students and determine report-card grades. One element of student evaluation often involves homework, and preparation for developing a homework policy can be done before school starts.

Prepare a homework policy in the form of a letter that is sent to parents at the start of the school year (see Chapter 14). The homework policy should explain why homework is assigned, explain the types of homework you will assign, inform parents of the amount and frequency of homework, provide guidelines for when and how students are to complete homework, let parents know you will positively reinforce students who complete homework, explain what you will do when students do not complete homework, and clarify what is expected of the parents (Sarka & Shank, 1990).

10. *Backup materials.* It is useful to have some backup materials available when instruction takes less time than anticipated, when a change of plans is necessary, or when students finish their activities early. These backup materials may be related to the particular topics being covered at the time. Many teachers have a collection of puzzles, educational games, discussion questions, brain teasers, creative writing, word searches, and riddles. You can gather these materials before school starts.

11. *Opening class routine.* Students often perform better when they know that a particular routine will be regularly followed at the start of class. You can decide on the particular actions to be taken. You may need to take attendance, make announcements, and attend to other tasks at the start of the class period. The purpose of having a routine is to provide an orderly transition as students enter the room and get ready for instruction. Some teachers have students review vocabulary words or other problems related to the curriculum while other tasks are performed.

12. *Folder for substitute teachers.* A substitute teacher will take your place when you are absent. It is important to prepare materials for substitute teachers to help support what they do, maximize the learning, and minimize any off-task behavior. Many teachers keep a folder for substitute teachers that includes important information. It can be kept on your desk with the plan book.

The type of material in a folder for substitute teachers varies, but the following information would be useful to include: a copy of the daily schedule, times for recess and lunch, a list of the classroom rules, a list of classroom procedures (e.g., morning opening, taking attendance, lunch count, lunch, dismissal, fire drills), a list of reliable students in each class period, hall-pass procedures (to go to the rest room, library, or office), information on where to find certain items (e.g., lesson plans, audiovisual equipment, supplies), others to contact for information or help (e.g., a nearby teacher with room number), and a list and description of students with special needs. Much of this information can be collected before school starts, and additional information can be added as needed.

Establishing a Plan to Deal with Misbehavior

With an understanding of classroom management and discipline, you will need to develop a plan for dealing with misbehavior in the classroom. A seven-step plan is presented here that begins with establishment of a system of rules and procedures. You need to provide a supportive environment during instruction and also provide situational assistance when students get off task. If the student does not get back on task, you need to move through advancing levels of punishment. If none of these actions works, you may need to involve other personnel.

TEACHERS IN ACTION

PREPARING FOR THE SUBSTITUTE TEACHER

Christine MacBurney, middle school language arts teacher, New Providence, New Jersey

I have an accountability system for the times I have a substitute teacher. This is a reporting sheet for the substitute to give me feedback on each class's behavior and academic progress. It includes a five-point rating scale for the class behavior and general cooperation along with space for noting specific student concerns. At the beginning of the school year, I tell the students about this reporting system and discuss their responsibility toward a substitute teacher in the event of my absence. I also tell them of specific repercussions if their behavior is less than ideal. I now find that my classes compete with each other for the best ratings and comments, knowing that I also reward the best class with a night free of homework.

You should deal with misbehavior in a way that is effective while also avoiding unnecessary disruptions. Researchers and educators have also proposed movement from low to high intervention when developing a plan to address misbehavior (e.g., Wolfgang, 1999; Levin & Nolan, 2000; Charles, 2002). Once the rules and procedures and a supportive classroom environment are in place, the teacher moves from low to high interventions as described below.

1. *Establish your system of rules and procedures.* Establish an appropriate system of rules and procedures as a foundation for dealing with discipline. It is vital that you select a system of rules and procedures appropriate to the situation. This system should incorporate reward or reinforcement for desirable behavior and the consequences of misbehavior.

No single approach is best for all teachers and all teaching situations. For instance, rules and procedures for a tenth grade English class would not be appropriate for a third grade class. Furthermore, the system needs to be consistent with established school and district policies and with your own educational philosophy, personality, and preferences.

2. *Provide a supportive environment during class sessions.* Once the system of rules and procedures has been established at the start of the school year, you need to maintain a supportive environment. Actions taken in the normal course of instruction are for the purpose of guiding and reinforcing students for positive behavior. You would follow them even in the absence of misbehavior.

Providing a supportive environment is accomplished primarily through cueing and reinforcing appropriate behavior and through getting and holding attention. Cueing and reinforcing involves stressing positive, desirable behaviors; recognizing and reinforcing desired behaviors; and praising effectively. Getting and holding attention necessitates focusing attention at the start of lessons; keeping lessons moving at a good pace; monitoring attention during lessons; stimulating attention periodically; maintaining accountability; and terminating lessons that have gone on too long. Treat students with dignity and respect, and offer challenging, interesting, and exciting classes.

3. *Provide situational assistance during class sessions.* Students may get off task during a lesson. This off-task behavior may be a form of misbehavior or a lapse in attention. Either way, you need to promptly provide situational assistance. *Situational assistance* denotes actions you take to get the student back on task with the least amount of intervention and disruption possible; it does *not* involve delivering aversive nonpunitive or punitive consequences. You should be alert to a lack of involvement in learning activities, prolonged inattention or work avoidance, and obvious violations of classroom rules and procedures. These behaviors can be dealt with directly and without overreaction.

Situational assistance can be provided by removing distracting objects, reinforcing appropriate behaviors, boosting student interest, providing cues, helping students through hurdles, redirecting the behavior, altering the lesson, and other approaches (discussed more fully in Chapter 11).

Some inappropriate behaviors are of such short duration and are so insignificant that they can be safely ignored. Your use of situational assistance might be considered a "forgiveness step" for the student by recognizing that the off-task behavior is minor or fleeting and by allowing the student to get back on task without penalty.

CLASSROOM DECISIONS

Before using mild responses for off-task behavior, teachers often provide situational assistance to get students back on task. What are the benefits for using situational assistance? How might situational assistance differ for first, seventh, and eleventh grades? How might cultural differences of students affect your decisions about the ways to provide situational assistance?

4. *Use mild responses.* If a student continues to be off task after situational assistance is provided, then you need to use mild responses that are intended to correct the student's behavior. These are not intended to be punitive. Mild responses may be nonverbal or verbal (see Chapter 11).

Nonverbal responses include ignoring the behavior, using signal interference, using proximity control, or using touch control. Verbal responses include reinforcing peers, calling on the student during the lesson, using humor, giving a direct appeal or command, reminding the student of the rule, and several other approaches.

5. *Use moderate responses.* If students do not respond favorably to mild responses and continue to exhibit off-task behavior, you need to deliver moderate responses (see Chapter 11). These punitive responses deal with misbehavior by removing desired stimulus so as to minimize the inappropriate behavior. Moderate responses include the use of logical consequences and various behavior modification techniques such as time-out and loss of privileges.

6. *Use stronger responses.* If moderate responses are insufficient, you need to move to a more intrusive type of intervention (see Chapter 11). These stronger responses are intended to be punitive, by adding aversive stimuli such as reprimands and overcorrection. The purpose of aversive stimuli is to decrease unwanted behavior.

7. *Involve others when necessary.* If all efforts have failed to get the student to behave properly, then you need to involve other persons in the process. This occurs most commonly with chronic or severe behaviors. You may consult or involve counselors, psychologists, principals and assistant principals, teaching colleagues, college personnel, mental health centers, school social workers, school nurses, supervisors and department heads, and parents. Their assistance and involvement will vary depending on their expertise.

Planning for the First Day

Starting the school year effectively is vitally important when establishing a system of classroom management. Several principles should guide your decisions about planning the start of the school year and your actions in the first few days of school (Emmer et al., 2000; Evertson et al., 2000; Good & Brophy, 2000; Burden, 2003).

1. *Plan to clearly state your rules, procedures, and academic expectations.* When students arrive in your class for the first time, they may have uncertainties. They will want to know your expectations for behavior and for academic work. They will want to know what the rules are for general behavior and also what the consequences are for adhering to or breaking the rules. Students also will wonder how you will monitor the rules and how consistently you will enforce them. They want to know what procedures exist for things such as going to the restroom, passing in homework, sharpening their pencils, talking during seatwork, and other specific activities. Furthermore, they will be interested in finding out about course requirements, grading policies, standards for work, and other aspects of the academic program.

Your philosophical perspective about classroom management will likely affect your decisions. You need to consider the degree to which you want to involve students in identifying the rules and procedures. Some teachers like to determine the rules before school starts; other teachers prefer to involve students in the discussion of the rules to develop a sense of ownership. Still other teachers let the students discuss and determine the rules themselves. You need to decide on your approach to the selection of rules and procedures prior to the start of school. It is especially important to take the necessary time during the first few days of school to thoroughly describe your expectations for behavior and work. Emphasize and be more explicit about desirable behavior in these discussions. Combine learning about procedures, rules, and course requirements with your initial content activities to build a good foundation for the school year.

2. *Plan uncomplicated lessons to help students be successful.* Content activities and assignments during the first week should be selected and designed to ensure maximum student success. By selecting relatively simple lessons at the start of the school year, fewer students are likely to need individual help. This allows you to focus on monitoring behavior and on delivering the appropriate consequences to shape and reinforce appropriate behavior. It provides you with opportunities to reinforce students for their academic work and to begin to develop positive relationships with students.

TEACHERS IN ACTION

CONDUCTING YOURSELF ON THE FIRST DAY

Beatrice Gilkes, high school computer science teacher, Washington, D.C.

The image that I project on the first day when the students enter is very important, so I take time to carefully plan what I am going to do. It is a day that is usually very hectic and filled with monumental record-keeping chores, statistical reports, and directions. In spite of these distractions, it is important that the students develop a positive image of me as a reasonable, caring, intelligent, and compassionate human being.

I use the following questions as a guide as I start planning for the first day and as I try to get to know my students:

- What do I really expect of my students?
- What do my students expect of me?
- What do I need to know about them?
- How can I plan for their interests, talents, and deficiencies?
- What will make me special to them?

3. *Keep a whole-class focus.* Plan activities for the first week that have a whole-class focus, as compared to activities that involve several small-group activities. Whole-class activities make it easier to monitor student behavior and performance. In this way, you can focus on reinforcing appropriate behavior and preventing inappropriate behavior.

4. *Be available, visible, and in charge.* You must be in charge of students at all times. Move around and be physically near the students, and maintain a good field of vision to see all students wherever you are located. Move around during seatwork to check on student progress.

■ ■ ■ ■ ■

CLASSROOM DECISIONS

Effective teachers are available, visible, and in charge. How could you exhibit this take-charge behavior as students come into the room and as you begin your opening announcements and activities in a lesson? How might your approach differ with a different grade level?

5. *Plan strategies to deal with potential problems.* Unexpected events can happen when meeting the students on the first day or days of school. These might include (a) interruptions by parents, office staff, custodians, or others; (b) late arrivals on the first day; (c) one or more students being assigned to your class after the first day; and (d) an insufficient number of textbooks or necessary materials. While you cannot foresee when unexpected events might occur, you can give advance thought to how you would deal with these common events if they happened.

Treat each unexpected situation in a calm, professional manner. This will serve as a good model for your students when they confront unexpected or challenging events. Treat students respectfully and deal with some of the needed details later. For example, you can ask a late enrolling student to take a seat and begin work, and then you could handle the particular enrollment procedures later.

6. *Closely monitor student compliance with rules and procedures.* By monitoring students closely, you can provide cues and reinforcement for appropriate behavior. Better classroom managers monitor their students' compliance with rules more consistently, intervene to correct inappropriate behavior more often, and mention rules or describe desirable behavior more often when giving feedback. Effective classroom managers stress specific corrective feedback rather than criticism or threat of punishment when students fail to comply with rules and procedures.

7. *Stop inappropriate behavior quickly.* Inappropriate or disruptive behavior should be handled quickly and consistently. Minor misbehavior that is not corrected often increases in intensity or spreads to other students. Quickly respond to inappropriate behavior to maximize on-task behavior. Act in a professional manner to settle the difficulty and preserve the student's dignity in front of the other students.

8. *Organize instruction on the basis of ability levels.* The cumulative record folders for students in your class will indicate the ability levels in reading, math, and other subjects.

Instructional content and activities should be selected to meet the ability levels of the students in the class.

9. *Hold students academically accountable.* Develop procedures that keep students accountable for their academic work. This may include papers to be turned in at the end of class, homework, in-class activities, or other means. Return the completed papers to the students promptly and with feedback. Some teachers give a weekly assignment sheet to each student. This sheet is completed by the student, checked by the parent, and returned to the teacher daily.

10. *Be clear when communicating information.* Effective teachers clearly and explicitly present information, give directions, and state objectives. When discussing complex tasks, break them down into step-by-step procedures for the students.

11. *Maintain students' attention.* Arrange seating so all students can easily face the area in the room where most of their attention needs to be held during instruction. Get the active attention of all students before starting a lesson. Monitor students for signs of confusion or inattention, and be sensitive to their concerns.

12. *Organize the flow of lesson activities.* Effective classroom managers waste little time getting the students organized for the lesson. They maximize student attention and task engagement during activities by maintaining momentum and providing signals and cues. They successfully deal with more than one thing at a time (e.g., talking with one student but also keeping an eye on the rest of the class).

Conducting the First Day

The first day of school is often a time of nervousness for teachers and students. Fortunately, you can make decisions about a number of issues as you prepare for the first day. Students, on the other hand, enter school on the first day with a lot of uncertainty; they will have questions (Wong & Wong, 1998):

- Am I in the right room?
- Where am I supposed to sit?
- What are the rules in this classroom?
- What will I be doing this year?
- How will I be graded?
- Who is the teacher as a person?
- Will the teacher treat me as a human being?

You can do a number of things on the first day to address these student concerns, as discussed below.

1. *Greet the students.* Stand by the classroom door before class begins. When students are about to enter your classroom, greet them with a smile and a handshake. As you do this, tell them your name, your room number, the subject or period, if needed; the grade level or subject; and anything else appropriate, such as seating assignments (Wong & Wong, 1998).

Your name, room number, section or period, and grade level or subject should be posted outside your door and on the chalkboard.

2. *Tell students about their seat assignments.* There are various ways to handle seat assignments for students. Some teachers prefer to let students select their seats, while other teachers prefer to assign seats. Either way, students should be told what to do as they enter the classroom for the first time. If you determine the seating assignment, there are several possible ways to inform students of their seat assignment as they enter the room. You might have a transparency showing on an overhead projector indicating the seating arrangement. A different transparency would be used for each of your class sections. Also have a copy of the seating chart in hand as the students are greeted at the door.

3. *Correct improper room entry.* Observe students as they enter the room and take their seats. Some students may not go directly to their seats or may behave inappropriately. It is important to ask a student who enters the room inappropriately to return to the door and enter properly.

Be calm, but firm; tell the student why this is being done, give specific directions, check for understanding, and acknowledge the understanding (Wong & Wong, 1998). The communication might be something like this:

Todd, please come back to the door. I am sorry, but that is not the way you enter our classroom everyday. You were noisy, you did not go to your seat, and you pushed Ann. When

---

TEACHERS IN ACTION

THE FIRST CLASS SESSION

Martin Miller, Jr., high school mathematics teacher, New Providence, New Jersey

There is no second chance to make a first impression. Planning for the first class session with your students takes as much time as the preparation for any other content lesson you will teach. The anxiety level for both teachers and students about that first day is high. Taking advantage of these feelings can make for a good beginning.

Students like to have guidelines on how the class will be run as well as what is expected of them academically. I always begin by welcoming the students into my class and immediately giving them something to do. I hand them their textbook and an index card. On the card, they write their name, address, telephone number, and book number.

While the students are filling out their cards and looking at the textbook, I set up my seating chart and verify attendance. Within ten minutes of meeting the students, I begin my first lesson. By keeping clerical chores to a minimum, I try to have more time on task. After a closure activity, somewhere in the middle of the class period I take a few minutes to explain how their grade will be determined, the rules of the class, and when extra help sessions are available.

Next, we deal with some curriculum content, and then I make a homework assignment. I tell the students that any homework assignment will be written on the chalkboard every day in the same location.

Setting high standards on the first day makes the following days easier. We will always need to monitor and adjust, but this will be within the framework set on the first day.

you enter this classroom, you walk in quietly, go directly to your seat, and get to work immediately on the assignment that is posted. Are there any questions? Thank you, Todd. Now please show me that you can go to your seat properly.

During this interaction, be sure to use the student's name and be polite with a "please" and "thank you."

4. *Handle administrative tasks.* Taking attendance is one of the first administrative tasks to be done at the start of the class period. Have the students raise their hands when called to indicate that they are present and to give you an opportunity to see the faces that go with the names. As you call each name, ask the student whether you pronounced it correctly.

After the first day of school, some teachers prefer not to take attendance at the start of class. Instead, they give an assignment that the students are to begin as soon as they enter the classroom. After the students are underway, the teacher can take attendance by visually scanning the room; the names do not need to be called. This approach, or one similar to it, takes very little time and allows students to move quickly into the academic work.

5. *Make introductions.* Students appreciate knowing something about the teacher. At the start of the class period, tell the students your name and some personal information, such as the number of years you have been teaching, professional development activities, family, personal interests and activities, hobbies, and other background information. This helps the students know you as a person and may be informative and comforting to them. This is also the time to let the students know that you are enthusiastic about working with them and that you will be reasonable and fair with them.

Some teachers like to use this opening time to have the students briefly introduce themselves. Some get-acquainted activities for students could be included on the first day to help promote good feelings.

6. *Discuss classroom rules and procedures.* All classrooms need rules and procedures if they are to run smoothly and efficiently. Rules should be taught on the first day of class to establish the general code of conduct. Post the rules in a conspicuous place in the classroom. If a letter has been prepared for parents that describes the rules and procedures, this should be given to the students so they can take it home.

Some classroom procedures may be taught on the first day of school, but many teachers prefer to teach procedures (e.g., distributing materials, getting ready to leave the classroom, handing in papers) over the next several school days instead (Leinhardt, Weidman, & Hammond, 1987). In this way, all the procedures are not taught at the same time, and students might be less overwhelmed and more likely to remember them when they are covered in several brief sessions. Procedures can be taught when the need for them first occurs. For example, when it is time to collect papers at the end of an activity, you could teach students the appropriate procedure.

7. *Present course requirements.* Before school started, you would have prepared the course requirements and syllabus. On the first day, students want to know what content will be covered and what is expected of them concerning grading. Take time to discuss the course content and some of the activities planned for the year. If you have prepared a syllabus, hand it out. Discuss the grading requirements concerning tests, homework, projects, and the like, and indicate what levels are needed for the various letter grades.

8. *Conduct an initial activity.* Depending on the amount of time available on the first day, many teachers plan an initial activity related to the curriculum. It should provide a review of some material that students had in the previous year, or may be a preview of content to be covered. Either way, the activity should be designed so that the students can complete it without much assistance and with much success. This leaves you free to monitor the students during the activity, to provide assistance when necessary, and to take corrective action on off-task behavior.

CLASSROOM DECISIONS

An initial activity will focus on some aspect of the curriculum. How might you provide variations of this activity based on the varied ability levels of the students? How might you relate the content to the various cultural backgrounds of your students? How might you modify the activity due to the varied learning styles of the students?

9. *End the class period.* A routine to end the class period is needed, and this must be taught to students. Procedures need to be established and time saved for actions such as returning books and supplies, disposing of scrap paper and cleaning up the classroom, and putting away books and other materials in preparation for leaving the classroom.

ORGANIZING YOUR CLASSROOM AND MATERIALS

Decisions about room arrangement must be made before students arrive on the first day of school. Before arranging the classroom, you should consider (a) the movement patterns of students throughout the classroom; (b) the need for students to obtain a variety of materials, texts, reference books, equipment, and supplies; and (c) the need for students to see the instructional presentations and display materials. Good room arrangement can help teachers cope with the complex demands of teaching by minimizing interruptions, delays, and dead times. Based on studies of effective classroom managers, there are four keys to good room arrangement (Emmer et al., 2000; Evertson et al., 2000).

1. *Use a room arrangement consistent with your instructional goals and activities.* You will need to think about the main types of instructional activities that will be used in your classes and then organize the seating, materials, and equipment compatibly. Teacher-led presentation, demonstrations, or recitations require students to be seated so that they can see the instructional area. In contrast, small-group work requires very different room arrangements.

2. *Keep high traffic areas free of congestion.* High traffic areas include the space around doorways, the pencil sharpener and trash can, group work areas, certain book shelves and supply areas, the teacher's desk, and student desks. High traffic areas should be kept away from each other, have plenty of space, and be easily accessible. For example, try not to seat a student next to the pencil sharpener because of the traffic in that area and the possibility for inappropriate behavior.

3. *Be sure students are easily seen by the teacher.* It is important that teachers clearly see students to identify when a student needs assistance or to prevent task avoidance or disruption. Clear lines of sight must be maintained between student work areas and areas of the room that the teacher will frequent.

4. *Keep frequently used teaching materials and student supplies readily accessible.* By having easy access and efficient storage of these materials, activities are more likely to begin and end promptly, and time that is spent on getting ready and cleaning up will be minimized. Establishing regulated storage areas can help to reduce the occurrence of students leaving materials in their desks or taking them out of the room.

5. *Be certain students can easily see instructional presentations and displays.* The seating arrangement should allow all students to see the chalkboard or overhead projector screen without moving their chairs, turning their desks around, or craning their necks. Place the primary instructional area in a prominent location to help students pay attention and to facilitate note taking.

Floor Space

A classroom typically contains many materials such as student desks, the teacher's desk, bookcases, tables, and activity centers that take up floor space. Consider the functions of the space and the four keys to good room arrangement to facilitate learning and to minimize interruptions and delays. Visiting other teachers' classrooms can provide ideas for effective ways to arrange the floor space in your own classroom.

A good starting point in planning the floor plan is to decide where you will conduct whole-group instruction. Examine the room and identify where you will stand or work when you address the entire class to conduct lessons or to give directions. This area should have a chalkboard, an overhead projector screen, a table for the overhead projector, a small table to hold items needed during instruction, and an electrical outlet. Consider the following items:

■ *Student desks.* Even if other arrangements are to be used later in the year, you might start the year with student desks in rows facing the major instructional area since it is easier to manage students with this pattern. Be sure all students can see the major instructional area without having their backs to the area and without having to get out of their seats.

It is important to keep student desks clear from high traffic areas. Avoid placing their desks near the door, pencil sharpener, trash can, and supply areas. Leave ample room for aisles between the desks to enable easy movement of students and yourself when monitoring seatwork.

■ The *teacher's desk.* Your desk should be situated so that you can see the students, but it is not essential that the desk be at the front of the room. Placement of your desk at the rear of the room, in fact, may help when monitoring students during independent work. Students facing away from you cannot tell when you are looking at them unless they turn around. As a result, students often assume their behavior is being very closely monitored. This tends to encourage students to stay at their assigned tasks. Instead of sitting at their desks during independent work, many teachers prefer to move around the room to monitor and assist students.

If you plan to work with individual students at your desk, you need to consider traffic patterns to and from the desk. Student desks should not be so close to yours that students will be distracted by other students approaching your desk or working with you there.

■ *Bookcases and filing cabinets.* These should be placed so students' visibility of chalkboards or relevant displays are not obstructed. They also should not prevent your monitoring students. If a bookcase contains frequently used items such as resource books, dictionaries, or supplies, then it should be conveniently located and monitored. If seldom used items are contained, an out-of-the-way place is best. If there is only one bookcase, it is helpful to use it for frequently used items.

■ *Activity centers or work areas.* An *activity center* is an area where one or more students come to work on a special activity. It may be in the form of a learning center or a computer work area. One or more tables are commonly used as the work surfaces in these areas. When selecting the placement of tables for this area, be sure that you can see all students in the work area, keep traffic lanes clear, and avoid congested areas. A center often will have special equipment such as tape recorders with headphones, a computer, a filmstrip projector, or other materials and supplies. Enough table and work space must be provided for students to work efficiently. It is useful to place the work area at the side or the back of the room and to the backs of other students.

Storage Space

Teachers and students use a wide variety of instructional materials. All of these materials are not used every day and must be stored when not in use. Therefore, storage space must be provided for textbooks and resource books, frequently used instructional materials, teacher's supplies and instructional materials, equipment, and infrequently used materials.

1. *Textbooks and resource books.* Some textbooks are not kept by students, and thus must be stored in the classroom for easy access when needed. In addition, resource books obtained from the school library, public library, or other sources may be available for student use. All of these books should be stored in a bookcase that enables easy access.

2. *Instructional materials.* Materials that students need will vary with the subject area that you teach. These may include rulers, scissors, special paper, pencils, staplers, tape, glue, and other supplies. Students may be expected to provide some of these supplies (and would keep them in their desks or bring them to class). As with textbooks and resource books, a storage location should be selected to enable easy access to the materials. Clearly labeled containers for each of the supply items are often very helpful in maintaining an orderly supply area. These materials may be stored on shelves of a bookcase or cabinet, or on a counter.

3. *Teacher supplies.* Supplies that only you would use should be kept in your desk or in storage areas used only by you. These supplies include items such as hall passes, attendance and lunch count forms, computer disks, computer programs, lesson plan book, tablets, file folders, and chalk. These items should be placed in secure places so students don't have access to them. For example, leaving hall passes on top of the teacher's desk makes it easy for students to take them for their own use.

■ ■ ■ ■ ■

SPOTLIGHT ON TECHNOLOGY

SPACE FOR MEDIA USE

When making decisions about how to use class-room floor space, arrangements for the use of instructional media need to be considered in the following areas:

1. *Seating and study areas.* Consider where students will be seated in the classroom to work or study and how they will be using instructional media and materials in relation to these work or study areas. Make provisions for students to work with different types of media on a variety of work surfaces (at their desks, at tables, even on the carpeted floor), in spaces that allow independent work (in study carrels), or in small group areas separated from the class by some type of divider.

2. *Space dividers and display areas.* Area dividers can be used both to separate spaces and to provide useful display surfaces and areas for shelving, storage, and projecting visuals. These dividers and display areas can enhance the use of instructional media. Room dividers also serve as useful display areas for certain nonprojected visuals, such as posters. Panels

of a divider also may be used for certain projected visuals for students working individually or in small groups.

3. *Arrangements for projection.* When using projected visuals with the entire class, make provisions for an appropriately sized screen, seating for comfortable viewing, ambient light so that the room is not entirely dark, and placement of the projector screen to limit extraneous light on the screen. When projecting for individual or small-group viewing, provide an appropriate screen. This can be a sheet of white matte-finish paper taped on a wall, on the side of a study carrel, or on some surface in the small group study area.

4. *Storing and accessing materials.* Keep and store materials only if they genuinely will be reused. Determine which materials should be kept in the classroom for immediate access and which can be held ready elsewhere (e.g., in another room in the building, at the teacher's home, or in another storage area). Next, decide how to store these materials (such as with some type of box or packaging).

TEACHERS IN ACTION

STORING AND DISTRIBUTING SUPPLIES

Eric Stiffler, seventh grade science teacher, Wichita, Kansas

I like to organize my science classes into ten groups, partly because I have ten large desks in my room. One work group for each table works very well. I assign each group a number (1–10) and a tray of materials which includes scissors, beakers, graduated cylinders, and rulers. I label each tray and each item in the tray with the number of the group.

When we get ready to do an activity, one student from each group goes to get their tray. No time is wasted explaining where the materials are. At the end of the class period, the students put the items back in their trays. I assign one student to check the trays and make sure that everything has been returned. This system has eliminated theft problems and has saved a great deal of time.

4. *Equipment.* An overhead projector, tape recorders, computers, or other instructional media are not commonly used every day. Therefore, these items must be stored when not in use.

5. *Infrequently used items.* Some instructional materials are used only one time a year. These include seasonal decorations (e.g., Halloween, Thanksgiving), bulletin board displays, or special project materials. Certain instructional materials may be used for only one unit, as in the case of a model of the human eye for a science class. Some teachers prefer to keep seasonal decorations or other infrequently used materials at their homes.

Bulletin Boards and Wall Space

Constructive use of bulletin boards and wall space can contribute to a positive classroom environment. This can be achieved by displaying relevant instructional material, assignments, rules, schedules, student work, and other items of interest. Many teachers involve students in the selection of content and the preparation of bulletin boards and the use of wall space. One approach is to select a different group of students to plan and prepare a bulletin board each month.

Some teachers prefer to dedicate a certain purpose for each bulletin board. For example, one bulletin board could be used to post classroom rules, a daily or weekly schedule, classroom helpers, lunch menus, a school map, emergency information, or any other procedural information. Another bulletin board could be used to display student work. A third type of bulletin board could be simply for decoration, with seasonal, motivational, or artistic items. Other bulletin boards can be used to post information and news articles about school or community events. In addition, bulletin boards can also be used to post content-related news articles, posters, or information.

Some of this material, such as a listing of classroom rules, can be placed on posters and displayed on the walls of the classroom if the content is not likely to change during the school year. On the other hand, designated areas of the chalkboard can be used to display student assignments or special announcements, because this information is likely to change daily.

SELECTING AND TEACHING RULES AND PROCEDURES

Think about all the traffic laws that govern the use of motor vehicles. Guidelines are set for ways to signal, turn, yield the right of way, pass other vehicles, and numerous other aspects of driving. These laws have been established in each state to ensure the safety of the driver and others. In a similar way, guidelines are also needed in the classroom to govern how the teacher and the students conduct themselves so that learning objectives are achieved and everyone is successful.

Rules and procedures are used to guide and govern student behavior in classrooms. Even in positive learning communities where students are actively involved in arranging their learning environment, rules and procedures are necessary to guide behavior. Teachers need to carefully consider what rules and procedures are needed in order to effectively manage the class.

Your philosophical perspective about teaching, classroom management, and discipline will greatly influence how you select rules and procedures. Teachers who prefer to take more control of the classroom decision making will likely select rules and procedures without consulting students. Teachers who prefer to involve students to some degree in the decision making will likely have a discussion with the students and then collaboratively decide on the rules and procedures. Teachers who are very student oriented may turn the discussion over to the students and let them determine the rules and procedures.

Many educators who have written about creating a learning community endorse student involvement in some classroom decision making, including the selection of rules and procedures. Alfie Kohn (1996), for example, maintains that teachers should create classroom learning communities by moving away from discipline through the use of student involvement. He would allow students to make choices and says that teachers need to develop a caring community and provide an engaging curriculum. Kohn's principles are consistent with the guiding model (low teacher control). Some degree of student involvement in the selection of rules and procedures helps to build ownership and commitment.

As you consider the information on rules and procedures, reflect on your philosophical perspective concerning discipline and classroom management. One model may represent your beliefs about child development and management of student behavior. This, in turn, will give you a perspective about the degree of control that you would want to take when determining rules and procedures.

Rules

Rules refer to general behavioral standards or expectations that are to be followed in the classroom. They are general codes of conduct that are intended to regulate individual behavior in an attempt to avoid disruptive behavior. Rules may be identified to guide the way students interact with each other, prepare for class, and conduct themselves during class. They are commonly stated in positive terms to guide student behavior. In addition to general rules, teachers sometime state rules for specific situations (e.g., gum chewing is not allowed).

■ *Examine the need for rules.* Rules provide guidelines for appropriate behaviors so that teaching and learning can take place. They should be directed at organizing the learning environment to ensure the continuity and quality of teaching and learning and not simply be focused on exerting control over students.

Rules are necessary to have teaching and learning take place, and they need to be realistic, fair, and reasonable. Rules that are selected should meet the following purposes: (a) the teacher's right to teach is protected; (b) the students' rights to learning are protected; (c) the students' psychological and physical safety are protected; and (d) property is protected (Levin & Nolan, 2000).

You need to examine the way you teach and the type of classroom environment you would like to maintain when considering rules. A number of factors should be considered, including your educational philosophy, the age and maturity of the students, school rules and expectations, the type of classroom climate to be developed, and the rationale for a particular rule.

■ *Select the rules.* After considering the need for classroom rules, you are ready to select rules that are appropriate for your classroom. Sample rules include: (a) follow the teacher's directions; (b) obey all school rules; (c) speak politely to all people; and (d) keep your hands, feet, and objects to yourself. These rules are probably appropriate for all grade levels (K–12).

Due to differences in student maturity and developmental levels, some rules may be needed only for certain grade levels. For example, students in the primary grades (K–3) often need direct guidance on many matters. Some additional rules that would be appropriate for these grades may include (a) follow directions the first time they are given, (b) raise your hand and wait to be called on, (c) stay in your seat unless you have permission to get up, and (d) do not leave the room without permission.

For departmentalized settings and grade levels, some rules about materials and starting class are often used, such as (a) bring all needed materials to class and (b) be in your seat and ready to work when the bell rings at the start of the period. A number of guidelines for selecting classroom rules are displayed in Table 10.2.

Consider the degree to which students will be involved in identifying classroom rules. Among other things, student involvement will be affected by the teacher's philosophical perspective. Many teachers do not provide for student choice in rule setting; teachers may clearly present the rules and discuss the rationale for them. Other teachers find that students have more commitment and adhere to the rules if they helped set the rules and consequences in the first place. Teachers can be effective managers whether or not they involve students in identifying classroom rules.

■ *Select rewards and consequences.* As previously mentioned, both rewards and penalties need to be identified for the classroom rules. Rewards may include a variety of reinforcers such as social reinforcers, activities and privileges, tangible reinforcers, and token reinforcers. Students need to be told that these reinforcers will be delivered if they follow the rules.

Similarly, students need to be told what consequences will be delivered if they choose to break a rule. When a student gets off task, first provide situational assistance in an effort to get the student back to work. If the student stays off task, then you should deliver mild responses such as nonverbal and verbal actions. If that does not work, you can move to logical consequences and other actions.

TABLE 10.2 Guidelines for Selecting Classroom Rules

1. Make classroom rules consistent with school rules.
2. Involve students in making the rules to the degree that you are comfortable and to the degree that the students' age level and sophistication permit.
3. Identify appropriate behaviors and translate them into positively stated classroom rules.
4. Focus on important behavior.
5. Keep the number of rules to a minimum (4 to 6).
6. Keep the wording of each rule simple and short.
7. Have rules address behaviors that can be observed.
8. Identify rewards for when students follow the rules and consequences for when they break the rules.

TEACHERS IN ACTION

STUDENT INVOLVEMENT IN SELECTING RULES, CONSEQUENCES, AND ACTIVITIES

Robb Scurrah, high school math teacher, Cottage Grove, Minnesota

The more I involve my students in setting the tone for the class, the better my classroom becomes. This involvement increases the students' sense of ownership and responsibility.

Using the school handbook as a guide at the start of the semester, I have groups of three to five students work on identifying our posted list of classroom rules and expectations. They also develop the range and level of consequences that they feel should apply when necessary. In addition, they select some positive, enjoyable class activities for appropriate breaks in the schedule.

The results of these discussion groups are put into a letter, and each student signs a copy that we keep in a class file. Since the students come up with the ideas themselves, they feel that they have a vested interest in making the plan work. When a student drifts from the boundaries that were defined, it usually takes just a quiet reminder about the expectations and how she or he was involved in the process. The appeal to student ownership and their developing sense of responsibility and maturity usually dampens any problems.

As compared to imposing standards on students, this collaborative process with the students has made my class a much better learning environment and a nicer place for me to teach.

■ *Teach and review the rules.* After the classroom rules have been identified, teach them in the first class session as if they were subject-matter content. This discussion should include an explanation of the rules, rehearsal, feedback, and reteaching. It is important that the students recognize the rationale for the rules and are provided with specific expectations for each rule. Specific guidelines for teaching and reviewing classroom rules are displayed in Table 10.3.

■ *Obtain commitments.* After teaching the rules to the students, you should have your students express their understanding of the rules and indicate their intention to follow the rules. This can be done in a variety of ways. One of the most effective is to have students

TABLE 10.3   Guidelines for Teaching and Reviewing Classroom Rules

1. Discuss the rules in the first class session.
2. Discuss the reasons for the rules.
3. Identify specific expectations relevant to each rule. Provide examples and emphasize the positive side of the rules.
4. Inform students of consequences when rules are followed and also when they are broken.
5. Verify understanding.
6. Send a copy of your discipline policy home to parents and to the principal.
7. Post the rules in a prominent location.
8. Remind the class of the rules at times other than when someone has just broken a rule.
9. Review the rules regularly.

sign a copy of the paper that lists the rules and includes a statement such as "I am aware of these rules and understand them." In this way, each student makes an affirmation of the rules. You can keep these signed sheets. An extra copy of the rules could be given to students for placement in their desk or in a notebook.

As discussed earlier, sending the discipline policy home to the parents is another means of obtaining a commitment to the policy. In this way, parents are informed of the policy at the start of the school year. Parents can contact you if they have any concerns or questions about the discipline policy. If not, the parents are asked to sign and return a form which states that they are aware of the rules and understand them (similar to the form their child could sign at school).

Procedures

Procedures are approved ways to achieve specific tasks in the classroom. They are intended to help students accomplish a particular task, rather than prevent inappropriate behavior as in the case of rules. Procedures may be identified to direct activities such as handing in completed work, sharpening a pencil, using the restroom, or putting away supplies. The use of procedures, or routines, has several advantages (Leinhardt et al., 1987): they increase the shared understanding for an activity between you and students, reduce the complexity of the classroom environment to a predictable structure, and allow for efficient use of time.

Some procedures may be sufficiently complex or critical, such as safety procedures for a laboratory or student notebook requirements, that you should provide students with printed copies of the procedures. Many procedures, however, are not written because they are very simple or their specificity and frequency of use allow students to learn them rapidly. As with rules, it is important to clearly state the procedures, discuss the rationale for them, and provide opportunities for practice and feedback, where appropriate.

■ ■ ■ ■ ■ ▬▬▬▬▬▬▬▬▬▬▬▬▬▬▬▬▬▬▬▬▬▬▬▬▬▬▬▬▬▬▬▬▬▬▬▬▬▬

CREATING A LEARNING COMMUNITY

CLASSROOM RULES

Some teachers select classroom rules themselves while other teachers involve students to varying degrees in identifying the rules. Involving students to some degree helps to create a learning community. If students are involved, teachers may have an open discussion, may provide one or two "must" rules as a starting point, or may take a variety of approaches from being completely open to being somewhat directive when determining the rules.

1. What are the advantages and disadvantages of teachers selecting the rules by themselves? Of teachers involving the students?

2. As a first year teacher, do you intend to involve students in identifying rules? If so, how involved will you allow the students to be in the process?

3. How will you determine the consequences for the rules that are identified? Should students be involved in selecting consequences?

■ *Examine the need for procedures.* As a first step, you must examine the need for procedures in your classroom. What activities or actions would benefit from having a procedure that would regularize student conduct in the performance of that action? To answer this key question, you might think about all the actions that take place in the classroom and identify those that would benefit from having an associated procedure.

Fortunately, you do not need to start from scratch in doing this assessment because research studies of classroom management in K–12 classrooms have resulted in a framework that can be used to examine and identify typical classroom procedures. A number of the specific areas that might need classroom procedures are displayed in Table 10.4, some of which are adapted from Weinstein and Mignano (1997), Emmer et al. (2000), Evertson et al. (2000), and Jones and Jones (2001).

■ *Select the procedures.* When examining the items in Table 10.4, you need to consider the unique circumstances in your classroom. The grade level, maturity of the students, your preference for order and regularity, and other factors may be taken into account when deciding which items will need a procedure. It may turn out that you will select many items from the table, because these items involve fairly standard actions in many classrooms.

After selecting the items needing a procedure, decide specifically what each procedure will be. You could draw upon your own experiences when deciding on the specific procedures. You might recollect your own schooling experiences, your observations of other classrooms, your conversations with other teachers, and your own teaching experience when determining what specific procedures would be appropriate and efficient.

■ *Teach and review the procedures.* Students should not have to guess if they need to raise their hands during a discussion or interpret subtle signals from you to determine what you want them to do. From the very first day of school, teach and review the various procedures that are needed. Leinhardt et al., (1987) found that effective teachers spend more time during the first four days of school on management tasks than on academic tasks.

There are several steps that serve as guides when teaching and reviewing classroom procedures with the students: (1) explain the procedure immediately prior to the first time the activity will take place; (2) demonstrate the procedure; (3) practice and validate understanding; (4) give feedback; (5) reteach as needed; (6) review the procedures with the students prior to each situation for the first few weeks; and (7) review the procedures after long holidays.

ESTABLISHING A COOPERATIVE CLASSROOM

When you walk into a classroom where students are actively engaged in learning and are co-operating with the teacher and others, you can almost feel the good vibrations given off by the class. Students want to be involved and productive, and they enjoy working together. This type of classroom, however, doesn't happen by chance. Teachers take deliberate actions to establish a cooperative, responsible classroom where students will choose to be cooperate and make efforts to be academically successful. Students need to feel that they are expected to be orderly, cooperative, and responsible. Developing a positive classroom climate is one of the most important ways to establish and maintain student cooperation and responsibility.

TABLE 10.4   Areas Needing Classroom Procedures

1. Room Use Procedures
   A. Teacher's desk and storage areas
   B. Student desks and storage for belongings
   C. Storage for class materials used by all students
   D. Pencil sharpener, wastebasket, sink, drinking fountain
   E. Bathroom
   F. Learning stations, computer areas, equipment areas, centers, and display areas

2. Transitions In and Out of the Classroom
   A. Beginning the school day
   B. Leaving the room
   C. Returning to the room
   D. Ending the school day

3. Out-of-Room Procedures
   A. Bathroom, drinking fountain
   B. Library, resource room
   C. School office
   D. Playground or school grounds
   E. Cafeteria
   F. Lockers
   G. Fire or disaster drills

4. Procedures for Whole-class Activities and Instruction, and Seatwork
   A. Student participation
   B. Signals for student attention
   C. Talk among students
   D. Making assignments
   E. Distributing books, supplies, and materials
   F. Obtaining help
   G. Handing back assignments
   H. Tasks after work is completed
   I. Make-up work
   J. Out-of-seat procedures

5. Procedures during Small-Group Work
   A. Getting the class ready
   B. Taking materials to groups
   C. Student movement in and out of groups
   D. Expected behavior in groups
   E. Expected behavior out of groups

6. Other General Procedures for Secondary Classrooms
   A. Beginning the class period
      (1) Attendance check
      (2) Previously absent students
      (3) Late students
      (4) Expected student behavior

(continued)

TABLE 10.4 Continued

   B. Out-of-room policies
   C. Materials and equipment
      (1) What to bring to class
      (2) Pencil sharpener
      (3) Other room equipment
      (4) Student contact with teacher's desk, storage, and other materials
   D. Movement of student desks
   E. Split lunch period
   F. Ending the class period
7. Other Procedures
   A. Classroom helpers
   B. Behavior during delays or interruptions

To develop a cooperative, responsible classroom, you can take actions to (a) build positive teacher–student relationships, (b) build group cohesiveness, (c) maintain attention and involvement, and (d) reinforce desired behaviors.

Much of what is known about encouraging and reinforcing appropriate behavior comes from studies concerning direct instruction. Less is known about how behavior can be encouraged and reinforced through other instructional approaches. Thus, this section relates primarily to direct instruction. It is possible that somewhat different techniques would be successful with other instructional approaches.

Building Positive Teacher–Student Relationships

A significant body of research indicates that academic achievement and student behavior are influenced by the quality of the teacher–student relationship (Jones & Jones, 2001). Students prefer teachers who are warm and friendly. Students who feel liked by their teachers are reported to have higher academic achievement and more productive classroom behavior than students who feel their teachers hold them in low regard.

This research suggests that you need to learn and conscientiously apply skills in relating more positively to students. The guidelines listed below will help you build positive relationships (Charles, 2000; Good & Brophy, 2000; Jones & Jones, 2001).

1. *Use human relations skills.* When learning to manage the classroom climate, appropriate *human relations skills* are needed. There are four general human relations skills that apply to almost everyone in all situations: friendliness, positive attitude, the ability to listen, and the ability to compliment genuinely (Charles, 2000). When working with students, also give regular attention, use reinforcement, show continual willingness to help, and model courtesy and good manners.

2. *Enable success.* Students need to experience success. Successful experiences are instrumental in developing feelings of self-worth and confidence toward new activities. Students need to be provided with opportunities to achieve true accomplishments and to realize significant improvements (Charles, 2000). Learning is increased when students experience high rates of success in completing tasks (Jones & Jones, 2001). Students tend to raise their expectations and set higher goals, whereas failure is met with lowered aspirations.

To establish moderate-to-high rates of success, (a) establish unit and lesson content that reflects prior learning; (b) correct partially correct, correct but hesitant, and incorrect answers; (c) divide instructional stimuli into small segments at the learners' current level of functioning; (d) change instructional stimuli gradually; and (e) vary the instructional pace or tempo to create momentum (Borich, 2000).

3. *Be invitational.* In their book *Inviting School Success,* Purkey and Novak (1996) maintain that teachers should develop attitudes and behaviors that invite students to learn. *Invitational learning* is centered on four principles: (a) people are able, valuable, and responsible and should be treated accordingly; (b) teaching should be a cooperative activity; (c) people possess relatively untapped potential in all areas of human development; and (d) this potential can best be realized by places, policies, and programs that are specifically designed to invite development, and by people who are personally and professionally inviting to themselves and others.

Teachers who adopt an invitational approach develop an environment anchored in attitudes of respect, care, and civility, and promote positive relationships and encourage human potential. You can be invitational in countless ways, such as through verbal comments, nonverbal behaviors, instructional approaches, and physical aspects.

4. *Use effective communication skills.* Positive teacher–student relationships are affected by the type of communication that takes place. Effective communication allows for caring interpersonal interactions as well as for achieving personal and academic goals. There are two aspects to communication: *sending skills* and *receiving skills.*

Sending skills take many forms. You send messages to deliver instruction, provide students with feedback about their academic performance, confront students about behavior that needs to be changed, present positive expectation, and for other purposes. When sending information, use descriptive rather than judgmental language.

Receiving skills are equally important. By effectively listening to students, you can help them feel significant, accepted, respected, and able to take responsibility for their own behavior (Jones & Jones, 2001). You can help students clarify their own feelings and resolve their own conflicts. Teachers, however, too often do not listen fully to students and provide quick answers rather than fully listening and helping the student.

Allow the student to talk without interruption while using acknowledging expressions such as "I see," "Uh-uh," or "Go on." Nonverbal expressions, such as eye contact and leaning toward the student, also let the student know that you are interested in what is being said.

You could also use a *paraphrasing technique* when listening to students. This means that you restate the student's ideas in your own words as a means to clarify the statements and to encourage the student to say more. You can also reflect on and summarize what is being said.

5. *Establish a safe, nonthreatening environment.* Students need to feel safe and secure in the classroom to be successful. They should know that you will not allow physical or verbal abuse by anyone. Without that protection from you, students will continually be concerned about their safety and thus will give less attention to academic responsibilities. A safe, nonthreatening environment is appropriate for learning and helps establish a good relationship with the students.

6. *Be fair and consistent.* Students want to be treated fairly, not preferentially. Your credibility is established largely by making sure that words and actions coincide and by pointing this out to the class when necessary. If students can depend on what you say, they will be less likely to test you constantly. Consistency does not mean that you always need to behave in the same way, but rather that your judgments be reliable and consistent.

7. *Show respect and affection to students.* You must like your students and respect them as individuals. Your enjoyment of students and concern for their welfare will come through in tone of voice, facial expressions, and other routine behavior. Middle and secondary teachers should make efforts to get to know students personally. Students who like and respect their teachers will want to please them and will be more likely to imitate their behavior and attitudes.

8. *Communicate basic attitudes and expectations to students and model them in your behavior.* Students tend to conform not so much to what teachers say as to what they actually expect. You must think through what you really expect from your students and then see that your own behavior is consistent with those expectations. If you expect students to be polite to each other, for example, you should treat your students in the same manner.

9. *Create open dialogue with students.* It is useful to create an open dialogue with students, but you need to decide how open and involved you wish to be with them. The degree of open dialogue may be determined by the students' age, and your own personality, among other factors.

CLASSROOM DECISIONS

Teachers vary in the degree that they share personal information and opinions with students in their classes. Suppose that you have travelled extensively in the United States and that you are responsible for teaching American history. In your everyday interactions with your students, how personal will you be with your students and what factors will you take into account when deciding on this? To what extent will you relate personal experiences to the curriculum? How might the grade level and cultural diversity of your students affect your decisions?

10. *Systematically build better relationships.* You can express interest in and concern for students by (a) monitoring the quality of your relationships with them, with a focus on maintaining a high rate of positive comments; (b) creating opportunities for personal discussions with them; and (c) showing your interest in activities that are important to them (Jones & Jones, 2001). For example, you could deliberately plan to talk with some students in each cooperative learning group as you walk around to be available for help and to monitor their behavior.

11. *Communicate high expectations.* Teacher behaviors that create positive expectations almost always enhance the teacher–student relationship, and behaviors that create negative expectations result in poor relationships and poor student self-concepts, and thus reduce learning. For example, students often put forth a solid effort when you say that work may be hard but also express confidence that the students will be able to do it.

12. *Create opportunities for personal discussions.* Other than through day-to-day activities, teachers often find it helpful to set time aside to get to know their students. Some possible activities include (a) demonstrate your interest in students' activities; (b) arrange for interviews with students; (c) send letters and notes to students; (d) use a suggestion box; (e) join in school and community events; and (f) introduce new students to adults in the school (Jones & Jones, 2001). Some teachers also make "good news" phone calls to parents of students who do all that is requested of them.

Building Group Cohesiveness

People in groups behave differently than they do individually. Groups seem to take on an identity and personality of their own, and group personalities are quite prone to change in response to group dynamics. When thinking of classroom management and establishing order, it is important to build and maintain group cohesiveness.

Group cohesiveness refers to the extent to which the group has a sense of identity and oneness. You can take the following actions to develop and maintain a positive sense of group purpose and enjoyment and to promote group cohesiveness (Charles, 2000; Jones & Jones, 2001).

1. *Encourage a sense of togetherness.* At the beginning of the year, try to develop the sense that the class is a unit that lives and works together, that all members are striving toward a common goal, that all face a common set of obstacles, that all benefit from helping each other, that all lose something when any member is unsuccessful, and that all can take justifiable pride in the accomplishments of the class.

2. *Identify the purpose of class activities.* Students resent busy work and spot it easily. It is important to convey a sense of purpose for class activities by identifying specific short-range goals (e.g., having a class project done by Friday; having every student get at least 90 percent correct on next week's exam). It is useful to tell students why they have a given assignment, because they usually accept it more readily.

3. *Highlight group achievement.* Learning activities can be organized so that they lead to group rather than individual achievement. For example, the work of the math class could be evaluated in terms of what the class as a whole has been able to achieve, or the progress of a cooperative learning group could be highlighted.

4. *Provide public recognition.* The sense of purposeful group behavior is greatly increased through *public recognition.* When students work on projects and receive public recognition for what they have done, their sense of purposeful and responsible behavior improves dramatically, with a corresponding reduction in apathetic and disruptive behavior.

TEACHERS IN ACTION

CLASSROOM MEETINGS HELP GROUP COHESIVENESS

Laurie Robben, fourth grade teacher, Greenwich, Connecticut

I am extremely proud of the positive rapport that I have with my students. One way that I instill mutual respect is through classroom meetings. Every Friday, I set aside at least 15 minutes for a class meeting. We all sit together on the floor, including myself, to show that no one's ideas are more important than another's.

Classroom meetings provide a time for students to share their feelings openly about their school experience, and issues can be positive or negative. An important rule is that if someone wants to say something negative about a particular student, the class is not allowed to talk about that conversation outside the confines of our meeting. This is to prevent a student from being badgered.

One example is Alex, a nine-year-old who desperately wants peer attention but resorts to behaving like a clown. In a recent meeting, students told him they were not comfortable with his clowning and wished that he would stop. I asked the class to share times when they enjoyed being with Alex, and they encouraged him to practice those behaviors more frequently. At the end of the meeting, Alex asked his peers, "Could you help me be better and tell me when I'm bugging you?" We talked about how to tell Alex. The class concluded that a person is more likely to respond if you ask nicely ("Alex, this is an example of something that bugs me. Please stop"). Improvement has been apparent since that meeting.

Since we regularly have class meetings, the students will give me updates on past issues, such as "Lunch is better now. Adam doesn't show us the food in his mouth anymore!"

Class meetings show the class that I care about them outside of the traditional academic areas. It also encourages them to listen to one another. And it allows me to use peer influence to encourage behavioral changes. We all win!

This recognition can be provided in a variety of ways, such as charting group gains, charting personal gains, informing parents, sharing in the classroom, and producing a class newsletter.

■ ■ ■ ■ ■

CLASSROOM DECISIONS

Group cohesiveness can be promoted when providing public recognition of individual and group work. If your math class just successfully finished a unit with group projects and individual papers, how might you communicate your students' success to parents? How might you provide both public and private recognition to accommodate students' preferences for attention? How might you let people outside your class know of these successes in a public way?

5. *Stress the satisfaction that the group offers.* Dramatize the many new and interesting things students can do in the group. When they complete a group activity, discuss how interesting it was and how more like it are to come. Instead of asking what was wrong with an activity, ask what they like best. For example, after an activity or discussion, you could mention how successful it was and ask the students why they think it was so successful—then highlight how good it feels for the group to work so well and be successful.

6. *Increase the person's prestige within the group.* The prestige of group membership can be emphasized by reminding students that they are now in a certain elementary grade or in the middle school, junior high school, or high school. Favorable evaluations of the group can be given by others such as the principal, a visiting speaker, or another teacher.

7. *Engage students in cooperative activities.* Having students participate in cooperative activities helps make the group more cohesive. Competitive activities within the classroom may make the group less cohesive. A number of resources are available on cooperative activities (Slavin, 1991; Sharan & Sharan, 1992; Baloche, 1998; Johnson & Johnson, 1999, 2000).

8. *Increase the frequency of interaction.* Increasing the frequency of interaction within the group makes it more attractive to individual members. Interaction is increased by having students work together on planning and carrying out cooperative projects.

9. *Provide activities that help create cohesive groups.* Groups do not become cohesive simply by members spending time together. You can use special activities, especially at the start of the year, to develop positive feelings about the group and the individual members. At the middle and secondary levels, you can use various get-acquainted activities, special events days, and cooperative group work.

Maintaining Attention and Involvement

To effectively manage a group of students, you need to capture and hold student attention and encourage ongoing involvement. *Attention* means focusing certain stimuli while screening out others. If students are not engaged in the learning process, it is unlikely that they will learn the material and it is possible that they will get off task and disrupt order. Recommendations for ways to maintain student attention and involvement come from a number of sources (e.g., Good & Brophy, 2000; Eggen & Kauchak, 2001; Jones & Jones, 2001); some of the following guidelines come from these sources.

1. *Use attention-getting approaches.* You can use certain strategies to capture students' attention at the start of a lesson. These *attention-getting strategies* can be used throughout the lesson to maintain student interest; they fall into four categories (Eggen & Kauchak, 2001): physical, provocative, emotional, and emphatic. Overuse of any one approach, however, reduces its ability to arouse and maintain attention.

(a) Physical attention-getters deal with any stimulus that attracts one or more of the senses (sight, sound, touch, taste). Pictures, maps, the chalkboard, music, and manipulative objects are examples. Even your movement and vocal expression can be considered to be physical stimuli. (b) Provocative attention-getters involve the use of unique or discrepant events. To create them, you could introduce contrasting information, play the devil's advocate, and be unpredictable to the degree that the students enjoy the spontaneity. (c) Emotional attention-getters are approaches aimed at involving students emotionally. This may be something as simple as calling the students by name. (d) Emphatic attention-getters place emphasis on a particular issue or event. For example, you might cue students to an issue such as, "Pay careful attention now. The next two items are very important."

CLASSROOM DECISIONS

To maintain student attention, you may deliberately create disequilibrium by introducing contrasting information, playing the devil's advocate, or being unpredictable. If you were teaching a social studies class, how might you create disequilibrium when discussing the role of the Supreme Court throughout the history of the United States? As a means to be provocative, how might you approach a discussion about the consequences of the absence of a Supreme Court in U.S. government? How might student differences in learning styles affect the way you approach this topic while simultaneously giving consideration to maintaining order?

2. *Arrange the classroom so that students do not have their backs to the speaker.* When presenting material during a lesson, students should be seated so that everyone is facing the presenter (who may be you, a student, or a guest). This may seem like a simple task, but too often classrooms are arranged so that students do not have a complete view of the presenter and the instructional medium. Not only is the presenter unable to see all the students, but the students are not able to observe all the presenter's nonverbal behaviors.

3. *Select a seating arrangement that does not discriminate against some students.* Some teachers may spend as much as 70 percent of their time in front of the classroom. As a result, students at the back of the classroom contribute less to class discussions and are less attentive and on task than those near the front. Involvement is more evenly distributed when high- and low-achieving students are interspersed throughout the room. You can enhance on-task behavior by carefully arranging the seating and moving around the room. You should experiment with seating arrangements to promote student attention and involvement.

4. *Monitor attention during lessons and provide situational assistance as necessary.* Students are much more likely to pay attention if they know you regularly watch them, both to see if they are paying attention and to note signs of confusion or difficulty. Regularly scan the class or group throughout the lesson. Kounin (1970) used the term *withitness* to characterize a teacher's ability to recognize what is happening in the classroom and communicate that awareness to the students. Withitness is the degree to which the teacher notices misbehavior, targets the correct student, and corrects misbehavior before it intensifies or spreads.

When students show signs of losing interest or getting frustrated, you should provide *situational assistance*—teacher actions designed to help students cope with the instructional situation and to keep students on task, or to get them back on task before problems become more serious. Situational assistance may include actions such as removing distracting objects, providing support with routines, boosting student interest, helping students through hurdles, altering the lesson, or modifying the classroom environment.

5. *Keep lessons moving at a good pace.* Delays in a lesson may be caused by actions such as spending too much time on minor points, causing everyone to wait while students respond individually, passing out equipment individually, and so forth. Attention wanders while students are waiting or when something they clearly understand is being discussed needlessly (as in lengthy review lessons). You need to recognize what causes delays and minimize them in an effort to keep the lesson moving at a good pace.

6. *Vary instructional media and methods.* Monotony breeds inattentiveness, and the repeated and perhaps exclusive use of one approach to instruction soon results in a classroom of bored students. Moreover, student achievement is increased when a variety of instructional materials and techniques are used (Good & Brophy, 2000). Varying media by using an overhead, chalkboard, videotapes, and computer presentations provides a more interesting approach to teaching any lesson.

7. *Stimulate attention periodically.* Student attention wanders when instruction becomes predictable and repetitive. You can promote continual attention as a lesson or an activity progresses. You can stimulate attention by cueing students through transitional signals that a new section of the lesson is coming up. For example, you might say "We have just spent the last 15 minutes considering what running water erosion is. Now let's look at the ways that farmers and other people try to stop this erosion." Or you can use challenging statements such as "Now, here's a really difficult (or tricky or interesting) question—let's see if you can figure it out."

8. *Show enthusiasm.* Your own enthusiasm is another factor in maintaining student attention. Enthusiasm can be expressed through vocal delivery, eyes, gestures, body movement, facial expressions, word selection, and acceptance of ideas and feelings. Teacher enthusiasm has been related to higher student achievement (Good & Brophy, 2000). Students often learn more from lessons that are presented with enthusiasm and expressiveness than from dry lectures.

You do not need to express a high degree of enthusiasm all the time. Depending on the circumstances of the lesson, you may vary the degree of enthusiasm being expressed. For example, there may be times during a lesson when you might be very animated and vocally expressive. Other times, you may choose to be very mild mannered.

9. *Use humor.* Students appreciate a certain amount of humor in the classroom, and the use of humor has been found to increase student achievement (Ziv, 1988). Occasional humor also helps maintain student attention. You may enjoy making silly statements or sharing funny experiences with your students. Be cautious that jokes are not used to tease or demean any student, even if expressed in a funny way, because the student may interpret these statements as being serious.

10. *Use questions effectively to maintain attention.* You can use questions to achieve various academic objectives. To maintain attention and encourage ongoing involvement, review the guidelines about questioning in Chapter 7.

11. *Maintain individual accountability.* Students should be accountable for being involved in lessons and learning all the material. It is helpful to ask a question or require the student to periodically make some kind of response (Good & Brophy, 2000). An unpredictable pattern in the way you handle questions or responses helps maintain individual accountability and causes students to be mentally engaged in the lesson and to be more attentive.

12. *Pay close attention when students talk and answer questions.* Use active listening skills. This often entails using nonverbal skills that indicate that you are interested in what students are saying. If you do not give attention and show interest when students answer questions, you communicate to them that what they have to say is not very important which, in turn, will discourage involvement. Nonverbal expressions of your interest might include nodding, moving toward the student, leaning forward, maintaining eye contact with the student, and showing interest in your facial expression. Verbal expressions of interest may include statements such as, "Uh huh," "I see," "That's a thoughtful answer," or "I appreciate your thorough, insightful answer."

13. *Reinforce students' efforts and maintain a high ratio of positive to negative verbal statements.* Students attend more fully if a positive learning environment has been created. One of the best means for accomplishing this is to respond positively to their efforts. Positive and encouraging statements are very important for all students, who can be motivated by positive reinforcement. On the other hand, a teacher who consistently belittles students' efforts creates a negative learning environment that will likely lead to inattention and off-task behavior. Make many more positive and encouraging statements than negative statements. Think about it from the students' point of view: Would you like to be in a classroom where you hear mostly negative or mostly positive statements?

14. *Vary the reinforcers being used.* You can reinforce students in many ways, including social reinforcers, activities and privileges, tangible reinforcers, and token reinforcers. These are described later in this chapter. Verbal praise is one of the most common approaches used as lessons are being delivered. Vary the way you give verbal statements of praise. Instead of repeatedly saying "Nice job" or "Good answer," you should use many different statements, including those that mention more specifically what the student did that was praiseworthy ("I really like the details in your answer").

15. *Terminate lessons that have gone on too long.* When the group is having difficulty maintaining attention, it is better to end the lesson than to struggle through it. This is especially important for younger students, whose attention spans are limited. Nevertheless, some teachers continue lessons in order to maintain a certain schedule. This can be counterproductive, since students may not learn under certain conditions and in any case will have to be taught again.

Teachers sometimes prolong a lesson to give each student an opportunity to participate. Instead, you should tell the class that those who do not participate on a given day will have an opportunity to participate on another day.

Reinforcing Desired Behaviors

A *reinforcer* is an event or consequence that increases the strength or future probability of the behavior it follows. Reinforcement is used to strengthen behaviors that are valued and to motivate students to do things that will benefit them.

It is important to recognize the general principle of reinforcement: *behaviors that are reinforced will be retained; behaviors that are not reinforced will be extinguished.* You need to carefully consider whom to reinforce, under what conditions, and with what kinds of reinforcement. Reinforcement is likely to be effective only to the extent that (a) the consequences used for reinforcers are experienced as reinforcers by the student; (b) they are contingent on the student achieving specific performance objectives; and (c) they are awarded in a way that complements rather than undermines the development of intrinsic motivation and other natural outcomes of behavior (Good & Brophy, 2000).

Several techniques of reinforcement are available, including social reinforcers, activities and privileges, tangible reinforcers, and token reinforcers. Many of these reinforcers can be used with both individual students and the entire class.

Social Reinforcers. *Social reinforcers* are positive consequences such as verbal or written expressions, nonverbal facial or bodily expressions, nonverbal proximity, and nonverbal physical contact. Social reinforcers are especially valued by students when given by people important to them. Social forms of approval are especially useful when reinforcing student behavior if you and the students have a good relationship. *Praise* is an expression of approval by the teacher after the student has attained something, and social reinforcers are often used to express this praise. Social reinforcement should always be contingent on performance of appropriate behavior. You should be specific about the behavior that resulted in the praise and the reasons for giving it.

Most social reinforcement should be done privately with the student, but some may be done publicly. You need to carefully consider student characteristics when deciding how to deliver praise. A seventh grader, for example, might be somewhat embarrassed being praised in front of the class.

Activities and Privileges. *Activity reinforcers* include privileges and preferred activities. After students complete desired activities or behave in appropriate ways, you can then reinforce them with various activities and privileges. Some of these reinforcers could be various jobs as a classroom helper. Activity reinforcers are often very effective for reinforcing the entire class. A list of sample activities and privileges that can be used as reinforcers is provided in Table 10.5.

It is important to verify that certain behaviors are desirable. When you and students are on good terms, students just performing certain tasks such as straightening the room or cleaning the chalkboards with you can be rewarding. Many other activities and privileges

TABLE 10.5   Examples of Activity and Privilege Reinforcers

PRIVILEGES	CLASSROOM JOBS
Playing a game	Distributing or collecting papers and materials
Helping the teacher	Taking attendance
Going to the library	Adjusting the window shades
Decorating a bulletin board	Taking a note to the office
Working or studying with a friend	Watering the plants
Reading for pleasure	Stapling papers together
Using the computer	Erasing the chalkboard
Writing on the chalkboard	Operating a computer or projector
Earning extra recess time	Cleaning the erasers

have an intrinsic value that do not depend on a student's relationship to you. Running errands, studying with a friend, going to the library, being first in line, or choosing an activity are each likely to be a positive incentive that produces satisfaction in its own right. You may have students fill out a sheet at the beginning of the school year to identify activities and reinforcers that they would appreciate.

Tangible Reinforcers. *Tangible, or material, reinforcers* are objects valued in and of themselves: certificates, awards, stars, buttons, bookmarkers, book covers, posters, ribbons, plaques, and report cards. Food also may serve as a tangible reinforcer: cookies, sugarless gum, popcorn, jelly beans, peanuts, candy, or raisins.

If you are interested in using food (M & Ms, cookies, etc.), recognize some cautions. Some parents may object to certain foods (such as those high in sugar), and there may be cultural differences related to food. Students may be allergic to certain foods, and there may be health and state regulations governing dispensing food in schools.

Since tangible reinforcers serve as external or extrinsic reinforcement, their use should be limited. Other types of reinforcers are generally more available and more reinforcing in natural settings than tangible reinforcers. When you give awards, it is a good idea to distribute them so as to include a good number of the students. Don't give awards only for outstanding achievement; award for improvement, excellent effort, good conduct, creativity, and so on.

Token Reinforcers. A *token reinforcer* is a tangible item that can be exchanged for a desired object, activity, or social reinforcer at a later time. Tokens may be chips, points, stars, tickets, buttons, play money, metal washers, happy faces, or stickers. The back-up reinforcer is the reward for which tokens can be exchanged. Token reinforcement is useful when praise and attention have not worked. Tokens are accumulated and cashed in for the reinforcer.

KEY TERMS

Activity center	Invitational learning	Reinforcer
Activity reinforcers	Misbehavior	Rules
Attention	Off-task behavior	Sending skills
Attention-getting strategies	Order	Skeleton plan
Classroom management	Paraphrasing technique	Social reinforcers
Course syllabus	Praise	Tangible or material reinforcers
Discipline	Procedures	Token reinforcers
Group cohesiveness	Public recognition	Withitness
Human relations skills	Receiving skills	

MAJOR CONCEPTS

1. Classroom management involves teacher actions to create a learning environment that encourages positive social interaction, active engagement in learning, and self-motivation.

2. Order means that students are performing within acceptable limits the actions necessary for a particular classroom event to be successful.

3. Establishing order begins by preparing for the start of the school year, organizing the classroom and materials, and selecting and teaching rules and procedures.

4. Organizing your classroom and materials involves decisions about floor space, storage space, and bulletin boards and wall space.

5. Rules refer to general behavioral guidelines or expectations that are to be followed in the classroom. Procedures are approved ways to achieve specific tasks in the classroom.

6. To develop a cooperative, responsible classroom, teachers can take actions to (a) build positive teacher–student relationships, (b) build group cohesiveness, (c) maintain attention and involvement, and (d) reinforce desired behaviors.

DISCUSSION/REFLECTIVE QUESTIONS

1. What are the benefits of planning uncomplicated lessons at the start of the school year? What might happen if the lessons are too challenging?

2. What are the merits of having a plan for systematically dealing with misbehavior?

3. What are the merits and disadvantages for placing students' seats in rows?

4. What are the advantages and disadvantages of involving students in the selection of rules and procedures?

5. What might teachers do to provide an inviting atmosphere for learning?

SUGGESTED ACTIVITIES

For Clinical Settings

1. Identify tasks you would like to have performed by classroom helpers. Establish a procedure for showing the students what to do in these roles and for rotating these roles to other students every week or two.

2. For your grade level or subject area, select the classroom rules that you prefer to use. Next, develop a plan for teaching these rules to the students on the first day of class.

3. For your grade level or subject area, select the classroom procedures you prefer to use for the areas identified in Table 10.3.

4. Prepare a lesson plan for a class that you might teach. Next to the appropriate part of the lesson plan, make notations for actions that you could take to maintain student attention.

For Field Settings

1. Find out what policies exist in the school district and the school for student conduct and academic expectations (e.g., homework).

2. Talk to two or more teachers to determine what rules and specific procedures they use. Obtain any printed guidelines that they provide students.

3. Talk to teachers to identify specifically how they begin the school year and establish their classroom management system. Identify what they do prior to the start of school, what they do on the first day or first class session, and how they handle the first two weeks of school.

4. Talk with several teachers to see how they reinforce desired student behaviors.

USEFUL RESOURCES

Burden, P. R. (2003). *Classroom management: Creating a successful learning community* (2nd ed.). New York: Wiley & Sons.

Provides a comprehensive K–12 review of ways to create a learning community. It carries a practical, realistic view of decisions teachers make about getting organized for management, planning for management, managing when conducting the class, and restoring order after misbehavior.

Wong, H. K., & Wong R. T. (1998). *The first days of school: How to be an effective teacher.* Mountain View, CA: Harry K. Wong Publications.

Includes a number of practical suggestions to prepare for the school year and to conduct the opening days of school. Covers characteristics of effective teachers, positive expectations, classroom management, lesson mastery, and professional development.

WEB SITES

- 101 things you can do the first three weeks of class.

  http://www.udel.edu/cte/101things.htm
- Classroom management as it relates to computer usage

  http://www.athena.ivv.nasa.gov/project/teacher/manage
- Temple University information on classroom management

  http://www.temple.edu/CETP/temple_teach/cm-intro.html
- Practicing teachers offer tips

  http://www.pacificnet.net/~mandel/ClassroomManagement.html
- Classroom management plans

  http://www.geom.umn.edu/~dwiggins/plan.html
- Ideas for many aspects of classroom management

  http://www.angelfire.com/ks/teachme/classmanagement.html

- Classroom Management/Discipline—an overview of major management practices.

  http://cis.georgefox.edu/sheadley/edpage/web/edmB/classmanage.html
- The Innovative Classroom provides management tips

  http://www.innovativeclassroom.com/Class_Management/
- Google.com and other search engines. You can use a search engine to explore any topic in this chapter.

  http://google.com

  http://yahoo.com

  http://excite.com

  http://search.netscape.com

  http://altavista.com

  http://askjeeves.com

CHAPTER ELEVEN

CLASSROOM DISCIPLINE

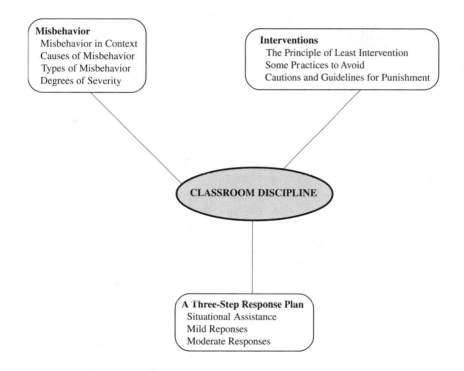

Misbehavior
  Misbehavior in Context
  Causes of Misbehavior
  Types of Misbehavior
  Degrees of Severity

Interventions
  The Principle of Least Intervention
  Some Practices to Avoid
  Cautions and Guidelines for Punishment

CLASSROOM DISCIPLINE

A Three-Step Response Plan
  Situational Assistance
  Mild Reponses
  Moderate Responses

OBJECTIVES

This chapter provides information that will help you to:

1. Recognize that misbehavior needs to be seen in the context of the circumstances and requires considerable interpretation.

2. Determine the causes of misbehavior.

3. Identify the types and degree of severity of misbehavior.

4. Describe the principle of least intervention.

5. Identify certain disciplinary practices to avoid.

6. Recognize the limitations of punishment and guidelines for it effective use.

7. Identify ways that situational assistance can be provided.

8. Determine ways to apply mild and moderate responses to misbehavior.

**PRAXIS/Principles of Learning
and Teaching/Pathwise**

The following principles are relevant to content in
this chapter:

1. Creating a climate that promotes fairness   (B1)

2. Establishing and maintaining rapport with
students   (B2)

3. Establishing and maintaining consistent standards of classroom behavior   (B4)

4. Making the physical environment as safe and
conducive to learning as possible   (B5)

INTASC

The following INTASC standards are relevant to
content in this chapter:

1. The teacher uses an understanding of individual
and group motivation and behavior to create a
learning environment and encourages positive
social interaction, active engagement in learning,
and self-motivation.   (Standard 5)

2. The teacher uses knowledge of effective verbal,
nonverbal, and media communication techniques
to foster active inquiry, collaboration, and supportive interaction in the classroom.   (Standard 6)

Even with an effective management system in place, students may lose interest in the
lesson and get off task. You must be prepared to respond with appropriate strategies to restore order. To provide a context for your decision making in this area, you should first understand misbehavior in context, the causes and types of misbehavior, and the degrees of
severity that are exhibited. Next, you should understand how interventions might be used.
Finally, this chapter addresses these issues and proposes a three-step response plan to misbehavior.

MISBEHAVIOR

Misbehavior is any student behavior that is perceived by the teacher to compete with or
threaten the academic actions at a particular moment. Misbehavior creates disruptions in
the academic flow of classroom activities, but not every infraction of a rule is necessarily
misbehavior. Therefore, misbehavior needs to be seen as action in context and requires a
considerable amount of interpretation when decisions are made about the misbehavior.

First, it is important to recognize that the best way to deal with discipline problems
is to avoid them in the first place. Teachers should develop challenging, interesting, and exciting lessons and treat students with dignity and respect. You should also establish an effective classroom management system, as described in other chapters. If misbehavior then
occurs, teachers can consider the guidelines and principles presented in this chapter.

Misbehavior in Context

Students who are off task are not performing the planned instructional activity. They may
be pausing to think about an issue, daydreaming, or doing other things that are nondisrup-

tive but prohibit them from being engaged in the instructional activities. Students who are off task need to be addressed differently than students who are purposely misbehaving and interfering with the academic activities. You may need to intervene to stop the misbehavior. Recognize that your decisions about interventions are complex judgments about the act, the student, and the circumstances at a particular moment in classroom time.

Some student actions are clearly misbehavior and require teacher intervention. In many cases, however, the situation is not quite as simple. Some student actions that appear to be quite similar are reacted to differently by teachers when the actions are performed by different students at different times or in different contexts (Doyle, 1986).

The key to understanding misbehavior is to view what students do in the context of the classroom structure. Not every infraction of a rule is necessarily misbehavior. For instance, inattention in the last few minutes of a class session will often be tolerated because the lesson is coming to an end. You would most likely intervene when inattention is evident earlier in the class.

Misbehavior, then, needs to be seen as "action in context" (Mehan et al., 1982) and requires interpretation based on what the teacher knows about the likely configuration of events. You need to make reliable judgments about the probable consequences of students' actions in different situations. Consistency in your response does not mean that you need to behave in the same way every time, but rather that your judgments are reliable and consistent.

Causes of Misbehavior

One way to understand classroom control is to determine *why* students misbehave. In some cases, the reasons are complex and personal and perhaps beyond your comprehension or control. But some misbehavior comes from common, general causes that can be anticipated.

1. *Health factors.* Student behavior problems may be related to health factors. Lack of sleep, an allergy, illness, or an inadequate diet may greatly affect the student's ability to complete assignments or interact with others. For some children, sugar has an effect on their behavior and may result in hyperactivity.

2. *Physical impairments.* Physical impairments, such as a vision or hearing loss, paralysis, or a severe physiological disorder, may also contribute to behavior problems.

3. *Neurological conditions.* Some students may have a mental disorder that affects their behavior. For example, attention deficit disorder is a mental condition in which the area of the brain that controls motor activity does not work like it should. This is one of the most common childhood mental disorders and affects about 4 percent of school-aged children, according to the National Institute of Mental Health. Such students may be inattentive (are easily distracted, don't follow directions well, shift from one unfinished task to another, and seem not to be listening), hyperactive (talkative, fidgety, and squirmy), and impulsive (don't wait their turn, blurt out answers, and engage in dangerous activities without considering the consequences). Children born with fetal alcohol syndrome may be hyperactive or impulsive, and crack babies (children born to women who used crack during pregnancy) may exhibit similar behaviors.

■ ■ ■ ■ ■ ■

CLASSROOM DECISIONS

You have a student in your classroom who has attention deficit disorder. What would you do to understand the nature of the student's condition? Where would you go to seek out information about ways to deal with this student in the classroom? What adjustments might you consider in your classroom management and discipline plan for this student?

4. *Medication or drugs.* Medication or drugs, whether legal or illegal, may also be a factor. Over-the-counter medicine for nasal congestion, for example, may cause a student to be less alert than usual. Alcohol or drug abuse also may contribute to unusual behavior at school.

5. *Influences from the home or society.* Conditions in the student's home may be related to behavior problems. Student behavior problems may be associated with a lack of adequate clothing or housing, parental supervision and types of discipline, home routines, or significant events such as divorce or the death of a friend or relative. Factors in the community or in society also may contribute to student behavior problems. There has been considerable concern and debate over the effects of television on the beliefs and conduct of children. Violence on television is seen by some to influence students to be more aggressive.

6. *School and classroom factors.* School factors can be related to behavior problems. This includes factors such as the curriculum; effectiveness of teachers, administrators, and staff; school routines; adequacy of facilities; and even other students in the classroom. The physical arrangement of the classroom, temperature, noise, and lighting may affect student behavior. Student crowding may also be involved. Instructional factors may be the most important of all the physical factors that directly affect student behavior. They include the classroom learning climate, the appropriateness of the curriculum and instructional materials, and the effectiveness of the instructional delivery. When students' developmental needs are not being met, there is an increased chance for misbehavior.

TEACHERS IN ACTION

ELEMENTS OF THE SETTING AFFECT BEHAVIOR

Debra Young Stuto, sixth grade teacher, Omaha, Nebraska

To be effective in handling students, you must take the time to understand the causes of the behaviors and misbehaviors. For example, there was no way that Quincy would learn anything on the day that we had fishsticks for lunch. Quincy *hated* fishsticks. It took me several weeks of horrible scenes every Friday to fit fishsticks with Quincy's misbehavior.

Quincy was the oldest child of several little brothers and sisters, and his mother recently had a new baby. There was no way that he was going to have a sack lunch from home on fishstick days. So, on Thursday night I made Quincy a peanut butter and jelly sandwich as I made my own son's sandwich, and I put it on his desk in the morning so that it was there when he walked in. Neither of us mentioned it, and every Thursday I do the same thing. Now Quincy can learn on fishstick days.

Teachers sometimes needlessly create disciplinary problems by the way that they manage and conduct their classes. These inappropriate behaviors include being overly negative, maintaining an authoritarian climate, overreacting to situations, using mass punishment for all students, blaming students, lacking a clear instructional goal, repeating or reviewing already learned material, pausing too long during instruction, dealing with one student at length, and lacking recognition of student ability levels. While few teachers can avoid all these behaviors all the time, effective teachers recognize the potentially damaging effects on classroom order and discipline. Being aware of these characteristics is the first step to avoiding them. It is useful to periodically reflect on your own teaching behavior to determine if you are taking actions that are contributing to inattention or misbehavior.

Types of Misbehavior

Inappropriate behavior by individual students can be classified into four general categories:

1. *Hyperactivity:* defined as a high level of activity and nonaggressive contact, often due to neurological dysfunctions. Behaviors include (a) unable to sit still and fidgets, (b) talks too much, (c) cannot wait for pleasant things to happen, (d) constant demand for attention, (e) hums and makes other noises, (f) excitable, (g) overly anxious to please, and (h) awkward and poor general coordination.

2. *Inattentiveness:* the inability to complete work and activities, has a high level of distractibility. Behaviors include (a) doesn't stay with games and activities, (b) doesn't complete projects, (c) inattentive and distractible, (d) doesn't follow directions, (e) withdraws from new people and is shy, (f) sits fiddling with small objects, and (g) unable to sit still and fidgets.

3. *Conduct disorder:* the inability to accept correction, the tendency to tease others, and a high level of defiance. Behaviors include (a) doesn't stay with games and activities, (b) cannot accept correction, (c) teases others, (d) discipline doesn't change behavior for long, (e) defiant and talks back, (f) moody, (g) fights, and (h) has difficulty in handling frustration.

4. *Impulsivity:* has constant demand for attention, has an orientation to the present, and is unpredictable. Behaviors include (a) reckless and acts carelessly, (b) has lots of accidents, and (c) gets into things.

Degrees of Severity

Misbehavior in schools ranges from severely to mildly disruptive behavior. Severely disruptive behavior and crime in schools may involve violence, vandalism, robbery, theft, and drug use. These behaviors typically occur outside the classroom in places such as the lunch room, corridors, or outside the building. Moderate levels of misbehavior involve tardiness, cutting class, talking, call-outs, mild forms of verbal and physical aggression, inattentiveness, and failure to bring supplies and books. Most misbehavior is comparatively mild and is related to attention, crowd control, and getting work accomplished in the classroom.

When selecting an appropriate response to misbehavior, it is important that teachers take into account the degree of severity of the misbehavior. Severity can be gauged by factors

MODIFICATIONS FOR DIVERSE CLASSROOMS

THE EFFECT OF CULTURAL DIFFERENCES

The cultural background of students will likely affect the way that they interact with teachers and other students, respond to authority, use language, and conduct themselves in formal or informal settings. A student action that you view as disruptive or disrespectful might not be viewed that way by the student. The cultural differences between the teacher and the students have the potential to create difficulties when dealing with off-task behavior or misbehavior.

1. What can you do as a first-year teacher to better understand the cultural characteristics of your students? How can your students help? How can other teachers, administrators, or parents help?
2. How might this cultural understanding of your students cause you to modify what you do as a teacher?
3. In relation to off-task behavior and misbehavior, how might you need to modify your approaches based on the various cultural backgrounds of your students?

such as appropriateness, magnitude, intent, and extent to which a behavior differs from what is expected in a particular setting (Evans, Evans, & Schmid, 1989). The degree of your response should match the degree of severity of the misbehavior. Teachers sometimes ignore certain minor misbehaviors because the response may be more disruptive than the misbehavior.

INTERVENTIONS

The teacher must decide when and how to intervene when students are off task or misbehaving. An *intervention* is an action taken by the teacher that is intended to stop the disruptive actions and return the student to the academic activities.

Intervention decisions are typically based on the teacher's knowledge of who is misbehaving, what the misbehavior is, and when it occurs. Decisions about the intensity of the intervention may depend on the student's history of inappropriate behavior. However, you should not automatically jump to conclusions if an incident involves a student with a history of behavior problems.

Decisions to intervene are often made under conditions of uncertainty. That is, early cues may be ambiguous, yet the teacher has only a limited amount of time to make a judgment and act. To reduce uncertainty, teachers sometimes categorize students in terms of their persistence and their visibility in the social structure of the group. It is helpful to discuss the problem with the student to clarify the problem from both your perspective and the student's before considering possible interventions.

Interventions are used to repair order rather than create order, involve complex decisions about the probable consequences of particular actions by particular students at specific moments in the activity flow of a class session, and can themselves disrupt order.

TEACHERS IN ACTION

DISCUSS THE PROBLEM WITH THE STUDENT

Claudia Swisher, high school English teacher, Norman, Oklahoma

When I need to correct some specific student behavior or to deal with a problem, I always tell the student to "Meet me in the hall." I have learned that confrontations in class are set up as power plays, and the student has little reason to try to correct the behavior in front of the class. I don't explain the reasons for calling the student into the hall and don't answer any questions in the room. Once the student and I are in the hall, I explain my concern and focus on what needs to be done when we both return to the classroom.

I don't allow the student to change the subject or excuse the behavior. I do listen, and I have often found that I have misunderstood some aspect of the behavior.

If more privacy is needed, I will track down a student during my planning period and ask his or her current teacher for a few minutes. The student and I may walk the halls, sit in an empty room, or sit outside. Many misunderstandings can be worked out in this way, and my students know that I respect their feelings.

I know that dealing with these problems in private keeps both the student and me safe from an audience and allows us to be honest. By the end of the year, my students know that "Meet me in the hall" isn't the first step to a confrontation, but an attempt to solve a little problem before it becomes too big for us.

The Principle of Least Intervention

The *principle of least intervention* states that when routine classroom behavior is being handled, misbehaviors should be corrected with the simplest, least intrusive intervention that will work (Slavin, 2000). If the least intrusive intervention does not work, then you move up to a more intrusive approach. The main goal is to handle the misbehavior in an effective manner that avoids unnecessarily disrupting the lesson. To the extent possible, the lesson should continue while misbehavior is handled.

How do you apply this principle of least intervention? When you notice students starting to lose interest in the lesson or beginning to get off task, you can provide situational assistance—actions to help the student cope with the situation and keep on task. If the student then is off task, you can select mild responses to get the student back on task. If mild responses are not effective, you can use moderate responses. Based on the principle of least intervention, this continuum of teacher responses is displayed in Table 11.1, and details are provided later in this chapter.

Some Practices to Avoid

Research and practice suggest that some strategies are inappropriate or unsuccessful when trying to restore order. In a comprehensive review of the literature concerning behavior management techniques, Weber and Roff (1983) found that disadvantages outweigh the advantages for the use of harsh reprimands, threats, and physical punishment. Furthermore,

TABLE 11.1   A Three-Step Response Plan to Misbehavior Using the Principle of Least Intervention

TEACHER RESPONSE	STEP 1 PROVIDE SITUATIONAL ASSISTANCE	STEP 2 USE MILD RESPONSES	STEP 3 USE MODERATE RESPONSES
Purpose	To help the student to cope with the instructional situation and keep the student on task	To take nonpunitive actions to get the student back on task	To remove desired stimuli to decrease unwanted behavior
Sample actions	Remove distracting objects Provide support with routines Reinforce appropriate behaviors Boost student interest Provide cues Help student over hurdles Redirect the behavior Alter the lesson Provide nonpunitive time-out Modify the classroom environment	Nonverbal responses ■ Ignore the behavior ■ Use nonverbal signals ■ Stand near the student ■ Touch the student Verbal responses ■ Call on the student during the lesson ■ Use humor ■ Send an I-message ■ Use positive phrasing ■ Remind students of the rules ■ Give students choices ■ Ask "What should you be doing?" ■ Give a verbal reprimand	Logical consequences ■ Withdraw privileges ■ Change the seat assignment ■ Write reflections on the problem ■ Place student in time-out ■ Hold student for detention ■ Contact the parents ■ Have student visit the principal

practitioners have identified additional approaches that have questionable effectiveness. The message is clear—teachers should avoid the following practices.

1. *Harsh and humiliating reprimands.* A harsh reprimand is very negative verbal feedback. Teachers may get carried away with this verbal thrashing and humiliate the student. Research reports suggest that the use of harsh reprimands is a very ineffective, inefficient, and costly strategy for modifying student behavior. Harsh reprimands include speaking to the student in an exceptionally stern manner, yelling, and screaming. All of this may be done to the point where the student may be humiliated. Teachers sometimes give harsh reprimands when they have lost their emotional control in response to the misbehavior.

2. *Threats.* A *threat* is a statement that expresses the intent to punish the student if the student does not comply with the teacher's wishes. Most practitioners and researchers believe the disadvantages of using threats outweigh any possible benefits. Teachers may warn students to alert them to potential consequences, but a threat often expresses more severe consequences than would normally be expected and may be stated when the teacher has lost emotional control.

3. *Nagging.* Continual or unnecessary scolding of a student only upsets the student and arouses the resentment of other students.The teacher may consider these scoldings to be mini-lectures, but they are seen as nagging from the students' point of view.

4. *Forced apologies.* Forcing a student to express an apology that is not felt is a way of forcing him or her to lie. This approach solves nothing.

5. *Sarcastic remarks.* Sarcastic remarks are statements that the teacher uses to deride, taunt, or ridicule the student. While the teacher may consider such remarks as a means of punishment, they create resentment, may lower the student's self-esteem, and, in fact, may lower the esteem of the teacher in the eyes of the students.

6. *Group punishment.* *Group punishment* occurs when the entire class or group is punished because of the misbehavior of an individual. Peer pressure is intended to help modify the behavior of the individual. Group punishment is difficult to use effectively, and the undesirable side effects are likely to outweigh the advantages. It forces students to choose between the teacher and one of their classmates. Many students will unite in sullen defiance of the teacher and refuse to blame the classmate if group punishment is used. Even if the students go along with the teacher, the technique engenders unhealthy attitudes.

7. *Assigning extra academic work.* When assigning extra academic work as a punishment, the teacher implies that the work is unpleasant. This extra work is often in the form of homework that is not normally required. The student then associates schoolwork with punishment. This is not the message teachers should convey.

8. *Reducing grades.* Penalizing a student academically for misbehavior again creates an undesirable association. Students who are penalized for misbehaving may develop an attitude of "What's the use?" toward academic work. Furthermore, reducing grades for misbehavior confounds the grade, which is intended to report only the student's academic progress.

9. *Writing as punishment.* After students misbehave, teachers may have them copy pages out of a dictionary, encyclopedia, or other book, or have students write a certain statement ("I will not do such and such again.") a number of times. Unfortunately, this approach leads to hostility by the students, gives the impression that writing is a bad thing (English teachers would get upset about the message being conveyed here), and is not logically linked to what the students may have done.

10. *Physical labor or exercise.* A teacher may use pushups or some other physical action as punishment. However, the teacher may not be familiar with the student's physical abilities, and the student could get hurt. In addition to concerns about the student's safety, having students do extra exercises in physical education in response to misbehavior may cause the student to lose interest in the physical activities when the teacher assigns them as punishment.

11. *Corporal punishment. Corporal punishment* is a strategy in which the teacher inflicts physical pain on the student in an attempt to punish the student for misbehaving. Paddling, spanking, slapping, and pinching are examples.

There are many disadvantages to using physical consequences (Hyman, 1990, 1997). Inappropriate behavior may be suppressed only temporarily, and appropriate behaviors may be suppressed as well. Other negative behaviors often emerge, such as escape (running away from the punisher), avoidance (lying, stealing, cheating), anxiety, fear, tension, stress, withdrawal, poor self-concept, resistance, and counteraggression. The student also may suffer physical harm. Furthermore, physical punishment may also serve as a model of aggressive behavior for the student. Because of these disadvantages, *physical consequences should not be used.* Many districts have a policy either prohibiting the use of corporal punishment or establishing specific guidelines for its limited use.

Cautions and Guidelines for Punishment

The later steps of the Principle of Least Intervention may involve punishment. *Punishment* is the act of imposing a penalty with the intention of suppressing undesirable behavior. There are two procedures for achieving this purpose: (a) *withholding positive reinforcers or desirable stimuli* through techniques such as logical consequences and behavior-modification approaches such as time-out and loss of privileges; and (b) *adding aversive stimuli* through actions by which students receive a penalty for their behavior. Withholding positive reinforcers is considered to be less harmful than adding aversive stimuli. Withholding positive reinforcers represents a *moderate response* to a student's misbehavior, while adding aversive stimuli represents a *severe response.*

Especially for beginning teachers, dealing with misbehavior that requires moderate or severe responses can be very troubling. It is often helpful to talk with the principal, other teachers, or school counselors to obtain ideas and advice for dealing with students who exhibit more serious misbehavior. In addition, it is often useful to contact the student's parents at any point to inform them of any concerns you might have and to solicit their help in working with the student.

The effects of punishment are limited and specific. Much evidence shows that punishment can control misbehavior, but by itself will not teach desirable behavior or even reduce the desire to misbehave (Slavin, 2000). Punishment does not teach the student appropriate behavior, and it often has a transitory effect in suppressing inappropriate behavior. It allows the student to project blame rather than accept responsibility for behavior.

Punishment should not be applied when misbehavior is not disruptive or when problems exist because students do not know what to do or how to do it. It is used in response to repeated misbehavior. Even with repeated misbehavior, punishment should be avoided when students are trying to improve.

You should express confidence in the students' ability to improve, and punish only as a last resort when students repeatedly fail to respond to more positive treatment. Apply punishment as part of a planned response, and not as a means to release your anger or frustration.

The following factors are important to consider when effectively using punishment.

1. *Discuss and reward acceptable behaviors.* Acceptable behaviors should be emphasized when classroom rules are first discussed. Make it clear to students why the rules exist. Discuss the reasons for not engaging in behavior considered to be inappropriate. Most students will behave appropriately if they know what is expected.

2. *Clearly specify the behaviors that will lead to punishment.* Clarifying acceptable behaviors for the students may not be enough. To help the students to understand, examples of behaviors that break the rules and lead to punishment should be identified and discussed.

3. *Use punishment only when rewards or nonpunitive interventions have not worked or if the behavior must be decreased quickly because it is dangerous.* Punishment should be used as a last resort when other techniques have failed.

4. *Administer punishment in a calm, unemotional manner.* If you deliver punishment while still emotionally upset, you may select an overly harsh punishment and may also provoke the student into further inappropriate reactions. Punishment should not be an involuntary emotional response, a way to get revenge, or a spontaneous response to provocation.

■ ■ ■ ■ ■ ▬▬

CREATING A LEARNING COMMUNITY

MOVING FROM COMPLIANCE TO BUILDING COMMUNITIES

In *Beyond Discipline: From Compliance to Community* (1996), Alfie Kohn makes an articulate and passionate argument for the reduction of punishment. He challenges educators to ask this question when planning to work with students: "What do they require in order to flourish, and how can we provide those things?" Kohn says teachers should focus on developing caring, supportive classrooms where students participate in problem solving, including problems about behavior. He advises teachers to develop a sense of community in their classrooms.

1. If you were to adopt Kohn's ideas, how would that affect your selection of rules and procedures and your selection of consequences for infractions?
2. To contribute as members of the learning community and participate in decision making, what knowledge and skills would students need to have?
3. How would you justify to parents your classroom approaches for which students have so much say in how the class is run?

5. *Deliver a warning before punishment is applied to any behavior.* The warning itself could reduce the need for the punishment. If the student does not correct the behavior after the warning, punishment should be delivered at the next occurrence.

6. *Apply punishment fairly with everyone who exhibits the targeted behaviors.* You should treat both sexes the same way and low-achieving and high-achieving students the same way.

7. *Apply punishment consistently after every occurrence of the targeted misbehavior.* Behaviors that reliably receive punishment are less likely to be tried by students than behaviors that occasionally go uncorrected.

8. *Use punishment of sufficient intensity to suppress the unwanted behaviors.* Generally, the greater the intensity is, the longer-lasting the effect. But this does not mean that you need to resort to extreme measures. For example, the loss of positive reinforcement because of inappropriate behavior is better than shouting "don't do that" with increasing intensity.

9. *Select a punishment that is effective, that is not associated with a positive or rewarding experience, and that fits the situation.* Not all aversive consequences that you select may be seen as punishment. Some students, for instance, might think that it is a reward to be placed in a time-out area in the classroom. In this case, a different consequence should be used that is not seen by the student as being positive or rewarding. Also, don't overreact to mild misbehavior or underreact to serious misbehavior. The seriousness of the misbehavior, the student, and the context of the situation need to be taken into account.

10. *Avoid extended periods of punishment.* Lengthy, mild punishment such as missing open study time for a week, may have a boomerang effect. Punishment with a short duration is more effective.

CLASSROOM DECISIONS

Let's assume that you have taken a teaching position in a school that has a history of discipline problems. You need to develop a set of rules, procedures, and consequences to establish an appropriate learning environment. Punishment can be used to suppress undesirable behavior. What guidelines will you establish for yourself for the appropriate and effective use of punishment? What might you do to reinforce or support desired behavior?

A THREE-STEP RESPONSE PLAN

When off-task behavior and misbehavior occur, a three-step response plan can be followed as a means to restore order and get the students back on task. The three steps described here are based on the principle of least intervention discussed earlier (see Table 11.1). You provide situational assistance as the first approach to get the student back on task, and then sequentially apply mild and moderate responses. If misbehavior continues after moderate responses are applied, other interventions may be needed. In these cases, it is useful to discuss the situation with the principal and school counselor.

Situational Assistance

Students sometimes pause from the instructional task to look out the window, daydream, fiddle with a comb or other object, or simply take a brief mental break from the work. In these examples, the students are not misbehaving—they are simply off task for a short time. You should take steps to draw the student back into the lesson and to keep the student on task.

To communicate to the student that you have noticed off-task behavior, you should first provide *situational assistance*—actions designed to help the students cope with the instructional situation and to keep them on task or to get them back on task before problems worsen. Problem behaviors thus can be stopped early before they escalate or involve other students.

If students remain off task after situational assistance is provided, move on to *mild responses.* These nonverbal and verbal, nonpunitive responses are designed to get the student back on task. The continuum of responses to misbehavior (see Table 11.1) illustrates that situational assistance is the starting point when dealing with off-task behavior.

In an early work on behavior management intervention, Redl and Wineman (1957) identified 12 behavior-influence techniques designed to manage surface behaviors. Their work has been expanded and reorganized by others, including Burden (2003), Levin and Nolan (2000), Weinstein (2003), and Weinstein and Mignano (1997). The organization of this section represents a synthesis of these suggested techniques.

1. *Remove distracting objects.* Students sometimes bring objects to school that may be distracting, such as combs, keys, or magazines. When you see that these objects are keeping the students from the assigned tasks, simply walk over to the student and collect the object. The student should be quietly informed that the object can be picked up after class. Be kind and firm; no discussion is necessary. Inform students that they should store such objects in an appropriate place before school.

2. *Provide support with routines.* Students appreciate and often find comfort in knowing what is going to happen during the class period or during the day. They like to know where, when, why, and with whom they will be at various times. It is helpful to announce and post the daily schedule. Changes in the schedule should be announced in advance, if possible. Even for a single lesson, students often appreciate knowing at the start what activities are planned for the lesson. Knowing the schedule provides students with a sense of security and direction. Routines for entering and leaving the classroom, distributing classroom papers and materials, and participating in group work contribute to this sense of security.

3. *Reinforce appropriate behaviors.* Students who have followed the directions can be praised. This communicates to the student who is off task what is expected. A statement such as "I'm pleased to see that Juan has his notebook ready for today's lesson" communicates to others what is expected. Appropriate behavior is reinforced while simultaneously

TEACHERS IN ACTION

NONPUNITIVE RESPONSES

Janet Kulbiski, kindergarten teacher, Manhattan, Kansas

After reading Jane Nelsen's book *Positive Discipline* (Ballantine Books, 1996), I changed my attitude about misbehavior and tried some different behavior management strategies in my classroom. I now see misbehavior as an opportunity for teaching appropriate action.

Several of Nelsen's techniques have been very helpful in my classroom. I use natural and logical consequences, allow students choices, and redirect misbehavior. Natural consequences occur without intervention from anyone, such as when a child does not wear his coat and then gets cold. Logical consequences, by contrast, require intervention connected in some logical way to what the child did. If a child draws a picture on the table, a logical consequence would be that the child cleans it up.

It is important to give students choices whenever possible. This gives them a sense of control and worth, but all choices must be acceptable to you. For example, "Please, put the toy on my desk or in your backpack."

Redirecting student behavior involves reminding them of the expected behavior. For example, instead of saying, "Don't run," I say, "We always walk." Eliminating "Don't" from my vocabulary has helped a lot.

When I deal with misbehavior, I try to always use the situation as an opportunity for the child to learn the expected behavior. My goal is to leave the child feeling good about himself or herself and equipped to handle the situation appropriately next time.

---

giving a signal to students who are off task. This approach is more commonly used in elementary classrooms; middle and secondary students may consider it to be a little juvenile.

4. *Boost student interest.* Student interest may wane in time as the lesson proceeds. You should express interest in the student's work when the student shows signs of losing interest or being bored. Offer to help, noting how much work has been completed, noting how well done the completed part of the task is, or discussing the task. These actions can help bring the student back on task. Interest boosting is often needed when students do individual or small-group classwork.

For example, when a student appears to be off task while working in a small group, you could walk over and ask how the group is doing. Also, you might ask the student a question about the group's progress. Take a matter-of-fact, supportive attitude when trying to boost student interest.

5. *Provide cues.* Sometimes all the students are asked to do one thing, such as to prepare their materials or to clean up at the end of class, and cues can be given in these cases. *Cues* are signals that it is time for a selected behavior. For example, you may close the door at the start of class as a cue that instruction is about to begin and that everyone is expected to have all materials ready. Or the lights could be flipped or a bell sounded to signal time to begin cleanup or to finish small-group work.

For these situations, you can select an appropriate cue and explain its use to the students. Using the same cues consistently usually results in quick responses. You are conveying behavioral expectations and encouraging constructive, on-task behavior.

CLASSROOM DECISIONS

Imagine that your English class is working in groups using cooperative learning techniques for a seven-day project. When the students come into the room, they immediately go to their groups and start work. On some days and during some of the class sessions, you need to give some information to all students. How can you use a cue as a signal for students to stop work at that point and pay attention to you? Also, how can you give a cue that it is time to prepare to leave the class at the end of the class period?

6. *Help students over hurdles.* Students who are experiencing difficulty with a specific task need help in overcoming the problem—helping them over a hurdle—to keep them on task. *Hurdle helping* may consist of encouraging words from you, an offer to assist with a specific task, or making available additional materials or equipment. For example, in a seatwork activity in which students need to draw several elements, including some straight lines, you might notice that one student is becoming upset that her lines are not straight. You could help her by handing her a ruler. In this way, you help before the student gives up on the assignment or becomes disruptive.

7. *Redirect the behavior.* When students show signs of losing interest, you can ask them to answer a question, to do a problem, or to read as a means of drawing them back into the lesson. Students should be treated as if they were paying attention and should be reinforced if they respond appropriately. It is important not to embarrass or ridicule students by saying that they would have been able to answer the question if they had been paying attention. Simply by asking a content-related question, students will recognize that you are trying to draw them back into the lesson. Redirecting student behavior back into the lesson discourages off-task behavior.

8. *Alter the lesson.* Lessons sometimes do not go as well as you would like, and students may lose interest in the lesson for a variety of reasons. The lesson needs to be altered in some way when students are seen daydreaming, writing notes to friends, yawning, stretching, or moving around in their seats. This allows for a change of activities such as small-group discussions or games that students like and require their active participation. Select a different type of activity than the one that has proven to be unsuccessful. When you alter the lesson early, you are able to keep student attention focused on the lesson and maintain order. For example, if a whole-class discussion proves to be unsuccessful, you might have students work in pairs on a related issue that still deals with the lesson's objectives.

In your initial planning, take student interests and abilities into account and provide a variety of activities in each lesson. The need to alter the lesson once underway is thereby minimized. It is helpful to have several types of activities planned in each lesson, some requiring active student participation. Consider the length of time allocated to each activity by taking into account the students' age and maturity.

9. *Provide nonpunitive time-out.* Students who become frustrated, agitated, or fatigued may get off task and disruptive. When you notice this happening, you could provide a nonpunitive time-out. A *time-out* is a period of time that the student is away from the instructional situation to calm down and reorganize his or her thoughts. The student then returns to the task with a fresh perspective. This time-out is not intended to be a *punitive response* or a punishment for the off-task behavior.

When a time out is needed, you could ask the student to run an errand, help you with something, go get a drink, or do some other task not related to the instructional activity. Be alert to students showing signs of frustration and agitation and be ready to respond quickly.

Sometimes it is useful to have a small area of the room specifically designated for time-out. This could be a desk placed off in a corner, partially hidden by a filing cabinet. The student could go to this semiprivate area in an effort to calm down and prepare to continue with the lesson. You could suggest that the students be allowed to go to this area when they think they need it. Students who use the corner for nonpunitive time-out should be allowed to decide themselves when they are ready to return.

10. *Modify the classroom environment.* The classroom environment itself may contribute to off-task behavior. The arrangement of the desks, tables, instructional materials, and other items in the classroom may give rise to inefficient traffic patterns or limited views of the instructional areas. Other factors include the boundaries between areas for quiet student and group projects and access to supplies. In addition, both your actions and those of your students may affect their behavior.

Once misbehavior develops, you may need to separate the students or change the setting in some way. Examine the disturbance and identify the element that contributes to it. Modification in the classroom arrangement may include moving tables, student desks, or the storage area.

Mild Responses

Students may misbehave even after you have developed a system of rules and procedures, provided a supportive instructional environment, and given situational assistance to get misbehaving students back on task. In that case, mild responses should be used to correct the student's behavior. *Mild responses* are nonpunitive ways to deal with misbehavior while providing guidance for appropriate behavior. Nonverbal and verbal mild responses are meant to stop the off-task behavior and to restore order. The three-step response plan shown in Table 11.1 illustrates the movement to more directive responses if situational assistance is not successful.

Nonverbal Responses.   Even with situational assistance, students may get off task. Nonverbal responses are taken as a nonpunitive means to get the student back on task. *Nonverbal responses* may include planned ignoring, signal interference, proximity control, and touch control. These approaches are taken in increasing order of teacher involvement and control.

Shrigley (1985) studied 523 off-task behaviors, and found that 40 percent of the behaviors could be corrected by the nonverbal responses discussed here. Five percent of the behaviors where corrected by ignoring the behavior, 14 percent were corrected by signal interference, 12 percent by proximity, and 9 percent by touch control. Nonverbal approaches successfully extinguish many off-task behaviors. If these approaches do not work, higher control approaches such as verbal interventions need to be used.

■ ■ ■ ■ ■ ■

CLASSROOM DECISIONS

As your class is working in small groups, you notice two students in one group who are off task. How could you respond nonverbally to get the students back on task? What factors might affect your decision on the particular method? If you were making a presentation to the whole class when misbehavior took place, what nonverbal responses might you take?

1. *Ignore the behavior.* Intentionally ignoring minor misbehavior is sometimes the best course of action as a means to weaken the behavior. This is based on the reinforcement principle called *extinction;* that is, if you ignore a behavior and withhold reinforcement, the behavior will lessen and ultimately disappear. Minor misbehaviors that might be ignored are pencil tapping, body movements, hand waving, book dropping, calling out an answer instead of raising a hand, interrupting the teacher, whispering, and so on. Behaviors designed to get your attention or that of their classmates are likely candidates for extinction, or ignoring the behavior.

Ignoring the behavior is best used to control only behaviors that cause little interference to teaching/learning, and it should be combined with praise for appropriate behavior. Extinction is inappropriate for behaviors (e.g., talking out, aggression) reinforced by consequences that you do not control, or for behaviors (violence) that cannot be tolerated during the time required for extinction to work (Kerr & Nelson, 2002). If the behavior continues after a reasonable period of planned ignoring, you should be more directive.

There are limitations to ignoring the behavior. One risk is that students may conclude that you are not aware of what is happening and may continue the behavior. While you may ignore the behavior and do not give the student the desired attention, other students may give such attention. Furthermore, the student may continue the behavior for a while after you ignore it; however, if the deliberate ignoring is effective, the student will eventually stop the behavior. For some behaviors, extinction is too slow to be of practical value. Aggressive or hostile behaviors may be too dangerous to ignore.

2. *Use nonverbal signals.* A nonverbal signal can be used to communicate to the disrupting student that the behavior is not appropriate. Signals must be directed at the student. They let the student know that the behavior is inappropriate and that it is time to get back to work.

Nonverbal signal interference may include making eye contact with the student who is writing a note, shaking a hand or finger to indicate not to do some inappropriate action, holding a hand up to stop a student's calling out, or giving the "teacher look." These actions should be done in a businesslike manner. You need to move to the next level of intervention if these disruptive behaviors persist.

3. *Stand near the student.* Your physical presence near the disruptive student to help the student get back on task is *proximity control.* This is warranted sometimes when you cannot get the student's attention to send a signal because the student is so engrossed in an inappropriate action. For example, a student may be reading something other than class-related material or may be writing a note. While doing this, the student may not even look

TEACHERS IN ACTION

USING BODY LANGUAGE AND "THE TEACHER LOOK"

Lynne Hagar, high school history and English teacher, Mesquite, Texas

I am a small woman, but I can effectively control 30 senior students just by using my voice and my body language. When I want a certain behavior to stop, the first thing I do is to look at the student. Even if that student is not looking at me, he or she eventually becomes aware that I am staring. Then I point at the student and nonverbally indicate that the behavior is to stop. A finger placed on my lips indicates that talking needs to stop.

Often, a questioning or disapproving look or gesture can stop undesirable behaviors right there. I may have to move into a student's personal space or comfort zone to stop a behavior, but a combination of a look and physical proximity are effective about 90 percent of the time. I might even casually rest my hand on the student's desk, never stopping teaching, and stay put for a minute or so until I'm sure the student is back on task.

My advice is to practice "the look" in the mirror until you get it right. It shouldn't be a friendly look, but it doesn't have to be angry either. Learn to say in your manner, "I am in charge here."

Also, move around the classroom. Getting close to your students is essential, not only when you are correcting them but also when you want to reassure them or reinforce their positive feelings about you and your classroom. A friendly touch on the shoulder as you are helping a student with a problem or a hug when a student has a big success can go miles toward cementing your positive relationship with that student.

up at you. As a result, signals will not work. While conducting the lesson, walk around the room and approach the student's desk. It is then likely that the student will notice your presence and put the material away without a word being spoken.

Some proximity-control techniques may be somewhat subtle, such as walking toward the student, while other approaches, such as standing near the student's desk, are more direct. If students do not respond to proximity control, you need to move to a more directive level of intervention.

4. *Touch the student.* Without any verbal exchange, you may place a hand on a student's shoulder in an effort to achieve calm, or take a student's hand and escort the student back to his or her seat. These are examples of *touch control*—mild, nonaggressive physical contact that is used to get the student on task. It communicates that you disapprove of the action. Touch control may redirect the student back into the appropriate behavior, such as repositioning the student's hand where it belongs—on the desk.

When deciding whether and how to use touch control, you may take into account the circumstances of the behavior and the characteristics of the students when deciding whether and how to use touch control. Students who are angry or visibly upset sometimes do not want to be touched, and some do not want to be touched at any time. How well touch will be received depends on where it occurs and how long it lasts. A touch on the back, hand, arm, or shoulder is acceptable to many students, whereas touch to the face, neck, leg, chest, or other more personal areas are often not acceptable. Brief touch is con-

TEACHERS IN ACTION

STANDING NEAR THE STUDENT

Claudia Swisher, high school English teacher, Norman, Oklahoma

I have learned that being physically close to students is a powerful tool for keeping them on task. During class discussions or seatwork, I walk up and down the rows, spend time at the very back of the room, and even may sit in empty seats. It takes my students some time to get used to this since they seem more used to seeing their teacher as a stationary object; but they will turn around during discussion to find me in the room.

I can easily give assistance to a reluctant student if I see someone is struggling. It is easy to give pats on the back when I am among the students. Re-luctant students find it difficult to avoid involvement when I am right there near them.

No one is threatened by my presence beside or behind them. I am able to quietly deal with many behaviors that interfere with learning, such as sleeping, social note writing, talking, ignoring the lesson, drawing instead of listening, reading another book, or doing other homework. While roaming the room, I can easily correct, redirect, encourage, and praise my students without distracting the entire class.

sidered acceptable; the longer the touch, the more it becomes unacceptable, and it may even be considered a threat. Talk to your principal to be certain that you understand the guidelines and legal considerations of appropriate touching.

Verbal Responses.   Although nonverbal mild responses may be effective, verbal responses can be used as nonpunitive, mild responses to misbehavior. Their purpose is to get the student back on task with limited disruption and intervention. Various verbal responses are described below.

1. *Call on the student during the lesson.*   You can recapture a misbehaving student's attention by using his or her name in the lesson, such as "Now, in this next example, suppose that John had three polygons that he...." You could ask a question of the student to recapture the student's attention. Calling on the student in these ways allows you to communicate that you know what is going on and to capture the student's attention without citing the misbehavior.

Be cautious—students' dignity should be preserved. If you call on students in these ways only when they misbehave, they will sense that you are just waiting to catch them misbehaving, and this strategy will backfire by creating resentment (Good & Brophy, 2000).

2. *Use humor.*   Humor can be used as a gentle reminder to students to correct their behavior. Humor directed at the situation or even at yourself can defuse tension that might be created due to the misbehavior. It can depersonalize the situation and thus help resolve the problem. You must be careful that the humor is not sarcastic. *Sarcasm* includes statements that are directed at or make fun of the student; these statements are intended to "put down" or cause pain to the student. Instead, humor is directed at or makes fun of the situation or the teacher. The student may then reconsider his or her actions and then get back on task.

3. *Send an I-message.* An I-message verbally prompts appropriate behavior without giving a direct command. Gordon (1991) developed this technique for verbally dealing with misbehavior. An I-message is a statement you make to a misbehaving student.

An *I-message* has three parts: (a) a brief description of the misbehavior; (b) a description of its effects on you or the other students; and (c) a description of your feelings about the effects. For example, you might say, "When you tap your pen on the desk during the test, it makes a lot of noise, and I am concerned that it might distract other students."

I-messages are intended to help students recognize that their behavior has consequences on other students and that you have genuine feelings about the actions. Since I-messages leave the decision about changing one's behavior up to the student, they are likely to promote a sense of responsibility.

4. *Use positive phrasing. Positive phrasing* is used when inappropriate off-task behavior allows you to highlight positive outcomes for appropriate behavior (Shrigley, 1985). This usually takes the form of "When you do X (behave in a particular appropriate way), then you can do Y (a positive outcome)." For example, when a student is out of her seat, you might say, "Renee, it will be your turn to pick up supplies when you return to your seat."

Through the use of positive phrasing, you redirect students from disruptive to appropriate behavior by simply stating the positive outcomes. In the long run, students begin to believe that proper behavior does lead to positive outcomes.

5. *Remind students of the rules.* Each classroom needs to have a set of rules governing student behavior, along with a set of consequences for breaking them. When students see that consequences of misbehavior are in fact delivered, reminders of the rules can help them get back on task because they do not want the consequences. When one student is poking another student, for example, you might say, "Delores, the classroom rules state that students must keep their hands and feet to themselves." This reminder often ends the misbehavior because the student does not want the consequence. If the inappropriate behavior continues, you must deliver the consequence, or the reminder will be of little value because students will recognize that there is no follow-through.

6. *Give students choices.* Some students feel defensive when confronted about their misbehavior. As a result, you can give them choices about resolving the problem. This allows the student to feel that he or she settled the problem without appearing to back down. All the choices that you give to the student should lead to resolution of the problem.

If a student is talking to another nearby student, you might say, "Harvey, you can turn back in your seat and get back to your project, or you can take the empty seat at the end of the row." In this way, Harvey has a choice, but the result is that he gets back to work in his seat or in the seat at the end of the row.

7. *Ask "What should you be doing?"* Glasser (1992) proposes that teachers ask disruptive students questions in an effort to direct them back to appropriate behavior. When a student is disruptive, you might ask "What should you be doing?" This question can have a positive effect because it helps redirect the student back to appropriate behavior.

TEACHERS IN ACTION

GIVING STUDENTS CHOICES

Terri Jenkins, middle school English teacher, Hephzibah, Georgia

Avoiding conflict is important for classroom survival. This is especially true if the student is trying to seek power or attention. By giving the student a choice in resolving a problem, you defuse the situation and avoid a conflict.

For example, a student may be talking with a neighbor while you are giving instructions. You might say, "Brian, I really need quiet while I am giving directions so that everyone can hear. You have a choice: (1) you may remain where you are and stop talking to Mary, or (2) you may reseat yourself somewhere else in the classroom. Thanks." Then you should walk away.

In this way, students have the power to make a choice. They do not feel challenged and usually respond appropriately. The behavior stops, and little instructional time is lost. Choices should not be punitive or rewarding; they should be designed to stop the misbehavior.

When giving choices, you should be polite and courteous, being careful that the tone of your voice is emotionless. After stating the choices, you should say thank you and then walk away from the student. In this way, it becomes obvious that you expect the student to comply.

Of course, some students may not answer this question honestly or reply at all. In that case, you should make statements related to the question. For example, "Keith, you were swearing and name calling. That is against our classroom rules. You should not swear or call names of others." If the student continues to break the rule, then appropriate consequences should be delivered.

8. *Give a verbal reprimand.* A very straightforward way to have the students stop misbehaving is to simply ask or direct them to do so. This is sometimes called a *desist order* or a *reprimand,* and is given to decrease unwanted behavior. Verbal reprimands are effective with many mild and moderate behavior problems, but by themselves are less successful with severe behavior disorders (Kerr & Nelson, 2002).

A *direct appeal* involves a courteous request for the student to stop the misbehavior and to get back on task. You might say, "Martina, please put away the comb and continue with the class assignment." A direct appeal often gives the student a sense of ownership for deciding to get back on task and to do as you requested. The student feels a sense of responsibility.

As an alternative, you could use a *direct command* in which you take the responsibility and give a direction in a straightforward manner, such as "Wayne, stop talking with your friends and get to work on the lab activity." With the direct appeal and the direct command, the student is expected to comply with your directions. If the student defies your request or command, you must be prepared to deliver an appropriate consequence.

Soft reprimands, audible only to the misbehaving student, are more effective than loud reprimands in reducing disruptive classroom behavior (Kerr & Nelson, 2002). Soft, private reprimands do not call the attention of the entire class to the misbehaving student and also may be less likely to trigger emotional reactions.

Moderate Responses

Following situational assistance and mild nonverbal and verbal responses, students might continue to misbehave. In that case, moderate responses should be used to correct the problem. The three-step response plan shown in Table 11.1 illustrates the movement to more directive responses if mild responses are not successful.

Moderate responses are intended to be *punitive ways* to deal with misbehavior *by removing desired stimuli* to decrease the occurrence of the inappropriate behavior. Moderate responses include logical consequences and behavior-modification techniques. Since student behaviors that warrant moderate responses are more problematic than mild misbehaviors, it is often useful to discuss specific problems with the principal, other teachers, or the school counselor. Parents can be contacted at any point in an effort to inform them of their child's actions and to solicit their help.

A *logical consequence* is an event arranged by the teacher that is directly and logically related to the misbehavior (Dreikurs, Grunwald, & Pepper, 1982). The consequence should be reasonable, respectful, and related to the student action. For instance, if a student leaves paper on the classroom floor, that student must pick it up off the floor. Or, if a student breaks the rule of speaking out without raising his or her hand, you would ignore the response and call on a student whose hand is up. Or, if a student marks on the desk, the student is required to clean the marks off. Students are more likely to respond favorably to logical consequences because they do not consider the consequences mean or unfair.

You may tell the student what the consequence is right after the behavior occurs. For example, "Milton, you left the study area a mess. You need to clean it up at the end of class." As an alternative, you may give the student a choice when inappropriate behavior is noticed. This tells the student that the inappropriate behavior must be changed or, if it is not changed, that a particular consequence will occur. For example, you may say, "Joellen, you have a choice of not bothering students near you or having your seat changed."

When given a choice, students will often stop the inappropriate behavior. This approach can be very effective because the student feels a sense of ownership in solving the problem, and the issue is over quickly. Of course, if the problem behavior continues, you must deliver the consequence that you stated to the student.

At the start of the school year, you should think of two or three logical consequences for each of the classroom rules and inform students of these consequences. Logical, reasonable consequences are preplanned, and you are not under the pressure of thinking up something appropriate at the time the misbehavior occurs.

Because of the variety of rules that you might develop, you might select a wide range of logical consequences; some may be considered behavior-modification approaches, which are discussed in more detail later in this chapter. Some examples of logical consequences include the following:

■ *Withdraw privileges.* As a regular part of the classroom activities, you may provide your students with a number of special privileges such as a trip to the library, use of a computer, use of special equipment or a game, service as a classroom helper, or other valued privileges. If the misbehavior relates to the type of privilege offered, a logical consequence would be to withdraw the privilege. For example, if a student mishandles some special equipment, then the student would lose the privilege of using the equipment.

■ *Change the seat assignment.* Students may talk, poke, or interact with other students in nearby seats. Sometimes a problem occurs because certain students are seated near each other. Other times, just the placement of the seats enables easy interaction. If inappropriate interaction occurs, a logical consequence would be to relocate the student's seat.

■ *Have the student write reflections on the problem.* It is often useful to ask the student to reflect on the situation to help the student recognize the logical connection between the behavior and the consequences. You may ask the student to provide written responses to certain questions; this might be done during a time-out.

These questions may include: What is the problem? What did I do to create the problem? What should happen to me? What should I do next time to avoid a problem? Other questions may require the student to describe the rule that was broken, why the student chose to misbehave, who was bothered by the misbehavior, what more appropriate behavior could be chosen next time, and what should happen to the student the next time the misbehavior occurs.

Written responses to these or similar questions help students see their behavior more objectively and promote more self-control. You may choose to have the student sign and date the written responses for future reference. The written responses can be useful if the parents need to be contacted at a later time.

■ *Place the student in a time-out.* Sometimes a student is talking or disrupting the class in such a way that interferes with the progress of the lesson. In such a case, the student could be excluded from the group; this is called a *time-out.* Removing the student from the group is a logical consequence of interfering with the group. An area of the room should be established as the time-out area, such as a desk in a corner or partially behind a filing cabinet. As a general rule, time-out should last no longer than 10 minutes.

TEACHERS IN ACTION

USING AN OOPS SHEET FOR REFLECTIONS

Lisa Bietau, fourth grade teacher, Manhattan, Kansas

When my students misbehave, I sometimes ask them to fill out an OOPS Sheet to have them reflect on their behavior. OOPS stands for an "Outstanding Opportunity for a Personal Stretch." The sheet has a place for their name and date at the top. Then there are several other areas that the student needs to fill in: (1) Describe the problem. (2) What other choices did you have to settle the situation without difficulty? (3) How might you handle this differently if it happens again?

After the student fills out the OOPS Sheet, I meet with the student privately to briefly discuss the situation and to review the options and solutions that the student wrote. This reflection and discussion with me helps the students to understand my expectations and to recognize that they have a responsibility to consider reasonable options when they meet a challenging situation.

I sign the OOPS Sheet and make a copy for my files. The original is then sent home with the student to obtain the parent's signature. All the student's privileges are suspended until the signed sheet is returned. If the sheet is not returned the next day, I call the parents and another copy is sent home, if necessary. I have found that students show more self-control after completing the OOPS Sheet.

■ ■ ■ ■ ■

CLASSROOM DECISIONS

During a lesson in your classroom, a student has continually made noises, distracted other students, and interfered with the lesson. You decide to place the student in the time-out area of your room for several minutes. What factors might you take into account when deciding what you will have the student do while in time-out? How will you help the students to see that this action is a logical consequence of the disruptive behavior? How might your decisions be affected by your grade level?

■ *Hold the student for detention. Detention* means detaining or holding back students when they normally would be free to go and do other things. The student is deprived of free time and perhaps the opportunity to socialize with other students. Detention may include remaining after class or staying after school.

Detention can be a logical consequence for student behaviors that waste class time. A student might be asked to work on the social studies paper that was not completed during class due to inappropriate behavior. Students will soon see the logic that time wasted in class will have to be made up later, on their own time in detention.

Make sure the student understands the reasons for the detention. It should logically fit the offense, and the time should not be excessive. Twenty to thirty minutes after school would be reasonable. Confer with the student and work out a plan to help the student avoid detention in the future and to move toward self-control.

Detention after school can be viewed as unreasonable if the student misses the school bus and is subjected to the hazards of the highway on the way home, or if the parents instructed the student to return home immediately after school. Consider these and related issues when preparing to use after-school detention.

■ *Contact the parents.* If a student shows a pattern of repeated misbehavior, then you may need to contact the parents or guardians. The logic here is that if all earlier attempts to extinguish the misbehavior do not work, it is appropriate to go to a higher authority. Parents may be notified by a note or a letter to inform them of the problem and to solicit their involvement or support. You may choose to call the parents instead. If the situation is fairly serious, a conference with the parents may be warranted.

■ *Have the student visit the principal.* In cases of repeated misbehavior or serious misbehavior such as fighting, students may be sent to the school office to see the principal. The principal may talk with the student in an effort to use his or her legitimate authority to influence the student to behave properly. Some schools have specific procedures to be followed when students are sent to the principal. When the behavior problems reach this point, additional personnel, including the school counselor or psychologist and the parents, need to be consulted to help the student.

KEY TERMS

Corporal punishment	Desist order	Direct appeal
Cues	Detention	Direct command

Extinction	Logical consequence	Punitive response
Group punishment	Mild responses	Reprimand
Hurdle helping	Misbehavior	Sarcasm
Hyperactivity	Nonverbal responses	Situational assistance
I-message	Positive phrasing	Threat
Impulsivity	Principle of least intervention	Time-out
Inattentiveness	Proximity control	Touch control
Intervention	Punishment	

MAJOR CONCEPTS

1. Misbehavior is any student behavior that is perceived by the teacher to compete with or threaten the academic actions at a particular moment.

2. Misbehavior ranges from mildly to severely disruptive behavior, and the degree of the teacher response should match the degree of severity.

3. The principle of least intervention states that when dealing with routine classroom behavior, misbehavior should be corrected with the simplest, least intrusive intervention that will work. If that does not work, then move up to a more intrusive approach.

4. Research and practice suggest that some strategies are inappropriate or unsuccessful when trying to restore order.

5. Due to inherent problems in the use of punishment, teachers should follow certain guidelines when using punitive responses.

6. Situational assistance is designed to help students cope with the instructional situation and to keep them on task.

7. Mild responses are nonpunitive ways to deal with misbehavior while providing guidance for appropriate behavior. Nonverbal and verbal approaches can be used.

8. Moderate responses deliver punishment as a means to restore order.

DISCUSSION/REFLECTIVE QUESTIONS

1. Provide some examples to illustrate how the context of the misbehavior might affect the teacher response.

2. Identify ways in which the teacher may contribute to the occurrence of misbehavior.

3. How might the cause of the misbehavior affect the teacher's choice of an appropriate response?

4. What are the benefits of providing situational assistance?

5. What are the benefits and disadvantages of intentionally ignoring the misbehavior?

6. How can teachers justify the use of punishment?

7. What are the arguments for and against using corporal punishment?

8. What are the merits and disadvantages of moving in a three-step response plan from providing situational assistance to using moderate responses?

SUGGESTED ACTIVITIES

For Clinical Settings

1. Review Table 11.1 and consider additional examples for teacher responses at each of the three steps.

2. Identify examples of student behavior for which mild responses would be appropriate.

3. Consider what types of punishment you might use in your teaching, and identify guidelines that you will follow for their use.

For Field Settings

1. Talk with students at several grade levels to identify reasons why they might misbehave and effective teacher responses.

2. Talk with teachers at several grade levels to see how the grade levels and subject areas might affect their handling of misbehavior.

3. Talk to teachers to identify ways they use situational assistance and mild and moderate responses to misbehavior.

USEFUL RESOURCES

Burden, P. R. (2003). *Classroom management: Creating a successful learning community* (2nd ed.). New York: Wiley & Sons.

Provides a comprehensive K–12 review of ways to establish, maintain, and restore order in the classroom. It carries a practical, realistic view of decisions teachers make about getting organized for management, planning for management, managing when conducting the class, and restoring order after misbehavior.

WEB SITES

- Tips on managing student behavior and effective interventions from the Kentucky Department of Education.

  http://www.state.ky.us/agencies/behave/homepage.html

- Teacher's encyclopedia of behavior management

  http://www.state.ky.us/agencies/behave/encyndex.html

- Schoolwide and classroom discipline

  http://www.nwrel.org/scpd/sirs/5/cu9.html

- You can handle them all

  http://www.disciplinehelp.com

- Positive behavior interventions and support

  http://www.pbis.org

- Dr. Mac's Amazing Behavior Management Advice Site

  http://maxweber.hunter.cuny.edu/pub/eres/EDSPC715_MCINTYRE/715HomePate.html

- Links to articles concerning student discipline

  http://www.effectivediscipline.com/

- A variety of techniques

  http://www.education-world.com/a_curr/curr155.shtml

- Links to articles and advice regarding classroom discipline

  http://www.proteacher.com/030002.shtml

- This collection of Northwest Regional Educational Lab (NWREL) resources focuses on safe schools.

  http://www.nwrel.org/comm/topics/safe.html

- Helpful classroom discipline information

  http://www.adprima.com/managing.htm

CHAPTER TWELVE

ASSESSING STUDENT PERFORMANCE

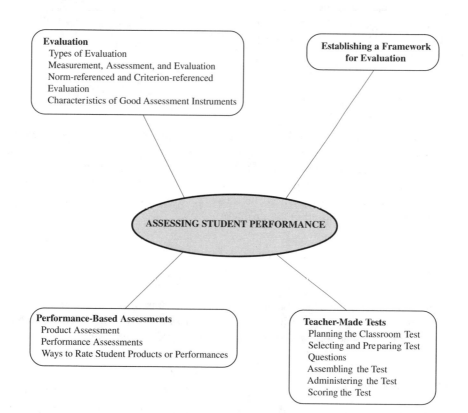

OBJECTIVES

This chapter provides information that will help you to:

1. Define evaluation, measurement, and assessment.
2. Establish a framework for effective evaluation.
3. Identify ways to use formal and informal assessment strategies.
4. Select ways for performance-based evaluation.
5. State guidelines for preparing teacher-made tests.

PRAXIS/Principles of Learning and Teaching/Pathwise

The following principles are relevant to content in this chapter:

1. Creating or selecting evaluation strategies that are appropriate for the students and that are aligned with the goals of the lesson   (A5)

2. Monitoring students' understanding of content through a variety of means, providing feedback to students to assist learning, and adjusting learning activities as the situation demands   (C4)

INTASC

The following INTASC standard is relevant to content in this chapter:

1. The teacher understands and uses formal and informal assessment strategies to evaluate and ensure the continuous intellectual, social, and physical development of the learner.   (Standard 8)

Student evaluation is necessary to help teachers determine the degree to which educational objectives have been achieved and to help teachers know their students as individuals. As you consider student evaluation, a number of questions come to mind. What is evaluation? How do teachers prepare for evaluation? How can performance-based evaluation be conducted? How can teacher-made tests be prepared and administered? These questions will be explored in this chapter.

EVALUATION

Before teachers conduct evaluation in their classrooms, it is important to recognize that there are several types of evaluation, that there is a difference between measurement and evaluation, and that norm-referenced and criterion-referenced tests can be used.

Types of Evaluation

There are three types of evaluation, each serving a different purpose and each being conducted at different times (Linn & Gronlund, 2000). First, *diagnostic evaluation* is necessary at the start to determine their individual levels of competence, to identify those who have already achieved mastery of the requisite learnings, and to help classify students into tentative small groups for instruction.

Second, *formative evaluation* is used to monitor learning progress during instruction and to provide continuous feedback to students and parents. To obtain the necessary information, you may use commercially prepared tests, your own criterion-referenced tests, observations, or other techniques. Formative evaluation is typically quite comprehensive in the examination of the content. If formative evaluation is to provide useful guidance to the teacher and student, it should include frequent assessment to provide systematic feedback on progress (Tanner, 2001).

CLASSROOM DECISIONS

Students in your class will likely have a wide range of prior knowledge about the content in the next unit you will teach. In an effort to more effectively plan content and experiences in the unit, how can you obtain information and diagnose the students' prior knowledge? How might you enable students to contribute to the planning of the unit? How might the grade level that you teach affect your response to these questions?

Third, *summative evaluation* is at the end of a unit, marking period, or course to (a) determine the extent of the students' achievement and competence, (b) provide a basis for assigning grades, and (c) provide the data from which reports to parents and transcripts can be prepared. Summative evaluation typically examines the student's broad ability as compared to the detailed examination of each component in formative evaluation.

Measurement, Assessment, and Evaluation

Although measurement and evaluation are related, they are nevertheless different. *Measurement* is the process used to obtain data concerning student learning. For instance, a paper-and-pencil test is used to measure the achievement of a student, but other types of data collection can be used, such as performance-based measures. The term *assessment* is commonly used as a synonym for measurement. Assessment, however, often is viewed by educators as having more emphasis on authentic, alternative, or performance-based measurement as compared to teacher-made tests.

Evaluation is a process in which the teacher uses information derived from many sources to arrive at a value judgment. Evaluation may be based on measurement data, but also might be based on other types of data such as questionnaires, direct observation, written or oral performance ratings, or interviews.

The differences between measurement and evaluation can be illustrated when you determine a grade at the end of a marking period. Throughout the marking period, you will measure student performance by a variety of means. Then you would place these measures within a grading system to determine the student's grade. The grading system actually reflects the value judgment concerning the student's measures.

Norm-referenced and Criterion-referenced Evaluation

Norm-referenced evaluation is used to interpret a score of an individual by comparing it with those of other individuals. Ranking students is the primary issue. For example, a teacher would use a norm-referenced test to compare the reading abilities of students before forming reading groups. A norm-referenced test finds a student's performance level in relation to levels of others on the same test. Many standardized achievement and aptitude tests are norm-referenced instruments.

In contrast, *criterion-referenced evaluation* is used to interpret a person's performance by comparing it to some specified criterion such as a performance standard. Individual mastery is the primary issue. The object is to determine whether the student can or cannot perform at a certain standard. How well others perform on the same standard is not considered.

Characteristics of Good Assessment Instruments

The effectiveness of any measuring device depends upon its validity, reliability, and practicality (Airasian, 2001).

   1. Validity. *Validity* deals with the extent to which a measuring device measures what it purports to measure. While there are several types of validity, teachers are usually most concerned with content validity. Content validity refers to the degree to which an instrument samples the subject matter in the area to be measured or the degree to which it coincides with the instructional objectives that are to be measured. This is typically the only type of validity used in teacher-made tests and other measures. To determine content validity, you would examine the outline of instructional objectives and check the congruence with the test questions. High content validity would mean that there is a good match between test questions and instructional objectives covered in class. Low content validity would mean that there is a poor match.

   2. Reliability. *Reliability* deals with the consistency of results. The more consistent the results, the higher the reliability of the test. If you administer a reliable test and shortly after readminister an equivalent form of the same test, students should score roughly the same as they did in the first test.

   All measuring devices have some type of error. Measurement error may come from errors in the instrument, errors in the use of the instrument, and errors emanating from the subject's response. The more objective the scoring of a test, the more reliable the score. Factors that may act to make a test less reliable are the length of a test (i.e., very short tests are not very reliable), the ambiguity of directions and questions, and an overload of questions that are too difficult or too easy. Variability in the students' responses may also be affected by temporal factors such as poor motivation, lack of interest, improper test environment, poor emotional set, and illness.

   3. Practicality. *Practicality* refers to the ease of administering the measuring device, the time required, the energy expended to collect the data, and the ease with which the data can be interpreted. For instance, an essay test may be easily prepared by the teacher but the time required to grade it may make such a test impractical. Conversely, an objective test can be graded relatively quickly but may take much longer to prepare.

ESTABLISHING A FRAMEWORK FOR EVALUATION

Even before instruction begins, you need to establish a framework for student evaluation by addressing the following issues.

   1. *Identify the reasons for assessing student performance.* A classroom test, for instance, can serve a variety of purposes, such as judging student mastery, measuring growth over time, ranking pupils in terms of their achievement, and diagnosing student difficulties. Different purposes lend themselves to various evaluation measures. Therefore, it is essential that you know the major use of the evaluation results.

2. *Plan to gather information for both formative and summative evaluation.* Formative evaluation should be frequent to provide feedback about the student's developing knowledge and skills. In fact, all scores for formative evaluation may not need to be recorded for the report card grade. Summative evaluation is more comprehensive and is conducted at selected concluding points, such as at the end of a chapter or unit. Scores from summative evaluation are tallied as part of the report card grade.

3. *Identify course content that is to be evaluated.* This content is often included in a course curriculum guide. This content will be translated into instructional objectives for daily lesson plans. These objectives will likely be written for the cognitive, psychomotor, and affective learning domains.

4. *Relate the evaluation to the prestated objectives.* Each objective should be evaluated, but the means for gathering evaluation information will vary depending on the stated objectives and the purpose of the evaluation.

5. *Include evaluation measures in all three learning domains.* Instructional objectives should be written for each of the three learning domains, and each of these objectives should be evaluated. Different types of evaluation instruments are often used to measure student performance in each domain. The cognitive domain is often evaluated through the use of (a) tests developed by teachers themselves, (b) achievement tests developed by local, regional, or state agencies, which may or may not be normed, and (c) nationally standardized tests and scales. Skills in the psychomotor domain are evaluated through performance and product tests.

Objectives in the affective learning domain are more difficult to evaluate than objectives in the other domains. Techniques often used include attitude scales, opinion polls, questionnaires, open-ended questions, checklists, observation, group discussion, anecdotal records, interviews, and role playing. Observation of students in the process of performing a particular task can also provide useful information concerning their attitudes toward the task.

6. *Use multiple approaches when gathering assessment information.* Do not rely only on teacher-made tests. Also use performance-based assessments when appropriate.

7. *Devise an evaluation plan before instruction.* This will guide your planning and preparation for the class sessions. Then communicate the objectives and evaluation criteria to the students.

PERFORMANCE-BASED ASSESSMENT

As an alternative to teacher-made tests, teachers can measure student learning by assessing products that students prepare reflecting their learning or by assessing actual student performances designed to demonstrate their learning; this is *performance-based assessment.* Once the student produces the product or conducts the performance, teachers then need to use various types of rating scales or checklists to translate the student performance into some type of score.

Since performance-based assessments are seen to be alternatives to teacher-made tests, terms such as alternative assessment, authentic assessment, and direct assessment have been used to describe performance-based assessments. There are two types of performance-based assessments: product assessment and performance assessment (see Table 12.1).

Product Assessments

Instead of students completing a traditional paper-and-pencil test, students are asked to prepare a product reflecting their learning, and teachers then complete a rating scale or compose written comments to assess student learning as reflected in the product. Product assessments include (a) directions that outline the nature of the products that students will develop, (b) the product itself, which students prepare, and (c) a rating scale of some kind that assesses the nature of the student product. There are many types of products that students might be asked to prepare. Some of the more common types of student products are discussed here.

Portfolios. A *portfolio* is a collection of a student's work over time that demonstrates mastery of specific performance criteria against which the tasks in the portfolio can be judged. The student systematically chooses and compiles work products that go into the portfolio. Work products may include items such as reports, letters, drawings, journals, and other documents. Portfolios are intended to actively involve students in learning, develop self-assessment skills, and provide insights to students and teachers on progress and accomplishment (Burke, 1999; Popham, 2002).

You can guide students through portfolio development by identifying the characteristics of good academic work, applying criteria for good work to their own work, using peer-revision groups to refine and assess their work, and selecting work so that the portfolio creates a portrait of the student as a learner. Teachers who have implemented portfolios

TABLE 12.1 Performance-Based Assessments

Students present products or conduct some type of performance to demonstrate their learning.

PRODUCTS	PERFORMANCES
Portfolio	Oral presentation
Work sample	Presentation with media
Project or report	Science lab demonstration
Research paper	Athletic demonstration
Science lab report	Musical, dance, or dramatic presentation
Log or journal	Debate
Model	Demonstration of specific tasks
Media products (computer presentation file, audio or videotape)	Participation in an event
	Interview with the student

report that (a) students have a richer, more positive and expanded sense of their progress, (b) assessment becomes collaborative rather than competitive, (c) teachers obtain a richer, clearer view of their students over time, and (d) records of what students are actually doing are available to teachers (Tierney, Carter, & Desai, 1991).

Some teachers think that portfolios are only appropriate for use in the elementary grades, but teachers at the middle and secondary levels have also used portfolios successfully. Geometry portfolios, for example, might include work that displays problem solving, communication, or other skills. Language arts and social studies portfolios might include writings and other projects that offer evidence of progress and goal setting.

Work Samples.   Gathering work samples provides a longitudinal record of student progress. Work samples might include (a) written work such as a report, test, or story, (b) artwork, (c) tape recordings, (d) a construction project done in art, industrial arts, or an appropriate subject, or (e) other types of finished products depending on the subject area. Using work samples probably occurs more in the elementary grades, but teachers in certain secondary subject areas may use work samples as well.

Experience Summaries.   In experience summaries, students record what they have learned from a particular experience. Teachers and students may do this cooperatively. For instance, after going on a field trip to an art gallery, the class could identify facts and concepts that they learned. This listing would be useful for you to determine the extent of student learning.

Logs or Journals.   While experience summaries are used for one event, logs or journals are kept on a continuing basis. Students might keep a journal to record their insights,

---

TEACHERS IN ACTION

EVALUATING WITH WORK SAMPLES

Joan Spiker, first grade teacher, Manhattan, Kansas

To evaluate student handwriting and creative writing in first grade, I have kept dated writing samples. I collect monthly samples of handwriting and keep them in individual student folders. The student reviews the samples in the folder, and then I conference with the student to set goals for the next month. The folders are also used to report progress at parent-teacher conferences.

Nearly all the creative writing in first grade is in the form of little books constructed by the students. All the books are dated and kept in special individual writing cubbies (i.e., commercial cardboard shoe keepers). When a little book is completed and shared, it is given a sticker and placed in the student's cubby. All the books through the year are kept and can easily be reviewed by the authors themselves, other students, the teacher, or parents. The collection is reviewed in student conferences and in parent-teacher conferences to evaluate progress and set goals. This strategy works well for handwriting and for creative writing because the students have a dated accumulation of work to use as a basis for self-evaluation.

conclusions, and feelings about their classroom experiences. The class can log daily progress concerning learning activities in a notebook or on a chart. This provides a running account of work in the unit and can be used to review and check on previous plans and decisions as the unit progresses.

Projects, Reports, or Papers.   Students might prepare various types of projects, reports, or papers that reflect their learning. These products often involve a number of skills and are developed over more than one class period.

Models.   Students may prepare models concerning people, places, or topics being addressed in class. The models may contain information and represent certain aspects of their learning.

Media Products.   Working individually or in groups, students are asked in many classrooms to prepare an audiotape, videotape, or computer-assisted presentation concerning some aspect of the curriculum. The final media product will represent certain aspects of student learning.

Performance Assessments

Similar to product assessments, teachers will complete a rating scale or compose written comments to assess student learning reflected in a performance that students are asked to conduct. Performance assessments include (a) directions that outline the nature of the products that students will develop, (b) the product itself, which students prepare, and (c) a

---

TEACHERS IN ACTION

EVALUATING WITH JOURNAL QUESTIONS

Hildie Brooks, seventh and eighth grade health teacher, Manhattan, Kansas

For the past several years, I have been testing my health students with a strategy I call "journal questions." On Monday of each week, I write a journal question on the chalk board, and the students must write a minimum of three paragraphs in response to the question of the week. The questions are based on the concepts developed during the previous week. The students must identify, explain, and support their own ideas. The emphasis is not on one correct answer, but on the ability of the student to express his or her own ideas. For example, in the seventh grade class, the journal question one week dealt with why do people *start* to use mind-altering drugs and whether there are any good reasons to start to use drugs.

There are numerous benefits to this type of evaluation. The students learn to think for themselves instead of spitting back memorized facts and figures. The students must support their opinions without fear of being put down for their opinions. The students will apply information discussed in class in order to support their opinions. One of the most enjoyable aspects is being able to get to know the students in a more intimate way through the writing of their own ideas.

rating scale of some kind that assesses the nature of the student product. There are many types of performances that students might be asked to conduct. Some of the more common ones are discussed here.

Oral or Mediated Presentations.   Students may be asked to prepare a report on a selected topic and then present it to the rest of the class. Sometimes these reports include instructional media (e.g., overhead transparencies, computer-assisted presentations). The teacher may choose to rate the actual presentation as a way to gauge student learning.

Actual Demonstrations.   Students may be asked to demonstrate their skill in some type of athletic, musical, dance, or dramatic performance. Or skill needs to be demonstrated in a science lab, a computer class, or any other class where the student's learning is best reflected in actual performance.

Participation in an Event.   Sometimes a group of students or the entire class is involved in an activity in which students exhibit certain knowledge and skills through their participation. A student's knowledge and skill in forensics or debate, for instance, can be seen through participation.

Interviews.   Interviews and individual conferences can be used to evaluate cognitive skills as well as attitudes and values. Students sometimes express ideas and feelings during interviews that they might not otherwise state.

TEACHERS IN ACTION

HAVING STUDENTS REFLECT ON THEIR OWN PERFORMANCE

Mary Kim Schreck, high school American literature teacher, Bridgeton, Missouri

Teachers often reflect on how they handled themselves with students to consider how they might improve, what they could build on, or what needs to be repeated. Since this type of reflection is so valuable for teachers to improve, why not structure opportunities for students to reflect on their own performance?

I have often asked my students for reflective evaluations of projects, but I recently came upon another way of obtaining student self-reflections that resulted in a great deal of enthusiasm and insightful comments. It involves students asking interview questions of themselves. I have students identify questions about the project or unit. Then the students interview themselves and write down their answers to their own questions.

I give them a couple guidelines as they create their questions about the project or unit: (a) ask a minimum of five questions that require more than a yes or no answer, and (b) have one question go back to an answer already written, and ask for more information or elaboration.

I also give students some samples of topical areas where they might create their questions, such as questions about the quality of their work, their favorite part of the literature, the time line of events, and areas of difficulty and how they dealt with them. Students find that they have a great deal to say, and they enjoy the interview structure.

Ways to Rate Student Products or Performances

It is easy to say that it is a great idea to gather student products or to ask students to perform in certain ways as a means to demonstrate their learning. However, teachers may find it challenging to specify the actual observable criteria that demonstrate student learning and to determine what the actual rating approaches will be. Some guidelines are provided in this section.

Selecting Rating Criteria.   The following guidelines can be used when selecting observable criteria for products or performances (Airasian, 2000).

1. *Select the performance or product to be assessed and either perform it yourself or imagine yourself performing it.* This step will help you to understand the actual student actions that would need to be completed.
2. *List the important aspects of the performance or product.* The most important behaviors or attributes should be reflected in the rating criteria.
3. *Try to limit the number of performance criteria that can reasonably be observed and assessed.* Each item needs to be assessed, so limit the number of performance criteria to 10 to 15.
4. *If possible, have groups of teachers think through the criteria as a group.* This step will save time and will help to produce a more complete set of criteria than that produced by any single teacher.
5. *Express the criteria in terms of observable student behaviors or product characteristics.* Be specific when stating the criteria.
6. *Avoid vague and ambiguous words, such as correctly, appropriately, and good.* Avoid working that can lead to multiple interpretations.
7. *Arrange the performance criteria in the order in which they are likely to be observed.* This will save time when observing and maintain focus on the performance.
8. *Check for existing performance criteria before constructing your own.* Preexisting criteria might be available for your use.

Rating Approaches.   Various approaches can be used to rate student products or performances. The most commonly used approaches are reviewed here.

1. *Rating scales.* A *rating scale* allows a teacher to judge student performance along a continuum, rather than as a dichotomy (present/not present). The rating scale may be numerical (e.g., 1 through 4), descriptive (using a range of words to reflect the criteria), or a combination of the two. Instead of merely indicating the presence or absence of a trait, as in a checklist, rating scales enable you to indicate the status or quality of what is being rated.

A *rubric* is a type of rating scale used to judge student performance on a continuum. Rubrics can be created in many ways to describe the levels of student performance based on the performance criteria. Rubrics often have more thorough ways of describing each performance level than simple rating scales. The thorough descriptions of performance criteria in rubrics provide considerable guidance for the students as they prepare their products or performances. See Tables 12.2 and 12.3 for examples.

TABLE 12.2   Rubric Template

CRITERIA	RUBRIC RATING			
Criterion 1 (enter the criterion description here)	1	2	3	4
Criterion 2	1	2	3	4
Criterion 3	1	2	3	4
Criterion 4	1	2	3	4

Note: Some rubrics have the number rating at the top of the columns and a unique narrative description under each rating for each criterion. This provides more clarity about what is needed for each rating.

2. *Checklists.* A *checklist* is a written list of performance criteria. A teacher reviews the student product or performance to determine which criteria are met. A checkmark indicates that the criterion was met; if it is not, the item is left blank. A checklist enables you to note quickly and effectively whether a trait or characteristic is present, but it does not permit you to rate the quality or frequency of a particular behavior. When that additional information is needed, you may want to use a rating scale or an anecdotal record.

3. *Anecdotal records.* An *anecdotal record* is a written account of events and behaviors that the teacher has observed concerning the student's product or performance. Only those

TABLE 12.3   Sample Rubric Rating Scales

NUMERICAL SCALES				
0	1	2	3	4
1	2	3	4	5
NUMERICAL SCALE WITH VERBAL DESCRIPTORS				
1	2	3	4	
Weak	Satisfactory	Very Good	Excellent	
VERBAL DESCRIPTORS				
Needs improvement	Satisfactory	Good	Excellent	
Novice	Adequate	Competent	Exemplary	

observations that have special significance and cannot be obtained from other assessment methods should be included in an anecdotal record. Anecdotal records should contain factual descriptions of what happened, when it happened, and under what circumstances the behavior occurred. The interpretation of the behavior and the recommended action should be noted separately. Each anecdotal record should contain a record of a single incident.

5. *Participation charts.* A *participation chart* is intended only to indicate the degree of involvement and the type of involvement in classroom discussion or activities. A typical form has students' names on one axis and the degree and frequency of involvement on the other axis. The charts are not intended to indicate why students participate.

TEACHER-MADE TESTS

To achieve the purpose of teacher-made tests, you need to carefully plan the test and then select and prepare test questions. Next, you would need to assemble, administer, and score the test.

Planning the Classroom Test

The preparation of a classroom test involves many decisions. Advance attention to the following decision areas will likely result in an improved test (McMillan, 2001).

1. *Decide on the purpose of the test.* To be helpful, classroom tests must be related to the teacher's instructional objectives and procedures. Classroom achievement tests serve a variety of purposes, such as (a) judging the students' mastery of certain knowledge and skills, (b) measuring growth over time, (c) ranking students in terms of their achievement, (d) diagnosing student difficulties, (e) determining the effectiveness of the curriculum, (f) encouraging good study habits, and (g) motivating students. These purposes are not mutually exclusive.

2. *Decide on what is to be tested.* What should be tested? The answer depends on the instructional objectives and what has been stressed in class. As noted previously, the table of specifications should be determined *prior to instruction,* and this should serve as the basis for preparing a test. The table of specifications includes instructional objectives and content. The relative emphasis on the three domains of learning should be reflected in the table of specifications. Furthermore, an effective test should include only questions that address important outcomes of instruction.

3. *Prepare a table of specifications showing the content and objectives to be tested.* A *table of specifications* identifies the intended outcomes of instruction; it specifies objectives or behaviors that the student should attain by the end of the instruction and the content related to these objectives. These statements should be precisely stated to clearly convey intentions. Summative evaluation, then, is intended to examine the degree of success with which the objectives were achieved by the students.

When making a test, the table of specifications is intended to identify the scope and emphasis of the test, to relate the objectives to the content, and to construct a balanced test. The table of specifications should be prepared *before instruction* and can even be distributed to students. The table of specifications displayed in Table 12.4 indicates the number of test questions in each learning domain for each content area in a sample unit in science.

CLASSROOM DECISIONS

When planning a unit, how can your preparation of a table of specifications help you to prepare instructional objectives in all appropriate learning domains for each content area within the unit? When you prepare a test, how might you use that same table of specifications to ensure that there are test questions that cover all the learning domains in all the content areas in the unit?

4. *Decide on when to test.* The use of the test results will determine the frequency of testing. If used in formative evaluation, students should be given short, criterion-referenced tests frequently to keep you apprised of the students' performance and identify those in need of additional or remedial instruction. Summative evaluation would be conducted less often.

TABLE 12.4   Table of Specifications for a Weather Unit in a Middle School Earth Science Class

OBJECTIVES / CONTENT	KNOWS			UNDERSTANDS	INTERPRETS	TOTAL NUMBER OF ITEMS	PERCENT OF ITEMS
	Basic Terms	*Weather Symbols*	*Specific Facts*	*Influence of Each Factor on Weather Information*	*Weather Maps*		
Air pressure	1	1	1	3	3	9	15
Wind	1	1	1	10	2	15	25
Temperature	1	1	1	4	2	9	15
Humidity and precipitation	1	1	1	7	5	15	25
Clouds	2	2	2	6		12	20
Total number of items	6	6	6	30	12	60	
Percent of items	10	10	10	50	20		100

MODIFICATIONS FOR DIVERSE CLASSROOMS

MODIFYING TEST QUESTIONS FROM TEXTBOOK PUBLISHERS

Companies that publish textbooks commonly prepare a teacher's edition that includes objectives, suggested instructional activities, and other useful information. Sometimes a set of test questions is also included for each chapter in the book, including multiple choice, true and false, matching, and other types of questions.

1. What are the advantages for teachers to use these questions in their entirety as the test for their students once the unit is completed?

2. What might be the disadvantages for using the teacher's edition tests when testing students in your class? Or conversely, why would teachers want to create their own test questions?

3. Recognizing the diversity among your students, what are some ways that you might modify your approach to testing and test question preparation to accommodate the diverse learners?

To some extent, the frequency of testing is affected by institutional regulations on marking and reporting grades to parents. More frequent evaluation is superior to less frequent evaluation. Teachers in secondary schools sometimes communicate with each other in an effort to stagger the days when students are tested so several tests are not scheduled for the same day.

5. *Decide what kinds of questions to use.* There basically are two item formats: essay and objective (multiple choice, matching, true–false). Some item formats are less appropriate than others for measuring certain objectives. Therefore, carefully consider the advantages and disadvantages of each item format. These will be discussed in greater detail in a later section.

6. *Decide how many questions to include in the test.* The length of a test will vary according to its purpose, the kinds of items used, the reliability desired, the length of testing time available, and the age and ability of the students. Formative tests would be more in-depth and frequent than summative tests. As explained later, the time to complete different item formats varies. The longer the test, the more reliable it tends to be, but only so many items can be completed within a 50-minute class period. The age and ability of the students also must be considered.

7. *Decide on the level of difficulty for questions included in the test.* The difficulty of a test should depend to a large extent upon its purpose. Item difficulty will not be a factor in the selection of test items if the test results are to be used to describe the status of individual students. However, test difficulty is a consideration when the test results are to be used to differentiate among students in terms of their achievement.

8. *Decide on the format of the test.* You need to decide about mechanical and formatting features of the test, such as grouping and arranging test items, directions for answering questions, distribution of correct responses, the layout of items, and other aspects. These will be discussed in a later section.

Selecting and Preparing Test Questions

There are two categories of test questions: essay and objective. *Essay questions* may include short-answer or restricted responses (about a half page), discussion or extended responses (about two to three pages), or oral responses. *Objective questions* may include multiple choice, matching, true–false, and short-answer (a single word or several words). Since some item formats are less appropriate than others for measuring certain objectives, teachers should carefully consider the advantages of each type of item format.

Test questions might be included in the teacher's edition of the textbook, and you might consider using them. Carefully examine test items included in the teacher's edition to be sure they are worded effectively, are at the proper levels of the learning domains being tested, are directed at content which was covered during instruction, and are at the appropriate reading level for your students.

Essay Questions.   Two common types of essay questions are the restricted response and the extended response. *Restricted response essay questions* establish limits for the form and scope of the student answers. Students are often asked to discuss one specific aspect of an issue and to limit their answers to perhaps half a page. Restricted essay questions are useful for measuring comprehension, application, and analysis (Stiggins, 2001).

Extended response essay questions, by contrast, have no limits placed on the student concerning the points to discuss or the organization used in the answer. Extended response questions require students to call upon factual knowledge, evaluate this knowledge, organize the ideas, and present these ideas in a logical, coherent way. Skills in synthesis and evaluation are effectively tested with this type of question.

A variety of mental processes can be evaluated through the use of essay tests. From simple to higher-order skills, these include (a) what, who, when, which, and where; (b) list; (c) outline; (d) describe; (e) contrast; (f) compare; (g) explain; (h) discuss; (i) develop; (j) summarize; and (k) evaluate.

There are advantages and disadvantages to the use of essay questions. Advantages include the fact that they are comparatively easier and less time consuming to prepare than objective tests, require that student supply the answer rather than simply select the answer, measure higher-order thinking, and stimulate creativity and freedom of expression.

But there are several disadvantages of essay questions. First, they generally sample content in a limited way. Three essay questions may not sample unit content as thoroughly as 50 multiple-choice questions. Therefore, essay tests that have several questions requiring short answers are preferable to a test that has few questions requiring lengthy answers. Second, essay questions are vulnerable to unreliable scoring. This problem of reader reliability can be minimized by careful construction of the test question and by setting up specified scoring procedures. Third, the student does not always understand the question and therefore is not sure how to respond, or is not able to put all appropriate ideas on paper in the given time. Fourth, essay questions require a great deal of time to read and score.

Writing Essay Questions.   To minimize the problems associated with essay questions, it is important to carefully prepare essay questions using the following guidelines:

1. *Reserve adequate time to prepare test questions.* Allow sufficient time to thoughtfully prepare each question and to be certain that each measures the intended objective, is

worded in a simple and clear manner, and is reasonable and can be answered by the students.

2. *Precisely define the direction and scope of the desired response.* This can be done by (a) delimiting the area covered by the question; (b) using descriptive, precise words in the question such as outline, illustrate, define, or summarize (as compared to the term "discuss"); (c) guiding the student into a certain direction by indicating what should be considered and presented in the answer; and (d) indicating the length of the answer (typically one-half page to two pages per question).

3. *Indicate the point value of each question.* Students need to know the point value of each question to be able to decide how much time to spend on the question.

4. *Use essay questions to measure objectives that can not be measured as well with other item formats.* As compared to other item formats, essay questions are especially useful in assessing students' understanding in the upper levels of the cognitive domain such as application, analysis, synthesis, and evaluation.

5. *Use many questions requiring relatively brief answers as compared to just a few questions involving long answers.* Brief answers (about one-half page) provide for a broader sampling of content, tend to discourage bias when some teachers grade for quantity rather than quality, enable the teacher to read the answers more rapidly and reliably, and also enable the teacher to direct the student to the desired response area.

6. *Take into consideration the time needed for an adequate response and the time available for the testing period.* Students need to have an appropriate amount of time to write out their responses to all questions.

7. *Adapt the length of response and the complexity of the answer to the maturity of the student.* The depth and breadth of the responses from fifth-graders certainly would be different from responses expected from tenth-graders.

8. *Do not provide optional questions on an essay test.* Providing options for the student undermines the basic function of summative tests (e.g., comparing the performance of students in a common area). Furthermore, it is difficult to construct questions of equal difficulty.

9. *Decide in advance how the essay questions will be scored.* In addition to the substance of student answers, decide how grammar, spelling, punctuation, handwriting, composition, and clarity of expression will be scored.

10. *Prepare a scoring key.* When preparing test questions, also identify what topics should be included in student responses to each essay question and then determine relative points for weak, average, or strong answers.

Evaluating Essay Questions.   The usefulness of a carefully constructed essay test can be undermined by improper grading procedures and standards. Essay tests must be reliably graded with either the analytical method or the rating method. In the analytical method, the teacher identifies all the specific points or topics that should be included in an appropriate answer. The student's score is determined by the number of points or topics that were included in the response to the essay question.

The rating method also involves the teacher identifying the points to be included in the answer, but the wholeness of the response is emphasized. Several student papers are selected to reflect the range of responses on a given question. These papers serve as anchor points as the other papers are read and rated. Papers may be read using a two-point scale (acceptable–unacceptable) up to a five-point scale (with steps going from superior to inferior). With the five-point scale, the teacher will place students' papers in one of these five piles upon reading student responses. It is preferable that each paper be read and rated twice. The rating method is effective when a large number of essays are to be read.

When evaluating essay questions, you should consider the following guidelines.

1. *Check the scoring key against actual responses.* Before scoring actually begins, read a few randomly selected papers to determine the appropriateness of the scoring key. Adjustments might be made in the key based on actual responses. The key should not be changed once actual scoring begins.
2. *If spelling, penmanship, grammar, and writing style of the responses are to be scored, it should be done independently of the subject matter content in the responses.*
3. *Score the students' responses anonymously.* If possible, conceal the student's name as each paper is evaluated in an effort to reduce biases.
4. *Evaluate one question at one time for all students.* This is designed to eliminate the *halo effect,* a general impression of high, medium, or low quality that might carry over from one response to another for each student. This practice also enables the teacher to more easily keep in mind the standards that are being applied for a particular question.
5. *Shuffle test papers before grading each question.* The ratings given to preceding papers sometimes affect the way teachers rate the next paper to be evaluated. Therefore, shuffle test papers before grading the next test question to try to minimize the effects of the preceding grades.
6. *Try to score all responses to a particular question without interruption.* In order to keep the standards clearly in mind, the papers should be read without excessive interruption or delay.
7. *Whenever possible, conduct two readings of the test and use the average as the final score.* Two independent readings simply helps improve the reliability of the test score. Of course, this may not be realistic at the secondary level if you have 125 student papers to evaluate.
8. *Provide comments and indications of correct answers.* By providing comments, you can provide students with more information about their progress, motivate them, indirectly teach them, and also help to explain the system of grading and determining scores.
9. *Set realistic standards.* Be sensitive to being overly generous or overly demanding as you review student responses.

Objective Questions. The most common types of objective test items are multiple choice, matching, true–false, and short answer.

Multiple Choice. A multiple-choice question has two parts: (a) a stem, which contains the problem, and (b) a list of suggested answers. The stem is typically in the form of a question or an incomplete statement. The incorrect responses are often called distracters. Generally four or five responses are listed and all but one is a distracter.

TEACHERS IN ACTION

SENDING E-MAILS TO YOUR STUDENTS ABOUT HOMEWORK AND TESTS

Pebble Richwine, high school science teacher, Miami, Oklahoma

We live in a computer age, and it seems that everyone now has an e-mail address. At the beginning of the year, I have my students fill out an information sheet, and I ask them for their e-mail address on a voluntary basis. In this way, I can send updates of classroom activities, schedule changes, or school updates. I also give students my home e-mail address.

Last year, we had three snow days before the semester final exams. I e-mailed the corrected schedule to each student, and this helped alleviate undue stress when the students returned to class. In addition, I have e-mailed hints or guides about tests and quizzes and have sent them helpful Web sites. I also receive questions about homework or other issues. The use of the e-mail has improved communication and has created some excitement when the students wonder what I will send them next.

From the list of responses provided, the student selects the one that is correct or best. Some questions have only one possible answer that is correct. In other questions, students are asked to identify the most appropriate, or best, answer from the choices given.

The *direct question format* has several advantages because it forces the teacher to state the problem clearly in the stem, it reduces the possibility of giving the student grammatical clues, and it may be more easily handled by younger and less able students because less demand is placed on good reading skills. The *incomplete statement format* can also be effectively used. In this case, the stem must be clear and meaningful and not lead into a series of unrelated true–false statements. A reverse (or negative) version of the direct question format and the incomplete statement format asks the student to select the one incorrect choice from a list of correct choices.

There are several advantages of multiple-choice questions. They (a) can test students in several levels of the cognitive domain, (b) can be scored quickly and accurately, (c) are relatively efficient in term of the number of questions that can be asked in a given amount of time and the space needed to present the answers, (d) can test a wide range of topics in a short time, and (e) are not significantly affected by guessing.

There are several disadvantages to multiple-choice questions. First, they are very difficult to construct and plausible sounding distracters are hard to find. Second, there is a tendency by teachers to write only factual recall questions. Of all the selection-type objective tests, multiple-choice items require the most time for the student to respond. Finally, test-wise students perform better than do non-test-wise students.

Consider the following guidelines when writing multiple-choice questions.

1. Use either a direct question or an incomplete statement as the item stem. A direct question is often preferable.
2. Write items in clear and simple language.
3. Make the response choices as brief as possible.

4. Include only one correct or best answer to every item.
5. With an incomplete statement, place the choices at the end of the statement.
6. Include four to five response choices.
7. State only plausible response choices.
8. List the responses choices below the stem in a vertical, easy-to-read format.
9. Use letters for the response choices.
10. Avoid a pattern of answers.

Matching.   Matching questions consists of a set of directions, a list of stems or numbered items (e.g., statements, phrases, words, incomplete sentences), and a list of choices (e.g., words, phrases, numbers). Students are required to make an association between each premise and the choices.

Matching questions are well suited to test knowledge in terms of definitions, dates, names, events, and other matters involving simple relationships. Since they require relatively little reading time, many questions can be asked in a limited amount of testing time. Matching questions are also easy to score. The range of test material can be broad, and guessing is limited.

There are some disadvantages to matching questions. They may encourage serial memorization rather than association. It is also sometimes difficult to get clusters of questions that are sufficiently alike that a common set of responses can be used. It is sometimes difficult to avoid giving clues, and too many items may be confusing to the students. Furthermore, matching questions are not well adapted to measure students' understanding of concepts, or their ability to organize and apply knowledge.

The following guidelines will assist you in preparing matching questions.

1. List the homogeneous premises on the left and the options to be matched on the right.
2. List the premises and choices in some logical or systematic order (e.g., alphabetically, chronologically).
3. Keep the list of premises and responses relatively short (the optimum is five to eight items to be matched).
4. Provide extra responses to reduce guessing.
5. The stem should include the longer and more involved statements and the response choices should be short and simple.
6. Number each stem and use capital letters for each response choice.

True–False.   A true–false item is simply a declarative statement to which the student responds by indicating whether it is true or false. One variation asks the student to correct false statements to make them true; these are often called modified true–false.

True–false questions have a number of advantages including the fact that they are good for students who are poor readers; can cover a large amount of content in a given testing period; generally provide high reliability; can be scored quickly and reliably; are adaptable to most subject areas; and can be constructed to measure the higher mental processes of understanding, application, and interpretation.

There are several disadvantages in the use of true–false questions. Scores may be unduly influenced by guessing. True–false items are often susceptible to ambiguity and misinterpretation, resulting in low reliability. The questions lend themselves to cheating more often than some other types of questions. Some statements are not entirely true or false, and thus specific determiners are often added to the questions.

To help overcome some of the disadvantages, the following guidelines can be used when writing true–false items.

1. Be sure that the item is absolutely true or false, without qualifications or exceptions.
2. Avoid loosely worded and ambiguous statements.
3. Highlight the central point of the question by placing it in a prominent position in the statement.
4. Avoid negative statements whenever possible.
5. Avoid making true statements consistently longer than false statements.
6. Avoid a disproportionate number of either true or false statements.

Short Answer. Short-answer or completion questions require students to provide a word or phrase. They are typically in the form of a direct question or a completion statement.

Short-answer questions reduce the chance that the student will guess the correct answer, and test items are relatively easy to construct. On the other hand, short-answer items are more difficult to score than other types of objective tests. There is also an emphasis on vocabulary and recall of information.

Use the following guidelines when constructing short-answer questions.

1. Generally, it is better to use a direct question rather than a completion statement.
2. Use short-answer questions to measure only the recall of important information.
3. Have the statement lead to one or two specific words or phrases.

TEACHERS IN ACTION

PREPARING AND GRADING A TEST

Dave Sampson, high school biology teacher, Marysville, Kansas

I obtain content for exam questions from the class notes, vocabulary words of the chapter, and the chapter review questions. Exams usually have fifty questions and include objective questions such as multiple choice, matching, completion, and listing. I use diagrams for identification of structures. I also use actual dissection specimens in a section of the test I call "What is it?" For these, I place the specimen in a display box and have numbered pins stuck in various parts that the students need to identify.

As a change of pace, I occasionally use a question called "Just for Thought." These are rid-dles or problems to work out, and they have nothing to do with the test content. Students can use them to replace one incorrect response from the exam. Students really enjoy the "Just for Thought" questions and sometimes do those first just to get relaxed at the start of the exam.

Without exception I return the corrected papers the following school day, and we go over the exams, make corrections, and settle any differences that may develop. I believe this procedure also serves as a good learning tool.

4. For completion statements, in general place the blanks near or at the end of the sentence.
5. For completion statements, do not require more than one or two completions to be made in any one test item.
6. When omitting words to make an incomplete statement, leave enough clues so the student knows that the answer selected is correct.

Assembling the Test

The mechanical features of a test—how the questions are grouped and arranged, what directions are given, and how the test was formatted—are no less important than the test items themselves. Careful attention to these aspects will enhance the value of the test as an evaluation tool and will also help save you time and effort.

Grouping and Arranging Test Items.   For most classroom purposes, test items can be arranged by a systematic consideration of the type of items used, the learning outcomes measured, the difficulty of the items, and the subject matter measured. First, all questions of an item format should be grouped together because it requires the fewest sets of directions, it is the easiest for the students because they retain the same mental set throughout each section, and it greatly facilitates scoring. Second, when two or more item formats are used in a test, they should be sequenced in the following order (Linn & Gronlund, 2000):

1. True–false or alternative response items
2. Matching items
3. Short-answer items
4. Multiple-choice items
5. Interpretive exercises
6. Essay questions

Arranging the sections of a test in this order produces a sequence that roughly approximates the complexity of the learning outcomes measured, ranging from simple to complex.

Third, within each item format, questions related to the same instructional objective should be grouped together. Fourth, items within each item format should be arranged in order of ascending difficulty. Therefore, both the sections and the items within the sections are arranged in an ascending order of difficulty throughout the test.

Writing Test Directions.   Directions should indicate what the students should do, how they are to do it, and where they should record their answers. Furthermore, the directions should indicate the time to be allocated to the test, the value of each test item, and whether or not they should guess at any answers they are unsure of. When determining test directions, teachers can use the following guidelines:

1. Provide a specific set of written directions for each item format.
2. Indicate the basis for the student answering the question.

3. Indicate how the student is to record the answers.
4. Indicate the point value of each question in an item format.
5. Indicate the purpose of the test, the length of time available, and whether students should guess. These issues could be verbally announced as compared to being written on the test paper.

Formatting and Reproducing the Test.   The visual display of the test items on the paper can affect time and effort the students expend and also the teacher's time during scoring. Use the following guidelines when formatting, typing, and reproducing a test.

1. Space items so they are easily read, answered, and scored with the least amount of difficulty.
2. Items should be numbered consecutively throughout the test.
3. Make sure all items have generous borders.
4. Keep all stems and options on one page.
5. For matching questions, have the list of premises and choices on the same page.
6. The most convenient method of response in true–false, matching, and multiple-choice questions is circling the correct answer.
7. Avoid a definite response pattern to the correct answer.
8. If no answer sheet is used, one side of the page should be used for responses to all objective questions, regardless of the item format.
9. Use a typewriter or a letter-quality printer to make the most legible-quality print.

■ ■ ■ ■ ■

SPOTLIGHT ON TECHNOLOGY

TEST MAKING WITH COMPUTER SOFTWARE

Computer software is available for making tests. Although the features and capabilities of the software vary, they commonly provide the following:

■ Allow entry of multiple-choice, matching, true–false, essay, fill in the blank, and scenario questions to create a bank of test questions. Questions can be easily modified.

■ Enable shuffling of questions to create multiple versions of the same tests with corresponding answer keys.

■ Enable the selection of individual questions or a random selection by question type, chapter, and level of difficulty.

■ Allow figures or text passages to be imported at needed locations.

Test-making software is typically password protected and is available for Macintosh and MS-DOS computers.

1. What advantages might you experience with the use of this software?
2. What disadvantages or problems might exist?
3. How might you use this test-making computer software?

Administering the Test

The physical and psychological environment should be conducive for students to demonstrate their achievement of learning outcomes. Bearing this in mind, consider the following guidelines when administering a test.

1. Provide comfortable testing conditions such as adequate light, ventilation, temperature, quiet, and work space.
2. Do not promote test anxiety by giving warnings about the importance of the test or by threatening the students.
3. Avoid giving a test just before or after a long vacation or some other important school event.
4. During the test, provide reminders about the time remaining.
5. Discourage cheating through careful proctoring and other means.
6. Do not talk unnecessarily before the test.
7. Keep interruptions to a minimum during test.
8. Avoid giving students hints about any test item.
9. At the start of the test, indicate what the students should do once they complete the test.

Scoring the Test

Guidelines were presented earlier for evaluating essay tests. Scoring objective tests can be done by machine or by hand. Some schools have facilities to score tests by machines which read students' responses off computer cards.

When scoring tests by hand, you have a few options. If the students write their answers on the test sheets themselves, you can simply create an answer key by using a blank test to write the correct answers. It is extremely helpful, as noted earlier, to have all the answers in one column, such as on the left side of the page. In this way, you can hold the answer key next to the student's test and mark the errors. If the student is asked to write the letter of the correct answer, you should draw a line through the incorrect answer and then add the letter of the correct answer. But if all letter choices are given at the left of the question and students are expected to circle the correct answer, you can easily see an incorrect answer and then indicate the error by circling the correct answer. In this way, in one stroke of the pen, the student knows the choice was incorrect and is also given the correct answer.

A scoring stencil can also be used in a similar way to cover all choices except the correct answer. You then can see which items were correctly marked by the students and place a mark on the correct choice when the students have chosen another response.

You could have students place their answers to objective questions (multiple choice, true–false, matching) on computer cards and use scanning systems to score the tests. This can save considerable time, especially when you have many tests to score such as at the middle and secondary levels. The cards that the students complete are run through a scanning machine and each card is scored. Most scanning systems can generate item analysis of the questions and a class roster with the score. Some scanning systems allow entering the scores from performance-based assignments (essays, special projects, oral exams, homework) with the machine-scored questions to obtain a combined score. The most sophisticated systems include software to scan, score, handle surveys, and develop a gradebook.

Regardless of the scoring method selected, the scoring key or answer key should be prepared and checked well in advance of the administration of the test. Generally, each item should have equal weight.

KEY TERMS

Anecdotal records	Formative evaluation	Practicality
Assessment	Measurement	Rating scale
Checklist	Norm-referenced evaluation	Reliability
Criterion-referenced evaluation	Objective questions	Rubric
Diagnostic evaluation	Participation chart	Summative evaluation
Essay questions	Performance-based assessment	Table of specifications
Evaluation	Portfolio	Validity

MAJOR CONCEPTS

1. Student evaluation helps teachers to determine the degree to which educational objectives have been achieved.

2. There are three types of evaluation: diagnostic, formative, and summative. Each serves a different purpose and each is conducted at different times.

3. Measurement or assessment is the process used to obtain data concerning student learning. Evaluation is the process of making a value judgment about student learning based on the measurement and assessment data.

4. Measurement or assessment approaches must be valid and reliable. Validity deals with the extent to which a measuring device measures what it purports to measure. Reliability deals with consistency—whether you would get about the same student results if you repeated the assessment.

5. Even before instruction begins, teachers need to establish a framework for student evaluation.

6. Performance-based assessment involves assessing student learning by examining products that students prepare to reflect their learning or by assessing actual student performances designed to demonstrate their learning.

7. When using performance-based assessment, teachers must specify the criteria by which the student products or performances will be rated, and then they must prepare the actual rating forms.

8. A table of specifications identifies objectives in all three learning domains that the student should attain by the end of instruction and also the content related to these objectives.

9. Student evaluation should be related to instructional objectives that are included in the table of specifications.

10. Guidelines for planning the classroom test, selecting and preparing test items, assembling the test, and administering and scoring the test can aid in effective measurement.

DISCUSSION/REFLECTIVE QUESTIONS

1. Recall examples in your own schooling when you took part in diagnostic, formative, and summative evaluation.

2. Describe how the terms *measurement* and *evaluation* differ.

3. Why is it useful to have a variety of assessment measures when evaluating student learning?

4. List factors that would help maintain high reliability of a test. Similarly, list factors that would help maintain high validity of a test.

5. What are the advantages and disadvantages of using products and performances to assess student learning?

6. What are the advantages of using a table of specifications when preparing a test?

7. What factors should be considered when deciding whether to use essay questions on a teacher-made test?

SUGGESTED ACTIVITIES

For Clinical Settings

1. Prepare a table of specifications for *this* chapter that includes learning objectives and content.

2. Prepare three questions for each of the following for a test on this chapter: true–false, short-answer, multiple-choice, and essay questions.

3. Identify the instruments of evaluation that would be appropriate when evaluating student outcomes in an art class.

4. Construct a rubric that could be used in assessing a short story.

For Field Settings

1. Ask one or more teachers to discuss the way they evaluate students. Analyze their responses in relation to the framework for evaluation discussed in this chapter.

2. Talk with several teachers about the ways that they conduct product or performance assessments. Ask specifically about rating criteria and rating forms.

3. Obtain one or more teacher-made tests and critique them based on the guidelines discussed in this chapter for planning the test, selecting and preparing test items, and assembling the test.

4. Talk to one or more teachers to obtain ideas for administering and scoring teacher-made tests.

USEFUL RESOURCES

Airasian, P. W. (2001). *Classroom assessment: Concepts and applications* (4th ed.). New York: McGraw-Hill.

Shows how assessment principles apply to the full range of teacher decision making.

Burke, K. (1999). *The mindful school: How to assess authentic learning* (3rd ed.). Arlington Heights, IL: Skylight Professional Development.

In a workbook format, it addresses learning standards and multiple ways to assess students, including portfolios, performance tasks and rubrics, teacher-made tests, logs and journals, checklists, and conferences.

Gronlund, N. E. (1998). *Assessment of student achievement* (6th ed.). Boston: Allyn & Bacon.

Serves as a practical guide for assessing the intended outcomes of instruction. Emphasis on teacher-made assessments and performance assessments.

Linn, R. L., & Gronlund, N. E. (2000). *Measurement and assessment in teaching* (8th ed.). Upper Saddle River, NJ: Prentice Hall.

> Provides thorough coverage of all aspects of measurement and assessment. Many examples and guidelines are included.

Montgomery, K. (2001). *Authentic assessment: A guide for elementary teachers.* New York: Longman.

> A concise yet thorough guide about various ways to conduct authentic assessment. Topics include rubrics, portfolios, authentic tasks, and others.

Tanner, D. E. (2001). *Assessing academic achievement.* Boston: Allyn & Bacon.

> Examines all aspects of assessment for classroom use. Includes using assessment information to inform instruction, standards and outcomes, ethical considerations, authentic assessment, and the computer as an assessment tool.

WEB SITES

- Numerous assessment resource links

  http://www.col-ed.org/smcnws/assessment.html

- An array of assessment links; focus on rubrics

  http://www.grand.k12.ut.us/curric/rubrics.html

- Great links to alternative assessment sites; testing, standards, portfolio

  http://www.mel.lib.mi.us/education/edu-assess.html

- Links to alternative assessment sites

  http://www.district44.dupage.k12.il.us/assess.html

- First in the Nation assessment resource links

  http://www.iptv.org/FINELINK/hotlinks.html

- The National Center for Fair and Open Testing; an advocacy organization working to end the abuses, misuses, and flaws of standardized testing and to ensure that evaluation of students and workers is fair, open, and educationally sound

  http://www.fairtest.org/

- The National Center for Research on Evaluation, Standards, and Student Testing

  http://www.cse.ucla.edu/

CHAPTER THIRTEEN

GRADING SYSTEMS, MARKING, AND REPORTING

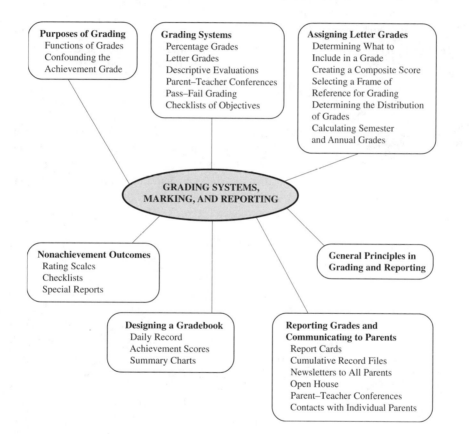

Purposes of Grading
Functions of Grades
Confounding the
Achievement Grade

Grading Systems
Percentage Grades
Letter Grades
Descriptive Evaluations
Parent–Teacher Conferences
Pass–Fail Grading
Checklists of Objectives

Assigning Letter Grades
Determining What to
Include in a Grade
Creating a Composite Score
Selecting a Frame of
Reference for Grading
Determining the Distribution
of Grades
Calculating Semester
and Annual Grades

GRADING SYSTEMS,
MARKING, AND REPORTING

Nonachievement Outcomes
Rating Scales
Checklists
Special Reports

**General Principles in
Grading and Reporting**

Designing a Gradebook
Daily Record
Achievement Scores
Summary Charts

**Reporting Grades and
Communicating to Parents**
Report Cards
Cumulative Record Files
Newsletters to All Parents
Open House
Parent–Teacher Conferences
Contacts with Individual Parents

OBJECTIVES

This chapter provides information that will help you to:

1. State the purposes of grading.

2. Describe the features of the various types of grading systems.

3. Determine the steps that are taken when assigning grades.

4. Identify nonachievement outcomes and determine how they can be measured and reported.

5. Describe information that needs to be recorded in the gradebook and how it can be formatted in an efficient manner.

6. Determine ways to report grades and effectively communicate to parents.

--- ■ ■ ■ ■ ■

PRAXIS/Principles of Learning and Teaching/Pathwise

The following principles are relevant to content in this chapter:

1. Monitoring students' understanding of content through a variety of means, providing feedback to students to assist learning, and adjusting learning activities as the situation demands   (C4)

2. Communicating with parents or guardians about student learning   (D4)

INTASC

The following INTASC standards are relevant to content in this chapter:

1. The teacher understands and uses formal and informal assessment strategies to evaluate and ensure the continuous intellectual, social, and physical development of the learner.   (Standard 8)

2. The teacher fosters relationships with school colleagues, parents, and agencies in the larger community to support students' learning and well-being.   (Standard 10)

It is not sufficient to simply gather information about student performance through teacher-made tests, portfolios, work samples, or other approaches. You must determine the grade for the student's work, place that grade within a grading system, and then report the grade to the student's parents. *Marks* or *grades* are summative, numerical, or quasi-numerical symbols that represent a student's performance in a marking period or a course and become a part of the student's permanent records. The terms *mark* and *grade* are frequently used interchangeably.

It is important to differentiate a mark or a grade from a score. *Scores* are assigned for a specific report, homework assignment, or test that is done while instruction is still taking place; this is formative evaluation. *Grades* are used in summative evaluation to represent the extent of the student's achievement and competence after instruction has occurred.

You will decide on the type of information to gather to evaluate students, how heavily to weigh each of the sources of information, and which frame of reference (i.e., criterion-referenced, norm-referenced, or potential standards) to use in assigning the grades. This information may come from homework, tests, quizzes, written or oral reports, or other measures. The choice of the grading system is often made by the school district and is reflected in the format used on the report cards.

When addressing the issue of grading student performance, you will need to make decisions about a number of factors. What are the purposes of grading? What types of grading systems can be used? How are grades to be assigned? How are nonachievement outcomes reported? How can a gradebook be formatted, and how can information be recorded in it? How is student progress to be reported to parents? These factors will be examined in this chapter, along with some general principles about grading and reporting.

PURPOSES OF GRADING

Grades convey information concisely, without needless detail. They also must be able to communicate information to a number of diverse audiences who use the grades for different purposes. The major audiences include students, parents, school administrators, counselors, other schools, college admission officers, and prospective employers. Each of these audiences uses grades in a somewhat different manner.

Functions of Grades

Grades and other reports of student progress serve several functions (Airasian, 2001; Carey, 2001). The two major purposes of grades are to provide information and to aid in making administrative decisions within the school, but there are other purposes as well. Regardless of the purpose, all papers should be graded and returned promptly.

1. *Informational functions.* Grades are used to inform students and parents about the student's academic progress. This feedback should enable students to judge their performance, lead to modification of their behavior, differentiate strong and weak areas of their performance, and serve as reinforcement for jobs well done. Grades inform parents about their child's performance, and also may provide the basis for questions to ask the child's teacher. This information enables parents to give their children needed emotional support and encouragement. These summary reports also give parents the basis for helping the children make sound educational plans.

2. *Administrative functions.* Grades are used for a variety of internal administrative purposes by the institution where they are assigned. They are used for determining promotion and graduation, awarding honors, deciding on admission to special courses and programs, and determining eligibility for scholarships and extracurricular activities, including athletic competition.

3. *Guidance functions.* By looking at a student's entire record, the student and a counselor may determine strengths, weaknesses, and interests. Counselors use this information to help students develop better self-understanding and make more realistic educational and vocational plans. This information could be used to make decisions about enrollment in certain courses or programs and about potential careers.

4. *Sorting and selecting functions.* Grades are often used when choosing individuals for academic honors, fellowships and awards, employment, advanced education in colleges and universities, and participation in various professional institutional activities. These decisions are competitive, and the decision makers are typically from an institution other than the one where the grades were assigned. Employers and admission officers from colleges and universities use grades to determine whether an individual will be hired or admitted.

5. *Motivational functions.* Periodic progress reports can contribute to student motivation by providing short-term goals and knowledge of results. How motivating the reports are likely to be, however, depends on the nature of the report and how it is used. If a single letter grade is used and students are threatened with low grades unless they study harder, the results are likely to be negative. However, when the reports are viewed as opportunities to check on learning progress, they are likely to have positive motivational effects.

6. *Research functions.* An often overlooked function of grades is the role they play in educational research. In research on student selection, grades are used as the criterion against which a predictor variable is validated (e.g., using high school grades as a predictor of success in college). Grades are also sometimes used in curriculum research and evaluation by using student success as an index of student performance.

Confounding the Achievement Grade

When trying to create a comprehensive index of student progress, some teachers might combine scores on conduct and achievement, thinking that improves the accuracy of students' grades, but the exact opposite occurs. The combining of these variables confounds, or mixes up, the meaning of the grade. Therefore, the meaning of the grade for achievement is compromised, and valid interpretation becomes difficult. There are four common ways that teachers confound achievement grades (Carey, 2001). You should avoid the following practices.

1. *Treating practice tests and homework as summative evaluation.* As discussed in the last chapter, diagnostic, formative, and summative evaluation serve different purposes. You would not consider using diagnostic evaluation data as the basis of a report card grade since that information is used to make placement and planning decisions. In a similar way,

■ ■ ■ ■ ■

CREATING A LEARNING COMMUNITY

DISCUSSING PURPOSES OF GRADING WITH YOUR STUDENTS

With a learning community, it is not the teacher *against* the students; it is the teacher *with* the students. In a learning community, everyone works together to promote student learning. One way to do that is to discuss the reasons for actions that are taken in the classroom.

Students know that assessment has to take place, but you can build understanding and commitment to assessment by discussing the reasons for assessment and the ways that the students might benefit. For example, formative assessment measures student learning as you proceed through a unit and provides feedback about areas of strength and weakness in the student performance prior to the final, summative assessment. Formative assessment performance is recorded, but may not be used to calculate the report card grade (scores from unit tests and projects may be used for the final, summative evaluation). Once students know the reasons for formative assessment and realize that it shows their development and will not be used for the report card score, they will feel less pressured and more willing to participate.

In addition, there may be various ways to involve students in the development of assessments in an effort to build their understanding and commitment to assessment in a learning community.

1. How might you go about discussing the reasons for formative and summative assessment in your classroom?
2. How might you ask for your students' preferences for the types of assessments to be used in your classroom? How might you ensure that you follow up by using their recommendations?
3. How might you actually involve your students in the preparation of various types of assessments?

formative evaluation data is intended to give the students and teacher feedback about student performance while instruction is still taking place. Unfortunately, teachers often combine formative evaluation data with summative evaluation data to determine the grade for the marking period or course. This combination of formative and summative evaluation data confounds the meaning of the grade.

Since the purpose of practice tests, homework, and related assignments used in formative evaluation is rehearsal, they are premature measures of achievement. Consequently, students' scores on practice tests tend to be lower than their scores on legitimate post-tests. Teachers who confound practice and achievement in this way usually attempt to minimize this negative influence by reducing the percentage that practice tests or homework contribute to the composite score, eliminating the lowest practice test score, providing opportunities for extra credit, or a combination of these three strategies.

2. *Administering unannounced post-tests.* Some teachers use unannounced post-tests, called pop quizzes, as a means to keep students studying on a regular basis rather than cramming before a scheduled test. Unfortunately, this practice confounds actual achievement and study habits. Student scores tend to be lower on unannounced tests as compared to their performance on scheduled tests. Teachers who use unannounced tests generally need to develop strategies to counter their negative influence.

3. *Reducing post-test scores due to misbehavior.* This practice confounds achievement with conduct. Unacceptable student behavior may include cheating on a test, talking or being disruptive during a test, or submitting assignments late. Teachers usually alter the earned score to teach the student that such misbehaviors will not be tolerated. Instead of reducing earned scores, alternative strategies should be used for encouraging honesty, consideration, and promptness. Many districts have a separate area of the report card to record behavior and citizenship.

4. *Using extra-credit assignments to alter grades.* Extra-credit assignments are those not required of all students in the regular conduct of the classroom, and these assignments may be used as the basis for altering the student's grade. This practice, however, confounds student achievement and effort. A higher grade that a student would earn through the use of extra-credit assignments actually masks the student's actual mastery level. Some teachers view extra-credit assignments as opportunities for the student to show added mastery or special skills.

■ ■ ■ ■ ■

CLASSROOM DECISIONS

Treating practice tests and homework as summative evaluation and using extra-credit assignments are two ways that achievement grades are confounded. What will be your policy on the use of these procedures?

Rather than using unannounced quizzes to promote regular study, what procedures could you use to achieve this purpose? How might you achieve this purpose with the use of various student groupings (in pairs or in groups of three)?

GRADING SYSTEMS

Effective grading and reporting should provide the type of information needed by the reports' users and present it in an understandable form. Depending on the purpose of the grade, as described earlier, some users of grades prefer comprehensive and detailed reports while other users prefer a single mark. As a consequence, most grading systems represent a compromise between the detailed information and the concise report. A *grading system* is the manner in which the students' achievement is reported (McMillan, 2001). There are several commonly used grading systems, as discussed in the following sections (Linn & Gronlund, 2000). Regardless of the procedure used, you should inform your students of the grading system that you will be using and clearly describe what your grading procedures and requirements will be.

Percentage Grades

In the percentage grading system, the teacher assigns a number between 0 and 100; often this number is supposed to correspond to the percentage of the material that the student has learned. A disadvantage of this approach is the difficulty in making distinctions of less than 4 to 7 points out of the 100. Consequently, during the 1930s and 1940s many school districts switched from numerical to letter grades.

Letter Grades

Letter grades have become the most commonly used grading system to represent a student's achievement. In this system, a single letter (e.g., A, B, C, D, F) is used to represent a student's achievement. There are at least two variations of the A-to-F grading system. One involves the use of a single number (e.g., 5, 4, 3, 2, 1) to represent the same meaning as the A-to-F. Another variation is the use of only two letters such as S (satisfactory) and U (unsatisfactory). This approach is most commonly used in elementary schools.

While concise and convenient, this system has shortcomings: (a) the meaning of the grades is often unclear because they are a collection of such factors as achievement, effort,

---

TEACHERS IN ACTION

INFORMING STUDENTS ABOUT GRADING PROCEDURES

Jeanne Pohlman, high school mathematics teacher, Wichita, Kansas

At the start of the school year, I give my students a handout that describes my grading procedures and expectations. The handout outlines the weight for tests, quizzes, and homework. Procedures are described for obtaining extra help and for using a three-ring notebook. I also include information about materials needed in class and procedures that we will use when beginning class. The policies on tardiness and cheating are also included. I think it is important to clearly state all these guidelines and expectations.

and good behavior; (b) interpretation is difficult; and (c) letter grades have resulted in an undesirable emphasis on grades as ends in themselves (Linn & Gronlund, 2000).

But the letter grade system does have a number of benefits. First, it is relatively easy to translate from letter grading to percentage grading and back. This conversion is convenient for the teacher who is able to record all student information on a numerical basis, weigh and average this information, and then assign letter grades accordingly. Second, the symbols + and – may be used to represent more specificity in the grade. Third, letter grades can easily be averaged to form a summary index called a grade point average (GPA).

Descriptive Evaluations

Descriptive evaluations are qualitative descriptions of learning, skills, and abilities that characterize a student's work. These may be in the form of written reports that are sent to parents or are included in the student's cumulative record folder. These reports enable greater flexibility in reporting student progress to parents by indicating strengths, weaknesses, learning needs, and suggestions for improvement. Criticisms of this grading system center on (a) the need to wade through extensive documentation in an effort to differentiate students, (b) the validity of the descriptions being affected by the style and personality of the student, and (c) time and effort involved in writing the descriptions. Some grade cards, including computerized versions, provide a space for brief comments.

Parent–Teacher Conferences

To overcome the limited information supplied on traditional report cards, some schools regularly schedule parent–teacher conferences. Conferences are most widely used at the elementary level, particularly in the primary grades. As a variation of the parent–teacher conference, middle schools and junior and senior high schools often make arrangements for parents to meet teachers at the end of each marking period when report cards are distributed. Parent–teacher conferences are usually used to supplement report cards and various descriptive reports; they are not typically used as the sole grading system.

Pass–Fail Grading

Some high schools have permitted students to take courses on a pass–fail basis rather than on the traditional A-to-F system. Because the pass–fail grade is not included in their grade-point average, this system encourages students to explore new areas of study without the fear of lowering their grade point average. As a grade reporting system, this approach offers less information than the A-to-F system.

Checklists of Objectives

For more informative progress reports, some schools have replaced or supplemented the letter or percentage grading systems with a list of major objectives to be checked or rated. This approach is most commonly used at the elementary level. For instance, five major objectives might be listed for each subject area with a checklist for each objective indicating the level of performance (e.g., outstanding, satisfactory, needs improvement).

ASSIGNING LETTER GRADES

Since most schools use the A-to-F grading system, you will need to determine what will be included in a grade and then establish a way to determine a composite score for each student. Next, you will need to select the frame of reference that is used in grading and then determine a method of distributing the grades for all the students in the class. Finally, you will need to calculate semester and annual grades.

Determining What to Include in a Grade

Letter grades are likely to be most meaningful and useful when they represent achievement only (Linn & Gronlund, 2000). The interpretation of grades becomes very confused when extraneous factors such as effort, conduct, study habits, and practice are included with achievement. Descriptions of student learning and development will be more precise if only achievement is used in determining the grade.

Grades should be valid measures of achievement. An *evaluation measure* is the means by which a teacher gathers information about the students' achievement. Evaluation measures may include tests, quizzes, reports, homework, and other approaches. Tests and other evaluation measures should actually measure student learning outcomes of the course objectives. Letter grades should reflect the extent to which students have achieved the learning objectives specified in the course objectives, and these should be weighted according to their relative importance (Linn & Gronlund, 2000).

Creating a Composite Score

At the end of a marking term, you will need to combine evaluation measure scores into a score that reflects each student's achievement throughout the term. This summative evaluation score for the marking term is called a *composite score.* A composite score is created by combining two or more scores obtained from the evaluation measures.

There is no single way that must be used to calculate composite scores; instead, a variety of approaches are used by teachers. Regardless of the specific approach taken, teachers need to consider the four following steps as they develop a procedure that works best for them when creating a composite score (Linn & Gronlund, 2000; Carey, 2001).

1. *Select evaluation measures that will be used in determining the student's grade.* Measures of student achievement can be obtained through a variety of means such as tests, written or oral reports, homework, ratings, laboratory performance, and projects.

2. *Analyze the relationship between the evaluation measures.* Some evaluation measures may be worthy of carrying more weight as the grade is determined. Therefore, first examine characteristics of the evaluation measures. When considering the complexity of an evaluation measure, look at its scope and the difficulty level of goals it measures. The scope can be compared using the number of goals measured and the length of time between instruction and testing. Difficulty can be compared using the relative complexity of the goals measured by each evaluation measure.

When considering scope, quizzes administered immediately following instruction that measure only one instructional goal are the least complex. Unit tests measuring more

TEACHERS IN ACTION

CREATING A COMPOSITE SCORE

Leslie Berman, middle school science and language arts teacher, Dania, Florida

In my school, we are told to have at least two grades per week for each student and to be able to justify all our judgments about these grades. As a result, I have developed the following point system for grading.

I grade on a scale of 10 points as follows: 0 = nothing handed in; 1 point = a blank paper with a name on it and handed in; 2 to 5 points = minimal work completed and handed in; 6 to 10 points = gradable work completed and handed in.

I grade every piece of work that I assign; some I grade for correctness and some for simple completion. After 10 assignments, I list all of them on the board and give the students two days for make-up completion. Then I total the grades for the 10 assignments and close out the book on them. I even highlight the total in my gradebook for easier identification and later averaging. For each marking period, I average about 30 to 40 assignments. More important items, such as book reports, count in multiples of 10, such as 20 or 30. Tests are averaged separately.

At parent conferences, it is impressive to show so many grades and so many opportunities for success. The system is geared to help the students succeed, and it is based on immediate feedback. With this system, grades are less intimidating, and it helps alleviate some classroom pressure.

goals and spanning more time are more complex. Based on differences in complexity, a teacher might decide that a comprehensive final should contribute more to the composite score than any midterm exam; a midterm exam should contribute more than any unit test; and a unit test should contribute more than any quiz (Carey, 2001).

The difficulty of the goals being measured also has to be taken into account. Based on differences in skill level, you might decide to assign more weight to tests that measure more difficult goals. One test that measures several less difficult goals may be considered comparable in overall complexity to another test that measures fewer but more difficult goals.

3. *Determine the percentage to be contributed to the composite score by each evaluation measure.* You need to calculate the percentage that each individual evaluation measure will contribute to the composite score. For example, if there were six unit tests and the teacher had identified that unit tests would contribute a total of 33.3 percent to the composite score, then you would divide the percent of contribution by the number of unit tests. In this case, each of the six tests would contribute 5.55 percent to the composite score (6 tests × 5.55 percent = 33.3 percent). In a similar way, each of two midterm exams would be worth 16.65 percent if the total weight of midterm exams was to total 33.3 percent. Then, the final exam would be worth 33.3 percent. Figure 13.1 displays a sample for the way these percentages would be allocated for each evaluation measure. The example shown in Figure 13.1 includes only tests; teachers may want to include other measures such as homework and projects as part of the composite score.

Usually, it is a matter of professional judgment when deciding on the percentage to allocate to each of the evaluation measures that are part of the composite score. Some districts, however, have grading policies that prescribe the percentage to be allocated to final exams.

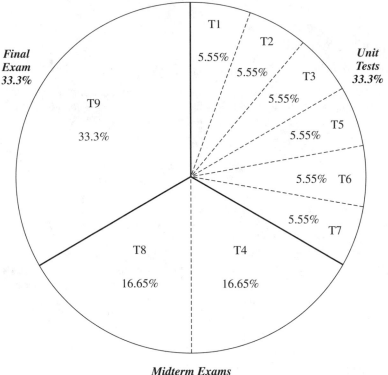

FIGURE 13.1   Percentage Contributed to the Term Composite Score by Each Test Category and Individual Test

Carey, L. M. (2001). *Measuring and evaluating school learning* (3rd ed.). Boston: Allyn & Bacon. Page 420. Reprinted with permission of Allyn & Bacon.

4. *Combine scores from evaluation measures into a composite score.* Although teachers may calculate a composite score in various ways, the objective is to combine the scores from each evaluation measure into a composite score.

The complicated part is to devise a system to have the scores from each evaluation measure reflect the appropriate relative weight when calculating the composite score. This composite-score calculation can be done in several ways. One way is to use a commercially prepared computer program to aid in these calculations. Grade analysis software such as this can automatically calculate composite scores using the relative weights that teachers specify for each evaluation measure. Such software can analyze and report data in a variety of ways. Second, you may calculate the average score for each type of evaluation measure and then calculate the composite score from these averages. Third, at the start of the marking term you may assign points for each individual evaluation measure that reflects the appropriate weight of the composite score. In this way, you need only to add up the total points at the end of the term to calculate the composite score. A drawback of this approach is that you will need to predetermine the exact type and number of evaluation

■ ■ ■ ■ ■

SPOTLIGHT ON TECHNOLOGY

CALCULATING GRADES WITH COMPUTER SOFTWARE

Grade analysis computer software is available for teachers to use when they calculate grades for the marking term, semester, or school year. While the capabilities of the software vary, they commonly calculate course grades with the weights teachers identify for the various evaluation measures, calculate statistics, rank students based on tests and the course, average homework and quizzes, alphabetize class rosters for various printouts, prepare progress reports for individual students, and other functions. The software is typically password protected and is available for Macintosh and IBM-compatible computers.

1. What advantages might a teacher experience with the use of such software?
2. What disadvantages or problems might exist with the use of computer grade analysis software?
3. How might you use this gradebook software?

measures to be used throughout the term. Fourth, you may identify a weight factor for each evaluation measure, calculate weighted scores for each measure, and combine weighted scores into a composite score. Fifth, you may devise a number of variations to these approaches or use completely different approaches in an effort to calculate a composite score.

Selecting a Frame of Reference for Grading

Teachers should consider three frames of reference when determining students' grades (Linn & Gronlund, 2000; Tanner, 2001).

1. *Criterion-referenced standards.* Assigning grades on a criterion-referenced basis involves comparing a student's performance to prespecified standards set by the teacher, usually indicated in percentages of material learned. Setting standards for criterion-referenced grading is a matter of professional judgment. With this approach, you would select score ranges for A to F that reflect outstanding, very good, satisfactory, very weak, and unsatisfactory achievement.

To some extent, this approach does involve comparisons with other individuals because standards have to be realistically set; they should be based on previous evidence of student performance. If the standards are set too high, many students will fail; if they are too low, students will achieve invalidly high grades. However, when preset standards are used, students do not compete with one another as they may when peer comparisons are made.

The criterion-referenced system of grading is more complex than it first appears. To use an absolute level of achievement as a basis for grading requires that (a) the domain of learning tasks be clearly defined, (b) the standards of performance be clearly specified and justified, and (c) the measures of student achievement be criterion referenced (Linn & Gronlund, 2000).

2. *Norm-referenced standards.* Assigning grades on a norm-referenced basis involves comparing a student's performance with that of a reference group, typically one's classmates. Therefore, the grade is determined by the student's relative ranking in the total group rather than by some absolute standard of achievement. Because grading is based on relative performance, the grade is influenced by both the student's performance and the performance of the group.

3. *Potential standards.* Grading students with respect to their potential involves several considerations: their apparent ability levels, their past performances, and the efforts they have made. Under this system, students would receive high marks if they perform well relative to their apparent abilities, improve considerably, or appear to be making extensive efforts.

Teachers often have difficulty in grading effectively using the potential standard method. Making reliable estimates of learning potential, with or without tests, is a challenging task because judgments of potential are likely to be contaminated by achievement to some unknown degree. It is also difficult to estimate improvement over short spans of time. Consequently, grades based on potential are not dependable due to the lack of reliability in judging achievement in relation to potential and due to problems in judging the degree of improvement.

CLASSROOM DECISIONS

As a beginning teacher, you will need to select one of the following as a frame of reference for your grading system: comparing a student's performance to predetermined standards set by the teacher, to performance by others in the class, or to the student's potential. Which would you select, and why?

Determining the Distribution of Grades

Once the frame of reference is selected, teachers need to decide how to distribute grades within that frame of reference. A number of guidelines exist for this task.

Criterion-referenced Grading.   When criterion-referenced grading is used, conditions for grading on an absolute basis must be met. These conditions include identifying the domain of learning tasks to be achieved, defining the instructional objectives in performance terms, specifying the standards of performance to be attained, and measuring the intended outcomes with criterion-referenced measurements.

The letter grades in a criterion-referenced system may be defined as the degree to which the objectives have been attained as illustrated here (Linn & Gronlund, 2000):

A = Outstanding. The student has mastered all of the course's major and minor instructional objectives.

B = Very Good. The student has mastered all of the course's major instructional objectives and most of the minor objectives.

C = Satisfactory. The student has mastered all of the major instructional objectives but just a few of the minor objectives.

D = Very Weak. The student has mastered just a few of the course's major and minor instructional objectives and barely has the essentials needed for the next highest level of instruction. Remedial work is desirable.

F = Unsatisfactory. The student has not mastered any of the course's major instructional objectives and lacks the essentials needed for the next highest level of instruction. Remedial work is needed.

Using the above definitions as a guide, point ranges must be determined for each letter grade. Some school districts have identified the point ranges for each letter grade. Often, it is left up to the professional judgment of the teacher.

There are a number of possibilities when determining the point ranges for each letter grade. For instance, you might determine the lowest passing score and then have an equal range of points for each letter grade, as illustrated in the samples in Table 13.1. The three samples show the lowest passing score of 60, 65, and 70; and each sample illustrates a fairly even number of points for each letter grade. Sometimes teachers prefer to have fewer points for an A, or have a decreasing range of points as the grade gets higher. Again, the range of points that a teacher selects is a matter of professional judgment.

With criterion-referenced grading, the distribution of grades is not predetermined. If all students perform well, all will receive high grades. If some students demonstrate low levels of performance, they will receive lower grades. Therefore, the distribution of grades is not determined by the student's relative position in the group but rather by each student's level of performance.

■ ■ ■ ■ ■ ■

CLASSROOM DECISIONS

In your class, you use a letter grade system of grading in which the students need to meet predetermined standards to earn the respective grades. One of your students comes in for extra help, tries hard, but still does not perform well. What would you do when it comes time to record the grade for the marking period? Under what conditions, if any, would you alter the grade?

TABLE 13.1   Sample Grading Standards

	COMPOSITE SCORE AND THE RANGE OF POINTS		
GRADE	*Sample 1*	*Sample 2*	*Sample 3*
A	90–100 (11 pts.)	92–100 (9 pts.)	93–100 (8 pts.)
B	80–89 (10 pts.)	83–91 (9 pts.)	85–92 (8 pts.)
C	70–79 (10 pts.)	74–82 (9 pts.)	77–84 (8 pts.)
D	60–69 (10 pts.)	65–73 (9 pts.)	70–76 (7 pts.)
F	Below 60	Below 65	Below 70

Adapted from Carey, L. M. (2001). *Measuring and evaluating school learning* (3rd ed.). Boston: Allyn & Bacon. P. 424. Reprinted with permission of Allyn & Bacon.

Norm-referenced Grading.   Norm-referenced grading involves the ranking of students in order of their overall achievement and assigning letter grades on the basis of each student's rank in the group. A common method for assigning norm-referenced grades has two steps.

1. *Determine what proportion of the class will receive each letter grade.* This task is not as simple as it first might appear because the teacher needs to take a number of factors into account as the selection of the proportions is made. As the starting point of these decisions, the normal bell-shaped curve can be used. Grading on the normal curve results in an equal number of As and Fs, and Bs and Ds.

In a classroom of 20 to 30 students, the use of norm-referenced grading may not be desirable because (a) the groups are usually too small to yield a normal distribution, (b) classroom evaluation instruments are usually not designed to yield normally distributed scores, and (c) the student population becomes more select as it moves through the grades and less-able students fail or drop out of school (Linn & Gronlund, 2000). Consequently, teachers who use norm-referenced grading consider additional factors such as the type of class (e.g., introductory or advanced), the type of student (e.g., gifted, average, or slow learning), or others. After considering these factors, teachers may use their professional judgment to adjust the percentages for each letter grade.

Recognizing that a variety of factors need to be considered, you can use the following as a guide when selecting the proportion of students to receive each letter grade (Linn & Gronlund, 2000).

A = 10–20% of the students
B = 20–30% of the students
C = 30–50% of the students
D = 10–20% of the students
F =   0–10% of the students

These percentage ranges are for illustration only. There are no simple ways for determining the ranges for a given situation.

2. *Make grade assignments based on the students' ranked scores.*   There are three steps to this process. First, using the percentage of students that you selected in the first step, determine the number of students that are to receive each letter grade. Second, rank students in the order of their achievement. This can be done by listing the scores in descending order and indicating a frequency tally by each score. And finally, assign the grade for each student based on his or her score and on the letter grade designation for that score based on the previous steps.

Calculating Semester and Annual Grades

At the end of two or more marking terms, term grades are combined into a semester grade. At the end of the year, semester grades are then combined into an annual grade. Teachers often calculate semester and annual grades in a way similar to that which they used to calculate the composite scores for each marking term. As noted previously, there is a great deal of variability among teachers in the way this is done.

One way to calculate semester and annual grades is to use a computer program to aid in grade analysis and record keeping. Second, you could take the average of the marking term grades to calculate the semester grade, or take the average of the marking term grades and the final exam to calculate the annual grade. Third, you could identify a weight factor for the marking terms, semester grades, and final exam; calculate weighted scores for each measure; and combine weighted scores into a composite score. Fourth, you may devise a number of variations to these approaches or use completely different approaches in an effort to calculate semester or annual grades.

NONACHIEVEMENT OUTCOMES

In addition to reporting achievement, teachers are often expected to measure and report student conduct. *Nonachievement outcomes* involve student conduct in areas such as effort, study habits, attitude toward learning, and citizenship. Most commonly, the report card used by the district will indicate the categories to be reported along with the manner in which the report will be made. Nonachievement outcomes typically reported include rating scales, checklists, and special reports; these same approaches may be used for recording achievement outcomes.

Rating Scales

Probably the most popular method of reporting judgments of effort, work habits, character traits, and other nonachievement information is a rating scale. For example, work habits, effort, and initiative can be rated as "superior," "average," or "unsatisfactory." Other items such as the respect for rights, property, and feelings of others could be rated on a three-step scale with "shows great respect," "shows proper respect," and "shows little respect." Rating scales on report cards may include three to five intervals for such traits as honesty, dependability, and leadership.

There are some disadvantages to the use of rating scales. First, ratings require considerable teacher time. Second, ratings are subject to the halo effect. This refers to the tendency of raters to consistently rate certain individuals positively and other individuals negatively regardless of the trait or characteristic being rated. This is a special danger when the teacher does not know the student well and consequently relies on general impressions of the student in making ratings of specific traits, or when a teacher lacks objectivity.

Checklists

A second procedure for reporting nonachievement outcomes is the checklist. A listing of specific behaviors or behavior patterns related to the traits to be judged is typically presented. While the checklist may include both desired and undesirable behaviors, it is more common for items to be stated all positively or all negatively.

For example, items listed under the heading of work habits might include positive statements such as uses time effectively, organizes work well, follows directions, uses resource material appropriately, and demonstrates the capacity for independent study. In contrast, a list of negative statements for work habits might include makes poor use of time, does not organize work well, distracts others, does not follow directions, fails to use resource materials appropriately, and lacks the capacity for independent study. Positive statements have the advantage of praising desired behavior. On the other hand, it is probably more informative to students and their parents to know what weaknesses in study habits a teacher perceives so that steps can be taken to remedy them.

Special Reports

An alternative to rating scales and checklists is the use of special report forms to communicate with parents and for use in cumulative student records. These are used when a teacher considers a student's behavior to (a) merit special commendation or (b) warrant a formal reprimand or warning. Special reports take less teacher time and energy than do ratings forms or checklists. To be used fairly and consistently, it is helpful to have a guide prepared by the district to assist teachers in making such reports. It is important that the reports not be viewed by students simply as a system for recording disciplinary problems.

CLASSROOM DECISIONS

Nonachievement outcomes may include items such as effort, study habits, attitude toward learning, and citizenship. Are there additional nonachievement outcomes that might be related to particular subject areas (e.g., physical education, social studies, science, art)? What kind of information will you need to gather for each nonachievement outcome, and how will you record it in your gradebook?

DESIGNING A GRADEBOOK

A *gradebook* includes three types of student behavior that teachers are usually expected to monitor and report: achievement, attendance, and conduct. Consequently, a gradebook documents students' progress throughout the school year. While teaching assignments and information requirements vary, most teachers need a daily record of students' attendance and other information related to classroom management, a record of achievement scores, and a record of conduct scores.

Your gradebook design should reflect the nature of your teaching assignment. A teacher who is assigned five different groups needs a gradebook that contains a daily log, a record of achievement scores, and a conduct record for each class. On the other hand, an elementary teacher who teaches five different subjects to the same group needs to create one daily log, one conduct record, and then a different achievement record for each subject (Carey, 2001).

While commercially produced gradebooks are available, many provide inadequate space for good documentation and are not formatted in ways that are the most efficient for the teacher. Consequently, you may be more satisfied with a gradebook that you construct using a large loose-leaf notebook; large block, two-sided graph paper; and divider pages

---

TEACHERS IN ACTION

DESIGNING A GRADEBOOK

Cindy Norris, sixth grade teacher, Manhattan, Kansas

When selecting a gradebook, I go for something simple, quick, and easily accessible! I don't use the regular gradebooks—they are printed too small, there is not enough room to write. Instead, I use a form which has a grid of boxes and place it in a 3-ring notebook. The names of the students go on the left of the horizontal lines. The top of the vertical lines include the assignment, points it was worth, and the date it was due. You can either buy professionally printed grids of various sizes, or you could prepare your own grid with the size of boxes that you prefer. The form I use is easy to write in. At the end of the grading period, I can pull the pages out of the notebook and put new pages in, ready for the next grading period.

Another advantage for using a 3-ring notebook for a gradebook is that you can use it for many other purposes—your teacher manual, important memos, rosters, etc. It's convenient to have all that information handy and in one notebook.

---

with tabs (Carey, 2001). After students' names are recorded on the first page, subsequent pages can be trimmed so the names remain visible as new pages are added. With this design, you can add new pages as needed, remove and store information from previous semesters, and insert records you might generate using the various computer programs available for gradebooks.

While there will be some variation due the nature of the your teaching assignment, an efficiently designed gradebook should have three sections to record (a) the daily record, (b) achievement scores, and (c) summary charts for the semester and the school year.

Daily Record

The *daily record* is used to document information about attendance, homework and classroom assignments, particular instances of conduct that you want to record, and other school matters (Carey, 2001). To prepare this section, select the information you will document, choose symbols that represent each type of information, create a legend for the symbols, list the class dates, and record the selected behaviors. A sample list of symbols for recording behaviors is shown in Table 13.2 along with an illustration of how to record these symbols in the daily log. The sample shown in Table 13.2 only includes symbols for negative behavior; teachers often include symbols for positive behavior as well.

You will also need a summary section for the marking term in which you record the frequency of each behavior over the term. A sample summary section of the daily record is displayed in Table 13.3.

Achievement Scores

The gradebook should also contain a section to record and summarize students' achievement scores on post-tests (e.g., tests conducted after instruction). Again, the amount and

TABLE 13.2   Sample Symbols and Format for Recording Behaviors

SAMPLE SYMBOLS FOR RECORDING BEHAVIORS

ATTENDANCE	*Study Habits*	*Participation*	*Conduct*
/ = Absent	H = Homework	M = Materials not present	A = Aggressive
(/) = Unexcused absence	(H) = Homework accurate	C = Clothing inadequate	D = Disruptive
X = Tardy	XH = No homework	P = Did not participate	CT = Cheating on test
(X) = Unexcused Tardy	IH = Inaccurate homework	T = Time wasted	
	CH = Homework not complete		
	LH = Late homework		

SAMPLE DAILY RECORD OF CONDUCT

Dates	9–1	2	3	4	5		8		9	10	11		12
Students							**H**					**Trip**	
Allen, B.					(/)		X	IH	X	P		ok	
Baker, J.							H	/				ok	

Adapted from Carey, L. M. (2001). *Measuring and evaluating school learning* (3rd ed.). Boston: Allyn & Bacon. P. 435–436. Reprinted with permission of Allyn & Bacon.

type of information that needs to be recorded will vary with the teacher's assignment. In general, the more complete the information recorded, the easier it is to determine the student's grade for the marking term, semester, and school year. A format is needed in the gradebook to systematically record necessary information.

Summary Charts

Another section of the gradebook is needed to record summary information for the semester and the school year. Selected information and summaries from the sections for daily

TABLE 13.3   Sample Summary Section of the Daily Record

Students	ATTENDANCE				STUDY HABITS					PARTICIPATION				CONDUCT		
	/	(/)	X	(X)	(H)	XH	IH	CH	LH	M	C	P	T	A	D	CT
Allen, B.	0	1	1	0	12	2	1	0	0	1	0	0	0	0	0	1
Baker, J.	3	0	1	0	2	4	6	1	2	7	0	2	0	0	1	0

Adapted from Carey, L. M. (2001). *Measuring and evaluating school learning* (3rd ed.). Boston: Allyn & Bacon. P. 437. Reprinted with permission of Allyn & Bacon.

TEACHERS IN ACTION

INFORMATION IN A GRADE BOOK

Gayle Bennett, high school English teacher, Manhattan, Kansas

A gradebook is used to record much more information than scores for tests and homework. First, a teacher must keep track of tardies and absences in the gradebook. Second, gradebooks can be used to record makeup work. Now, makeup work is an interesting phenomenon. Some teachers make up elaborate procedures such as two days to make up work for every day of excused absence. Forget that! I would never keep track of these. It would require an entire new notebook. Many teachers, including me, simply do not accept late work unless a student has an excused absence.

Third, gradebooks can be used to record when progress reports or down slips have been sent.

Down letters are used to report academic or other difficulties to parents. The pink copy of the down slip is kept and the date sent is recorded in my grade book.

Fourth, records for a variety of other actions may need to be kept in a gradebook. Records may need to be kept on in-school suspension assignments, regular reports for students with individualized educational plans, alphabetized lists of students whom you may take out of other classes for a club activity, bulletins listing students missing class due to sports and music events, and other information. Collectively, a gradebook holds much more information than grades.

---

records and for achievement scores will be transferred to this summary section. The summary section, therefore, will include summary information on the daily record, on the semester summary of achievement scores, and on the annual summary of achievement scores.

REPORTING GRADES AND COMMUNICATING TO PARENTS

Parents need to know how their children are progressing in school. In addition to reporting information about achievement and nonachievement outcomes, parents often want information about course content, instructional activities, grading procedures and student requirements, and special activities. By properly communicating with parents, you (a) fulfill your responsibility in telling parents of their children's progress, (b) explain the academic program to parents and solicit their understanding and assistance, and (c) enlist parents' help in educating their child.

Information about course content, instructional activities, grading procedures and student requirements, and special activities can be conveyed through the use of newsletters, open houses, and parent–teacher conferences. Achievement and nonachievement outcomes are communicated through report cards, and sometimes individualized letters to parents and parent–teacher conferences. A cumulative record file for each student is also maintained in the school as a source of information for the teacher and parents.

Report Cards

Report cards serve as the primary means to report to parents about their child's achievement and nonachievement progress (Stiggins, 2001). The district determines a number of aspects of *what* will be reported on the report cards and *how* the information will be reported. First, the district determines what achievement and nonachievement progress will be reported. Second, it determines what grading system will be used to report achievement progress. This may be in the form of letter grades, percentage grades, pass–fail, description evaluations, checklists of objectives, or other approaches. Third, it may determine the frame of reference (criterion-referenced or norm-referenced grading) to be used when assigning grades. Fourth, it may determine guidelines when calculating term or annual grades. For example, this may be in the form of a requirement to count a semester exam as 25 percent of the semester grade. Fifth, it may determine the percentages that should be used for each letter grade.

All of these decisions are beyond your control, and you need to be prepared at the end of the marking term to record information on the report card in the manner the district dictates. Some districts send progress reports to the parents halfway through the marking period. Beginning teachers, especially, should examine the district's report card for their grade level to see what information they are expected to report at the end of the marking term. Take this into account as you devise the evaluation system for your classroom.

Report cards differ in the way that nonachievement progress is reported. These reports vary considerably among districts and also by grade level. Report cards for the elementary grades, especially the primary grades of K–3, often have a number of nonachievement measures such as social development, work habits, effort, citizenship, academic readiness, and other areas. Report cards for the intermediate grades (4–6) have less emphasis on these items and have fewer items for teachers to report. Likewise, report cards for middle school, junior high school, and high school students have fewer items for reporting nonachievement information.

Cumulative Record Files

The school maintains a *cumulative record file* for each student as a source of information for the teacher and parents. The file for each student commonly contains one or more cumulative record cards recording the following information: (a) personal information (home address and telephone number, parents' names, parents' work addresses and phone numbers, the name of a person to contact in an emergency, and other useful background information); (b) information for each school year and in each subject area concerning the student's attendance, achievement (often including grades for each marking term, each semester, final exams, and final annual grades), nonachievement areas (often related to work habits, citizenship, and conduct); (c) the student's scores on various achievement tests or other standardized tests taken over the years he or she has been in school; (d) health; and (e) honors or participation in special activities. In addition, the cumulative record file often includes information about specially scheduled parent–teacher conferences and other anecdotal information.

The responsibility for updating the cumulative files for each student for each year varies among districts. For certain types of information, the school's secretarial staff sometimes enters the information. For other information, it is the classroom teacher's responsibility to have the file completely updated at the end of the school year. The balance of responsibility often depends on the situation in each individual school.

Cumulative record files serve several important purposes. First, the file provides the official record of a student's attendance, achievement, promotions, and graduation. It constitutes the basis for the student's transcript when transferring to another school. Second, the academic information can assist in determining each student's appropriate assignment to grade level or to specific classes. For instance, reading levels indicated for a student during second grade can help the classroom teacher make the appropriate reading group assignment when the student starts third grade.

Third, the data recorded in these records can help teachers understand the student's academic and social behavior. By examining these records, you may be able to identify special needs, distinguish between transient and permanent behavior tendencies, find out when a problem started, and discover clues concerning causal factors underlying a student's difficulties. And fourth, this record can help parents and teachers achieve a more objective and accurate picture of the student's achievements, special abilities, and special problems. Cumulative record files are also accessible to parents.

Newsletters to All Parents

At the start of the school year or a new course, teachers sometimes prepare a newsletter that would go to the parents of all the students in the class. This newsletter often includes information about the course content, instructional activities, and grading procedures and student requirements. Of course, the nature of the initial newsletter will vary with the grade level and the type of teaching assignment. As a guide, though, the newsletter may include a description of the following:

1. Course title or subject area(s)
2. Brief course or subject area description
3. Course objectives
4. A brief content outline
5. Typical learning activities
6. Grading procedures. This could include a listing of the types of evaluation measures to be used and the proportion of the marking term grade that each measure will carry. For example, tests (40 percent), homework (20 percent), project (20 percent), and quizzes (20 percent). In addition, the grading scale could be included indicating the percentages for each letter grade.
7. Materials that the student will need
8. Behavioral guidelines and expectations
9. The school telephone number. This is included as a convenience for the parents in the event they need to contact you.

It is important that you convey this information to the students as well. Students especially need to know grading procedures and guidelines and also behavioral expectations. During the school year, additional newsletters might be sent to all parents with information about special events, programs, or opportunities.

Open House

Many schools plan an open house near the beginning of the school year, inviting parents to come to the classroom and meet the teacher. Teachers commonly make a presentation to all the parents at one time and use this opportunity to convey the same type of information that was outlined in the newsletter described earlier. In fact, it is very helpful to have this same information printed and ready to distribute to parents when they arrive at the open house. The sheets that parents receive can then serve as the outline for the teacher's presentation at the open house.

The open house is typically not a time when teachers meet with individual parents about their child's progress. Some schools plan additional open houses later in the school year, but it is more common to have one open house at the start of the school year or the start of the semester.

CLASSROOM DECISIONS

Many school districts have an open house within the first few weeks of the start of the school year for parents to meet the teachers. What information would you convey in a 20-minute period to the parents who meet in a group with you in your classroom? What other ways might you continue to communicate with the parents throughout the school year?

Parent–Teacher Conferences

Many districts schedule parent–teacher conferences to permit teachers to explain students' grades and answer questions parents might have about their child's achievement, conduct, or attendance. At the elementary level, many districts have regularly scheduled parent–teacher conferences at least once and perhaps two or three times throughout the school year. These conferences are much less common at the secondary level.

In addition to parent–teacher conferences scheduled by the district, teachers or parents may initiate a conference to address some aspect of the student's progress.

When preparing for and conducting parent–teacher conferences, you should consider the following guidelines:

1. Prepare for the conference in advance.
2. Give the parents some idea in advance of the topic to be discussed.
3. Allow enough time for the conference.
4. Begin with a positive statement regarding the student.
5. Present the documentation for the grades.
6. Avoid becoming defensive when parents question the teacher's judgment.

7. Maintain an open mind to parents' ideas.
8. Listen to all that parents are saying (verbally and nonverbally) before responding.
9. Avoid overwhelming parents with the presence of other school personnel.
10. Avoid overwhelming parents with irrelevant material or use of jargon.
11. Avoid physical barriers such as a desk or uncomfortable chairs.
12. Follow up on commitments made during the conference. (Some teachers ask the parents to call back in a week or so.)

Contacts with Individual Parents

Teachers commonly contact individual parents through telephone calls or letters, and there are several reasons for doing this. First, you may want to invite the parents to a particular class activity or function, one in which their child is playing a significant role. Second, you may provide the parents with information about their child's academic work. Often, this concerns difficulties the student is having, and you may wish to discuss the issue with the parents to enlist their assistance and support. Do not overlook the importance of sending letters to parents that provide good news about the child's academic work. Many schools have forms or certificates that can be used to convey positive news. These do not take much of the teacher's time but make a big difference in the relationship that is established with the student and the parents.

Third, you may provide information about the conduct of the child. As with the letter concerning academic progress, these letters to parents should not be just for problems. Letters should also be sent that convey positive information concerning the child's conduct. Similarly, forms and certificates are often available for conveying good news concerning conduct. Fourth, you may send a letter asking that a parent–teacher conference be scheduled to discuss some aspect of the student's progress.

GENERAL PRINCIPLES IN GRADING AND REPORTING

The following general principles can serve as the basis of your system of grading and reporting.

1. Describe the grading requirements to the students. This includes providing information about the types of evaluation measures that will be used, the proportion of the marking term grade that each measure will carry, and percentages required for each letter grade.
2. Grades should represent academic achievement only. Do not alter grades due to student misbehavior.
3. Evaluate students at all levels of the cognitive domain.
4. Evaluate frequently throughout the marking term so that sufficient data concerning student achievement is obtained to determine the grades.
5. Communicate clearly to students what they will be evaluated on each time an evaluation is to occur.

6. Use many different evaluation measures. There should be a good balance of homework, classwork, quizzes, major tests, projects, and other appropriate evaluation measures.

7. Keep students informed about their progress throughout the marking term.

8. Devise an efficient format for the gradebook to accurately record all evaluation data and to simplify the task of calculating marking term, semester, and annual grades.

KEY TERMS

Composite score
Criterion-referenced standards
Cumulative record file
Daily record
Evaluation measure

Gradebook
Grades
Grading system
Marks
Nonachievement outcomes

Norm-referenced standards
Potential standards
Scores

MAJOR CONCEPTS

1. Grades convey information about a student's progress to students, parents, school administrators, counselors, other schools, college admission officers, and prospective employers. They serve informational, administrative, guidance, and sorting and selecting functions.

2. A grading system is the manner in which grades are reported. Grading systems include percentage grades, letter grades, descriptive evaluations, parent–teacher conferences, pass–fail grading, and checklists of objectives.

3. To assign grades, teachers must determine what to include in a grade, create a composite score, select the proper frame of reference for grading, and determine the distribution of grades.

4. Assigning grades on a criterion-referenced basis involves comparing a student's performance to prespecified standards set by the teacher. Norm-referenced grading involves comparing the student's performance with that of a reference group, typically one's classmates.

5. Teachers are often expected to measure and report on student's conduct in such areas as effort, study habits, attitude toward learning, and citizenship. These are often reported in rating scales, checklists, and special reports.

6. A gradebook should be designed and formatted for efficient recording and use of the daily record (e.g., attendance, homework and classroom assignments, conduct), a record of achievement scores, and summary charts for the semester and the school year.

7. Teachers need to be prepared at the end of the marking term to record information on the report card in the manner the district dictates. The district may specify a number of aspects of what is to be reported and how it is to be reported.

8. Besides reports cards, teachers can communicate to parents through newsletters, open houses, parent–teacher conferences, and contacts with individual parents. The student's cumulative record file can also serve as a source of information.

9. Teachers should describe the grading requirements to the students. This includes providing information about the types of evaluation measures that will be used, the proportion of the marking term grade that each measure will carry, and percentages required for each letter grade.

DISCUSSION/REFLECTIVE QUESTIONS

1. Suppose that a debate were being conducted on the topic of abolishing grades in elementary and secondary grades. List the reasons for and against this action.

2. What are the advantages and limitations for three types of grading systems: percentage grades, letter grades, and descriptive evaluations.

3. Why should teachers use a variety of evaluation measures during a marking term?

4. What are the advantages and limitations of assigning grades on a criterion-referenced basis?

5. For the grade level and/or subject area that you intend to teach, what type of nonachievement outcomes (e.g., conduct) would be appropriate to report? How would you measure these outcomes and report them?

6. What categories of information need to be included in the achievement score section of a gradebook?

7. What advantages would there be if the teacher prepared and distributed a newsletter at the start of the school year for parents concerning course content, learning activities, grading procedures, and student expectations?

SUGGESTED ACTIVITIES

For Clinical Settings

1. Select the types of conduct (e.g., effort, study habits, attitude toward learning, citizenship, or others) that you would want to measure and report on the report card for the grade level you intend to teach. Design a gradebook format to record information about this conduct. This should include a key for the information, a way to record the daily log, and a way to provide a summary of this information at the end of the marking term.

2. For your grade level and subject area, select evaluation measures for achievement you would use during a marking term and identify information concerning these that you would need to record in the gradebook. Next, design a gradebook that would enable you to record the required information and prepare marking term summaries.

3. Identify the percentages for each letter grade that you would use in the grade level and/or subject you intend to teach. State the rationale for lowest passing percentage and for the range of points at each letter grade.

4. Make a list of things you would need to do to prepare for a parent–teacher conference. Also list any materials you would need to have ready for the conference.

For Field Settings

1. Talk with one or more teachers to determine what evaluation measures they use, how they create a composite score for the marking term, what frame of reference they use when grading, and how they determine the distribution of grades within the class.

2. Examine the report card for a school district to see *what* achievement and nonachievement information is reported and *how* it is reported. Critique the report card for positive and negative aspects.

3. With the permission of the teacher, examine the cumulative record files for students in one class. Notice the type of information recorded and identify ways this information could be used.

4. Find out what the policy is for a school district on conducting open houses. Talk to one or

more teachers to see (a) what they do to prepare for the open house, (b) what special description sheets are prepared for parents, and

(c) how they actually conduct the open house presentation to parents.

USEFUL RESOURCES

Burke, K. (1999). *The mindful school: How to assess authentic learning* (3rd ed.). Arlington Heights, IL: Skylight Professional Development.

In a practical, workbook format, it addresses learning standards and multiple ways to assess students, including portfolios, performance tasks and rubrics, teacher-made tests, logs and journals, checklists, and conferences.

Gronlund, N. E. (1998). *Assessment of student achievement* (6th ed.). Boston: Allyn & Bacon.

Serves as a practical guide for assessing the intended outcomes of instruction. Emphasis on teacher-made assessments and performance assessments.

McMillan, J. H. (2001). *Classroom assessment: Principles and practice for effective instruction* (2nd ed.). Boston: Allyn & Bacon.

Shows how assessment principles apply to the full range of teacher decision making. Includes emphasis on high-quality assessments, assessing mainstreamed students, and assessments in each learning domain.

Montgomery, K. (2001). *Authentic assessment: A guide for elementary teachers.* New York: Addison Wesley Longman.

Provides a brief overview of authentic assessment, designing and using rubrics, portfolios, and using assessments in grading and reporting.

Popham, W. J. (2002). *Classroom assessment: What teachers need to know.* (3rd ed.). Boston: Allyn & Bacon.

Includes material dealing with the day-to-day decisions teachers make about assessment.

WEB SITES

- My gradebook.com is a Web-based teacher gradebook designed to enhance communication among teachers, students, and parents.

  http://www.mygradebook.com/

- GradeQuick: calculate grades, track attendance, create reports, and more

  http://www.jacksoncorp.com/gquick.html

- Grade guide for storing, retrieving, analyzing, and reporting students' grades

  http://www.alberts.com/AuthorPages/00004782/Prod_239.htm

- The Pretty Good Grading Program (elementary only)

  http://pggp.com/

CHAPTER FOURTEEN

WORKING WITH COLLEAGUES AND PARENTS

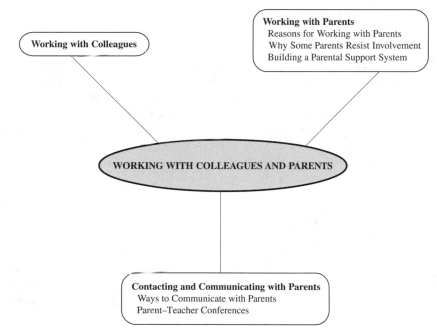

OBJECTIVES

This chapter provides information that will help you to:

1. Identify reasons why you would turn to colleagues for assistance.

2. Identify the reasons for contacting and interacting with parents.

3. Describe reasons why some parents resist involvement.

4. Determine ways that a parental support system can be developed.

5. Identify when to contact parents.

6. Determine ways to communicate with parents.

PRAXIS/Principles of Learning and Teaching/Pathwise

The following principles are relevant to content in this chapter:

1. Building professional relationships with colleagues to share teaching insights and to coordinate learning activities for students   (D3)

2. Communicating with parents or guardians about student learning   (D4)

INTASC

The following INTASC standard is relevant to content in this chapter:

1. The teacher fosters relationships with school colleagues, parents, and agencies in the larger community to support students' learning and well-being.   (Standard 10)

Can you imagine how challenging it must have been to teach in a one-room schoolhouse? There were so many responsibilities and challenges with the curriculum, instructional materials, and student behavior, and no one to turn to for help. Fortunately, teachers today have a number of colleagues that they can turn to for assistance concerning a variety of issues.

Parents can also be contacted for assistance when working with their child. In addition, teachers must take a variety of steps to contact and communicate with parents about the school program and the progress of their children. This chapter addresses ways to work with both colleagues and parents.

WORKING WITH COLLEAGUES

Teachers often need to turn to others for assistance when dealing with problems about student behavior, reading or language problems, media and instructional technology, students with special needs, curricular issues, instructional strategies, and numerous other issues. Depending on the issue, teachers may turn to one or more of these colleagues and resource people:

- Principals
- Counselors or psychologists
- Reading specialists
- Special education resource teachers
- Librarians
- Media specialists
- Curriculum specialists
- School or district committees
- District or community agencies
- School secretary
- Custodians

When dealing with a student who has significant misbehavior problems, for example, it is wise to consult with the principal, school counselor, or psychologist to obtain information and advice as you work with this challenging student. Sometimes, however, students do not respond to any of your strategies, and the misbehavior may continue to be chronic and serious. Deviant and disruptive behavior warrants referrals to outside help. In such cases, you may need to refer this student to the school counselor or psychologist when you recognize that a developing problem is beyond your professional expertise. Remember that you have not been trained to be a psychologist, counselor, or social worker, and you should not view yourself as a failure when referring the student to receive help from someone with appropriate training.

Before problem student behavior gets serious enough for these referrals, it is often helpful to have telephone calls and conferences with parents to inform them of the student behaviors and your actions and to solicit their assistance. In addition, the principal can counsel or intervene in various ways when handling a challenging student.

In serious cases, district and community agencies might need to be contacted to work with the school and the family. Many districts or city governments have an office of substance abuse and violence prevention and intervention, and its resources may be useful. Social workers are available in various community agencies. Other types of offices and organizations within the district or community might be contacted for help.

■ ■ ■ ■ ■

CLASSROOM DECISIONS

Let's assume that you have a student in your classroom who exhibits some of the classic characteristics of noncompliance and aggression. The student breaks rules, argues, makes excuses, delays, teases, fights, and is cruel to others. The problems may reach a point where they are considered serious enough to contact the principal, counselor, psychologist, or others. What criteria will you establish when deciding whether to seek outside help?

On the other hand, you may have a student with a disability or with special needs. In this case, you would contact the special education resource teacher for guidance and assistance. Or you might have a student who has limited English proficiency. Or you may want to integrate instructional technology into your instruction. Or you may have an interest to use a particular instructional approach, such as problem-based instruction. In all these cases, you would likely seek out colleagues in your school or district for assistance. Teaching should not be a solitary profession; you strengthen yourself when you turn to others for assistance. Keep in mind that your students will be ultimate beneficiaries of your willingness to seek out this assistance.

WORKING WITH PARENTS

Imagine that you are a parent and you and your family have just moved into the community during the summer. You have one child in third grade and another in seventh grade. Because you moved from another state, you are concerned that the curriculum might be quite different in this new district, and you wonder how your children will adjust to the new community and their new school and teacher. Wouldn't you want to talk to the teachers to share some of these issues? Wouldn't you like to hear about the curriculum and how the teachers will handle instruction? Wouldn't you like to maintain ongoing contact throughout the school year? Yes, of course!

Good communication with parents should be a priority because it keeps teachers and parents informed about what is happening. It also builds trust so that there can be a working partnership in the event that there are difficulties with the students. Although a teacher's primary responsibility is to work with students, it is important to communicate and interact with the students' parents throughout the school year. The reason for the communication will often determine the timing of the contact and the means by which the contact will be made.

At the start, we must recognize that children come from many types of family settings. Some come from two-parent families, but 25 percent come from one-parent families. One third of marriages are remarriages, and one out of four children has one or more stepparents (Swap, 1993). Some children are cared for by a combination of community caregivers, not in a traditional home. As a result of these various family settings, the term *parent* is used in this chapter in a broad sense to represent the adult or adults who have parental responsibility. Thus this definition of a parent could include the biological parents, foster or stepparents, a grandparent, an aunt or uncle, an older sibling, or a guardian.

Parents want their children to succeed in school and generally appreciate teachers' efforts to keep them informed and involved about academic and behavioral issues (Berger, 2000). Parental reactions to problems vary widely. Reactions are largely determined by individual experiences, life experiences, education and training, expectations, socioeconomic circumstances, and other factors. The reactions of the child, the teacher, and others also have a bearing on how the problem will be handled (Walker & Shae, 1999).

It is important to listen carefully to parents to identify their concerns and suggestions. Trust is developed when parents know that their ideas are recognized and understood. The full benefits of parent–school relationships are not realized without this interaction and collaboration.

What are the reasons for working with parents? Why is it important to understand the parents and their point of view? When should parents be contacted? What are the ways that teachers might communicate with parents? We will examine these questions in this chapter.

Reasons for Working with Parents

Students ultimately benefit from good communication and effective working relationships between the school and home. Parental involvement in their children's schooling has been associated with better attendance, more positive student attitudes and behavior, greater willingness to do homework, and higher academic achievement (Henderson & Berla, 1995).

There are several reasons why you would want to communicate with parents.

1. *To create open, two-way communication and to establish friendly relations.* Positive contacts with parents early in the year help establish positive, friendly relations. In this way, parents and teachers do not see each other as adversaries but as allies in helping the student be successful. Two-way communication can be fostered, and that will result in appropriate school-community relations that will benefit everyone involved.

2. *To understand the student's home condition.* Information about a student's home condition can help you decide on an appropriate course of action with the student. You may learn the parents are having marital problems, have limited ability to read or speak

English, exert excessive pressure for the child to excel academically, or tend to be abusive to the student when there are problems at school. Such factors can be important as you decide how best to help each student academically and behaviorally.

3. *To inform parents of academic expectations and events as well as student performance.* Parents appreciate knowing your policy concerning homework, late papers, and grading guidelines. They also like to know what content will be covered, when the quizzes or tests are scheduled, and what special events are scheduled. Introductory letters or a Back-to-School Night are helpful, as are newsletters devoted to special events, units to be covered, or the academic schedule. Finally, parents want to know how their children are doing. Report cards and conferences provide information periodically, but many parents appreciate learning about early indications of academic difficulties.

4. *To enlist parents' help with academic issues.* Teachers often seek help from parents at the start of the year. They may send a list of needed classroom and instructional supplies home to the parents to supplement purchases made by the school district. You may want to identify parents who might be available to serve as classroom aides or chaperones for regular or special events. This assistance may include preparing materials for bulletin boards, assisting during a field trip, and the like.

5. *To inform parents of disciplinary expectations and actions.* At the start of the year, teachers often inform parents of their disciplinary policy and their expectations for student conduct. As with the academic information at the start of the year, this communication is often accomplished through an introductory letter or a newsletter, or at the Back-to-School Night. If a student misbehaves, you may need to inform the parents of the situation without having to seek additional support and assistance from them.

6. *To enlist the parents' help in dealing with their children.* When students have difficulties, the parents should be contacted to identify ways they might help. When students misbehave, the parents should be contacted so that you can work together to help the student stay on task and be successful. Parents exert much influence on their children, and they can cooperate and support your actions.

You and the parents may both agree on strategies to help the child, to build the child's cooperation and commitment to address any problems. A behavior-modification program may be agreed on; as part of the plan, parents may withhold privileges or offer rewards at home. Parents have access to more attractive rewards than does the school, such as a videotape rental, a trip to the pool, or the purchase of an item of clothing. Establishing a plan of action with the student as an active participant and with the support of the parents is crucial for successful progress.

Why Some Parents Resist Involvement

As much as you would like the cooperation and support of parents when dealing with a student with academic or behavioral difficulties, you may find some parents apathetic or resistant to involvement. There are several possible reasons for parental resistance.

■ As students, some adults may have had unhappy experiences. They may view schools as being oppressive and not a place of hope for their children. These parents may consider it unlikely that school personnel can solve problems.

■ Parents of children who have a history of misbehavior may adopt coping mechanisms in an effort to deal emotionally with the problems (Walker & Shae, 1999). Their responses may point to self-doubt, denial, withdrawal, hostility, and frustration. These parents may resist involvement with all school personnel.

■ Some parents view teachers, principals, counselors, and other school personnel as the experts in addressing issues such as misbehavior (Turnbull & Turnbull, 2001). Consequently, they may resist involvement because they do not want to interfere with the actions taken by the teacher or other officials.

■ Some parents are threatened by the school itself and the bureaucracy. They may be intimidated by the size of the school, the need to report to the school office when visiting the school, the busy nature of the school, the lack of private areas for discussion, and other physical aspects of the school. As a result, these parents may resist involvement because they have a sense of discomfort about the school.

■ Diversity among the parent population and the sense of being different from school personnel may make parents uncomfortable in seeking contact with teachers or administrators (Swap, 1993). For example, Asian immigrant parents may think that communication with teachers is considered to be "checking up on them" and an expression of disrespect (Yao, 1988). Members of other ethnic groups, likewise, may feel out of place.

■ Some parents do not know what is expected of them or how they might contribute to their child's education. They may withdraw or become angry or frustrated when the school seems to be failing to meet their child's needs. They do not realize that the school would value their involvement.

■ Some parents do not become involved with the school for practical reasons. They may not speak English or have limited competency in English. They may not drive a car or have limited access to transportation. They may not have access to a babysitter or cannot afford one. Or they simply may be too tired after long days at work themselves.

CLASSROOM DECISIONS

Let's assume that you teach in a school that has much ethnic diversity, and that some parents do not attend the Back-to-School Night or the parent–teacher conferences at the end of the report-card periods. How do you find out why parents did not attend? If there are cultural perceptions prohibiting their attendance, how might you address this? How could you communicate to these parents that it is acceptable to attend such sessions and that their child would ultimately benefit from their attendance? What support might you seek from the principal in communicating with them?

Building a Parental Support System

It is helpful to identify ways you can build a parent support system so that you can communicate effectively with the parents and enlist their help when the need warrants. Joyce Epstein, a leading advocate of comprehensive parental involvement, identified six types of *parental involvement* (Epstein et al., 1997): (a) *Type 1: parenting,* helping all families establish home environments to support learning; (b) *Type 2: communicating,* designing more effective forms of communication to reach parents; (c) *Type 3: volunteering,* recruiting and organizing parent help and support; (d) *Type 4: learning at home,* providing ideas to parents on how to help the child at home; (e) *Type 5: decision making,* including parents in school decisions, developing parent leaders and representatives; and (f) *Type 6: collaborating with community,* identifying and integrating resources and services from the community to strengthen school programs, family practices, and student learning and development.

The National Parent Teachers Association (2000) maintains that parent involvement takes many forms, including (a) two-way communication between parents and schools; (b) supporting parents as children's primary educators and integral to their learning; (c) encouraging parents to participate in volunteer work; (d) sharing responsibility for decision making about children's education, health, and well-being; and (e) collaborating with community organizations that reflect schools' aspirations for all children.

It is important to counteract parental resistance. Recognizing that there are varying degrees of parental support and involvement, you will most likely try to build a support system by focusing on Epstein's Types 2 and 3—by communicating to reach parents and by seeking parent volunteers to help in various ways with academic issues. Other aspects of parental involvement are considered in other sources (Canter & Canter, 1991; Epstein, 1991; Swap, 1993; National PTA, 1997, 2000; Warner, 1997).

CONTACTING AND COMMUNICATING WITH PARENTS

As discussed previously, there are several reasons for working with parents. The timing of the contact will depend on the reason for it. There are three points to consider when contacting parents.

1. *Initial contact with all parents* would occur at the start of the year. These contacts would be designed to inform parents about the academic program, grading guidelines, the homework policy, rules and procedures, and other academic and behavioral expectations. Requests for additional classroom supplies and for parent volunteers for activities are generally made at this time. You could make these contacts through an introductory letter, a newsletter, Back-to-School Night, or other means.

2. *Ongoing contact with all parents* occurs throughout the year to provide information about content being covered in class, the schedule for tests or other evaluation requirements, field trips, the progress of the students, and so on. You may need additional parent volunteers throughout the year and may contact parents at various times as the need arises. These ongoing contacts could be made through a newsletter or information sheet, an open house, report cards, or other means.

3. *Contact with selected parents* needs to occur to inform them about unique concerns about their child's progress. These contacts may occur when there is either positive or negative news to report. You will often contact parents when there is a problem, yet it is easy to overlook contacting parents when there is good news to report. Parents especially appreciate reports of good news. If a problem arises later, parents are often more willing to support and cooperate with the teacher.

Ways to Communicate with Parents

There are many ways to communicate with parents, and the method may be affected by its purpose. To discuss a serious act of misbehavior, for example, you would probably not wait for a parent–teacher conference scheduled at the end of a report-card period to contact the parents but would likely call the parents immediately.

Much communication with parents occurs at the start of the year in the form of an introductory letter, a letter about classroom management and discipline, a Back-to-School Night, and information sheets. Ongoing communication may be through an open house, newsletters, notes and letters, phone calls, special events and informal contacts, sending home student work, report cards, home visits, and parent–teacher conferences. To contact parents about their child's academic work or behavior, you could call them or arrange for a special conference.

Table 14.1 is a summary of ways to communicate with parents that are discussed in the following sections.

Introductory Letter.   Teachers sometimes send an *introductory letter* home with the students to give to their parents during the first week of school prior to the Back-to-School Night. This letter is intended to serve as a brief welcome to the new year, include some basic information about the class, and invite the parents to the Back-to-School Night that will soon follow.

The letter may include some information about the schedule, homework, absences, and the curriculum. You may mention in the letter that more will be said about these and

TABLE 14.1   Ways to Communicate with Parents

1. Introductory Letter
2. Letter about Classroom Management and Discipline
3. Back-to-School Night
4. Information Sheets
5. Open House
6. Newsletters
7. Assignment Sheets
8. Individual Notes and Letters
9. Phone Calls
10. Web Sites and E-mail
11. Special Events and Informal Contacts
12. Sending Home Student Work
13. Report Cards
14. Home Visits
15. Parent–Teacher Conferences

other issues at the Back-to-School Night. A sample introductory letter to parents is displayed in Figure 14.1. You can adapt this letter for your particular situation.

Letter about Classroom Management and Discipline.   You need to share your plan for classroom management and discipline with the parents and the principal. If you expect them to be involved when you need them, they need to know that you have a plan and to be aware of your rationale for rules, positive recognition, and consequences.

September 4

Dear Parents:

Now that the school year has begun, I'd like to introduce myself. I am Melissa Riley, and I am your child's ninth-grade algebra teacher this year. I have taught in this school district for 14 years, and have taught pre-algebra, algebra, geometry, and trigonometry. I completed my undergraduate work at the University of Illinois and my master's degree at Kansas State University.

I want this to be a successful school year for you and your child. To ensure this success, it is important that we maintain open communication. Please do not hesitate to contact me if you have any questions or concerns. You could call me at school after dismissal between 3:30–4:30 p.m. at 555-7308. Or you could call anytime during the day and leave a message for me to call you back. My e-mail address is mriley@hotmail.com.

At various times throughout the school year, I will be sending a newsletter home with your child to provide information about classroom activities and special events. On a regular basis, your child will bring home graded assignments for you to look at. I also look forward to seeing you at the conference session which we schedule at the end of each report card period.

The annual Back-to-School Night for this school is scheduled for next Thursday, September 12, from 7:30–9:15 p.m. On that evening, you will have the opportunity to go through your child's schedule of classes in shortened 10-minute class periods. When you meet me during algebra class, I will share information about the curriculum, my approach to instruction, my academic expectations and procedures, my policy on discipline, and other issues. The books and materials that we will be using this year will also be on display. I encourage you to attend the Back-to-School Night because it will give you an opportunity to understand the mathematics program and become better acquainted with me.

Working together and keeping in good contact, I'm confident that this will be an exciting and successful school year. I look forward to meeting you at the Back-to-School Night.

Sincerely,

Melissa Riley

FIGURE 14.1   Sample Introductory Letter to Parents

TEACHERS IN ACTION

INTRODUCTORY LETTER TO PARENTS

Sherry Bryant, middle school social studies teacher, Rochester, New Hampshire

Have a letter ready to send home with the students on the first day of school to introduce yourself to parents and explain your goals for the year. Ask for parental support. Have them discuss with their child the goals, when and where they will do homework, and other aspects of the school work. Explain to parents that they are their child's main educators. Discuss the importance of their role in their child's life and mention that you value them. Ask the parents to fill out a questionnaire that will help you know what the parents' hopes are for their child. Give your phone number. Let the parents know that you welcome their calls, and let them know that you want to work with them so that this is a good year for their child.

At the start of the school year, you need to discuss rules, consequences, and other aspects of management with the students. A copy of this information sheet should be given to the students to take home to their parents. The letter should provide details of the classroom management and discipline plan and explain why it is important. Ask the parents to discuss the plan with their children, sign the plan, and return the signature portion to you. A sample letter to parents about classroom management and discipline is displayed in Figure 14.2. You may adapt that letter for your particular situation.

If the Back-to-School Night is scheduled early in the year, you may ask the parents to return the signature portion at that time. Or you may prefer to wait and present the letter to the parents at the Back-to-School Night and get the signatures at that time. Letters can then be sent home to parents who did not attend that evening.

Back-to School Night.   Many schools schedule a *Back-to-School Night* or Family Night during the first or second week so parents can receive information about the academic program, grading guidelines, the homework policy, rules and procedures, and other expectations. Requests for additional classroom supplies and for parent volunteers for activities are generally made at this time.

Some schools do not schedule a Back-to-School Night or, if they do, it comes later than the first or second week of school. As a result, you may find other ways to communicate with parents, since it is important to establish contact as early as possible. For example, a letter about classroom management and discipline might be expanded to include information that is commonly covered at a Back-to-School Night.

The scheduling of the Back-to-School Night is handled in different ways. For middle, junior high, and senior high schools, parents are often given their child's schedule, and they follow it just as the student would, but in shortened class sessions of 10 to 15 minutes. In this way, the parents see every teacher in the way that their child would during the school day. Teachers often use this time to present information to the parents about academic and behavioral guidelines and expectations.

Dear Parents:

Now that the school year has begun, I'd like to introduce myself and give you some information about how I conduct my classes. My name is Keith McKinsey, and I am your child's fifth-grade teacher. I have taught in this school district for eight years. I completed my undergraduate work at the Florida State University and my master's degree at Kansas State University.

To maintain an appropriate learning environment, I have established the following classroom rules which all students are expected to follow:

1. Follow the teacher's directions.
2. Keep your hands, feet, and objects to yourself.
3. Do not swear or tease.

To encourage students to follow the rules, I will recognize appropriate behavior with praise, various types of reinforcement, and notes or calls home to you. If students choose to break the rules, I have established an escalating series of responses ranging from gentle prompts and reminders, to the use of logical consequences, and to detention. In class, we have discussed these rules, the reinforcement for following the rules, and the consequences if the students choose to break the rules. My goal is to ensure success for your child. Working together, I'm confident that it will be an enjoyable and productive school year.

Please indicate that you understand this discipline plan by signing your name below and indicate the phone numbers where you can be reached during the day and evening. You might also discuss the rules to make sure your child understands them.

Please do not hesitate to contact me if you have any questions or concerns. You could call me at school after dismissal between 3:30–4:30 p.m. at 555-6188. Or you could call anytime during the day and leave a message for me to call you back. My e-mail address is kkeith@hotmail.com.

Sincerely,

Keith McKinsey

(Tear off and return the part below to Mr. McKinsey)

- -

I have read and understand Mr. McKinsey's classroom management plan, and I have discussed it with my child.

Parent/Guardian Signature _____   Date _____

Comments:

FIGURE 14.2   **Sample Letter to Parents about Classroom Management and Discipline**

Preparing for Back-to-School Night.   Back-to-School Night is often your first contact with the parents, so thorough preparation is necessary. There are many ways to prepare for this evening.

■ *Prepare your own introductory letter to parents about the Back-to-School Night in your classroom* (see the sample introductory letter in Figure 14.1). Do not rely only on notices which the school sends home. Some teachers like to have their students prepare special invitations for their own families.

■ *Make sure that the classroom looks attractive and neat.* Post your name and room number prominently on the door and the front chalkboard. Display samples of work by all students. Display copies of the textbooks and other instructional materials.

■ *Prepare a list of any instructional supplies or materials that parents might be able to provide.* This list will vary depending on the subject and grade level. It may include items such as rulers, buttons, a box of facial tissue, or other supplies. Have enough copies of the list to give to all parents.

■ *Prepare separate sign-up sheets for parents.* These may concern the need for a private, follow-up conference about their child; volunteers to help at special events such as field trips; volunteers such as guest speakers in class; or volunteers to provide various instructional supplies requested by the teacher.

■ *Plan a well-organized, succinct presentation.* Parents want to hear about your background and experience, behavioral and academic expectations, procedures for issues such as homework and absences, and other policies. Be sure to plan for time at the end of the presentation for questions.

■ *Prepare handouts for your presentation.* Parents will receive these handouts at the Back-to-School Night. Have enough copies of this material to give to all parents. A sample content outline of the presentation is shown in Table 14.2. Your handout should include details about issues such as those listed in Table 14.2. On the front page of the handout, in-

TEACHERS IN ACTION

BACK-TO-SCHOOL NIGHT

Jane Holzapfel, seventh grade computer literacy teacher, Houston, Texas

Many times teachers are unaware of situations in and outside of the classroom that affect students. Tell parents at the Back-to-School Night, the Open House, and at Parent–Teacher Conferences that they can help by writing notes to inform you of situations that are upsetting to their children or to ask questions about what is happening at school.

I also ask my students to write me a note when there is a problem, no matter how unimportant they may think it is. It is helpful to tell parents to ask their children to write the teacher a note when something is bothering them. With 170 students a day, we are often unaware of something that could be easily solved if we knew about it.

TABLE 14.2   Sample Content Outline for the Back-to-School Night Presentation

1. *Background about yourself*
   a. College training and degrees earned
   b. Professional experience, including length of teaching service, grade levels taught, where taught
   c. Personal information (e.g., family, hobbies, special interests or experiences)

2. *The curriculum, academic goals, and activities*
   a. Overview of the curriculum and the topics to be covered (Refer to the textbooks and related instructional materials on display in the room.)
   b. Your approach to instruction
   c. Instructional activities and any special events such as field trips or unique programs

3. *Academic expectations and procedures*
   a. Grading guidelines and procedures (how grades are determined)
   b. Grading requirements (e.g., tests, quizzes, homework, projects)
   c. Homework (purposes, how often, make-up policy, absences)
   d. When report cards are delivered
   e. Parent-Teacher conferences

4. *Discipline*
   a. Classroom rules
   b. Positive rewards
   c. Consequences for breaking the rules
   d. Incremental steps taken when misbehavior continues
   e. When parents will be contacted
   f. Parents need to sign the sheet concerning the classroom management and discipline policy.

5. *Ask parents to sign up for selected issues*
   a. For a private, follow-up conference about their child
   b. For parent volunteers for providing instructional materials and supplies
   c. For parent volunteers to help at special events such as field trips
   d. For parent volunteers such as guest speakers in class

6. *Express an interest to hear any ideas and concerns from parents at any time*

7. *Time for questions at the end of the session* (save several minutes if possible)

clude your name, the school phone number, and the times that you can be reached at the school at that phone number. Attach other related materials to this handout; these materials may include a sheet showing the daily or weekly class schedule, a sheet of needed instructional materials and supplies, or a sheet concerning the classroom management and discipline policy. To simplify distribution, staple all the handouts together as one set of materials sequenced in the order that you will cover the material during the presentation.

Conducting the Back-to-School Night.   Several guidelines should be taken into account when conducting the Back-to-School Night. Since your presentation is usually limited, possibly to only 10 to 15 minutes, it is important to plan how to conduct yourself.

Greet parents at the door, introduce yourself, and ask them to be seated. Begin your presentation using the handout which you previously prepared concerning your background, the daily and weekly schedule, the curriculum, academic goals and activities, academic expectations and procedures, discipline, and other issues. At the start, hand a copy of the handout to each parent.

Have parents sign up for individual follow-up conferences if they want to talk with you at length about their child. Back-to-School Night is not intended to deal with concerns about individual students. Allow time for parents to ask questions. This will be an opportunity for you to provide clarification about issues and to hear the concerns of parents.

Information Sheets.   Not all schools schedule a Back-to-School Night, and not all parents attend a scheduled Night. As a result, you can prepare a packet to send home that provides information about the curriculum, grading expectations and requirements, rules and procedures, the discipline plan, and other matters. The sheets may be the same as those given to parents who attend the Back-to-School Night, or a shortened version.

Open House.   Once or twice a year, most schools schedule an open house for parents to visit the classrooms during a particular evening to see their child's teacher, observe the classroom and samples of student work, and learn about books and materials being used. Some districts do not have a Back-to-School Night but instead schedule the first open house in mid-to-late September. At open house, teachers may give a formal presentation about the program, or schools may allow parents to drop in at any time during open house to informally discuss issues with the teacher.

Since open houses are conducted well into the school year, materials and projects that students have prepared can be displayed. Science fairs, for example, may be scheduled at the same time as an open house to provide an opportunity for parents to see students' science displays. Since some parents attending the open house may not have attended the Back-to-School Night, it is often useful to have extra copies of the handout provided at the Back-to-School Night to describe your policies.

Newsletters.   A newsletter periodically sent to all parents contains information about special events, content to be covered in the curriculum, tests or quizzes that are coming up, student projects, or other issues. Newsletters may be as brief as one page, or may be longer according to need. You can report accomplishments of the class and of individual students. Computers can be used to prepare the newsletters. Students could prepare the newsletter as a group or class project, under suitable circumstances.

Assignment Sheets.   Another way to communicate with parents is through an assignment sheet, which describes the assignments for the next week or two. The student is asked to show it to the parents. Some teachers may prefer that the parents sign the sheet and have it returned to school. This makes the students are fully aware of what needs to be turned in for evaluation, and they can make needed arrangements in their schedules; and the parents also are aware of what is happening.

Individual Notes and Letters.   Notes and letters are written to individual parents to discuss some particular issue about their child. You can use them to request that a conference be arranged with you, to invite parents to class functions, to inform parents about their child's work, or to offer suggestions.

Notes should be carefully written. They should be free of errors in spelling, grammar, and sentence structure. Furthermore, they should be brief, clear, honest, and factual. Educational jargon should not be used. Notes and letters are especially useful for contacting parents who are hard to reach by telephone.

Make sure that you address the letter with the correct names, since the parent and child may not have the same last name. If the parents do not read English, try to take steps to write the letter or note in their native language. Avoid writing a letter when you are upset about a classroom event; calm down first. Try to end with a positive statement about working together for the benefit of the child.

Be cautious about sending notes home to parents only when there is bad news to deliver. Certainly there are times when such notes need to be sent. You should also send notes home to parents with good news about the child's academic work or behavior. Brief, positive notes take only a few minutes to write to express pleasure about the child's performance. By systematically writing one or two notes to different parents each day, you will provide good news and help build positive relationships with the parents. Parents will usually talk with their child about the note, and the child may come to school the next day with a more positive attitude.

■ ■ ■ ■ ■ ▬▬▬▬

CLASSROOM DECISIONS

Sending notes or letters home to parents is one way to communicate with the parents. What types of information might you convey in the notes or letters? What guidelines will you establish for yourself about the content, the writing form, the frequency, and other factors? How might you need to vary these guidelines if you were teaching at the second, eighth, and twelfth grades, respectively?

TEACHERS IN ACTION

ASSIGNMENT SHEETS

Kathy Sublett, eighth grade history and language arts teacher, Anderson, California

It is important for students to know where they stand in their grades on a weekly basis. To give this weekly feedback, I provide students and their parents with an assignment sheet that shows the assignments that have been made, the ones the student turned in, and the ones due next. I inform parents about this at the Back-to-School Night and also in a memo that I send home.

There are two purposes of the assignment sheet. First, it helps remind students that they are responsible for their assignments. They only have to look at the sheet to see which assignments they are missing. Second, it is self-protection against irate parents who are amazed when they receive a deficiency notice for their child. I simply ask the parents to look at their child's assignment sheet to see what has not been turned in. The assignment sheets have helped defuse many tense situations. I can then ask the parents for their support in getting students to focus on their work.

Phone Calls.   Like notes and letters, telephone calls are made to parents to discuss a particular issue. The phone calls could request that a conference be arranged with you, to invite parents to class functions, to inform parents about their child's work, or to offer suggestions. As with notes and letters, be cautious about calling parents only when you have bad news. Also call parents when there is good news to report.

Phone calls can be quite brief because you only need to have two or three positive statements to share. They are not intended to be lengthy discussions about students. The parents should be asked to tell the child about the phone call.

There are times when you need to contact parents about the child's misbehavior. You need to plan ahead before making the call. The call should begin with a statement of concern such as, "Mrs. Erickson, I care about Kristina and I feel that her behavior in the classroom is not in her best interest." You then should describe the specific problem and present any pertinent documentation. You go on to describe what you are doing and have done to deal with the misbehavior. At this point, it is helpful to invite parental input by asking questions such as, "Has Kristina had similar problems in the past? Why do you think she is having these problems at school? Is there something going on at home that could be affecting her behavior?"

It is then useful to get parental input about how to solve the problem. State what you will do to help solve the problem and explain what you want the parent to do. Before ending the telephone conversation, you should let the parent know that you are confident that the problem can be worked out and tell the parent that there will be follow-up contact from you. Then recap the conversation.

Web Sites and E-mail.   Many schools have Web sites, and these may include links to a Web site for each teacher in the school. In these cases, teachers can place information on the Web site to communicate to students and parents about homework, class projects, grading policies, and many other issues.

As computer use becomes more common, many families have e-mail capability. Teachers can provide students and parents with their e-mail address to open this type of communication. Parents can contact the teacher with questions or comments through e-mail, and teachers can report student progress and other information to parents through e-mail.

Special Events and Informal Contacts.   Throughout the year, teachers and parents may attend many special events. These may include sporting events, concerts, plays, carnivals, craft displays, and others. Contacts with parents at these events may provide brief opportunities to share a few words about their child's work. These contacts are especially useful as progress reports and as a means of discussing a particular issue.

Sending Home Student Work.   You can inform parents about their child's academic progress by sending home completed and graded student work. Parents can see what you have covered, the child's work, and any notes or remarks you have made.

Sending home only completed worksheets may not be very enlightening to the parents. It is useful to send home a variety of materials including worksheets, tests, quizzes, homework, projects, lab reports, writing samples, artwork, or other types of student products. Be sensitive about notes or remarks you place on the papers. These notes are evaluative statements, but they should also include comments about good points and improvement as well as about areas still needing attention.

TEACHERS IN ACTION

CONSTRUCTIVE PHONE CALLS TO PARENTS

Kathryn Tallerico, former high school English teacher, now a teacher center director, Thornton, Colorado

As a tenth grader, Rudy was a bright student who had a history of being hostile, pouty, and downright rude. My two interdisciplinary teammates and I had a series of problems with her last year, and we eventually had a conference with her father.

This year, Rudy showed up in my Creative Writing class. I had to work hard to face her without prejudice and to assume that she would cooperate and succeed. Well, she did. Whether it was the class, the maturation process, or both, I'm not sure, but she had become a delight to teach.

After three months of bliss, I called her father and was able to sincerely praise her turnaround. I told her father how difficult it had been to like her the previous year. He simply said, "I know, I know. That's what she was like at home, too." Then he shared a bit about his personal hurt, and thanked me profusely for taking the time to bring my observations to his attention. I could hear the pride in his voice. I hung up glowing with the rare satisfaction of having witnessed a major growth within the short time I got to spend with an adolescent.

The next day at school, Rudy thanked me too. She said her dad let her know how much it meant to him. She added that it was very important to her that he know how much she had truly changed. Then I thanked her, and we hugged.

In retrospect, I sincerely believe that careful, honest discussion at all stages had laid the groundwork for Rudy's dramatic growth. I use four guidelines for myself when communicating with parents: (1) keep accurate records of the facts and rely on these when speaking to parents, (2) always have at least one truly kind or complimentary remark to make about the student, (3) record notes about the conversation and place a memo in a planner for a week or two ahead to provide the parent with follow-up information, and (4) ask the parent for information, help, and advice—communication must be two-way to be effective.

SPOTLIGHT ON TECHNOLOGY

USING TECHNOLOGY FOR COMMUNICATION

Increasingly, schools are using computer technology and Web pages to make information available to parents, students, and the public. Web page information about the school might include the school calendar; directories for teachers, administrators, and the staff; school policies; special events; and other information. Some schools make provisions so that each teacher has a Web page for use for his or her classroom. Teachers may post their syllabi, rules and procedures, notices about special events, listing of assignments or homework, Web links to useful resources, and much more. In addition, e-mail may be provided, opening up the capability to communicate within the school and also to students and parents at their homes.

1. If you had a Web page available for your use for your classroom, how might you use it? What information might you post?
2. When considering e-mail, what types of communication might you consider with students and parents? What provisions for communication will you make for homes that do not have Internet access?

Papers that are sent home with students to show their parents may not even get home or all the papers may not be shown to the parents. To overcome these problems, you might devise various ways to have parents sign a sheet to indicate that they have seen the material. For example, a parent response sheet might list the material being sent home, with a blank space for parents to sign and date. The student then returns the response sheet to you.

CLASSROOM DECISIONS

Sending graded student papers home for parents to see is one important means of communication. What guidelines will you establish for yourself concerning comments you place on the papers, the type of papers sent home, and the means to confirm that parents did receive the papers? How might you modify your procedures if a number of parents have limited English proficiency or if there were a variety of ethnic groups represented?

Report Cards.   Parents are informed of their child's academic performance when report cards are distributed. Most report cards have an area where you can either write a statement or indicate a code for a statement concerning effort and citizenship. As with notes, letters, and phone calls, you should be cautious about making only negative notes on report cards. Deserving students should receive positive notes.

When warranted, include notes on the report card to indicate the need to improve. Parents may call teachers shortly after report cards have been delivered if they have any question about them. Have documentation ready to justify what you have noted.

Home Visits.   Another means for personal contact with parents is through home visits, especially for parents who are reluctant to visit the school. This type of communication is not as popular as it once was due to changing social conditions and concerns about safety to the visiting teachers. Nevertheless, home visits allow you to inform the parents about the academic program and the child's progress. You may choose to make home visits to those parents who did not attend the Back-to-School Night or parent–teacher conferences. The handout prepared for the Back-to-School Night could be given to the parents. Visiting the student's home gives you insight into the family environment.

Some school districts have a home-visitation coordinator or a parent educator who is responsible for regularly visiting students' homes to discuss the child's progress in school, important events in the family's life, and ways parents can support and extend their child's learning.

It is important to know the community before making home visits because of concerns about safety. When the visits may prove beneficial, two teachers may visit the student's home together, or a teacher and a security guard may make the visit.

Parent–Teacher Conferences

Another important way of communicating with parents is through *parent–teacher conferences* to report information about progress, academic performance, or behavior. Many school districts schedule a day or two at the end of each report-card period for parent–

TEACHERS IN ACTION

SENDING GRADES AND UPDATES TO THE PARENTS

Pebble Richwine, high school science teacher, Miami, Oklahoma

To minimize the need for parents to call me and to better communicate with parents, I use a gradebook computer program that can generate reports for individual students. In this way, I can prepare a progress report on any student at anytime. I often send progress reports to the parents about a week before the official school mid-semester progress reports go out. My reports go to all parents, not just to the parents of students who are having some difficulty.

The report for each student from the gradebook program has three parts. First, the introduction reminds the parents that the grades are calculated on the basis of three averages: homework, quizzes, and tests. Second, a detailed list of the student's work is displayed, including the name of the assessment item, the maximum points possible, and points earned. Third, parents are asked to contact me if they have any questions. I include my school phone and my school and home e-mail address.

Since I have been sending these progress reports to the parents, I don't receive angry phone calls from parents due to a lack of information, but instead get calls asking how they can help their child. In this way, the student is then responsible to the parent concerning why they did not turn in three homework assignments.

To prevent a student from pulling these reports from the mailbox, I don't tell them when the progress reports will be sent to parents, and I also send the report as a single trifold, stapled sheet to camouflage the report. These progress reports have helped to improve communication with the parents.

teacher conferences so parents can meet individually with the teachers. Conference days are typically scheduled only for elementary grades; all parents are invited to attend these individually scheduled conferences.

Many middle schools, junior high schools, and high schools do not schedule parent–teacher conferences, but instead arrange for a block of time on one day at the end of the report-card period for parents to visit with each teacher on a drop-in basis. The ways to prepare for and conduct this session will be somewhat different than that used at the elementary level, but the general principles discussed here for preparing for this parental contact still apply.

In addition to the conferences conducted at the end of report-card periods, parent–teacher conferences are held with particular parents as the need warrants. When a student persistently misbehaves or has academic problems, you may ask the parents of that child to come to the school for a conference. Prior to having such a conference, you may want to meet with the student to work out a plan to address the problem. If this meeting with the student does not lead to resolution, then a meeting with the parents is warranted, and the student may be asked to also attend.

To have effective parent–teacher conferences, teachers should thoroughly prepare for the conference, take certain actions when conducting the conference, and provide appropriate follow-up. Guidelines discussed in the following sections center primarily on parent–teacher conferences to address academic issues. These guidelines would need to be adapted somewhat to address individually scheduled parent–teacher conferences concerning academic or disciplinary issues.

Preparing for the Conference.   Preparation for a drop-in conference with parents at the end of the report-card period will be different from preparation for an individually scheduled parent–teacher conference. Administrators in middle schools, junior high schools, and high schools commonly take steps to inform parents about the day and time for the drop-in conferences at the end of the report-card periods. Since these teachers have responsibility for many students, it is usually not feasible to have sample materials available for all students. Instead, teachers often have the gradebook on hand along with sample tests, quizzes, homework, and projects that students have completed throughout the marking period.

If an individual parent–teacher conference is needed, the teacher often calls the parents to select a day and time. Before the conference, the teacher may gather pertinent materials about the student and the situation. If it is an academic issue, the teacher may collect the gradebook and a sample of work done by the student, including tests, projects, and homework to be shown to the parents during the conference. If it is a behavioral issue, anecdotal record sheets and other documentation may be gathered.

Whether for a drop-in conference at the end of the report-card period or for an individually scheduled conference, the physical environment needs to be prepared for the session. You can arrange for these materials: (1) a table for the conference, (2) three or four adult-sized chairs for the table, and (3) a clean, tidy room.

Conducting the Conference.   Discussion and questions in the conference should be sequenced to develop rapport, obtain information from parents, provide information to parents, and summarize and follow-up. There are several guidelines to consider.

The following guidelines include a technique to sandwich your main messages in between good news or positive statements at the start and at the end of the conference. The parents who hear good comments at the start are then in a comfortable frame of mind. As the conference comes to a close, it is useful to summarize your main points and then conclude with additional positive statements.

1. *Begin the conference in a positive manner.* Walk up to the parents, introduce yourself, and welcome them into the room. Start the conference with a positive statement about the student, such as, "Emily really enjoys providing leadership for students in her small group when working on projects."

2. *Present the student's strong points before describing the matters needing improvement.* Highlight the student's strengths as you move into a discussion about his or her performance. Show samples of the student's work to the parents. Later, identify matters that need further improvement.

3. *Encourage parents to participate and share information.* Allow opportunities to ask questions and share information about the student. Pose questions to parents at various points of the conference to encourage their input.

4. *Plan a course of action cooperatively.* If the student needs to work on a particular issue, discuss the possible actions that you or the parents could take. Come to agreement about the course of action that each of you will take.

5. *End the conference with a positive comment.* Thank the parents for coming and say something positive about the student at the end of the conference.

6. *Use good human relations skills during the conference.* To be effective, you should be friendly and informal, positive in your approach, willing to explain in understandable terms, willing to listen, willing to accept parents' feelings, and careful about giving advice. You should avoid arguing and getting angry; asking embarrassing questions; talking about other students, teachers, or parents; bluffing if you do not know an answer; rejecting parents' suggestions; and being a "know it all" with pat answers (Linn & Gronlund, 2000).

Handling Conference Follow-up.   During the conferences, it is useful to make a list of follow-up actions. These actions may include providing more thorough feedback to the student during the next marking period, recommending additional readings to some students, providing certain parents with periodic updates on their child's performance, or a host of others. It is important to follow up in the ways that were identified during the parent–teacher conference.

KEY TERMS

Back-to-School Night
Introductory letter

Parent
Parental involvement

Parent–teacher conferences

MAJOR CONCEPTS

1. Teachers often need to turn to others for assistance when dealing with problems about student behavior, reading or language, media and instructional technology, students with special needs, curricular issues, instructional strategies, and numerous other issues.

2. Teachers work with parents to (a) understand the student's home condition; (b) inform parents of academic expectations and events as well as student performance; (c) enlist parents' help with academic issues; (d) inform parents of disciplinary expectations and actions; and (e) enlist parents' help in dealing with their children.

3. Parental resistance may be due to (a) the parents' unhappy experiences when they were students; (b) parental coping mechanisms in dealing with ongoing problems with their children; (c) the parents' view that educators are the experts; or (d) the parents' intimidation by the school and the bureaucracy.

4. The individual classroom teacher will most likely try to build a parental support system primarily by communicating to reach parents and by seeking parent volunteers to help in various ways with school-related issues.

5. The timing of the contact with the parents will be determined by the reason for the contact. The three main points of parental contact are (a) initial contacts with all parents at the start of the school year; (b) ongoing contacts with all parents throughout the school year; and (c) contact with selected parents concerning their child's academic or behavioral progress.

6. Initial communication with parents occurs at the start of the school year in the form of an introductory letter, a letter about classroom management and discipline, a Back-to-School Night, and information sheets.

7. Ongoing communication throughout the school year may occur with an open house, newsletters, notes and letters, phone calls, special events, informal contacts, sending home student work, report cards, home visits, and parent–teacher conferences.

8. To contact individual parents about their child's academic work or behavior, teachers often call the parents and sometimes arrange for a special parent–teacher conference to address the issues.

DISCUSSION/REFLECTIVE QUESTIONS

1. As a beginning teacher, would going to colleagues for assistance be seen as a sign of weakness and inability as a teacher? Why or why not?

2. How might information about a student's home condition help you as a teacher decide on an appropriate course of action with the student? How might this information create some problems for you?

3. When is an appropriate point to contact parents if a student is exhibiting mild misbehavior? Moderate misbehavior?

4. In what ways did your teachers in the middle and secondary grades contact and interact with your parents?

5. What are some ways that teachers can communicate with parents about academic expectations and events?

6. How can you communicate with parents who do not show up for Back-to-School Night or parent–teacher conferences?

SUGGESTED ACTIVITIES

For Clinical Settings

1. Prepare an introductory letter which you might send to parents at the start of the school year.

2. Assume that you will send four newsletters to parents during the school year. For each newsletter, select the month it will be sent and list the type of content that you might report in each newsletter. (Would you have regular features in each newsletter? What content might be unique to each issue?)

3. Prepare a letter that you might send to parents prior to a parent–teacher conference.

For Field Settings

1. Talk with several teachers about experiences they have had with parents who resist involvement. How did these teachers still communicate with these parents? What suggestions do they offer?

2. Ask several teachers to describe the ways that they prepare for and conduct the Back-to-School Night. What recommendations do they have to aid your preparation?

3. Talk with several teachers about their experiences preparing for and conducting parent–teacher conferences. What suggestions do they offer for your handling of the conferences?

USEFUL RESOURCES

Christopher, C. J. (1996). *Building parent–teacher communication: An educator's guide.* Lancaster, PA: Technomic Publishing Co.

Provides a thorough, practical perspective about all aspects of parent communication. Includes informing and involving parents, documentation, assessment, common problems encountered.

National PTA. (2000). *Building successful partnerships: A guide for developing parent and family involve-*

ment programs. Bloomington, IN: National Educational Service.

Provides specific, practical guidance for initiating and promoting all aspects of parent involvement. Includes issues such as communicating, volunteering, collaborating. Very useful resource.

Swap, S. M. (1993). *Developing home–school partnerships: From concepts to practice.* New York: Teachers College Press.

Provides a comprehensive overview and numerous practical suggestions for educators to strengthen school–parent relationships. Discusses benefits and barriers to parental involvement. Presents several models for this involvement. Useful resource.

Trunbull, E., Rothstein-Fisch, C., Greenfield, P. M., & Quiroz, B. (2001). *Bridging cultures between home and school: A guide for teachers.* Mahwah, NJ: Lawrence Erlbaum Associates.

Includes guidance for parent and family involvement, with special emphasis on addressing the cultural differences that may exist between the educators and the parents.

Warner, C. (1997). *Everybody's House—The schoolhouse: Best techniques for connecting home, school, and community.* Thousand Oaks, CA: Corwin Press.

Includes techniques for parent and family involvement. Considers barriers and ways to overcome them to promote good communication and involvement.

WEB SITES

- A PTA Resource: Making Parent–Teacher Conferences Work for Your Child

  http://www.pta.org/programs/edulibr/parteach.htm

- Toward More Productive Parent Teacher Conferences

  http://npin.org/pnews/1998/pnew1198/int1198c.html

- Ten Things You Should Never Do in a Parent–Teacher Conference

  http://www.nysut.org/newyorkteacher/backissues/1998-1999/981007parentconference.html

- National Parents Information Network (NPIN) provides access to research-based information about the process of parenting and about family involvement in education

  http://npin.org/

- Education Week on the Web indexed to a range of topics, including working with parents

  http://www.edweek.org/context/topics/

- Department of Education resources for parents, teachers, and the community

  http://www.ed.gov/

- Teachers Helping Teachers

  http://www.pacificnet.net/~mandel/

- Tips for parents on working with schools

  http://www.ed.gov/pubs/PFIE/families.html

- This collection of Northwest Regional Lab (NWREL) resources focuses on parent involvement.

  http://www.nwrel.org/comm/topics/parent.html

REFERENCES

CHAPTER ONE—INTRODUCTION TO TEACHER DECISION MAKING

Allen, D., & Fortune, J. (1966). An analysis of micro-teaching: New procedures in teacher education. *Micro-teaching: A description.* Stanford, CA: Stanford University.

Ambach, G. (1996). Standards for teachers: Potential for improving schools. *Phi Delta Kappan, 78*(1), 207–210.

Baloche, L. A. (1998). *The cooperative classroom: Empowering learning.* Upper Saddle River, NJ: Prentice Hall.

Berliner, D. C. (1987). Ways of thinking about students and classrooms by more and less experienced teachers. In J. Calderhead (Ed.), *Exploring teachers' thinking* (pp. 60–83). London: Cassell.

Beyer, L. E. (1984). Field experience, ideology, and the development of critical reflectivity. *Journal of Teacher Education, 35*(3), 36–41.

Borko, H., & Niles, J. (1987). Planning. In V. Richardson-Koehler (Ed.), *Educator's handbook: A research perspective* (pp. 167–187). New York: Longman.

Borko, H., & Shavelson, R. J. (1991). Teacher decision making. In B. Jones & L. Idol (Eds.), *Dimensions of thinking and cognitive instruction.* Hillsdale, NJ: Erlbaum.

Brady, M. (2000). The standards juggernaut. *Phi Delta Kappan, 81*(9), 648–651.

Byrd, D. M., & Adamy, P. (2002). Assessing the impact of standards: Overview and framework. In E. Guyton & J. Rainer (Eds.), *Yearbook for teacher education.* Washington, DC: Association of Teacher Educators.

Byrd, D. M., Foxx, S., & Stepp, S. L. (1990, April). *Journal writing: An analysis of levels of reflection.* Paper presented at the annual meeting of the American Educational Research Association, Boston.

Calderhead, J. (1988, April). *Reflective teaching and teacher education.* Paper presented at the annual meeting of the American Educational Research Association, New Orleans.

Carter, K., Doyle, W., & Riney, M. (1995). Expert–novice differences in teaching. In A. C. Ornstein (Ed.), *Teaching: Theory into practice* (pp. 259–272). Boston: Allyn & Bacon.

Clark, C. M. (1988, March). Asking the right questions about teacher preparation: Contributions of research on teacher thinking. *Educational Researcher, 17*(2), 5–12.

Clark, C. M., & Peterson, P. L. (1986). Teachers' thought processes. In M. C. Wittrock (Ed.), *Handbook of research on teaching* (pp. 255–296). New York: Macmillan.

Clift, R. T., Houston, R. W., & Pugach, M. C. (Eds.) (1990). *Encouraging reflective practice in education: An analysis of issues and programs.* New York: Teachers College Press.

Conle, C. (1997). Community reflection and the shared governance of schools. *Teaching and Teacher Education, 13*(2), 137–152.

Copeland, W. D. (1986). The RITE framework for teacher education: Preservice applications. In J. V. Hoffman & S. A. Edwards (Eds.), *Reality and reform in clinical teacher education* (pp. 25–44). New York: Random House.

Cruickshank, D. R. (1985). Uses and benefits of reflective teaching. *Phi Delta Kappan, 66*(10), 704–706.

Cuban, L. (1995). A national curriculum and tests: Consequences for schools. In *The hidden consequences of a national curriculum* (pp. 47–62). Washington, DC: American Educational Research Association.

Darling-Hammond, L. (1997). *Doing what matters most: Investing in quality teaching.* New York: National Commission on Teaching and America's Future.

Dewey, J. (1933). *How we think: A restatement of the relation of reflective thinking to the educative process.* Boston: Heath. (Reprint from 1909)

Doyle, W. (1990). Themes in teacher education research. In W. R. Houston (Ed.), *Handbook of research on teacher education* (pp. 3–24). New York: Macmillan.

Ferguson, R. (1991). Paying for public education: New evidence on how and why money matters. *Harvard Journal of Legislation, 28,* 465–498.

Freiberg, H. J., & Waxman, H. C. (1990). Reflection and the acquisition of technical skills of teaching. In R. T. Clift, R. W. Houston, & M. C. Pugach (Eds.), *Encouraging reflective practice in education* (pp. 119–138). New York: Teachers College Press.

Glickman, C. D. (1986). Developing teacher thought. *Journal of Staff Development, 7*(1), 6–21.

Glickman, C. D., Gordon, S. P., & Ross-Gordon, J. M. (2001). *Supervision and instructional leadership: A developmental approach* (5th ed.). Boston: Allyn & Bacon.

Griffin, B. J. (1997). Helping student teachers become reflective practitioners. *The Teacher Educator, 33*(1), 35–43.

Grimmett, P. P., MacKinnon, A. M., Erickson, G. L., & Riecken, T. J. (1990). Reflective practice in teacher education. In R. T. Clift, R. W. Houston, & M. C. Pugach (Eds.), *Encouraging reflective practice in education* (pp. 20–38). New York: Teachers College Press.

Harrington, H. L., Quinn-Leering, K., with Hodson, L. (1996). Written case analysis and critical reflection. *Teaching and Teacher Education, 12*(1), 25–37.

Hunter, M. (1984). Knowing, teaching, and supervising. In P. Hosford (Ed.), *Using what we know about teaching* (pp. 169–192). Alexandria, VA: Association for Supervision and Curriculum Development.

Hurst, J., Kinney, M., & Weiss, S. J. (1983). The decision making process. *Theory and Research in Social Education, 11*(19), 178–182.

Interstate New Teacher Assessment and Support Consortium. (1998). Next steps: Moving toward performance-based licensure in teaching. [Online] Available: http://www.ccsso.org/intasc.html.

Johnson, D. W., Johnson, R. T., & Holubec, E. J. (1994). *The new circles of learning: Cooperation in the classroom.* Alexandria, VA: Association for Supervision and Curriculum Development.

Kagan, D. M. (1995). Research on teacher cognition. In A. C. Ornstein (Ed.), *Teaching: Theory into practice* (pp. 226–238). Boston: Allyn & Bacon.

Kilgore, K., Ross, D., & Zbikowski, J. (1990). Understanding the teaching perspectives of first-year teachers. *Journal of Teacher Education, 41*(1), 28–38.

Kohn, A. (2000, September 13). Standardized testing and its victims. *Education Week, 20*(4), 46–47, 60.

Kounin, J. S. (1970). *Discipline and group management in classrooms.* New York: Holt, Rinehart & Winston.

Lampert, M., & Clark, C. M. (1990). Expert knowledge and expert thinking in teaching: A response to Floden and Klinzing. *Educational Researcher, 19*(5), 21–23.

Leino, J. (1995). Cooperative reflection in teacher education: A finish perspective. *Teacher Education Quarterly, 22*(1), 31–38.

National Board for Professional Teacher Standards (1987). *What teachers should know and be able to do.* Detroit: Author. [Online] Available: http://www.nbpts.org/

National Commission on Excellence in Education (1983). *A nation at risk: The imperative for educational reform.* Washington, D.C.: US Department of Education. [Online] Available: http://www.ed.gov/pubs/NatAtRisk/

National Commission on Teaching and America's Future (1996). *What matters most: Teaching for America's future.* New York: Author.

National Council for Accreditation of Teacher Education (2001). *Professional standards for the accreditation of schools, colleges, and departments of education.* Washington, DC: Author.

Newell, S. T. (1996). Practical inquiry: Collaboration and reflection in teacher education reform. *Teaching & Teacher Education, 12*(66), 567–576.

Pajak, E., (2001). Clinical supervision in a standards-based environment. *Journal of Teacher Education, 52*(3), 233–243.

Phi Delta Kappa. (n.d.). *Reflective teaching.* Bloomington, IN: Author.

Pugach, M. C. & Johnson, L. J. (1990). Developing reflective practice through structured dialogue. In R. T. Clift, R. W. Houston, & M. C. Pugach (Eds.), *Encouraging reflective practice in education* (pp. 186–207). New York: Teachers College Press.

Resnick, L. (1987). *Education and learning to think.* Washington, DC: National Academy Press.

Richardson, V. (1990). The evolution of reflective teaching and teacher education. In R. T. Clift, R. W. Houston, & M. C. Pugach (Eds.), *Encouraging reflective practice in education* (pp. 3–19). New York: Teachers College Press.

Ross, D. D. (1990). Programmatic structures for the preparation of reflective teachers. In R. T. Clift, W. R. Houston, & M. C. Pugach (Eds.), *Encouraging reflective practice in education* (pp. 97–118). New York: Teachers College Press.

Sabers, D., Cushing, K., & Berliner, D. C. (1991). Differences among teachers in a task characterized by simultaneity, multidimensionality, and immediacy. *American Educational Research Journal, 28,* 63–88.

Sapon Shevin, M. (1999). *Because we can change the world: A practical guide to building cooperative, inclusive classroom communities.* Boston: Allyn & Bacon.

Schön, D. A. (1987). *Educating the reflective practitioner.* San Francisco: Jossey-Bass.

Shavelson, R. J. (1976). Teacher decision making. In N. L. Gage (Ed.), *The psychology of teaching methods.* The seventy-fifth yearbook of the National Society for the Study of Education, Part I. Chicago, IL: The University of Chicago Press.

Shavelson, R. J., & Stern, P. (1981). Research on teachers' pedagogical thoughts, judgments, decisions, and behavior. *Review of Educational Research, 51*(4), 455–498.

Shepard, L. A., & Bliem, C. L. (1995). Parents' thinking about standardized tests and performance assessments. *Educational Researcher, 24*(8), 25–32.

Shulman, L. S. (1987). The wisdom of practice: Managing complexity in medicine and teaching. In D. C. Berliner & B. V. Rosenshine (Eds.), *Talks to teachers* (pp. 369–386). New York: Random House.

Simmons, J. M., & Schuette, M. K. (1988). Strengthening teacher reflective decision-making. *Journal of Staff Development, 9*(3), 18–27.

Tyler, R. W. (1950). *Basic principles of curriculum and instruction.* Chicago, IL: University of Chicago Press.

Wenzlaff, T. L., & Cummings, K. E. (1996). The portfolio as metaphor for teacher reflection. *Contemporary Education, 67*(2), 109–112.

Wildman, T. M., Niles, J. A., Magliaro, S. G., & McLaughlin, R. A. (1990). Promoting reflective practice among beginning and experienced teachers. In R. T. Clift, R. W. Houston, & M. C. Pugach (Eds.), *Encouraging reflective practice in education* (pp. 139–162). New York: Teachers College Press.

Yinger, R. J. & Clark, C. M. (1982). *Understanding teachers' judgments about instruction: The task, the method, and the meaning* (Research Series No. 121).

East Lansing, MI: Institute for Research on Teaching, Michigan State University.

Zeichner, K. M. (1981–1982). Reflective teaching and field-based experience in teacher education. *Interchange, 12*(4), 1–22.

Zeichner, K. M. (1987). Preparing reflective teachers: An overview of instructional strategies which have been employed in preservice teacher education. *International Journal of Educational Research, 11*(5), 565–576.

Zeichner, K. M., & Liston, D. P. (1987). Teaching student teachers to reflect. *Harvard Educational Review, 57,* 23–48.

Zeichner, K. M., & Tabachnick, B. R. (1981). Are the effects of university teacher education 'washed out' by school experience? *Journal of Teacher Education, 32,* 7–11.

CHAPTER TWO—THE FUNDAMENTALS OF PLANNING

American Association for the Advancement of Science (1993). *Benchmarks for science literacy: Project 2061.* New York: Oxford University Press.

Berliner, D. C. (1979). Tempus educare. In P. Peterson & H. Walberg (Eds.), *Research on teaching: Concepts, findings, and implications.* Berkeley, CA: McCutchan.

Berliner, D. C. (1988, Oct.). *Implications of studies of expertise in pedagogy for teacher education and evaluation.* Paper presented at the 1988 Educational Testing Service Invitational Conference on New Directions for Teacher Assessment, New York.

Borich, G. (2000). *Effective teaching methods* (4th ed.). Upper Saddle River, NJ: Prentice Hall.

Borko, H., & Niles, J. A. (1987). Descriptions of teacher planning: Ideas for teachers and researchers. In V. Richardson-Koehler (Ed.), *Educators' handbook: A research perspective* (pp. 167–187). New York: Longman.

Calderhead, J. (1984). Classroom management. *Teachers' classroom decision making* (pp. 21–45). London: Holt, Rinehart & Winston.

Calderhead, J. (1987). *Exploring teachers' thinking.* London: Cassell Educational.

Clark, C. M., & Peterson, P. L. (1986). Teachers' thought processes. In M. C. Wittrock (Ed.), *Handbook of research on teaching* (3rd ed.) (pp. 255–296). New York: Macmillan.

Clark, C. M., & Yinger, R. J. (1979). Research on teacher planning: A progress report. *Journal of Curriculum Studies, 11*(2), 175–177.

Clark, C. M., & Yinger, R. J. (1987). Teacher planning. In *Talks to teachers* (pp. 342–365). New York: Random House.

Clark, L. H., & Starr, I. S. (1996). *Secondary and middle school teaching methods* (7th ed.). Columbus, OH: Merrill.

Department of Education (1991). *America 2000: An education strategy.* Washington, DC: Author.

DiPardo, A. (1997). Of war, doom, and laughter: Images of collaboration in the public-school workplace. *Teacher Education Quarterly, 24*(1), 89–104.

Evertson, C. M., Neely, A. M., & Hansford, B. (1990). The act of teaching: From planning to evaluation. In C. B. Myers & L. K. Myers (Eds.), *An introduction to teaching and schools* (pp. 476–516). Ft. Worth, TX: Holt, Rinehart & Winston.

Freiberg, H. J., & Driscoll, A. (2000). *Universal teaching strategies* (3rd ed.) Boston: Allyn & Bacon.

Furner, J. (1995, April). *Planning for interdisciplinary instruction: A literature review.* Paper presented at the annual meeting on Effective Classroom Teaching, Tuscaloosa, AL.

Gagné, E. (1985). Strategies for effective teaching and learning. In *The cognitive psychology of school learning.* Boston: Little, Brown.

Gagné, R. M., Briggs, L. J., & Wager, W. W. (1992). *Principles of instructional design* (4th ed.). Ft. Worth, TX: Harcourt Brace Jovanovich College Publishers.

Gagné, R. M., & Driscoll, M. P. (1988). *Essentials of learning for instruction* (2nd ed.). Englewood Cliffs, NJ: Prentice Hall.

Good, T. L., & Brophy, J. E. (2000). *Looking in classrooms* (8th ed.). New York: Longman.

Gronlund, N. E. (2000). *How to write and use instructional objectives* (6th ed.). Upper Saddle River, NJ: Prentice Hall.

Illinois State Board of Education (1986). *State goals for learning and sample learning objectives.* Springfield, IL: Illinois State Board of Education.

Juarez, T. (1992). Helping teachers plan: The role of the principal. *NASSP Bulletin, 76*(541), 63–70.

Kagan, D. M. (1995). Research on teacher cognition. In A. C. Ornstein (Ed.), *Teaching: Theory into practice* (pp. 226–238). Boston: Allyn & Bacon.

Kellough, R. D., & Kellough, N. G. (1999). *Middle school teaching: A guide to methods and resources* (3rd ed). Columbus, OH: Merrill.

Lee, T. I., & Huang, I. (1997, March). *An interpretive study on instructional representations of a senior high school biology teacher.* Paper presented at the annual meeting of the National Association of Research in Science Teaching, Chicago, IL.

Leinhardt, G. (1986). *Math lessons: A contrast of novice and expert competence.* Paper presented at the annual meeting of the American Educational Research Association, San Francisco.

Leinhardt, G., Weidman, C., & Hammond, K. M. (1989). Introduction and integration of classroom routines by expert teachers. In L. W. Anderson (Ed.), *The effective teacher.* New York: Random House.

Marzano, R. J., Pickering, D. J., & Pollock, J. E., (2001). *Classroom instruction that works: Research-based strategies for increasing student achievement.* Alexandria, VA: Association for Curriculum and Development.

Merenbloom, E. Y. (1991). *The team process* (3rd ed.). Columbus, OH: National Middle School Association.

Morine, G., & Vallance, E. (1975). *A study of teacher and pupil perceptions of classroom interactions.* (BTES Special Report B). San Francisco: Far West Laboratory for Education Research and Development.

Morine-Dershimer, G. (1977, April). *What's in a plan? Stated and unstated plans for lessons.* Paper presented at the annual meeting of the American Educational Research Association, New York.

Morine-Dershimer, G. (1979). *Teacher plan and classroom reality: The South Bay study: Part 4* (Research Series No. 60). East Lansing, MI: Institute for Research on Teaching, Michigan State University.

Muth, K. D., & Alvermann, D. E. (1999). *Teaching and learning in the middle grades.* (2nd ed.). Boston: Allyn & Bacon.

National Center on Education and the Economy and the University of Pittsburgh (1997). *New standard student performance standards.* New York: Harcourt Brace.

National Council of Teachers of English & International Reading Association (1996). *Standards for English language arts.* Urbana, IL, and Newark, DE: Author.

National Council of Teachers of Mathematics (1989). *Curriculum and evaluation standards for school mathematics.* Reston, VA: Author.

National Education Goals Panel (1991). *The national education goals report: Building a nation of learners.* Washington, DC: Department of Education.

Neely, A. M. (1985). Teacher planning: Where has it been? Where is it now? Where is it going? *Action in Teacher Education, 7*(3), 25–29.

Neely, A. M. (1986). Integrating planning and problem solving in teacher education. *Journal of Teacher Education, 37*(3), 29–33.

Orlich, D. C., Harder, R. J., Callahan, R. C., & Gibson, H. (2001). *Teaching strategies: A guide to better instruction* (6th ed.). Boston: Houghton Mifflin.

Panaritis, P. (1995). Beyond brainstorming: Planning a successful interdisciplinary program. *Phi Delta Kappan, 76*(8), 623–628.

Peterson, P. L., & Comeaux, M. A. (1987). Teachers' schemata for classroom events: The mental scaffolding of teachers' thinking during classroom instruction. *Teaching and Teacher Education, 3,* 319–331.

Peterson, P. L., Marx, R. W., & Clark, C. M. (1978). Teacher planning, teacher behavior, and student achievement. *American Educational Research Journal, 15,* 417–432.

Popham, W. J., & Baker, E. I. (1970). *Systematic instruction.* Englewood Cliffs, NJ: Prentice Hall.

Reynolds, A. (1992). What is competent beginning teaching? A review of the literature. *Review of Educational Research, 62*(1), 1–35.

Rosenshine, B. (1980). How time is spent in elementary classrooms. In C. Denham & A. Lieberman (Eds.), *Time to learn.* Washington, DC: National Institute of Education.

Strother, D. B. (1984). Another look at time-on-task. *Phi Delta Kappan, 65*(10), 714–717.

Taba, H. (1967). *Teachers' handbook for elementary social studies.* Palo Alto, CA: Addison-Wesley.

Taylor, P. H. (1970). *How teachers plan their courses.* Hough, England: National Foundation for Education Research.

Tursman, C. (1981). Good teachers: What to look for. *Education USA* (Special Report). Arlington, VA: National School Public Relations Association.

Tyler, R. W. (1950). *Basic principles of curriculum and instruction.* Chicago: University of Chicago Press.

Wyne, M. D., & Stuck, G. B. (1982). Time and learning: Implications for the classroom teacher. *Elementary School Journal, 83*(1), 67–75.

Zahorik, J. A. (1975). Teachers' planning models. *Educational Leadership, 33*(2), 134–139.

CHAPTER THREE—TYPES OF TEACHER PLANNING

Anderson, L. W., & Krathwohl, D. R. (Eds.) (2001). *A taxonomy for learning, teaching, and assessing* (rev. ed.). New York: Longman.

Berliner, D. C. (1987). But do they understand? In V. Richardson-Koehler (Ed.), *Educators' handbook: A research perspective* (pp. 259–293). New York: Longman.

Bloom, B. S. (Ed.) (1984). *Taxonomy of educational objectives. Handbook I: Cognitive domain.* New York: Longman. [Originally published in 1956; renewed in 1984.]

Brown, D. S. (1988). Twelve middle-school teachers' planning. *Elementary School Journal, 89,* 69–87.

Callahan, J. F., Clark, L. H., & Kellough, R. D. (2002). *Teaching in the middle and secondary schools* (7th ed.). Columbus, OH: Merrill.

Clark, C. M., & Peterson, P. L. (1986). Teachers' thought processes. In M. C. Wittrock (Ed.), *Handbook of research on teaching* (3rd ed.) (pp. 255–296). New York: Macmillan.

Clark, C. M., & Yinger, R. J. (1979). Research on teacher planning: A progress report. *Journal of Curriculum Studies, 11*(2), 175–177.

Earle, R. S. (1996). Instructional design fundamentals as elements of teacher planning routines: Perspectives and practices from two studies. *Proceedings of Selected Research and Development Presentations at the 1996 National Convention of the Association of Educational Communications and Technology, Indianapolis, IN, 18,* 917–960.

Grant, T. J. (1996, April). *Preservice teacher planning: A study of the journey from learner to teacher in mathematics and social studies.* Paper presented at the annual meeting of the American Educational Research Association, New York.

Harrow, A. J. (1972). *A taxonomy of the psychomotor domain: A guide for developing behavioral objectives.* New York: Longman.

Hunter, M. (1984). Knowing, teaching, and supervising. In P. L. Hosford (Ed.), *Using what we know about teaching* (pp. 169–192). Alexandria, VA: Association for Supervision and Curriculum Development.

King, A. (1990). Enhancing peer interaction and learning in the classroom through reciprocal peer questioning. *American Educational Research Journal, 27,* 664–687.

Mager, R. F. (1997). *Preparing instructional objectives* (3rd ed.). Atlanta, GA: Center for Effective Performance.

Marzano, R. J., Pickering, D. J., & Pollock, J. E. (2001). *Classroom instruction that works: Research-based strategies for increasing student achievement.* Alexandria, VA: Association for Curriculum and Development.

Morine-Dershimer, G. (1979). *Teacher plans and classroom reality: The South Bay study, Part IV.* East Lansing, MI: Michigan State University, Institute for Research on Teaching.

Muth, K. D., & Alvermann, D. E. (1999). *Teaching and learning in the middle grades* (2nd ed.). Boston: Allyn & Bacon.

Rosenshine, B. V. (1987). Explicit teaching. In D. C. Berliner & B. V. Rosenshine (Eds.), *Talks to teachers* (pp. 75–92). New York: Random House.

Rosenshine, B. V., & Meister, C. (1995). Research on teacher cognition. In A. C. Ornstein (Ed.), *Teaching: Theory into practice* (pp. 134–153). Boston: Allyn & Bacon.

Yinger, R. J. (1980). A study of teacher planning. *Elementary School Journal, 80*(3), 107–127.

CHAPTER FOUR—THE INCLUSIVE AND MULTICULTURAL CLASSROOM

Banks, J. A. (2002). *An introduction to multicultural education* (3rd ed.). Boston: Allyn & Bacon.

Bhaerman, R. D., & Kopp, K. A. (1988). *The school's choice: Guidelines for dropout prevention at the middle and junior high school.* Columbus: National Center for Research in Vocational Education, Ohio State University.

Bloom, B. S. (1982). *Human interactions and school learning.* New York: McGraw-Hill.

Campbell, L., Campbell, B., & Dickinson, D. (1999). *Teaching and learning through multiple intelligences* (2nd ed.). Boston: Allyn & Bacon.

Catterall, J., & Cota-Robles, E. (1988). *The educationally at risk: What the numbers mean.* Palo Alto, CA: Stanford University Press.

Chapman, C. (1993). *If the shoe fits: How to develop multiple intelligences in the classroom.* Arlington Heights, IL: IRI/Skylight Training and Publishing.

Dunn, R., & Dunn, K. (1992). *Teaching secondary students through their individual learning styles: Practical approaches for grades 7–12.* Boston: Allyn & Bacon.

Fogarty, R. (1997). *Problem-based learning and other curriculum models for the multiple intelligences classroom.* Arlington Heights, IL: IRI/Skylight Training and Publishing.

Gardner, H. (1985). *Frames of mind: The theory of multiple intelligences.* New York: Basic Books.

Gollnick, D. M., & Chinn, P. C. (2002). *Multicultural education in a pluralistic society* (6th ed.). Columbus, OH: Merrill.

Good, T. L., & Brophy, J. E. (1995). *Contemporary educational psychology* (5th ed.). New York: Longman.

Grossman, H., & Grossman, S. H. (1994). *Gender issues in education.* Boston: Allyn & Bacon.

Lazear, D. (1991). *Seven ways of teaching: The artistry of teaching with multiple intelligences.* Arlington Heights, IL: IRI/Skylight Training and Publishing.

Lehr, J. B., & Harris, H. W. (1988). *At-risk, low-achieving students in the classroom.* Washington, DC: National Education Association.

Mendler, A. N. (2000). *Motivating students who don't care.* Bloomington, IN: National Education Service.

Redick, S. S., & Vail, A. (1991). *Motivating youth at risk.* Gainesville, VA: Home Economics Education Association.

Romero, M., Mercado, C., & Vazquez-Raria, J. A. (1987). Students of limited English proficiency. In V. Richardson-Koehler (Ed.), *Educators' handbook: A research perspective.* New York: Longman.

Slavin, R. E. (2000). *Educational psychology: Theory and practice* (6th ed.). Boston: Allyn & Bacon.

Sprinthall, N. A., Sprinthall, R. C., & Oja, S. N. (1998). *Educational psychology: A developmental approach* (7th ed.). New York: McGraw-Hill.

Sternberg, R. J. (1988). *The triarchic mind.* New York: Viking.

Torrance, E. P., & Sisk, D. A. (1997). *Gifted and talented children in the regular classroom.* Buffalo, NY: Creative Education Foundation Press.

Turnbull, H. R., Turnbull, A., Shank, M., Smith, S., & Leal, D. (2002). *Exceptional lives: Special education in today's schools* (3rd ed.). Upper Saddle River, NJ: Prentice Hall.

Woolfolk, A. (2001). *Educational psychology* (8th ed.). Boston: Allyn & Bacon.

CHAPTER FIVE—MOTIVATING STUDENTS

Ames, C. (1992). Classrooms: Goals, structures, and student motivation. *Journal of Educational Psychology, 84,* 261–271.

Aronson, E., & Patnoe, S. (1997). *The Jigsaw Classroom: Building Cooperation in the Classroom.* New York: Longman.

Blumenfeld, P. C., Puro, P., & Mergendoller, J. R. (1992). Translating motivation into thoughtfulness. In H. Marshall (Ed.), *Redefining student learning: Roots of educational change* (pp. 207–239). Norwood, NJ: Ablex Publishing Co.

Burden, P. R. (2000). *Powerful classroom management strategies: Motivating students to learn.* Thousand Oaks, CA: Corwin Press.

Campbell, L., Campbell, B., & Dickinson, D. (1999). *Teaching and learning through multiple intelligences* (2nd ed.). Boston: Allyn & Bacon.

Chapman, C. (1993). *If the shoe fits: How to develop multiple intelligences in the classroom.* Arlington Heights, IL: IRI/Skylight Training and Publishing.

Fogarty, R. (1997). *Problem-based learning and other curriculum models for the multiple intelligences classroom.* Arlington Heights, IL: IRI/Skylight Training and Publishing.

Gardner, H. (1985). *Frames of mind: The theory of multiple intelligences.* New York: Basic Books.

Keller, J. M. (1983). Motivational design of instruction. In C. M. Reigeluth (Ed.), *Instructional design theories and models: An overview of their current status.* Hillsdale, NJ: Erlbaum.

Lazear, D. (1991). *Seven ways of teaching: The artistry of teaching with multiple intelligences.* Arlington Heights, IL: IRI/Skylight Training and Publishing.

Lepper, M. R., & Hodell, M. (1989). Intrinsic motivation in the classroom. In C. Ames and R. Ames (Eds.), *Research on motivation in education* (Vol. 3). San Diego, CA: Academic Press.

Stipek, D. J. (2002). *Motivation to learn: Integrating theory and practice* (4th ed.). Boston: Allyn & Bacon.

CHAPTER SIX—DIFFERENTIATING YOUR INSTRUCTION

Cohen, E. G. (1994). *Designing groupwork: Strategies for the heterogeneous classroom* (2nd ed.). New York: Teachers College Press.

Good, T. L., & Brophy, J. E. (2000). *Looking in classrooms* (8th ed.). New York: Longman.

Gregory, G. H., & Chapman, C. (2002). *Differentiated instructional strategies: One size doesn't fit all.* Thousand Oaks, CA: Corwin Press.

Johnson, D. W., & Johnson, R. T. (1999). *Learning together and alone: Cooperative, competitive, and individualistic learning* (5th ed.). Boston: Allyn & Bacon.

Oakes, J. (1990). *Multiplying inequities: The effects of race, social class, and tracking on opportunities to learn mathematics and science.* Santa Monica, CA: RAND Corporation.

Silver, H. F., Strong, R. W., & Perini, M. J. (2000). *So each may learn: Integrating learning styles and multiple intelligences.* Alexandria, VA: Association for Supervision and Curriculum Development.

Slavin, R. E. (2000). *Educational psychology: Theory and practice* (6th ed.). Boston: Allyn & Bacon.

Tomlinson, C. A. (1999). *The differentiated classroom: Responding to the needs of all learners.* Alexandria, VA: Association for Supervision and Curriculum Development.

Tomlinson, C. A. (2001). *How to differentiate instruction in mixed-ability classrooms* (2nd ed.). Alexandria, VA: Association for Supervision and Curriculum Development.

Tomlinson, C. A., & Allan, S. D. (2000). *Leadership for differentiating schools and classrooms.* Alexandria, VA: Association for Supervision and Curriculum Development.

Wormeli, R. (2001). *Meet me in the middle: Becoming an accomplished middle-level teacher.* Westerville, OH: National Middle School Association.

CHAPTER SEVEN—DIRECT INSTRUCTIONAL STRATEGIES

Cooper, H. M. (1989). *Homework.* New York: Longman.

Cooper, H. M. (2001). *The battle over homework: Common ground for administrators, teachers, and parents* (2nd ed.). Thousand Oaks, CA: Corwin Press.

Dillon, J. T. (1988). Discussion versus recitation. *Tennessee Educational Leadership, 15*(1), 52–63.

Evertson, C. M., Anderson, C., Anderson, L., & Brophy, J. E. (1980). Relationship between classroom behaviors and student outcomes in junior high mathematics and English classes. *American Educational Research Journal, 17,* 43–60.

Fisher, C., Filby, N., Marlove, R., Coehn, L., Dishaw, M., Moore, J., & Berliner, D. C. (1978). *Teaching behaviors, academic learning time and student achievement: Final report of phase III-B. Beginning teacher education study.* San Francisco: Far West Educational Laboratory for Educational Research and Development.

Gage, N. L., & Berliner, D. C. (1998). *Educational psychology* (6th ed.). Boston: Houghton Mifflin.

Good, T. L., & Grouws, D. (1979). The Missouri mathematics effectiveness project. *Journal of Educational Psychology, 71,* 143–155.

Hunkins, F. P. (1995). *Teaching thinking through effective questioning* (2nd ed.). Norwood, MA: Christopher Gordon.

Hunter, M. (1976). *Improved instruction.* El Segundo, CA: TIP.

Hunter, M. (1981). *Increasing your teacher effectiveness.* Palo Alto, CA: Learning Institute.

Hunter, M. (1984). Knowing, teaching, and supervising. In P. L. Hosford (Ed.), *Using what we know about teaching* (pp. 169–192). Alexandria, VA: Association for Supervision and Curriculum Development.

Hunter, M. (1994). *Enhancing teaching.* New York: Macmillan.

Moore, K. D. (2001). *Classroom teaching skills* (5th ed.). New York: McGraw-Hill.

Roby, T. (1987). Commonplaces, questions and modes of discussion. In J. T. Dillon (Ed.), *Classroom questions and discussion.* Norwood, NJ: Ablex.

Rosenshine, B. V. (1987). Explicit teaching. In D. C. Berliner & B. V. Rosenshine (Eds.), *Talks to teachers* (pp. 75–92). New York: Random House.

Rosenshine, B. V., & Stevens, R. (1986). Teaching functions. In M. C. Wittrock (Ed.), *Handbook of research on teaching* (3rd ed.) (pp. 376–391). New York: Macmillan.

Tobin, K. (1987). The role of wait time in higher cognitive level learning. *Review of Educational Research, 57,* 69–96.

Wilen, W. W. (1991). *Questioning skills, for teachers* (3rd ed.). Washington, DC: National Education Association.

CHAPTER EIGHT—INDIRECT INSTRUCTIONAL STRATEGIES

Arends, R. I. (2000). *Learning to teach* (5th ed.). New York: McGraw-Hill.

Beyer, B. K. (1987). *Practical strategies for the teaching of thinking.* Boston: Allyn & Bacon.

Borich, G. (2000). *Effective teaching methods* (4th ed.). Upper Saddle River, NJ: Prentice Hall.

Bruner, J. S. (1966). *Toward a theory of instruction.* Cambridge, MA: Harvard University Press.

Dewey, J. (1910). *How we think.* Lexington, MA: D.C. Heath.

Doyle, W. (1990). Themes in teacher education research. In W. R. Houston (Ed.), *Handbook of research on teacher education.* New York: Macmillan.

Frederiksen, N. (1984). Implications of cognitive theory for instruction in problem solving. *Review of Educational Research, 54,* 363–407.

Gagné, R. M. (1985). *The conditions of learning and theory of instruction* (4th ed.). New York: Holt, Rinehart & Winston.

Jacobsen, D. A., Eggen, P. D., & Kauchak, D. P. (2002). *Methods for teaching* (6th ed.). Upper Saddle River, NJ: Prentice Hall.

Johnson, D. W., & Johnson, R. T. (1999). *Learning together and alone: Cooperative, competitive, and individualistic learning* (5th ed.). Boston: Allyn & Bacon.

Johnson, D. W., Johnson, R. T., & Holubec, E. J. (1994). *The new circles of learning: Cooperation in the classroom and school.* Alexandria, VA: Association for Supervision and Curriculum Development.

Johnson, D., Maruyama, G., Johnson, R., Nelson, D., & Skon, L. (1981). Effects of cooperative, competitive, and individualistic goal structures on achievement: A meta-analysis. *Psychological Bulletin, 89*(1), 47–62.

Joyce, B., Weil, M., & Calhoun, E. (2000). *Models of teaching* (6th ed.). Boston: Allyn & Bacon.

Lou, Y., Abrami, P. C., Spence, J. C., Paulsen, C., Chanvers, B., & d'Apollonio, S. (1996). Within-class grouping: A meta-analysis. *Review of Educational Research, 66*(40), 423–458.

Marzano, R. J., Pickering, D. J., & Pollock, J. E., (2001). *Classroom instruction that works: Research-based strategies for increasing student achievement.* Alexandria, VA: Association for Supervision Curriculum and Development.

Slavin, R. E. (1987). Ability grouping and student achievement in elementary schools: A best-evidence synthesis. *Review of Educational Research, 57,* 293–336.

Slavin, R. E. (1991). *Student team learning: A practical guide to cooperative learning* (3rd ed.). Washington, DC: National Education Association.

Slavin, R. E. (1995). *Cooperative learning* (2nd ed.). Boston: Allyn & Bacon.

Slavin, R. E. (2000). *Educational psychology: Theory and practice* (6th ed.). Boston: Allyn & Bacon.

Walberg, H. J. (1999). Productive teaching. In H. C. Waxman & H. J. Walberg (Eds.), *New directions for teaching practice and research* (pp. 75–104). Berkeley, CA: McCutchen.

CHAPTER NINE—MANAGING LESSON DELIVERY

Arlin, M. (1979). Teacher transitions can disrupt time flow in classrooms. *American Educational Research Journal, 16,* 42–56.

Berliner, D. C. (1987). Simple views of effective teaching and a simple theory of classroom instruction. In D. C. Berliner & R. Rosenshine (Eds.), *Talks to teachers* (pp. 93–110). New York: Random House.

Borich, G. (2000). *Effective teaching methods* (4th ed.). Columbus, OH: Merrill Publishing.

Brophy, J. E. (1998). *Motivating students to learn.* New York: McGraw-Hill.

Doyle, W. (1984). How order is achieved in classrooms: An interim report. *Journal of Curriculum Studies, 16*(3), 259–277.

Dubelle, S. (1986). *Effective teaching: Critical skills.* Lancaster, PA: Technomic Publishing Co.

Emmer, E. T., Evertson, C. M., & Worsham, M. E. (2000). *Classroom management for secondary teachers* (5th ed.). Boston: Allyn & Bacon.

Evertson, C. M., Emmer, E. T., & Worsham, M. E. (2000). *Classroom management for elementary teachers* (5th ed.). Boston: Allyn & Bacon.

Good, T. L., & Brophy, J. E. (2000). *Looking into classrooms* (8th ed.) New York: Longman.

Gump, P. V. (1987). School and classroom environments. In D. Stokols & I. Altman (Eds.), *Handbook of environmental psychology* (pp. 691–732). New York: Wiley.

Hunter, M. (1994). *Enhancing teaching.* New York: Macmillan.

Jones, V. F., & Jones, L. S. (2001). *Comprehensive classroom management: Creating communities of support and solving problems* (6th ed.). Boston: Allyn & Bacon.

Kounin, J. S. (1970). *Discipline and group management in classrooms.* New York: Holt, Rinehart & Winston.

Roehler, L., Duffy, G., & Meloth, M. (1987). The effects and some distinguishing characteristics of explicit teacher explanation during reading instruction. In J. Niles (Ed.), *Changing perspectives on research in reading/language processing and instruction.* Rochester, NY: National Reading Conference.

Rosenshine, B., & Stevens, R. (1986). Teacher functions. In M. C. Wittrock (Ed.), *Handbook of research on teaching* (3rd. ed.) (pp. 376–391). New York: Macmillan.

Savage, T. V. (1999). *Teaching self-control through management and discipline* (2nd ed.). Boston: Allyn & Bacon.

Shostak, R. (1999). Involving students in learning. In J. Cooper (Ed.), *Classroom teaching skills* (6th ed.) (pp. 77–99). Boston: Houghton Mifflin.

Smith, H. A. (1984). The marking of transitions by more- and less-effective teachers. *Review of Educational Research, 49*(4), 557–610.

Weinstein, C. S. (2003). *Secondary classroom management: Lessons from research and practice* (2nd ed.). New York: McGraw-Hill.

Weinstein, C. S., & Mignano, A. J. (1997). *Elementary classroom management: Lessons from research and practice* (2nd ed.). New York: McGraw-Hill.

CHAPTER TEN—CLASSROOM MANAGEMENT

Arnold, H. (2001). *Succeeding in the secondary classroom.* Thousand Oaks, CA: Corwin Press.

Baloche, L. A. (1998). *The cooperative classroom: Empowering learning.* Upper Saddle River, NJ: Prentice Hall.

Borich, G. (2000). *Effective teaching methods* (4th ed.). Upper Saddle River, NJ: Merrill/Prentice Hall.

Bosch, K. A., & Kersey, K. C. (2000). *The first-year teacher: Teaching with confidence (K–8)* (rev. ed.). Washington, DC: National Education Association.

Burden, P. R. (2003). *Classroom management: Creating a successful learning community* (2nd ed.). New York: Wiley & Sons.

Canter & Associates (1998). *First-class teacher: Success strategies for new teachers.* Santa Monica, CA: Author.

Charles, C. M. (2000). *Building classroom discipline* (7th ed.). Boston: Allyn & Bacon.

Christopher, C. J. (1991). *Nuts and bolts: Survival guide for teachers.* Lancaster, PA: Technomic Publishing Co.

Eggen, P. D., & Kauchak, D. P. (2001). *Educational psychology: Windows on classrooms* (5th ed.). Upper Saddle River, NJ: Merrill/Prentice Hall.

Emmer, E. T., Evertson, C. M., & Worsham, M. E. (2000). *Classroom management for secondary teachers* (5th ed.). Boston: Allyn & Bacon.

Evertson, C. M., Emmer, E. T., & Worsham, M. E. (2000). *Classroom management for elementary teachers* (5th ed.). Boston: Allyn & Bacon.

Good, T. L., & Brophy, J. E. (2000). *Looking in classrooms* (8th ed.). New York: Longman.

Johnson, D. W., & Johnson, R. T. (1999). *Learning together and alone: Cooperative, competitive, and individualistic learning* (5th ed.). Boston: Allyn & Bacon.

Johnson, D. W., & Johnson, R. T. (2000). *Joining together: Group theory and group skills* (7th ed.). Boston: Allyn & Bacon.

Jones, V. F., & Jones, L. S. (2001). *Comprehensive classroom management: Creating communities of support and solving problems* (6th ed.). Boston: Allyn & Bacon.

Jonson, K. F. (2001). *The new elementary teacher's handbook* (2nd ed.). Thousand Oaks, CA: Corwin Press.

Kohn, A. (1996). *Beyond discipline: From compliance to community.* Alexandria, VA: Association for Supervision and Curriculum Development.

Kounin, J. S. (1970). *Discipline and group management in classrooms.* New York: Holt, Rinehart & Winston.

Leinhardt, G., Weidman, C., & Hammond, K. M. (1987). Introduction and integration of classroom routines by expert teachers. *Curriculum Inquiry, 17*(2), 135–176.

Levin, J., & Nolan, J. F. (2000). *Principles of classroom management: A hierarchical approach* (3rd ed.). Boston: Allyn & Bacon.

Moran, C., Stobbe, J., Baron, W., Miller, J., & Moir, E. (2000). *Keys to the classroom: A teacher's guide to the first month of school* (2nd ed.). Newbury Park, CA: Corwin Press.

Purkey, W. W., & Novak, J. M. (1996). *Inviting school success: A self-concept approach to teaching, learning, and democratic practice* (3rd ed.). Belmont, CA: Wadsworth.

Roberts, M. P. (2001). *Your mentor: A practical guide for first-year teachers in grades 1–3.* Thousand Oaks, CA: Corwin Press.

Sarka, P. R., & Shank, M. (1990). *Lee Canter's back to school with assertive discipline.* Santa Monica, CA: Lee Canter & Associates.

Schell, L. M., & Burden, P. R. (2000). *Countdown to the first day of school* (2nd ed.). Washington, DC: National Education Association.

Sharan, Y., & Sharan, S. (1992). *Expanding cooperative learning through group investigation.* New York: Teachers College Press.

Slavin, R. E. (1991). *Student team learning: A practical guide for cooperative learning* (3rd ed.). Washington, DC: National Education Association.

Weinstein, C. S., & Mignano, A. J. Jr. (1997). *Elementary classroom management: Lessons from research and practice* (2nd ed.). New York: McGraw-Hill.

Williamson, B. (1998). *A first-year teacher's guidebook* (2nd ed.). Sacramento, CA: Dynamic Teaching Co.

Wolfgang, C. H. (1999). *Solving discipline problems.* (4th ed.). New York: John Wiley & Sons.

Wong, H. K., & Wong, R. T. (1998). *The first days of school: How to be an effective teacher.* Mountain View, CA: Harry K. Wong Publications.

Wyatt, R. L., & White, J. E. (2001). *Making your first year a success: The secondary teacher's survival guide.* Thousand Oaks, CA: Corwin Press.

Ziv, A. (1988). Teaching and learning with humor: Experiment and replication. *Journal of Experimental Education, 57,* 5–18.

CHAPTER ELEVEN—CLASSROOM DISCIPLINE

Burden, P. R. (2003). *Classroom management: Creating a successful learning community* (2nd ed.). New York: Wiley & Sons.

Doyle, W. (1986). Classroom organization and management. In M. C. Wittrock (Ed.), *Handbook of research on teaching* (3rd ed.) (pp. 392–431). New York: Macmillan.

Dreikurs, R., Grunwald, B. B., & Pepper, F. C. (1982). *Maintaining sanity in the classroom: Classroom management techniques* (2nd ed.). New York: Harper & Row.

Evans, W. H., Evans, S. S., & Schmid, R. E. (1989). *Behavior and instructional management: An ecological approach.* Boston: Allyn & Bacon.

Glasser, W. (1992). *The quality school: Managing students without coercion* (2nd ed.). New York: Harper-Perennial.

Good, T. L., & Brophy, J. E. (2000). *Looking in classrooms* (8th ed.). New York: Addison Wesley Longman.

Gordon, T. (1991). *Discipline that works: Promoting self-discipline in children.* New York: Plume (a division of Penguin).

Hyman, I. A. (1990). *Reading, writing, and the hickory stick: The appalling story of physical and psychological abuse in American schools.* Lexington, MA: Lexington Books.

Hyman, I. A. (1997). *School discipline and school violence.* Boston: Allyn & Bacon.

Kerr, M., & Nelson, C. (2002). *Strategies for managing behavior problems in the classroom* (4th ed.). Columbus, OH: Merrill.

Kohn, A. (1996). *Beyond discipline: From compliance to community.* Alexandria, VA: Association for Supervision and Curriculum Development.

Levin, J., & Nolan, J. F. (2000). *Principles of classroom management: A hierarchical approach* (3rd ed.). Boston: Allyn & Bacon.

Mehan, H., Hertweck, A., Combs, S. E., & Flynn, P. J. (1982). Teachers' interpretations of students' behavior. In L. C. Wilkinson (Ed.), *Communicating in the classroom* (pp. 297–321). New York: Academic Press.

Pittman, S. I. (1984, April). *A cognitive ethnography and quantification of teachers' plans for managing students.* Paper presented at the annual meeting of the American Educational Research Association, New Orleans, LA.

Redl, F., & Wineman, D. (1957). *The aggressive child.* New York: The Free Press.

Shrigley, R. L. (1985). Curbing student disruption in the classroom—Teachers need intervention skills. *National Association of Secondary School Principals Bulletin, 69*(479), 26–32.

Slavin, R. E. (2000). *Educational psychology* (6th ed.). Boston: Allyn & Bacon.

Weber, W. A., & Roff, L. A. (1983). A review of teacher education literature on classroom management. In W. A. Weber, L. A. Roff, J. Crawford, & C. Robinson (Eds.), *Classroom management: Reviews of the teacher education and research literature* (pp. 7–42). Princeton, NJ: Educational Testing Service.

Weinstein, C. S. (2003). *Secondary classroom management: Lessons from research and practice* (2nd ed.). New York: McGraw-Hill.

Weinstein, C. S., & Mignano, A. J., Jr. (1997). *Elementary classroom management: Lessons from research and practice* (2nd ed.). New York: McGraw-Hill.

CHAPTER TWELVE—ASSESSING STUDENT PERFORMANCE

Airasian, P. W. (2000). *Assessment in the classroom: A concise approach* (2nd ed.). New York: McGraw-Hill.

Airasian, P. W. (2001). *Classroom assessment: Concepts and applications* (4th ed.). New York: McGraw-Hill.

Burke, K. (1999). *The mindful school: How to assess authentic learning* (3rd ed.). Arlington Heights, IL: Skylight Professional Development.

Linn, R. L., & Gronlund, N. E. (2000). *Measurement and assessment in teaching* (8th ed.). Upper Saddle River, NJ: Prentice Hall.

McMillan, J. H. (2001). *Classroom assessment: Principles and practice for effective instruction* (2nd ed.). Boston: Allyn & Bacon.

Popham, W. J. (2002). *Classroom assessment: What teachers need to know* (3rd ed.). Boston: Allyn & Bacon.

Stiggins, R. J. (2001). *Student-involved classroom assessment* (3rd ed.). Upper Saddle River, NJ: Prentice Hall.

Tanner, D. E. (2001). *Assessing academic achievement.* Boston: Allyn & Bacon.

Tierney, R. J., Carter, M. A., & Desai, L. E. (1991). *Portfolio assessment in the reading-writing classroom.* Norwood, MA: Christopher-Gordon Publishers.

CHAPTER THIRTEEN—GRADING, MARKING, AND REPORTING

Airasian, P. W. (2001). *Classroom assessment: Concepts and applications* (4th ed.). New York: McGraw-Hill.

Carey, L. M. (2001). *Measuring and evaluating school learning* (3rd ed.) Boston: Allyn & Bacon.

Linn, R. L., & Gronlund, N. E. (2000). *Measurement and assessment in teaching* (8th ed.). Upper Saddle River, NJ: Prentice Hall.

McMillan, J. H. (2001). *Classroom assessment: Principles and practice for effective instruction* (2nd ed.). Boston: Allyn & Bacon.

Stiggins, R. J. (2001). *Student-involved classroom assessment* (3rd ed.). Upper Saddle River, NJ: Prentice Hall.

Tanner, D. E. (2001). *Assessing academic achievement.* Boston: Allyn & Bacon.

CHAPTER FOURTEEN—WORKING WITH COLLEAGUES AND PARENTS

Berger, E. H. (2000). *Parents as partners in education: Families and schools working together* (5th ed.). Upper Saddle River, NJ: Prentice Hall.

Canter, L., & Canter, M. (1991). *Parents on your side.* Santa Monica, CA: Lee Canter & Associates.

Epstein, J. L. (Guest editor). (1991). Parental involvement [Special issue]. *Phi Delta Kappan, 72*(5).

Epstein, J. L., Coates, L., Salinas, K. C., Sanders, M. G., & Simon, B. S. (1997). *School, family, and community partnerships.* Thousand Oaks, CA: Corwin Press.

Henderson, A. T., & Berla, N. (1995). *A new generation of evidence: The family is critical to student achievement.* Washington, DC: Center for Law and Education.

Linn, R. L., & Gronlund, N. E. (2000). *Measurement and assessment in teaching* (8th ed.). Upper Saddle River, NJ: Prentice Hall.

National PTA (1997). *National standards for parent/family involvement programs.* Chicago, IL: Author.

National PTA (2000). *Building successful partnerships: A guide for developing parent and family involvement programs.* Bloomington, IN: National Educational Service.

Swap, S. M. (1993). *Developing home–school partnerships: From concepts to practice.* New York: Teachers College Press.

Turnbull, A. P., & Turnbull, H. R. (2001). *Families, professionals, and exceptionalities* (4th ed.). Upper Saddle River, NJ: Prentice Hall.

Walker, J. E., & Shae, T. M. (1999). *Behavior management: A practical approach for educators* (7th ed.). Columbus, OH: Merrill.

Warner, C. (1997). *Everybody's house—The schoolhouse: Best techniques for connecting home, school, and community.* Thousand Oaks, CA: Corwin Press.

Yao, E. (1988). Working effectively with Asian immigrant parents. *Phi Delta Kappan, 70*(3), 223–225.

NAME INDEX

SUBJECT INDEX

teach and review, 262
violations, 246
Process, curriculum differentiation
techniques, 152
Process feedback, 169
Proctoring, 325
Product assessment, 307, 308–310,
326
types of, 308–310
ways to rate, 312–314
Products
curriculum differentiation
techniques, 152–154
of student cooperative practice,
180
Professional journals and
publications, 47–48
Progress, 226
Progressive differentiation, 42
Progress reports, 331, 339, 341, 347,
348, 373
Projected visuals, 256
Projecting blame, 287
Projects, 125, 138, 308, 310, 326,
367, 368. *See also* Independent
study.
for advanced learners, 154
as course requirements, 244, 252
definition, 195
as evaluation measure, 213
grade input from, 336, 349, 352
as indirect instructional
strategies, 185, 187,
195–196
informing parents about, 370, 374
long-term, 68
Promotion, 331, 349
Prompting questions, 174
Promptness, 333
Proximity control, 247, 284, 292,
293–295
Psychologist, referral to, 357
Psychomotor domain, 81, 86–88,
99, 307, 314, 315
evaluation instruments for, 307
Psychomotor skills, 99
Public recognition, 267, 268
Punishment, 249
cautions and guidelines for, 277,
286–288
corporal, 283, 286
definition, 286
degree of severity, 288
duration of, 288

effects of, 286
identifying, 259
mass (group), 281, 285
practices to avoid, 285–286
reduction of, 287
selecting, 288
Punitive responses, 246, 247, 259,
292, 297, 298

Quarter, 63
Questioning and dialogue, 17–19
Questionnaires, 305, 307, 364
Question prompts, 82
Questions and questioning,
174–177, 212. *See also* Test
and testing.
ambiguity of, 306
as backup material, 244
categories of test (2), 317
for clarification, 226, 227
clarity, 228, 229, 230
essay, 316, 317
formulating key, 197, 198
item difficulty, 316
to maintain attention, 175,
177, 271
matching, 316, 317
modification for diversity, 316
multiple choice, 316, 317
objective, 316, 317
open-ended, 307
optional, 318
parental, 365, 366, 368, 374
reciprocal, 177
as review method, 218
techniques for using, 175–177
true and false, 316, 317
types of, 175–177, 316
as verbal response to
inappropriate behavior,
296–297
Quizzes
grade input from, 330, 334, 336,
337, 339, 349, 352
informing parents about, 367,
368, 374
pop, 333
as review method, 218
sending home, 370, 373

Ranking of students, 305, 307,
339, 342, 343
in terms of achievement, 314
Rapport, 374

Rating approaches, for products or
performances, 312–314
Rating criteria, for products or
performances, 312
Rating grading method, 318–319
Ratings, as evaluation measure, 213
Rating scale, 308, 310–313, 329,
336, 343, 344
definition, 312
Reader's Guide, 220
Readiness, of students, 154–155
Receiving skills, 265
Recitation, 138, 178, 212
room arrangement for, 253
Record keeping, computer program
to aid in, 343
Redirecting behavior, 246
Reference group, 339, 341
Referral, to outside help, 357
Reflection, 9–11
and constructivist approach to
teaching, 14–15
definition, 20
to improve decision making,
9–12, 15–19
planning for instruction, 24
postplanning, 25
student, 14
on weekly plans, 11
Reflective teaching, 16, 17
Reflective thinking, Dewey's model
of, 192
Reflective writing, 16–17, 299
Reinforcers and reinforcement,
134–144
activities as, 259, 272, 273–274
of appropriate behavior, 246,
248–249, 264, 268, 284, 286,
289–290
back-up, 274
definition, 272
as function of grades, 331
peer, 247, 268
positive, 272, 273, 274
of positive behavior, 234,
272–274, 365
privileges as, 259, 272–274
social, 259, 272, 273
tangible, 259, 272–274
techniques, 273–274
token, 259, 272, 273
varying, 272
withholding positive, 286, 288,
293